DATE DUE

Demco, Inc. 38-293

The Visual Focus
of American Media Culture
in the Twentieth Century

Also by Wiley Lee Umphlett

The Sporting Myth and the American Experience: Studies in Contemporary Fiction

Mythmakers of the American Dream: The Nostalgic Vision in Popular Culture

The Movies Go to College: Hollywood and the World of the College-Life Film

Creating the Big Game: John W. Heisman and the Invention of American Football

American Sports Culture: The Humanistic Dimensions (Editor)

The Achievement of American Sport Literature: A Critical Appraisal (Editor)

The Visual Focus
of American Media Culture
in the Twentieth Century

The Modern Era, 1893–1945

Wiley Lee Umphlett

Madison • Teaneck
Fairleigh Dickinson University Press

Associated University Presses
2010 Eastpark Boulevard
Cranbury, NJ 08512

The paper used in this publication meets the requirements of the American
National Standard for Permanence of Paper for Printed Library Materials
Z39.48-1984.

Library of Congress Cataloging-in-Publication Data

Umphlett, Wiley Lee, 1931–
    The visual focus of American media culture in the twentieth century :
the modern era, 1893–1945 / Wiley Lee Umphlett.
      p. cm.
    Includes bibliographical references and index.
    ISBN 0-8386-4001-X (alk. paper)
    1. Mass media and culture—United States—History.   I. Title.
P94.65.U6U47 2004
302.23′0973—dc21

                                  2003012706

6/25/04

PRINTED IN THE UNITED STATES OF AMERICA

Contents

Preface and Acknowledgments

THIS BOOK IS A SOCIOCULTURAL HISTORY OF THE VISUALLY ORIENTED FORMS of American culture that have beguiled our society from the 1890s to the end of World War II. A main purpose of my work is to show how revolutionary technological advances during these years have been instrumental in helping create a unique culture of media-made origins. Then, too, by focusing on the culture's attraction to both traditional and new modes of visual expression as welcome diversions from the harsh realities of life, I attend to the American people's affinity for those special individuals whose talent, vision, and lifestyle introduced daring new ways to avoid the ordinariness of life by fantasizing it. Thus, my narrative, which begins in the socio-economically demanding urban milieu of the late nineteenth century, where the escapist lure of theatrical productions, the print forms of literary diversion, sporting activities, and a variety of public amusements had begun to flourish, recognizes these venues' creators, entertainers, athletes, and entrepreneurs as new celebrity types who contributed to a media-made, escapist-bent approach to life.

A main intent of the early modes and venues of mediated culture was to help meet both the inspirational and escapist needs of those confronting the day-to-day challenges that a capitalist society imposed on them. Bonded by a common desire to relish the balm of escapist diversion were a rising middle class, the working-class poor, and newly arrived immigrants seeking their place in the sun. Since the quest for escapist experience knew no class boundaries, even the well-to-do devoted considerable time to their own elitist leisure pursuits. And as the desires of a burgeoning consumer society were being tempered by rapidly developing technologies, new media-made pastimes and amusements appeared that would subtly democratize the social tastes and behavior of both the masses and those of higher estate. As my title suggests, then, this book traces the modern developments of the first half of the twentieth century that reveal how a media-made culture evolved in response to all citizens' inner need to transcend the realities of an increasingly challenging, complex world. As the upshot of a seemingly endless accumulation of widespread concerns and issues of social, economic, and political consequence, in spite of any progress made in the larger soci-

7

ety, these realities still continued to devolve on the individual, regardless of class.

Moreover, my narrative discusses the effects that a mediated culture as both a force and a mirror of social change have had on traditional American values. In this light, I examine the sociocultural impact of an ongoing democratization process that through its nurturing of a responsive mediated culture has gradually eroded the polar postures of the elite and mass cultures which prevailed in the 1890s, that is, when the hierarchical divisions of American culture were firmly in place and the view from the top was considered the only acceptable way of seeing and appreciating the arts. As a result of ongoing developments in media technology, though, the century's second half would see a wide range of fragmented subcultural escapist venues arise that markedly diverged from the more communally-oriented outlets and activities of the century's early years.

The democratization of social behavior that evolved since the 1890s was also mirrored in the mediated messages of consumer advertising and fashion styles that sought to acclimate their targeted audiences to the escapist dimensions of the good life, a related theme that this chronicle dwells on. How the arts and literature reacted to democratization is accorded a relevant place, too.

The unifying device for my analysis of media-made culture's impact on American life is a collective metaphor that I refer to as the *mediated vision.* Emblematic of media technology's response to the commonly felt need to transcend the wide gulf between dream and reality in American life, its way of "seeing" offered an escapist means for avoiding the discontents of the present, most often in the century's early years through venues that recalled the memories of a nostalgic past or anticipated the realization of a utopian future.

However, in the century's second half, postmodernist ways of fantasizing reality, enhanced by the growing visual power of media technology and the transient modes of self-indulgence that sought to make the present more tolerable by intensifying experience, would transform the mediated vision into fragmented variations of its former self, reflecting the sociocultural changes in American society since the tumultuous times of the 1960s. Not until this era would the societal status of minorities become a volatile issue, though women's progress toward social independence was such that the twentieth century could be designated the Century of the Woman. Throughout, though, the mediated vision would maintain its egalitarian outlook, cutting across the social fabric of class, gender, age, and race to unite individuals in a common desire for the solace of escapist experience. Indeed, by the century's end, the earlier escapist dreams created by the media-made culture would evolve into a way of seeing in which reality itself functioned as a fantasized form of escapist entertainment—the development of which is the subject matter for a proposed second book.

The roots of this study lay in a book I wrote in the 1980s that dealt with the nostalgic implications of American popular culture. I realized then that a subject which had played such a dominant sociocultural role in twentieth-century life was deserving of a much more in-depth examination. This present volume, then, was originally part of a much longer work intended to cover the evolving visual dominance of the mass media throughout the twentieth century. But because my biggest challenge lay in organizing a subject so vast that it permeated the entire realm of life in the last century, I decided to confine the significant developments of the century's first half to a separate volume. As this book's extensive bibliography attests, my research was aided in the main by the large number of media-related publications that appeared up to 2000, the calendar end of the twentieth century. Hopefully, my efforts will present the reader a coherent synthesis of the sociocultural forces that have contributed to the media culture's role in the democratization of the American experience. As intimated above, its ongoing visual impact is to be examined in an ensuing book covering the years from the postwar era to the end of the century.

Concerning my choice of illustrations to exemplify this book's strong visual focus, I have taken a cue from Roland Marchand's quote in my prologue that "the clichés of popular art of an era," in the public repetition of their fantasy aspects, may suggest "the shared daydreams of the society." Thus the rationale for the inclusion, mostly from my own personal collection, of a period's communally directed examples of such popular art forms as the poster, illustration, comics/cartoons, movie and consumer advertising, and the sheet music cover.

In addition to numerous associates who offered moral support during the writing of this book, I owe a debt of gratitude to certain individuals who helped it become a reality: Dr. Harry Keyishian, director of the FDU Press, whose faith in this project never wavered; Christine A. Retz, managing editor at AUP, whose editorial staff contributed a great deal toward making this a better book; and closer home, Mike Feenker, whose computer expertise proved invaluable in producing a manuscript to meet today's production standards. I am also indebted to the library resources of the University of West Florida, where I served the major part of my academic career. Though a relatively young institution, it is well on its way to well-deserved recognition in the area of scholarly research. Finally, I would like to dedicate this book to my wife Joyce who, as a believer in my writing endeavors from the very beginning of our relationship, has been an ongoing source of inspiration.

The Modern Era of Communal Venues
and Public Diversions

The White City was a pictorial and passive experience. In it you were
a spectator. . . . The Midway, on the other hand, was a rousing urban
drama, with fairgoers playing the parts of both actor and audience.
— Donald L. Miller, "The White City"

Movie palaces showcased an astonishing world of art and luxury to a
public eager to embrace it. Day after day, week after week, audiences
returned to experience these privileged realms of wealth and grandeur
for the modest price of a movie ticket.
— Barbara Stones, *America Goes to the Movies*

So long as we live in a class society, mass culture will remain
indispensable even to those who have learned to scorn it; we cannot
escape what is so much a part of the atmosphere in which we live.
— Irving Howe, "Notes on Mass Culture"

The vision of America . . . as the dynamic leader of the world, has
within it, the possibilities of such enormous human progress as to
stagger the imagination. . . . there is the picture of an America which
will send out through the world its technical and artistic skills.
Engineers, scientists, doctors, movie men, makers of entertainment. . . .
— Henry R. Luce, "The American Century"

The Visual Focus
of American Media Culture
in the Twentieth Century

Prologue: The Rise of Media-Made Culture in America

> There is considerable agreement that all media
> are estranged from values and offer nothing but
> entertainment and distraction—that, ultimately,
> they expedite flight from an unbearable reality.
> —Leo Lowenthal, "Historical Perspectives
> of Popular Culture"

THEODORE DREISER'S CLASSIC NOVEL *SISTER CARRIE*, FIRST PUBLISHED IN 1900 amid an air of controversy, opens with its central character Caroline Meeber on a train bound for Chicago. It is the centennial year of 1889, and the eighteen year old Carrie, "full of the illusions and ignorance of youth," is headed to the place she thinks will be the answer to all her dreams. As Dreiser characterizes his heroine: "A half-equipped little knight she was, venturing to reconnoiter the mysterious city and dreaming wild dreams of some vague, far-off supremacy."[1]

Carrie's "wild dreams" derived from a modernist mind-set, a collective posture that was transforming American life toward the end of the nineteenth century and on into the early part of the twentieth. Living in a small town or on a farm may have offered a more sheltered, familiar way of life to many people at the time, but the opportunities the city promised were growing harder to resist. The sociocultural conflict between the deep-rooted values of small-town/rural life and the mediated attractions of an urban lifestyle had fomented a way of seeing that either reconciled or disregarded the gulf between dream and reality in American life. Emanating from a basic discontent with the present, or the way things are, this outlook—metaphorically termed the *mediated vision* in this book—has been a pivotal force in fostering the media-made culture of the twentieth century.

A fanciful counterpoint to Carrie's quest was captured in L. Frank Baum's popular children's story, *The Wonderful Wizard of Oz*, also published in 1900. Dorothy Gale, a Midwestern girl like Carrie, is whisked away by a tornado to a dreamland kingdom. But the magical world of Oz, with all its unexpected pitfalls, holds very little enchantment for Dorothy, and her prolonged sojourn there centers around the attempt to return to her rural roots in Kansas. As she reminds the Scarecrow: "No matter how dreary and gray our homes are, we people of flesh and blood would rather live there than in any other country, be it ever so beautiful. There is no place like home."[2] Diametrical to Carrie's expectations of her future in the city, Dorothy's yearning for the security of her past posits the other side of the mediated vision's rationale for rejecting the present: to seek the past's stability through nostalgia.[3]

Although these two works of fiction markedly differ in their respective realistic and fantasized perspectives, both suggest how the uncertainties of existence can conjure up the illusions of desire or the solace of memory to avoid the realities of the present. Aided by the proliferating breakthroughs in technology during this era, such a posture was receptive to new forms of escapism that cultivated a symbiotic relationship with the mediated vision. It was an association that would help alleviate the social and economic demands the urban milieu exacted upon the newly arrived city dweller, whether domestic or immigrant. In this psychologically alien environment created by industrialization, the disenchanted experiences of new arrivals from the hinterland and the social isolation of ethnic groups from abroad found relief from the emotional pain of adjustment by relating to the evolving escapist modes of the mediated culture and their power to transcend reality.

By the 1890s, then, a variety of entertainment venues had developed that as products of consumption provided vicarious escape through their ability to inspire illusions and dreams about the past and the future. For example, historical fiction in the Victorian tradition that glamorized the past in novels and magazines naturally responded to the mediated vision's growing demand for illusions and dreams. The graphic appeal of the popular magazine's cover art, along with its persuasive interior ads for products urging the consumer to realize the future in the present, conspired to formulate a new kind of visual escapism. As another way to escape the demands of the workaday world, popular songs of the time were composed for both the vaudeville stage and the parlor piano to trigger fond memories or inspirational dreams that even the illiterate immigrant might delight in.

Theodore Dreiser, himself a small-town emigré to the big city, realized from his own experience that the impersonal urban environment was a laboratory where Carrie Meeber's illusions would be put to the ultimate test. In contrast to her kindred working-class daydreamers who are victimized by social forces and who strive to realize their personal goals against hopeless economic odds, Carrie ironically succeeds at the expense of her more well-to-do paramour. Although a classic of its kind, her story of success through happenstance is but one version of the mediated vision's refusal to accept the considerable distance between illusion and reality in life.

The collective significance of Carrie's attraction to city life is symbolized at the novel's beginning in Dreiser's description of Chicago as a Mecca-like place whose "many and growing commercial opportunities gave it widespread fame, which made of it a giant magnet, drawing to itself, from all quarters, the hopeful and the hopeless—those who had their fortunes yet to make and those whose fortunes and affairs had reached a disastrous climax elsewhere. . . . Its population was not so much thriving upon established commerce as upon the industries which prepared the way for others."[4]

The magnetic place that was Chicago at the close of the century is where this history begins, covering the years from the advent of the nation's model showplace, the Columbian Exposition of 1893, to the end of the second World War, revealing how a mediated culture has mirrored the predominant fantasy images and illusions of this communally oriented era. As the older media-made forms evolved and newer ones originated, their proponents, in responding to the ever changing outlook of the mediated vision, were commercially motivated to interpret reality not only in a generally fantasized way but in an increasingly visual manner, as, most obviously, in the movies' more immediate sense of illusion. Throughout the first half of the century, then, the communal focus of the mediated vision demanded idealized images and romanticized interpretations of experience. However, the societal uprooting of two World Wars and two later politically divisive conflicts would culminate in the social upheavals of the 1960s. And as society grew increasingly problematic, bureaucratized, and fragmented, the mass-mediated forms of the culture would begin to display the characteristics of postmodernism, reflecting a breakdown of traditional values and the divisions between the elite and mass cultures—the subject matter of this project's planned second volume.

Following up on the events Daniel Boorstin calls the Graphic Revolution of the nineteenth century, then, the ensuing sections relate how media technology continued to develop and produce the escapist experiences that modern life would not only expect but demand. The upshot was a mediated culture in which images and daydreams predominated, relentlessly expanding their seductive spell. Roland Marchand comments in his provocative study of the visual power of American advertising that "the clichés of popular art of an era, particularly if they are dramatically and repeatedly paraded before the public eye, may induce individuals to recapitulate in their own fantasies some aspects of the shared daydreams of the society."[5] In the 1890s' urban milieu this visual phenomenon was stimulated by such mediated sources of shared fantasies as vaudeville, the newspaper comic strip, and especially that grandiose repository of cultural contradictions between the past, present, and future—the Chicago World's Fair. While the static vision of photography evolved into the motion picture by the early years of the twentieth century and the aural modes of the phonograph recording and radio began to complement each other by the 1920s to create mediated daydreams of their own, by the 1950s television and its spin-offs would generate undreamed-of ways to fantasize reality as a packaged consumer product. But, as this book observes, the mediated vision's mission to fill "our lives not with experience but with images of experience," saw it fulfilled most communally at first in the ritual of going to the movies.[6]

The sections that follow focus on how the creators, disseminators, and opportunists of the mediated culture shaped these images in the way they believed their audiences wanted to perceive them, as suggested by the most current "shared daydreams of the society." Enhanced by an incredible, ever-developing, visually oriented technology, then, the media forms that responded to the escapist desires of the mediated vision not only blurred the lines between fantasy and reality, they narrowed the gulf between the elite and mass cultures. Both these ongoing phenomena, whose ultimate implications are yet to be realized, are germane to the central focus of this book.

1

The 1890s—Setting the Stage for a Media-Made Culture

The world's greatest achievement of the departing century was pulled off in Chicago. The Columbian Exposition was the most stupendous, interesting, and significant show ever spread out for the public.

—George Ade

DURING THE LAST DECADE OF THE NINETEENTH CENTURY, THE CITY OF CHICAGO was an unregulated, sprawling metropolitan area whose raw vitality had been wrought by the catalyst of industrialization, urbanization, and technological development. As such, it was a mirror of what was happening to the country at large, epitomizing its rapid sociocultural transformation into a modern urban nation. As a strategic connection point between the commercial centers of the East and the developing towns of the western territories, Theodore Dreiser's Chicago, in preparing "the way for others," was a natural location as a manufacturing center, and with the coming of the stockyards, a marketplace for the cattle ranches to the south. It was also a hub for the expanding national railroad network that by 1900 would encompass nearly 200,000 miles of track. Consequently, Chicago quickly developed into a convenient jumping-off place for the vast flow of immigrants who had passed through New York's Ellis Island in quest of the American Dream, if not to be realized in the East, then surely in the burgeoning towns and cities of the Midwest. Even American farmers who had grown disillusioned with the rural way of life were making their way to these places in search of a more rewarding future. Or so they thought, somewhat in the vein of Dreiser's small-town dreamer, Carrie Meeber.

But many of these hopefuls would soon take on the disenchanted outlook of Baum's Dorothy Gale, as devious forces, such as Chicago's cheap labor market, conspired to exploit workers in a brutal capitalistic system designed to make the most of any profiteering opportunity. Although Upton Sinclair's investigative novel *The Jungle* (1906) would expose the wretched working

19

conditions as well as the unsanitary procedures of the meatpacking plants, not long after, poet Carl Sandburg's earthy imagery ironically expressed the cultural contradictions inherent not only in the city of Chicago but in the American experience itself. Sandburg's visually inspired poetry revealed a Whitmanesque awareness of both the elevating and unifying as well as the corrupting and disconnecting elements of a modern capitalistic society—a place of paradox within the scope of the mediated vision, where the ideal and the real could coexist.

THE "STUPENDOUS" SHOW OF 1893

As though to transcend the anomalies and vagaries of a consumer-oriented society, the city of Chicago staged its own special homage to American culture and modern technology in 1893 with the opening of the Columbian Exposition, a world's fair belatedly commemorating the four hundredth anniversary of Columbus's discovery of the New World. The construction of an awe-inspiring "White City" of classically designed buildings, crisscrossed by a complex system of placid lagoons, was graphic testimony to the ingenuity and efficiency of American know-how. It was also a vivid example of the preoccupation with illusion that had characterized the American experience from its beginnings. In this visually overwhelming atmosphere, onlookers sensed that they had arrived at the city of the future—a utopian place that stood in marked contrast to the country's growing urban centers and their attendant social ills. The reality behind the appearance, though, was that the fair's grandiose facade was just that—a kind of theatrical stage set made of fibrous plaster that was slated to be torn down soon after the show's closing. But during the six months of its existence the Columbian Exposition was a visually compelling showcase of America's obsession with the lure of the past and the promise of the future, pointing up significant clues to the disposition of the mediated vision at this time.

Relative to where the country might be headed in a progressive sense, the most impressive attractions were those devoted to the latest achievements in technology. The 1876 centennial fair at Philadelphia had extolled the wonders of the telegraph, the typewriter, and the telephone—all revolutionary instruments of mass communication. But with big city streets transformed into a veritable forest of poles and wires by the 1890s, the telephone had clearly made the greatest impact on interpersonal communication, attesting to a new aural relationship between place and distance. Similarly, the mysterious force of electricity, as it was exploited at the Chicago Fair, demonstrated a new kind of visual fantasy through its power to transform the night into an escapist milieu. Thomas Edison's lightbulb had been around since 1878, but it had taken a while for most people to relate to its

This promotional poster, which celebrates the Chicago Exposition's focus on modern achievements in technology and culture as well as its homage to the past, also suggests the 1890s' visionary outlook on the future's promise. Courtesy Library of Congress.

way of encapsulating electricity as a kind of controlled fire. By driving back the darkness of night this miraculous form of energy expanded not only the physical but the fantasy horizons of the mediated vision more dramatically than any other technological breakthrough up to that time.[1]

Of course, the Fair's daylight splendor mesmerized visitors as well. From the moment one passed through the White City's entrance and confronted its architectural jewel—the gleaming dome of the Administrative Building— the eye was continually challenged by a seemingly endless promenade of grandiose structures, each devoted to a special interest or exhibit. That most of the fair's buildings would be dismantled after its closing had little or no effect on the public's enthusiastic reception of their highly idealized appearances. Regionalist writer Hamlin Garland was so impressed that he wrote his rural parents to make a trip to the fair a high priority. Frank Baum, who had moved to Chicago in the early 90s from his failed business enterprises in the Dakota territories, attended the fair and undoubtedly envisioned in this special world of illusionary escape the basic ingredients for his imaginary Land of Oz. Another dreamer of exotic lands and lost civilizations who was exposed to the wonders of the fair was a youthful Chicagoan named Edgar Rice Burroughs. In some twenty years he would create one of the mediated culture's most enduring characters: Tarzan, the lord of an African jungle that never was.

Other imposing attractions reflected the visual mania for symbolic art and idealized monuments. As though to emulate the Statue of Liberty, that newest emblem of the nation's democratic ideals overseeing the harbor of New York City since 1886, the various murals, mosaics, and statues (of which the most impressive was Daniel French's Statue of the Republic gracing the Main Basin) were purposely designed and positioned to stimulate the eye and arouse the emotions. While these neoclassical forms inspired strong patriotic feelings and pride in the country's accomplishments, they also suggested the legacy of an older European culture, resurrected in a showplace where past actualities paradoxically clashed with modern achievements and future possibilities.

As a result, there were those who contended that this blatant kind of imitation and slavish devotion to classical ideals should have been supplanted by an indigenous architectural style that promoted America's rising status in the family of nations. The most outraged voice was that of architect Louis Sullivan, whose Transportation Building stood out as the fair's most visually original edifice. To exemplify his modernist philosophy of design that form should follow function, Sullivan had created a spectacular golden gate to his building, not only to reflect national purpose but to symbolize one of the American people's most cherished values: the freedom of personal mobility to pursue the promise of the American Dream. Sullivan's modernist plans for the high-rise buildings he created in St. Louis and Chicago during the 90s foreshadowed the most visible symbol of modern capitalism and the aspirations of the urban future—the soaring skyscraper. Though the neoclassic style would remain a force in American architecture until the 1930s, a noted European visitor echoed Sullivan's personal vision in commenting that Chicago's proliferating high-rise office buildings represented "a new sort of art—an art of democracy made by the masses for the masses."[2] As an art form of the mediated vision, it would soon dominate the urban scene.

The "Natural Stage" of New York City

It was Chicago's more sophisticated counterpart, New York City, that would ultimately become the nation's showplace for architectural and engineering achievements impressive to the eye. Not just the skyscraper, soon to be its most conspicuous feature, but such visible symbols of progress as the Pennsylvania Railroad's temple-like station and the expansion bridge—most strikingly expressed in the flowing lines of the Brooklyn Bridge, which was not only a technological feat, but also an artistic triumph. As in other large cities, a wider perspective on the urban scene was provided by new modes of transportation. Electrification brought an end to the horse car and introduced the trolley and the elevated train as a more efficient means of mass mobility both within the city and to outlying areas. The coming of mass transportation systems drew complete strangers together in the immediate experience of relating to and observing not only each other but the passing scene. In *A Hazard of New Fortunes* (1890), the story of a Boston family's uneasy transition to life in New York City, W. D. Howells describes the reactions of the novel's central character and his wife while riding the Third Avenue elevated. Their observations take on a theatrical perspective as they catch intimate views of working-class life through tenement windows: "a family party of workfolk at a late tea, some of the men in their shirt-sleeves; a woman sewing by a lamp; a mother laying her child in its cradle; a man with his head fallen on his hands upon a table; a girl and her lover leaning over the windowsill together."[3]

Mass transportation's communal frame of reference also offered opportunities for city dwellers to access the amusement venues of the expanding mediated culture, all of which the New York area had in variety and abundance, especially during the evening hours. As the Chicago Fair graphically demonstrated, any physical entity could be visually enhanced at night by electrification. So the city of New York was quick to realize the commercial potential of transforming its amusement centers and entertainment attractions along Broadway into a visually exciting area at night. As the popularity of vaudeville and the theater's star system peaked and media coverage of their personalities and the social scene proliferated, that New York innovation, the late-hour cabaret or nightclub, was becoming a popular venue for displaying the badge of celebrity as well as a place frequented by the type of person who desired both to be seen and to see others of kindred spirit. In this glamorous nightlife milieu that sprang up during the 90s, the modern spirit of mediated self-promotion challenged the still pervasive constraints of the Victorian consciousness. Lit up by the magical force of electricity, the cabarets, lobster houses, and theaters along the "Great White Way" transformed the night into a time for escapist adventure when private fantasies and secret desires might find an outlet.[4] Thus, the dining palaces of Delmonico's, Rector's, Luchow's, and the Waldorf-Astoria spoke elegantly to the promise of the night. At this time, though, only the well-to-do could afford to dine in the restaurants where millionaire James B. "Diamond Jim" Brady exercised his mammoth eating habits. In that area of Broadway he dubbed the "Street of the Midnight Sun," Brady's gluttonous consumption of food epitomized an age when dining out was not only an escapist adventure for the rich, but also an ostentatious way to promote societal status and the aggrandizement of self.

Attesting to New York's growing social appeal in the 1880s and 90s, a Wall Street banker declared that this city "is to the immense domain of the American Republic, a natural stage . . . for the great drama of civilization on this Continent."[5] As a mediated catalyst for this "great drama," then, New York was evolving into a mythical place where anything that socially and culturally mattered was either happening or could happen. Because of its growing fantasized aura, New York was becoming the city that other Carrie Meebers in the hinterland daydreamed about, simply because they believed their personal dreams could be realized in such a magical place. As a city of vertical aspirations, symbolized by its plethora of high-rise buildings, New York and its cosmopolitan air outshone Chicago's earthier milieu as a more culturally appealing mecca to the dreamers who yearned for future fame as an author, artist, actor, or in some other self-directed calling. A character in *A Hazard of New Fortunes* pointedly expresses this collective feeling: "There's only one city that belongs to the whole country, and that's New York."[6]

CHICAGO'S OTHER FAIR—THE MIDWAY PLAISANCE

Harbingers of the American people's growing attachment to amusements that catered to escapist desires were clearly in evidence at the adjunct to Chicago's White City—the mile-long strip known as the Midway Plaisance. By introducing the basic elements of the modern amusement park—unity of purpose within a diversity of attractions on a grandiose scale—this sector proved a big hit with visitors. In marked contrast to what they saw at the White City's educational exhibits, those who frequented the Midway indulged in such entertaining outlets as listening to the ragtime stylings of composer/pianist Scott Joplin or taking in Florenz Ziegfeld Jr.'s initial venture into show business, promoting strongman Eugene Sandow's amazing feats of strength. Or even more sensational for males, ogling the erotic bellydance routines of North African dancing girls—in particular the "hootchy-kootchy" routine of one of them who went by the name of Little Egypt.

If the custom of the time was to idealize women according to prevailing Victorian aesthetic tastes, the Midway's risqué bellydance was indicative of a shift in social attitude—a growing tolerance toward public display of the scantily clad female body. It was culturally acceptable for seminude women to appear in staged tableaux depicting classical scenes from antiquity, but since the 1870s the low comedy and satirical acts of burlesque had been playing to a growing legion of appreciative males. In fact, by the late nineteenth century these shows were openly promoting female sexuality.[7] Thus, Little Egypt's daring dance was yet another sign of the trend toward presenting women performers more as glorified sex objects than for any real talent. The female figure was also being erotically displayed in popular magazines to advertise products of interest to males. Through its visual focus in both entertainment and consumer advertising into and throughout the twentieth century, open display of the female body would mirror the mediated vision's evolving social attitudes toward human sexuality.

Even though the social role of women was still very much under the sway of Victorian constraints, ambivalent attitudes were beginning to surface as to just how far their proper role should extend beyond the conventions of marriage and the home. Thus, the White City's exhibit of women's achievements in the arts and crafts presaged radical change in the societal scene. In challenging the illusions that society had long perpetuated about them, many women were not only expressing their special creative talents but beginning to voice their concerns about their lack of political equality. Arising from the ferment of modernism, women's revolt against antiquated social conventions would play a major role in both their political and sexual emancipation in the coming new century.

The fact that the Midway's commercial attractions proved to be as popular as the White City's educational exhibits pointed up the receptive market for forms of amusement that could involve the individual in a communal way. A prime example of technology's growing role in creating mechanized amusement of this type was the visually dominant steel wheel that towered 264 feet above the Midway. Named for its inventor, George W. Ferris, the giant conveyance afforded riders at its apex a panoramic view of Chicago for as far as the eye could see. The irony of such a visual treat lay in the contrast between what one saw in the adjacent dream world of the White City and the congestion and squalor of the real world beyond. The nearby view of the recently opened University of Chicago also suggested the cultural divide between educational opportunity and urban vulgarity. But as a highly spectacular visual experience, Ferris's wheel looked ahead to other mechanized marvels designed to captivate the mediated vision, particularly the Coney Island venues and later theme parks of the twentieth century that would profit by the example set by the Midway Plaisance.

Such settings also provided a natural showplace for both rising and recognized entertainers, of whom the most storied showman to appear was William "Buffalo Bill" Cody. During the years 1883–1916, he headed up one of the most popular and successful productions in the field of commercial entertainment, mainly because its Wild West extravaganza's colorful troupe of cowboys and Indians responded to the mediated vision's nostalgia for the vanished American frontier. The show's main objective was to re-create what pioneer life in the American West was like through dramatizations of real-life events. Due to the emotional impact this spectacular show had on those who saw it, and even those who read or heard about it, the Buffalo Bill version of the "Wild West," along with the Western tale of the dime novel, kept the myth of the Frontier alive, as well as its justification of the American belief in Manifest Destiny.

Historian Frederick Jackson Turner, who announced that the Frontier had run its course in his landmark lecture to a society of academic peers at the fair, spoke from an innate nostalgic feeling for the significance of the West in America's past—that confronting its challenges had been highly instrumental in developing the national character. But in the sense of mythic space, the metaphor of the Frontier and its continuing challenge to look ahead to the future was of equal import. Despite the cultural impact that the myth of the West had on the American imagination at the time, who could have foreseen the ultimate visual connection between Buffalo Bill's Wild West production and one of the Midway's most popular attractions—the peep-show machine in which, for the price of a penny, one could see horses in motion? For here were the essential ingredients of one of the Western myth's most enduring contributions to the mediated vision's fascination with the Frontier concept—the Western film.

The Sociocultural Impact of the Chicago Exposition

Even though the major intent of those who had planned the White City was to suggest an inspirational vision of cultural unity and national destiny, the Chicago fair turned out to be, ironically, a "reflector of the country's confusing variety of conflicting cultural patterns."[8] As a grandiose monument to illusion, the White City was the idealized vision of Chicago's socially elite who had it designed to perpetuate the prevailing cultural tastes of the time. This end was undoubtedly the reason for the exclusion of any exhibits pertaining to African American cultural achievements. One that would have far-ranging impact on the mediated culture was ragtime music, but because it was of such low repute at the time, its performance was relegated to the Midway complex. Thus, the fair unwittingly revealed a class consciousness that extended from the White City's elitist standards of taste at one pole to the Midway's mass appeal at the other. In time, the mediated vision would play a prime role in cutting across these sociocultural differences.

During its existence, the fair attracted people from all walks of life (over twenty-five million from a population of seventy million at the time)—many of whom had little comprehension of its latent cultural significance. Nevertheless, the nouveaux riches of the Chicago businessmen/industrialists who had generated the financial backing for the Exposition not only saw the enlightenment of fairgoers as its cultural mission but the validation of their own cultural status. In fact, the nation's wealthy had long flaunted their elitist role as cultural custodians through their unabashed adulation of European culture. By assiduously acquiring its artifacts, paintings, and statuary, these capitalistic predators of the arts exploited the past to make its icons an integral part of their social identities in the present. This paradoxical duality of purpose was demonstrated in the White City's exhibits of modern technological triumphs staged amid a neoclassic setting that ironically paid high tribute to the past.

The mediated influence of the Columbian Exposition was sufficiently widespread for it to become the model for numerous American fairs of international scope. Though the apparent purpose of a fair was to create a "symbolic universe" in which "all collective events" were displayed "in a cohesive unity that includes past, present, and future,"[9] Atlanta's Cotton States and International Exposition in 1895 placed more emphasis on present progress through its vision of the New South's industrial and technological advances. Not to be outdone, the Midwest played host to the Trans-Mississippi and International Exposition in Omaha in 1898 to justify America's venture into colonialism and ensure future progress in world affairs. The nation's fondness for large-scale fairs as a way to visualize the achievements of American culture would continue in a big way on into the twentieth century. In leaving their imprint on the mediated culture, the prototypal expositions of the late nineteenth century ironically promoted the concept of a community of shared social experiences through both their elitist and popular attractions, thus presaging the democratizing effects of the movies and radio.

This shared sense of community was most apparent in the fairs' adjunct areas that featured sideshows, vaudeville acts, mechanical amusements, and even ethnic villages showing how people from other cultures lived. If cultural progress was the dominant theme of the American fairs, then their planners concurred that living examples from primitive societies considered backward by Western standards would not only entertain but educate fairgoers as to the superiority of the American way of life. Clearly, during this time of pervasive racism the day of a politically correct cultural tolerance and adherence to it lay far in the future.

THE AMBIVALENT VISION OF PHOTOGRAPHY

By the 1890s, photographic technology, which had advanced significantly since the days of the primitive daguerreotype, was conditioning the mediated vision to the paradoxical perception that what it saw in a photograph was more real than the subject it portrayed. Yet, in momentarily capturing an image, freezing it as a point in time, the camera was simultaneously dealing with reality and illusion. Thus, it prefigured what lay ahead for the mediated vision in the communally shared escapist experience of the movies' way of fantasizing reality.

George Eastman's marvelous Kodak camera, which came into widespread use during the 1890s, helped its owners merge reality and illusion by recording cherished moments of their personal lives. In reacting to the flood of social experiences generated in American life, people discovered Eastman's inexpensive Brownie camera as a way to "see" themselves as performers indulging in leisure activities that transported them beyond their everyday identities. They also used the camera to capture life's more formalized moments, the results of which were poignantly displayed in the photo album's ritualized history of family members from the cradle to the grave. But the narcissistic poses of old-time photos showing their subjects' inclination toward self-promotion through an air of studied informality suggest an innate desire to dramatize life as spontaneous play. By preserving a world lost in time, the camera's miraculous photograph expanded the horizons of the mediated culture by bequeathing valuable historical information to the future as well as nostalgic insights into the lifestyles of the past. Though photography would soon be transformed into a modernist art form, the Kodak camera, which visitors to the fairs of the 1890s brought in abundance, helped create an "art" of the people whose output offered the mediated vision an intimately visual connection with the past.[10]

THE PARADOX OF LITERARY REALISM
AS ENTERTAINMENT

Photography's visual influence was also evident in the trend toward realism in both painting and fiction during this time. To portray life as they envisioned it, certain novelists rebelled against the Victorian conventions of prolix description and formalized narration, taking on the perspective of a camera's eye to focus on the immediate drama of human relationships. A notable example of this end was the fiction of William Dean Howells. Although his sense of realism was tempered by the time's genteel social standards, Howells's urban scenes were presented in an explicitly staged manner that markedly contrasted with the impressionistic realism and complex style of his contemporary Henry James. Accordingly, in *A Hazard of New Fortunes,* Howells describes a New York tenement district in such a vivid manner it suggests a scene by the emerging Ashcan School of artists who painted and illustrated the social behavior of the urban masses in the streets and wherever they might congregate during this era.[11]

Although the main intent of Howells's fiction is to depict the concerns of upper middle-class life, his pictorial attention to the lifestyle of the urban masses as essential to a panoramic picture of his times sensitized the mediated vision to the environmental tensions that urban life could impose on both the well-to-do and commoners alike. The result was writing of a visually compelling nature that despite its serious intent made for a highly entertaining reading experience.

Though another of Howells's literary contemporaries, Mark Twain, was widely celebrated as a humorist, his personal insights into the devious side of human nature resulted in some of the classics of American literature. As a former journalist, Twain forged a media-oriented way with words that was photographic in its visual control of description. Also his unerring ear for earthy dialogue contributed to a unique writing style for his day, not to mention the influence it would have on the craft of later writers. Since the time of Howells and Twain, in fact, visually concrete writing has been a hallmark of both serious and popular American fiction that, in its control of illusion, involves the reader in a startling sense of immediacy.

Foreshadowing this kind of writing was the first-person, camera-eye technique Mark Twain employed in the *Adventures of Huckleberry Finn* (1884), a work inspired by his unflagging memory of the way things were during his adolescence. A clue to the nostalgic source of Twain's visual power appears in a passage from his autobiography in which he describes his ability to "call back" the look, odors, and sounds of the natural scene as well as "the snapshot glimpses of disturbed wild creatures scurrying through the grass."[12] The "snapshot glimpses" that characterize Mark Twain's realism combined nostalgic recall with the visual honesty of the camera's eye to forge a technique that endeared him to both the mediated vision and the critics. To the former his fiction was highly entertaining, and to the latter, it had something meaningful to say in a well crafted manner.

The fiction of both Howells and Twain conditioned the mediated vision to an understanding that the realities of life could be instructively entertaining when presented as visually compelling narrative. But both authors offered contrapuntal viewpoints of their day's cultural conflict between an older way of life and the vagaries of modernism. Howells, who rose from his Midwestern origins to become an urban sophisticate and literary guru, elected to write about those involved in the challenges and consequences of progress. On the other hand, Twain, who took his frontier background with him throughout his life as a nostalgic retreat from the demands of modern living, satirized those who capitalized on the spoils of progress to point out the folly of self-aggrandizement. Through the innocent eyes of his iconic character Huckleberry Finn he prophetically envisioned the impact of inevitable social change while nostalgically lamenting the passing of the old order. Although both writers' works represented a transitory stage between an older and a newer way of American life, they utilized the visual power of literary realism not only to inform readers of the significant issues and concerns of their changing times but, in light of the mediated culture's demands, to entertain them.

The conflict between illusion and reality was a major concern of other notable fiction writers in the 1890s. In *Maggie: A Girl of the Streets* (1893), Stephen Crane produced one of the first novels to undermine the mediated vision's idealized perception of urban life, as he also did with its illusions about the heroics of war in *The Red Badge of Courage* (1895), ironically one of the leading best sellers of the decade. Prophetically, the visual intensity of Crane's writing style revealed a modernistic sense of movement within the boundaries of time and space, anticipating the shifting narrative focus of the movies, only a few years away from realization in the films of D. W. Griffith.

To some writers of the time, the Darwinian concept of environmental stimulus played a major role in determining their characters' reactions to the conflict between illusion and reality. Theodore Dreiser, in fact, dramatizes Carrie Meeber's urban milieu almost as if it were a character unto itself that holds a demonic, unbending control over her fate. In his terse description, for example, of the Chicago business district where Carrie seeks a job near the beginning of her story, the adversarial role of the city is quite clear: "The entire metropolitan centre possessed a high and mighty air calculated to overawe and abash the common applicant, and to make the gulf between poverty and success seem both wide and deep."[13] Carrie's uncertain situation becomes even more precarious as the city which she perceives to be her deliverer evolves into an unfeeling, detached adversary, emblematic of Dreiser's own uncompromising posture toward the "wide and deep" divide between illusion and reality in American life. Indeed, writers like Dreiser and Crane, in drawing on the real-life image of the city as a formidable force in American life, helped remind the mediated vision that only its illusions about life could provide a temporal means of escape from present straits.

REGIONALISTS AND ROMANTICS: PRESERVING AND FANTASIZING THE PAST

Shunning urban experience to entice their readers into an appreciation for the diversity of life in America were the local-color fiction writers—or, as they were also referred to, the regionalists. In reaction to the modernist trends of their time, these writers displayed a strong visual sense of place and its inherent effect on character, and toward the close of the nineteenth century every area of the country had talented representatives. In the South, Joel Chandler Harris, in his popular moralistic tales related by the amiable black slave Uncle Remus, presented a nostalgic picture of plantation life in the antebellum South. Ironically, Harris's deft handling of Negro dialect helped reinforce the stereotypical image of the black character featured in the fiction of mediated culture. By the 90s, in fact, the African American of the urban scene had become a mediated character type that extended from the minstrel show tradition to vaudeville, popular songs, cartoons, advertising art, toys, and jokes—all perpetuating the era's racist image of the black as a childlike simpleton who accepted his lot in life without question.

While some Eastern regionalists, such as Sarah Orne Jewett, found a loyal following in an elitist journal like the *Atlantic Monthly,* Bret Harte brought the West to the rest of the country in the popular stories he had been publishing since the 1870s, most representatively in his collection *The Luck of Roaring Camp* (1872) and later in the *Saturday Evening Post.* Harte's fiction generated character types who would pervade the Western genres of fiction and film, for example, the suave gentleman gambler, the lone gold prospector, and the "good" prostitute as an habitué of the town saloon. In effect, regionalist writing attempted to preserve a way of life that was passing and, in the face of modernism, would soon be no more. In appealing to the nostalgic side of the mediated vision, its art lay in the vivid recollection of what its authors had seen and known. Regional novelist Willa Cather recognized a kindred spirit when she assessed the visual motivation of Sarah Orne Jewett's fiction and its rural Maine setting: "She early learned to love her country for what it was. What is quite as important, she saw it as it was. She happened to have the right nature, the right temperament, to see it so— and to understand by intuition the deeper meaning of all she saw."[14] Any of the stories in Jewett's most popular collection, *The Country of the Pointed Firs* (1896), would substantiate Cather's comments, as an intense desire to record her area's peculiarities predominates, as it does in all local-color fiction. Later, Willa Cather, inspired by her prairie youth, would lend her voice to this tradition.

The Popularity of Escapist Fiction and the Rise of Nonfiction

While many Americans in the 1890s were reading the escapist novels of British writers Arthur Conan Doyle, Anthony Hope, Rudyard Kipling, and Robert Louis Stevenson, American fiction writers were beginning to crack the best-seller realm with works inspired by exotic settings, the romance of history, and religion. The tradition of inspirational fiction with a religious theme begun in the 1880s with Lew Wallace's epical *Ben-Hur* was updated by Charles M. Sheldon's *In His Steps* (1897), a dramatized sermon that challenged readers to model their lives after the example of Jesus for the reward of eternal life. Christianity's widespread appeal as a panacea for the trials and tribulations of this world resulted in a large following for inspirational reading matter, as it would continue to do in periods of personal and social crises during the new century.

But it was the historical romance, typified by such popular novels as Charles Major's *When Knighthood Was in Flower* (1898) and Paul Leicester Ford's *Janice Meredith* (1899) that was the most widely read fiction of the 1890s. Relying on a style best termed as romanticized realism to reinterpret the past, the most popular as well as prolific writer of the genre was F. Marion Crawford. Theorizing in 1893 why romanticism should be the proper mode of the novel, he wrote: "the realist proposes to show men what they are; the romanticist tries to show men what they should be. . . . For my part, I believe that more good can be done by showing men what they may be, or can be, by describing their greatest weaknesses with the highest art."[15] Crawford's naive theory may have fallen far short of producing the "highest art," but one thing was certain about his kind of writing at the time. It found a highly receptive audience that preferred a romanticized world of the past to the actual one of the present.

Of course, the future held a special lure about it as well. An unconventional novel that became a best seller during the 90s was Edward Bellamy's *Looking Backward* (1888), in which its central character awakens in the year 2000 to find a utopian world free of class conflict and other social problems that had beset the late Victorian age. The future as a symbol of evolving progress was a favorite topic of the time, to which numerous magazine articles attested. Best-selling nonfiction also played a part in the individual's quest for self-improvement, exemplified by an inspirational tract like Elbert Hubbard's *A Message to Garcia* (1899) and a plethora of self-help guides to practical, successful living, the kind of book whose widest appeal to the mediated vision lay just ahead in helping it adjust to the challenges of a new century.

A major reason for nonfiction's growing popularity was a more receptive climate created by a spreading literacy. Due to a nationalized public school system, correspondence study courses, and lending libraries, the public was becoming acclimated to more challenging reading matter in both books and magazines. Naturally, profit-motivated publishers responded to the demand, orienting the mediated vision to an inexpensive way to broaden its cultural horizons as well as pursue its escapist inclinations.

Sensing that the time was right for more entertaining fare directed toward a middle-class audience, publisher Frank A. Munsey came up with a general interest periodical in the early 90s. Naming it after himself, he modeled its content after the Sunday newspaper supplements, promoting its strong visual slant with an abundance of pictorial content. The success-driven Munsey was no stranger to the publishing business. In 1882 he had produced the *Golden Argosy,* a magazine for juveniles in which the first issue revealed his preoccupation with the American success story in a rags-to-riches serial by Horatio Alger Jr. It established a tradition carried on in the nonfiction features of *Munsey's* that focused on the achievements of contemporary businessmen and industrialists whose climb to success paralleled Frank Munsey's own humble start as a telegraph operator in a remote area of Maine to become a millionaire New York publisher.

What really assured Munsey's continued success and future reputation was his introduction of the prototypal pulp journal in 1896. When the *Golden Argosy* started to fail, he converted it to the broader reading interests of a general audience. After shortening its name to *Argosy,* Munsey would respond to the escapist fancies of the mediated vision over the ensuing years by publishing fiction in all the popular genres: the adventure tale, the historical romance, the detective mystery, the Western, and the emerging forms of fantasy and science fiction, either as short stories or as serialized versions. Contending that the story itself is more important than the paper it is printed on, Munsey assured the profitability of his venture by publishing *Argosy* on rough wood pulp paper (hence the term "pulp" to categorize such magazines) of over one hundred pages selling for ten cents a copy. Realizing, too, that dramatically exciting cover illustrations would help sell his magazine, Munsey established both the image and format of countless pulp imitations to follow. He has since been rightly designated "the father of the pulp magazine," without whom "there might never have been a Tarzan, Sam Spade, Doc Savage, Zorro, or Shadow."[16] Thus, the major reason for Munsey's publishing success, in spite of the ruthless business methods attributed to him, was his innate feel for the kind of cheap, readily accessed entertainment the mediated vision demanded at the time. His fanciful stories may not have aspired to high literary standards, but their sense of how pure escapism could captivate lured many a reader into the fabulous world of the pulp writer.

Fiction for Everybody:
The Legacy of the Dime Novel

The prototypal source of the escapist fiction appearing in *Argosy* and its imitators was the dime novel that had been responding to the fantasy demands of a spreading mediated culture since the middle of the nineteenth century. Eager for stories set in America and fascinated by the fabled image of the vanishing frontier, many readers, especially city dwellers, found the fantasized Wild West depicted in the tales of colorful characters like Deadwood Dick and Deadshot Dave an exciting world of escape. As the product of pioneer publishing companies like Beadle and Adams, Frank Tousey, and Street and Smith, staffs of writers were assigned to create stories about an area of the country most of them had never seen. But a vivid imagination was their main asset, and it, coupled with technological advances in fast-speed printing, spurred publishers to produce millions of these pocket-sized paperbacks from the 1860s to the late 90s when they began to be supplanted by the growing popularity of the pulp magazine. Read by untold numbers of youths as well as adults, the dime novel, so called after the standard price of a copy though many sold for five cents, strived to give readers all they were looking for in terms of exciting action and escape from the humdrum world of their daily lives.[17]

During the early days of the dime novel the most popular hero of the Western genre was Buffalo Bill Cody, whose sensational exploits were fabricated by numerous writers, chief of whom was E. Z. C. Judson, writing under the pseudonym of Ned Buntline. If William Cody himself invented the "Wild West," it was Judson who concocted the popular frontier image of "Buffalo Bill," introducing it to Chicago theater patrons in his 1873 melodrama *Scouts of the Plains*. Although the play was a flop, audiences were taken by the Buffalo Bill character, and in this fascination one of the most persistent legends of the mediated culture was born. Soon, the illustrations accompanying Colonel Prentiss Ingraham's tales about Buffalo Bill had such a visual impact that it was said Cody himself matched his style of dress to the way it appeared in the illustrations. Whether apocryphal or not, the real-life Cody, who wore his blonde hair long with a goatee, buckskin jacket, and broad-brimmed hat, became the living symbol of the Western hero. The image projected by both Cody and the dime novel merged to establish the mediated vision's conception of the cowboy—an idealized character who kept the traditions and values of the past alive in the present.

By the 1880s and 90s the rapidly evolving urban scene had created a complex social milieu conducive to new subject matter structured around appropriate heroic styles. Pursuant to the heightened interest in city-spawned personalities, then, the private detective's most popular representative, the title character of Street & Smith's *Nick Carter Detective Library,* came on the scene in 1891. In effect, Nick Carter was the frontier hero removed to urban environs where he confronted the problem of crime with methods of Western justice. Despite his talent as a master of disguise, Nick kept his readers on edge through his involvement in perilous predicaments fomented by an endless round of villains seeking to do him in. As a forerunner of the pulp superhero, too, he relied on feats of strength and athletic ability to subdue his foes. A wide knowledge of languages and marksmanship skills with a variety of weapons also came in handy in times of need. As the American answer to Sherlock Holmes, Nick Carter became the mediated culture's longest-running series detective while adapting his personal lifestyle to changing social behavior over the years, from the pulp to the paperback era. Though in his beginnings Nick was a clean-living representative of the dime novel hero, the one thing that remained constant throughout his long career was the violent atmosphere of his tales. Fearing the tales' morally corrupting influence on young readers, many parents, educators, and social critics called for their suppression, a portent of things to come.

However, one dime novel hero seemed to be created to counter public opinion of this sort. Amid the ongoing expansion of higher education during the latter years of the nineteenth century, a growing interest in the collegiate experience arose, mainly in its social side generated by the media's attention to competitive athletics. The most popular dime novel hero who responded to the sports fantasies of American youth from 1896 on into the new century was Frank Merriwell, author Gilbert Patton's paragon of clean living and fair play. Writing under the pen name of Burt L. Standish, Patton unwittingly created a character of momentous mythical significance in his personification of the ideal traits of the man of action that Americans admired. Frank, in fact, represented an idealized sports world that was becoming an escapist refuge for young males, especially for those who dreamed of emulating Frank's sensational feats on the athletic field. As not only a larger than life model of physical courage, self-discipline, and team play in leading his school, Yale, to victory in the major sports of his day, he was incredibly honest and upright in all his interpersonal dealings off the field as well. The upshot of Frank's popularity was the inception of numerous other juvenile series featuring a central character who excelled in school/college sports.

If the Frank Merriwell character exemplified an overly idealized code for success in athletics and, by extension, in life itself, the youthful heroes depicted in the fiction of Horatio Alger Jr. set an even more fantasized standard for achieving success in business and life. Alger's tales of young boys out on their own, confronting the challenges and overcoming the pitfalls of urban life, had been appearing since the 1860s, so that by the 90s he had become the country's most popular author of juvenile fiction. He was also the most prolific, publishing not only in the dime novel format but in popular magazines and books. During Alger's career, in fact, over one hundred novels appeared in his name.

Horatio Alger's stories were really romanticized moral tracts played out within a predominant urban setting. In contrast to Theodore Dreiser's conception of the city as an impersonal environment oblivious to one's personal goals, Alger's city is a place where obstacles can actually enhance the opportunity to get ahead, provided one is possessed of the essential qualities of pluck, daring, and hard work. Ironically, though, it is mainly luck rather than the moralistic experience of hard work that enables an Alger hero to succeed. As Marcus Klein has noted, Alger's stories repeatedly relate how their central characters find themselves in "the right place at the right time to catch a thief, or to aid in an accident, or to help a stranger who has a reward to offer, or, more typically, to discover that he is the lost or true heir."[18] To Alger, though, good fortune came only to those who had the wherewithal to profit from life's unexpected situations. Had not many of the country's most successful businessmen and political leaders once been poor boys whose drive and ambition placed them in the right kind of fortuitous circumstances that led to a higher station in life? Long after his death in 1899, Alger's name would remain a cultural metaphor, the legacy of his naive but highly popular approach to dramatizing a philosophy of success considered integral to the American way. Indeed, Alger's code is still looked upon by many as the key to success even though they may never have heard of its progenitor.

Like Howells and Dreiser, Alger contributed a great deal to the mediated vision's conception of city life as well as its mythology. He was adept at describing the busy movement of the New York streets while suggesting the depravity that lurked around the corner of certain disreputable areas, offering a variety of temptations for his goal-oriented youths to avoid. In a way, Dreiser's Carrie Meeber and Alger's self-motivated heroes are alike in that their mutual attainment of success and respectability is due largely to circumstance rather than any real moral striving on their part. This was a major reason why the moralists denounced *Sister Carrie* on its publication and librarians conspired to keep Alger's books out of the hands of young readers, labeling them less than uplifting because of their sensational elements.

After publisher Edward Stratemeyer introduced the "Rover Boys Series for Young Americans" in 1899, he went on to build a publishing syndicate that would never be surpassed in the number and variety of series titles addressed to young readers. Inspired by the Horatio Alger tales he had read in his youth, Stratemeyer devised a formulaic format for the Rover Boy series that defined the conventions of most juvenile fiction over the next fifty years. Traditional juvenile characters had been drawn in the image of a mischievous self-assertive type like Huckleberry Finn or Frances Hodgson Burnett's socially approved Little Lord Fauntleroy. Both these popular fictional figures of the 1880s helped sensitize adults to a growing realization of adolescents' place in society. But as American youth began to think and act more independently in looking for ways to avoid the daily routine of school and home, Stratemeyer came up with the idea of structuring his series books around socially liberated characters. Though largely unsupervised by their parents, these intelligent, enterprising youths come across as models of decorous behavior while involved in suspenseful adventures and mysteries whose successful outcome is usually intended to emphasize the value of teamwork in resolving a problem or getting a job done. In cultivating a youthful version of the mediated vision, Stratemeyer introduced readers to a wide array of series books by such house names as Arthur M. Winfield (the Rover Boys Series) and Laura Lee Hope (the Outdoor Girls Series). Responding to the escapist desires of both boy and girl readers well into the new century, the Stratemeyer Syndicate's output would mirror American youth's diverse interests and social behavior in rapidly changing times.

One of the biggest inspirations for juvenile fiction during the last quarter of the nineteenth century was technological discovery. Inspired by the ingenious Thomas A. Edison in the main, this great age of invention spawned an appealing dime novel inventor to introduce young readers to the promise of future wonders. Indeed, Frank Reade Jr.'s array of marvelous inventions anticipated such achievements as the automobile, airplane, and submarine. The author of Frank's imaginative tales, which had been appearing since the late 1870s, was Luis P. Senarens, an American Jules Verne singularly obsessed with the possibility of flight, a highly fanciful topic for his day. Accordingly, Senarens had his hero roaming the globe in inventions like an "electric air canoe." Labeled "scientific romances" at the time, the output of Senarens, Verne, and British writer H. G. Wells, just coming into his own in the 90s, presaged a new fantasy genre for the mediated culture called science fiction.

Helping inculcate traditional values about the American way of life, magazine fiction addressed to a juvenile audience also performed an instructive as well entertaining function. In this area, the most respected was *St. Nicholas,* whose pages carried stories by celebrated authors like Louisa May Alcott, Joel Chandler Harris, and Mark Twain. Editor Mary Mapes Dodge, herself the author of the classic children's novel *Hans Brinker,* published stories whose dramatic intent was visually enhanced by notable illustrators of the day such as Howard Pyle, Palmer Cox, and Arthur Rackham. Starting out in 1873 on a long run that would last until 1939, *St. Nicholas* attracted a loyal following who would grow up fondly remembering what they had read in its pages as well as seen in both the realistic and fanciful illustrations that accompanied the stories. For many readers, then, *St. Nicholas* was their introduction to the escapist realm of the mediated vision.

The 1890s was a golden age of fiction addressed to either an adult or juvenile audience. Although social change would modify literary tastes over

THE FIVE CENT

WIDE AWAKE

LIBRARY

Entered according to Act of Congress, in the year 1883, by FRANK TOUSEY, in the office of the Librarian of Congress, at Washington, D. C.

Entered at the Post Office at New York, N. Y., as Second Class Matter.

No. 553 | COMPLETE | FRANK TOUSEY, PUBLISHER, 34 & 36 NORTH MOORE STREET, N. Y. | PRICE | Vol. 1
NEW YORK, April 12, 1893. | ISSUED EVERY WEDNESDAY. | 5 CENTS |

FRANK READE AND HIS STEAM HORSE.

By "NONAME."

In addition to its role in formulating the Western and the detective story, the dime novel also heralded the science-fiction genre. Author's collection.

the coming years, this time's popular fiction, in its intent of helping the reader transcend the ordinariness of everyday life, accomplished this end mainly through a visually directed narrative style—a compelling kind of writing that could make even a story set in the mundane present intensely entertaining.

FANTASIZING AND SELLING THE GOOD LIFE IN A GROWING CONSUMER CULTURE

A more tangible way to make the present palatable was through the acquisition of desirable material goods, provided one had the means to purchase them. In the 1890s the mail-order catalog came into its own as a readily available medium whose imagery of consumer desire was indoctrinating remote sectors of the country into the pleasures of materialistic wish fulfillment. Indeed, after thumbing through the profusely illustrated catalog circulated by the Chicago-based Montgomery Ward Company, many families in small towns and rural areas were induced into ordering items of their choice that might range from an insignificant novelty to a parlor piano. Geared to the middle-class purchasing power of that day, which was quite low by later standards, a piano, for example, could be purchased for less than a hundred dollars.

As the model for a system of marketing consumer products to remote areas of the nation, Ward was successful enough to attract a rival competitor in another Chicago company. Richard W. Sears, who parlayed his mail-order watch business into the billion dollar Sears, Roebuck Company, had a special knack for sensing what the average consumer was looking for in self-enhancing merchandise. Thus his catalog's text and sharply engraved product illustrations were alluring enough to hook many a customer in the hinterland. Capitalizing on both the expanding railroad network and, by 1896, rural free mail delivery of his catalog, Sears and new partner Julius Rosenwald (A. C. Roebuck had sold his interests in 1895) built their business into over 100,000 orders a day by century's end.

Facetiously referred to as the "farmer's bible" but more aptly as the "housewife's wish book," the mail-order catalog projected a visual kind of educational appeal. Through it, many isolated rural residents received their initiation into the mediated vision's perspective on the good life awaiting them in the beckoning urban world. Its allure was maximized by the enticingly pictured fashions, furniture stylings, household appliances, popular fiction, musical instruments, sporting goods, and, of course, children's toys and games. Those able to afford the purchase of two of the catalog's most popular items—the stereoscope and the phonograph—could enjoy both visual and aural access to the escapist diversions of the outside world. Small-town/rural folk may have had their spiritual needs nurtured by what they read in the Bible, but their materialistic dreams were visually enhanced by the mail-order catalog.

For urban area residents who had the means to shop directly for the material goods that the nation's rapidly developing consumer culture was producing, the big-city department store sufficed as an awesome showplace during the 90s. Here the late Victorian preoccupation with abundance and excess found a highly visible repository of merchandise as spectacle. By affording potential customers the opportunity to indulge in the escapist practice of "just looking," thus complementing a store's intent of attracting them off the street through alluring window displays, this ritual often enticed a browser into making a purchase. Such a mood is captured in *Sister Carrie* when Dreiser describes his heroine's reaction to the bounty of goods on display in a Chicago store. She reveals a side of herself that transcends class lines in this compelling ethos of consumerism—the desire to promote one's lot in life through material possessions.

It was during the Christmas season that magnanimous display and ornate decoration galvanized dormant consumer impulses to purchase more goods than at any other time, especially from the children's sections that stocked the popular toys and board games of the time. Intended to be both didactic and entertaining, many of them, such as the Milton Bradley Company's *Checkered Game of Life* and the Parker Brothers' *Game of Christian Endeavor,* mirrored the moral tone of the middle class, reducing the serious message of how to live an upright life to a level that even a small child could understand. Other colorfully designed games inspired by work, travel, new inventions, and historical themes had an educational side in alerting players to an exciting world undergoing dynamic change. Toys also reflected current trends, particularly in the area of transportation, as trains, model ships, and cast-iron vehicles of all kinds made their appearance. While boys were taught the virtue of thrift through the large number of mechanical banks sold, girls were reminded of their domestic role through the traditional dolls and toys that related to household duties. But an ominous sign of what lay ahead for boys in the real world showed up in the form of toy soldiers, popguns, warship models, and even military uniforms. By the new century, board games and toys had become an integral part of a middle-class child's upbringing, usually presented as a reward for model behavior and thus a tangible symbol of the mediated vision's traditional goal of self-improvement.

With the introduction of the Santa Claus image at this time, the big stores capitalized on this visual icon as a mediator between the spiritual meaning of Christmas and the commercial realities of a consumer society. A literary prototype had appeared in 1883 in Clement Moore's popular poem about a family visitation from St. Nicholas on Christmas Eve. But illustrator Thomas Nast's visual conception of the Santa Claus character had greater impact, prompting stores to hire ruddy-faced, overweight men to dress in the likeness of Nast's image and allow children the opportunity to make their wish lists known to them as a reward for "being good." To the mediated culture the spirit of Christmas, as it was personified in the popular image of Santa Claus, heralded the promise of a consumer-oriented society, providing yet another way to fantasize it.

Recognizing the growing purchasing power of women as well as their attraction to the shopping experience, stores announced periodic sales in newspaper display ads directed at the female eye. But compared to the well-to-do shopper whose venture to a department store was a form of escapist entertainment, women of lesser estate exercised a more practical bent in the ritual of bargain hunting; for them, the five-and-dime store that F. W. Woolworth had established in 1879 was a thrifty answer to certain household needs. His success demonstrated that there was a great deal of money to be made selling mass-produced items such as kitchenware as well as notions and novelties, provided they were offered cheaply enough. In addition to their rock bottom prices, Woolworth's stores relied on a simple marketing technique. In them, customers discovered open inspection counters whose items were arranged in such eye-appealing fashion that they practically sold themselves. Promoting his stores' stock through this method of visual seduction became a Woolworth hallmark, and as a result many a customer found the five to ten cent price for even a useless knickknack hard to resist. In fact, this system worked so profitably for Woolworth that he soon expanded it into a nationwide chain store operation. By 1913 his fortune was great enough for him to erect a "monument"—New York's Woolworth Building—to a success story that had all the earmarks of an Horatio Alger tale, as exemplified by Woolworth's rise from a poor farm boy to the status of a multimillionaire. The world's tallest structure at the time, Woolworth's sixty-story "Cathedral of Commerce," as it was dubbed, stood as a highly visible symbol of the capitalist message that had grown so appealing to the mediated vision: In America, wealth and the good life were in reach of anyone willing to work hard enough to achieve them.

PROMOTING THE GOOD LIFE THROUGH ADVERTISING

All the emerging commercial enterprises of this time were heirs of the new pictorial system of print advertising that had followed the development of mass production methods and the urbanization of America following the Civil War. Foremost among the basic needs of city dwellers, of course, were canned and packaged food items. But promoting and selling them called for recognizable brand names, both on the can or package and in the advertising process, whose primary goal was to single out a product's worth over its competition. To facilitate this mission as well as to counter the overblown promotional style of patent medicines that had invaded magazines, newspapers, and posters, advertising agencies began to play a key role in showing companies how to inform consumers of the supposed merits of their products. Accordingly, agency head J. Walter Thompson set out to promote highly visible and credible identities for companies with quality products to market. He accomplished his goal mainly through the widespread circulation of simple symbols and designs whose repetitious appearances in newspapers, magazines, and posters created immediate recognition and a pervasive awareness of a product's identity. Another factor in this ongoing visual process was the proliferation of product logos and ads on trade cards, serving trays, calendars, fans, clocks, and numerous novelties.

By the 1890s, popular magazines, more so than newspapers, had become national vehicles for the ad agencies to promote a product's worth, conditioning the mediated vision to identify trademarks and logos as referents to quality. In effect, these symbols heralded a new visual language that would become increasingly psychological in its persuasive manner of informing a potential customer why a particular product was the key to good health, social standing, or job success. As these were the things that really mattered to the mediated vision in its avid pursuit of the American Dream, the symbols of commerce that Thompson helped promulgate were intended to condition consumers to what the good life was all about. Over the years the advertising messages and imagery of these products would not only mirror their roles in promoting the good life but also record the mediated vision's changing social perspectives toward it.

Pursuant to technological advances in the use of color in print, magazine publisher Cyrus Curtis and such editors as George H. Lorimer and Edward Bok had little difficulty in accepting its role as a visual stimulus in pictorial advertising. Sensing the dynamic change that a consumer-oriented society was undergoing, these men tailored the advertising content of their magazines accordingly. Bok, in particular, bolstered the advertising revenue of the *Ladies' Home Journal* through his realization that women were a natural sales source for home products. Also capitalizing on this perception was the agency of N. W. Ayer and Son, which consolidated the functions of advertising broker, copywriter, and artist to create ads in which woman as the dominant symbol of American home life was paired with a product designed to ease her housekeeping drudgery. Because many popular magazines carried both articles related to family life and fiction inspired by women's escapist interests, they were not only a reliable advertising medium but a domestic mirror of their times.

By reflecting the social values of the consumers to which they were directed, magazine advertisements stand as a visual record of the country's transformation from an agrarian society to one that was highly industrialized and urbanized. They also reveal how the mediated vision adapted to changing consumer values—particularly in the shift from traditional assumptions about social behavior to more sophisticated, if frequently controversial, attitudes toward a product's social role, such as tobacco and alcohol.

The need to nationalize advertising resulted in large part from the nation-wide expansion of the chain store, whose marketing success now depended on the transportation of goods via an extended railway network to store locations. Along with the advent of nationally identified retailers functioning as viable markets to meet the demands of a burgeoning consumer society, a variety of advertising media, other than the magazine, was utilized to announce the availability of a multitude of products, whether consumers needed them or not.

The most ubiquitous advertising during the 1890s was circulated by the poster, which was enjoying a renaissance inspired by such figures of the European Art Nouveau movement as Henri Toulouse-Lautrec and Alphonse Mucha. To capitalize on its direct promotional power, the poster was placed in highly visible locations, publicizing everything from beer to bicycles. As a result, urban pedestrians and trolley commuters were visually inundated by posters affixed to the sides of buildings and fences as well as the trolleys themselves. American artists Will Bradley and Edward Penfield were among the more prominent to adapt the highly stylized modernist method of Art Nouveau illustration to advertising as, for example, in the posters they did to promote the safety bicycle as a recreational vehicle for both men and women. As the ownership of a bicycle had special meaning for women who sought to counter the era's social code limiting their involvement in physical activities, advertising that pictured women cycling was a major factor in making it socially acceptable and lowering the barriers against cross-gender leisure participation.

The poster also played a significant role in publicizing entertainment venues such as vaudeville, theatrical events, sporting activities, and the traveling circus. While high-speed printing advances assured its mass production for posting, the chromolithographic process revealed how color could enhance a poster's eye appeal. Indeed, the colorful poster that promoted a melodramatic play by focusing on its most exciting highlights was a strong factor in attracting patrons to it.

But the promise of the product that poster advertising promulgated had a downside as well. The ugly outdoor clutter accruing from its widespread, random posting precipitated an antisignage movement dedicated to ridding the urban scene of what it considered a distracting eyesore. Although a leasing system was initiated to regulate the visually intrusive images of commerce and popular culture, the pattern for the omnipresence of outdoor advertising in the coming century can be clearly seen in the eye-assaultive poster displays of the 1890s.

In 1891 the first electric sign appeared on Broadway, and by 1893 such commercial entreaties had become so prevalent that the "Great White Way" was coined to describe the area around Broadway and Twenty-Third Street. Among the most eye-catching at this time was the H. J. Heinz sign atop the Flatiron Building. Spread across a fifty-foot area was the shape of a gigantic pickle outlined by green bulbs with the name *Heinz* spelled out in white. Below it were highlighted many of the fifty-seven varieties of the company's pre-prepared foods. As another electronic innovation that helped fantasize the urban night, it conditioned the city dweller to a new kind of visual seduction that was becoming consonant with the urban scene. Thus the dynamics of the Heinz sign announced the arrival of the age of advertising ballyhoo. It also projected an escapist appeal that the mediated culture, falling increasingly under the spell of getting and spending, found very much to its liking.[19]

Entertaining a Mediated Audience through Theatrical Venues

Posters that advertised the various modes of theatrical entertainment in the 1890s offer sociocultural clues to the kinds of shows that had the greatest visual and aural appeal to theatergoers. Providing large-scale audiences with what they wanted to see and hear had begun with the minstrel show's popularity after the Civil War, but by the 80s it was being eclipsed by vaudeville. In its heyday, though, the uniquely American form of minstrelsy, in which white performers appeared in blackface, treated patrons to a full evening of comedy, song, and dance. The image of the blackface performer became so popular that even after the minstrel show's demise many vaudeville stars continued to appear in blackface as late as the 1920s. In analyzing the racist attitudes of the time, David Nasaw has observed that on stage the blackface performer's functional role was to be laughed at in order to allow all-white audiences to revel in their cultural superiority. Their "derisive laughter at the superstitions, the stupidities, the misuse of language and logic, the sentimentality and inherent childishness" these performers affected helped reinforce the prevailing stereotypes of blacks.[20] At a time when the dominant white posture set the standards for social behavior, it generally ignored African Americans as an integral part of the mediated culture. In a short while their music would demonstrate just how much a part of it they were.

Although vaudeville, a variety show format with roots in both the British music hall and minstrelsy, continued to expand with urbanization, it would find itself fighting for survival following the movies' growing popularity in the early years of the new century. Until the 1930s, though, hundreds of vaudeville houses on a national circuit played to the escapist desires of the mediated vision, while many urban theaters presented programs on a continuous basis for as little as five and ten cents a seat. Little wonder, then, that by the 90s vaudeville, whose program ranged from such varied turns as those featuring acrobats, jugglers, and magicians to animal and novelty acts, singers, and comedians, had become the nation's favorite source of live entertainment.

Respecting vaudeville's comedy turns, ethnic comics were headliners, due mainly to their peculiar brand of humor that cast them as social misfits, a role that middle-class audiences found highly amusing. Between 1890 and 1900, Ellis Island processed so many immigrants that by the end of the decade one-third of the country's total population was foreign-born. From this influx emanated the comedian of European extract who stood out as a distinct type until his idiosyncrasies were assimilated into the cultural mainstream. As he recounted the social mishaps of his new life in America, his heavily accented distortions of the English language were complemented by his exaggerated physical antics. Visually, this kind of humor looked ahead to the slapstick episodes of the 1920s' silent film comedy, while aurally it anticipated the radio comedy of the 1930s. Although magazine illustrators and newspaper cartoonists presented their visual impressions of Irish, Italian, German, and Yiddish types to the mediated culture, it was the vaudeville comics who brought them to life.

While vaudeville entrepreneur Tony Pastor featured comics in his programs, he made sure their routines were suitable and proper for audiences of both women and children. However, Pastor was not averse to exploiting the charms and talents of women performers. Among the most popular was singer-actress Lillian Russell, whose stage presence and widely publicized celebrity lifestyle, enhanced by her relationship with the ebullient "Diamond Jim" Brady, personified the glamorous side of the so-called Gay Nineties. But Russell's singing performances were more conventional than the wildly abandoned (at least for the time) song-and-dance routines of Eva Tanguay, whose signature song, "I Don't Care," epitomized her attitude toward social mores. Both performers helped inaugurate two culturally diverse images of the American female entertainer that would permeate the media culture of the upcoming century. Of course, Tanguay's model would prove to be the more conducive to controversy.

Even as early as 1866, the socially acceptable appearance of scantily dressed women on the American stage had originated in the New York production of *The Black Crook* at Niblo's Garden. This landmark show also represented the first major step toward the development of an American musical comedy tradition. And despite the moralists' outcry over the two hundred leotard-attired women who pranced seemingly nude about the stage, the production was a resounding success. Bolstered by a spectacular array of visual effects, it drew patrons to nearly five hundred performances over a sixteen-month period, and between 1868 and the 90s it was revived eight times. Due to its exciting combination of music and dance, along with a dazzling showcase of that day's conception of female beauty, *The Black Crook* anticipated Florenz Ziegfeld's *Follies* revue by appealing to the American theatergoer's attraction to grandiose staging effects that stimulated the visual and aural senses. The upshot was an intensely sensual viewing experience that audiences saw as the theater's ultimate escapist trip at the time.

However, American musical theater during the late nineteenth century was, for the most part, still under the sway of European-styled productions, as evidenced by Lillian Russell's popular roles in the operettas of Offenbach and Gilbert and Sullivan. But by the 1890s the originality and vitality of the American creative spirit, inspired by the escapist demands of the mediated vision, began to explore the possibilities for a uniquely American musical form. That native sources could provide appropriate material for musical theater had been demonstrated in *The Brook* (1879), which, after the manner of regionalist fiction, cast rural characters in their natural setting while they danced and sang songs with vernacular lyrics. Soon, the musical comedy genre was asserting itself as a natural medium for the introduction and purveyance of popular music.

During the late 90s, when the motion picture's development as a narrative mode was still some years away from realization, popular theater was enjoying one of its richest periods. A major reason was the ascendancy of melodrama, which, through its reaffirmation of traditional values, was the mediated vision's most appealing dramatic form. In particular, its conventional portrayal of the conflict between innocence and deception, often epitomized as a struggle between poor, well-meaning people and the rich and powerful, was especially popular with rural/small-town audiences. In effect, the melodramatic play depicted a problematic world that by its happy ending sought to show life as it should be. Typically, in one of the late nineteenth century's most popular plays, *Hazel Kirke,* the title character manages to end up triumphant despite the multitude of personal crises she has endured. This prototype of later radio soap opera drama not only provided a cathartic outlet for audiences' pent-up emotions, it transformed the problems of life into visually compelling entertainment. In general, plots were based on the combination of such situations as a long-suffering heroine (as in *Hazel Kirke*), a wrongfully accused hero, and the nefarious deeds of a villain. Regardless of any plot variation, vindication was necessarily attained by play's end, much to an audience's delight in seeing the real world improved upon.[21]

By the 90s the most popular productions of the genre, such as the long-running play based on Harriet Beecher Stowe's abolitionist novel, *Uncle Tom's Cabin,* were capitalizing on updated technical effects. While its outdated premise was still being dramatized in 1899 by innumerable repertory companies, the innovative technical developments of urban productions allowed for more realistic scenes and spectacular events to be staged as were also, for example, the suspenseful buzz-saw escape in *Blue Jeans,* the exciting horse race in *The Luck of the Run,* and *Ben-Hur*'s sensational chariot race. Both these latter scenes were made possible by treadmills that created the illusion of on-stage motion. Thus the implementation of such technology made a cliff-hanger predicament sensational enough to keep drawing patrons and guarantee a longer production run.

By experimenting with innovative ways to stage dramatic productions, then, popular theater of the 1890s was conditioning the mediated vision to appreciate spectacle on a grand scale. Earlier, impresario Imre Kiralfy, an Hungarian immigrant, had introduced spectacular theater in his productions of *Around the World in 80 Days* (1875), *The Fall of Rome* (1888), and *Columbus and the Discovery of America* (1891). Some were of such grandiose proportions they were presented outdoors in collaboration with the Barnum and Bailey Circus. The rage for historical pageantry would continue into the new century, looking ahead to the epic films of Hollywood and the mediated culture's next great visual medium of escapist entertainment.

Although the plays offered by a traveling repertory company were staged on a limited technical scale, this shortcoming hardly mattered to naive hinterland audiences, especially if a play was structured around their favorite theme—rural/small-town innocence confronting and overcoming big-city chicanery and deception. This formula usually featured a country bumpkin type whose natural, down-home manner ultimately won out over any kind of duplicity. Here, in essence, was the dramatic version of the mediated vision's natural conflict between an idealized pastoral past and the increasingly complex present. Two of the late nineteenth century's longest-running plays, *The Old Homestead* and *Rip Van Winkle*, were emblematic of this contrapuntal situation. The latter production, which starred one of the era's most heralded actors, Joseph Jefferson, was the archetypal story of this conflict as based on the Washington Irving tale (see my prologue, note 3). In effect, both plays reaffirmed the notion of the past as a time when things were less complicated and thus more appealing than the unfathomable present.

A featured attraction of the New York productions and traveling troupes that staged them in major cities around the country was the mediated star system of the American theater. Focusing on the matinee idol—the male actor adulated by women who attended a play's afternoon performance—these plays promoted such popular icons of the day as John Drew, James K. Hackett, and William Gillette. The latter's natural manner in portraying the title character in *Sherlock Holmes* (1899) attempted to humanize Arthur Conan Doyle's famous detective, even allowing for a romantic relationship between Holmes and the feminine lead, a naturally appealing situation to matinee patrons.

Anticipating the promotional efforts of the Hollywood studio system, the lithograph poster publicizing a stage celebrity's latest play aroused the mediated vision's growing curiosity about his or her private life. Journalists who focused on this fascination by writing newspaper/magazine stories about notable performers started another popular media tradition that would culminate in the kind of material featured in the newspaper tabloid and movie/ra-

dio fan magazine. Such coverage led entrepreneurs to recognize the box office rewards to be had from exploiting a star's off-stage activities and eccentricities. Florenz Ziegfeld, one of the up-and-coming star makers, would soon
offer an apocryphal contribution to tabloid journalism's flair for sensationalism by relating that his paramour, singer/dancer Anna Held, bathed in milk.
Even champion prizefighters John L. Sullivan, Bob Fitzsimmons, and James
J. Corbett capitalized on their athletic reputations to become popular actors.
Despite their lack of acting talent, these boxers' widely publicized triumphs
in the ring were enough to assure their on-stage popularity, especially Corbett whose good looks helped him attain the status of a matinee idol. Sensing an entertainment connection between athletic heroes and theatrical stars,
leading theater magazines of the day began devoting a significant amount of
space to sporting events. From the perspective of the mediated vision, both
sports and stage celebrities were now comparable to the time's millionaires
in personifying the success stories that the promise of the American Dream
inspired.

In contrast to the mission of the elitist Lyceum clubs that sponsored lec-
tures on specialized topics, the Chautauqua movement, which had started out
in the idyllic lake setting of upstate New York in the 1870s, soon evolved into
an educational/entertainment circuit that brought well-known speakers, musicians, cultural envoys, and entertainers of various talents to small-town/ru-
ral assemblies across the country. Seemingly in the best interests of the mediated vision, the Chautauqua equated the quest for self-improvement with
leisure activity. At heart, the idea of Chautauqua represented an opportunity
to get away from the demands of modern living and return to the pastoral ideal
that renewed one's inner spirit in a stimulating oasis of intellectual enrich-
ment and recreational good feeling. Thus, by responding to the self-devel-
opment goals of the mediated vision, the Chautauqua helped transform the
learning experience into a form of communally shared edification and entertainment.

POPULAR MUSIC'S GROWING VISUAL ORIENTATION

Singing performers of the vaudeville stage in the 90s helped promote a new
kind of mass-mediated music that originated in an area of New York City soon
to be known as Tin Pan Alley. This name, some said, was inspired by the ca-
cophony of piano music emanating from the open windows of the sheet music publishing houses. By the turn of the century self-made tunesmiths began congregating here by the score, composing and producing a seemingly
never-ending stream of formulaic songs for an ever-expanding appreciative
audience. By plugging these songs to well-known entertainers in hopes that
their performances would popularize them, the songwriters' ultimate goal was

to sell their tunes as recordings and sheet music for the parlor piano. This instrument, in fact, had grown so popular as a source of home entertainment that "between 1890 and 1900 the number of pianos in use in American homes increased more than five times as fast as the population."[22] To respond to this growth rate the sheet music industry began turning out songs as fast as the composers could create them, ranging from sentimental ballads to novelty tunes and, by the end of the century, ragtime numbers. Not until the sales of phonograph recordings began to cut into those of sheet music did the piano fade as a home entertainment medium. But during its ascendancy to something of a status symbol, the piano's conventional place in the family parlor reflected American middle-class respect for cultural gentility and the feeling of sociability its playing generated.

The sales success and popularity of a Tin Pan Alley song depended a great deal on the right aural combination of melody, lyrics, and rhythm. But certain visual factors were instrumental as well. The eye-catching chromolithograph of a thematic scene, pretty girl, or photograph of a well-known entertainer/singer made the sheet music cover a unique social reflector of its times. Listeners were also compelled to cultivate a highly personal identity with certain songs heard either alone or in social gatherings. Indeed, the songs whose lyrics blended so readily with their melodies possessed the aural power to conjure up mental images of remembered occasions from the past. "After the Ball," which was first heard in the longest-running musical production of the nineteenth century, *A Trip to Chinatown* (1890), was one of the time's most exemplary ballads whose popularity can be ascribed to its ideal match of narrative and melodic sentiment. Although composer Charles K. Harris claimed to have based his song on a real-life incident, he revealed an innate feel for his time's taste by embellishing the song's tale of unrequited love with unabashed sentiment. As a result, it became the nation's first major song hit, attested to by its voluminous sheet music and recording sales.

In the 90s, a song's theme—whether sentimental, romantic, nostalgic, or humorous—clearly reflected the escapist mood of the times. In fact, all the oversized, colorfully illustrated sheet music covers that adorned the parlor piano—from a pretty girl's face for a romantic ballad like "Down by the Old Mill Stream" to the flamboyant historical scenes for a rousing E. T. Paul march—would persist as strong visual evidence of the 1890s' popular taste in music. But the close of the century saw another kind of eye-catching sheet music art showing up on the parlor piano that unwittingly connoted imminent social change—the racially suggestive cover for a ragtime tune.

By the last decade of the nineteenth century the ingredients for the principal forms of African American music—ragtime, blues, and jazz—that had long been fermenting in the South were preparing to indoctrinate the American people into a new kind of musical experience. The melting pot of New Orleans had brought together the celebratory music of the marching brass band and the syncopated ragtime piano to produce Dixieland jazz, a merging of improvisational playing styles that presaged the advent of the modern dance orchestra. Too self-expressive and exuberant to be confined to one area, jazz soon found its way to the cabarets and nightspots of Chicago and New York, where it met with an enthusiastic reception. Tin Pan Alley, anticipating the money to be made in responding to the growing popularity of this dynamic new sound, began producing hundreds of hybrid versions of ragtime songs that would ultimately result in a widespread cultural acceptance of this uninhibited, earthy kind of music and its seemingly visual way of expressing itself. Although Scott Joplin was the most accomplished ragtime composer (his "Maple Leaf Rag," 1899's biggest hit, sold a million copies of sheet music), Ben Harney was the performer who helped turn ragtime into a national fad, mainly from the exposure he received appearing in New York entertainment venues and publishing an instructional manual for playing ragtime on the piano, the instrument that best accommodated its complex stylings. Though African Americans now enjoyed a new sense of mobility, their subjection to social segregation motivated them to cultivate their own version of the mediated vision. Indeed, they continued to expand on the roots of their musical heritage, assuaging the pain of urban isolation through the new kind of music they were boldly introducing to a spreading mediated culture.

In the 90s black performers who kept the minstrel tradition alive in their own shows found lucrative ways to exploit song publishing and recorded music. But such monetary rewards came at the price of condoning the racist posture of the so-called "coon" songs at the peak of their popularity during this time. Racist overtones notwithstanding, the distinguishing characteristics of jazz-styled music, particularly its syncopated rhythm and the incorporation of street language into its lyrics, would make an indelible mark on popular music, extending from Tin Pan Alley to vaudeville, musical comedy, and beyond.

That this kind of music would have a seminal influence in originating new dance steps was only natural. By the 90s, black minstrel shows were turning the tables on white culture by ending their performances with a rendition of the traditional cakewalk that plantation blacks had created as a parody of the Southern gentry's dress and manners. Put to a ragtime beat, it brought a show to a rousing, crowd-pleasing close, as featured in the all-black musical comedies of 1898—*A Trip to Coontown* and *Clorindy, or the Origin of the Cakewalk.* The black version of musical comedy not only introduced the cakewalk to a wider audience, its modernist, improvisational expression loosened the Victorian constraints on ballroom dancing, which up to this time had been dominated by the ritualistic, sedate movements of the European waltz. Though Dixieland's lively, foot-tapping beat inspired new forms of ballroom dance, the abandoned manner it encouraged between the sexes brought down public censure on those who engaged in it as downright godless frivolity.

The plaintively styled lyrical expression known as the blues also followed blacks from the rural South to the city. While the traditional Negro spiritual's lyrics that dated back to slave days attempted to transcend earthly trials and tribulations through the promise of a heavenly reward, the blues lament addressed life in the here and now, projecting a dark mood arising from the social inequities of living in a racist society or the emotional pain suffered from a lovers' quarrel or breakup. The blues style would play an influential role in the alienated, modernist perspective of much popular music in the twentieth century, relating directly to the mediated vision's ongoing discontent with life in the present.

Echoes of the Negro spiritual, recognized as an influential force in American folk music by 1900, continued to show up in the evolving gospel music of the black church, which would play no small part in the development of secular music. White composers also produced a popular version of religious music inspired by the Christian life and the celestial reward awaiting those who adhered to its teachings. As a result, the 1890s saw an outpouring of fundamentalist gospel hymns that were sung regularly at revival meetings. Although High Church denominations frowned on allowing the newer forms of nontraditional music into the sanctity of their services, D. L. Moody, a leading evangelist of the time's revival movement, expressed the opinion of many churchgoers when he commented: "Singing does at least as much as preaching to impress the word of God upon people's minds."[23] The emotional side of religious experience was naturally receptive to musical expression, reflecting the Gospel message's passionate appeal of an afterlife that transcended the uncertainties of life in the here and now.

Thus, all varieties of popular music in the 1890s contained the power not only to inspire but to amuse through lyrics structured around graphic visual metaphors. Whether through sheet music or recordings, the rendition of a song presented the listener a kind of aural photograph that generated memories associated with a particular time and place. As André Millard remarks in his history of recorded sound, "nothing brings home the immediacy of the cultural experience of the past like its sounds."[24]

THE PHONOGRAPH'S ROLE IN DEMOCRATIZING AMERICAN MUSIC

By the late 90s many memorable songs heard on the vaudeville stage and in musical theater were enjoying extended popularity as recordings for the phonograph as well as sheet music for the piano. While Thomas Edison's invention of a medium for recording and replaying sound in 1877 was a major breakthrough in communications technology, he had envisioned more practical uses for his "talking machine" than just musical entertainment. But in

1889 a mass-directed use for it as a musical medium supplanting the player piano was realized in the public placement of coin operated models. This marked the beginning of the commercial age of electronic entertainment and the mediated vision's acceptance of it as an immediate way to complement leisure time with a pleasant listening experience.

Widely advertised as a socially essential household item, the phonograph was manufactured and marketed by three major companies—Edison, Victor, and Columbia, all of which also produced recordings. Although the Edison name was considered a sign of quality in itself, Victor would eventually gain the upper hand in sales. In fact, its Victrola model grew popular enough for the public to make it the generic name for a record player. Regardless of make, though, the phonograph, even as a piece of furniture, would function as both a status symbol and an escapist venue, supplanting the primacy of the parlor piano.

In this acoustic age of the hand cranked or battery operated player, Edison experimented briefly with the 78–rpm disc recording, but his company would ultimately fail as a competitor due to its stubborn commitment to promoting the cumbersome cylinder recording. In the meantime the disc recording that Emile Berliner had introduced in 1887 was becoming the record customer's more acceptable format, and the Victor Talking Machine Company realized at once its marketing potential.

While recording lists helped fuel the ongoing conflict between the elite standards of high culture and mass tastes, the increasing escapist demands of the mediated vision had begun to plant the seeds for the gradual democratization of American music. Though Victor capitalized on the elitist appeal of operatic music at this time, it and the other recording companies also realized the commercial advantages in giving the general public the kind of music it most wanted to hear. Naturally, sentimental ballads, novelty tunes, and topical songs topped the company lists, but also near the top was a category then referred to as "race" music. It included the comic songs recorded by coon shouters, so labeled in that day of the acoustic recording because singers had to raise their voices to be clearly recorded. Since political correctness was obviously far from being a social issue at this time, the recording companies' commercial interests catered to whatever appealed to listeners as best-selling escapist entertainment

As popular music of the 1890s was primarily defined and popularized by its reception on the vaudeville stage, sentimental songs aimed at immigrant patrons, especially the Irish homesick for the old country and rural newcomers to the city looking back to simpler times, were naturals for the phonograph. Even though poverty had been a prime motivator for starting a new life in America or departing the rural scene, it was never a deterrent to inspiring music that idealized the way things had been. Thus the nostalgic affinities of the mediated vision were a major factor in determining much of the music produced by the recording companies at this time.

Another dominant force in the recorded music of the era was the dynamic two-step beat of "March King" John Philip Sousa's compositions. During this generally conservative time, when patriotism and sentiment were openly expressed feelings, the live band concert in an outdoor setting attracted a wide following, especially in the summer in small towns across the country. A Sousa march on such a program was ritually anticipated, and the dynamics of performance attendant to a number like the "Washington Post March" (1891) were as visually exciting and inspiring as they were aurally. As a result, Sousa's emotionally charged marches were best sellers as both sheet music and recordings during the decade. Also as enhancements to the patriotic fervor generated by the Spanish-American War in 1898, they fostered an intensely nationalistic air. The American military would be forever indebted to the rousing music of John Philip Sousa, whose marches were played whenever and wherever a parade or patriotic ceremony was in order.[25]

As the earliest form of electronic entertainment responding to the escapist desires of the mediated vision, the phonograph, in helping democratize American musical taste, ironically transformed the communal experience of a live concert into one that was more private and personalized to the solitary listener. And as a visually oriented relationship, it allowed the listener to return to an escapist world of nostalgic memories as well as inspirational dreams—a realm happily distanced, if only temporarily, from the self-limiting demands of everyday life.

THE DUAL ROLE OF THE DAILY NEWSPAPER

By the last decade of the nineteenth century the ongoing demand for immediate sources of information about contemporary events found the most efficient and entertaining medium to be the metropolitan daily newspaper. By also proving itself as a democratizing force, the newspaper not only addressed the special interests and concerns of the socially elite and literate middle class, it provided a cheap tutorial instrument for newly arrived immigrants eager to learn the rudiments of the English language and accustom themselves to the social ways of their new country. This socializing process might be realized through such visually inspired venues as illustrated advertisements, the pictorial layouts that accompanied hard news, feature stories, sporting reports, and a new form of pictorial narrative called the comic strip.

Although it reported the current events and political issues considered "news," the urban newspaper was a highly competitive enterprise that sought to attract a daily readership through a diversity of regular features carried for the sole purpose of amusement. In addition to their human interest stories, many readers took to certain New York papers' sensationalized reports of crime, scandal, and social gossip, all seemingly intended to entertain as they informed. With a tradition dating back to the penny paper of the 1830s, the reportage of crime and scandal was hardly new to American journalism. But in the 90s, the competition among the large number of papers serving a growing urban area like New York resulted in all-out attempts to report the socially subversive side of the news to increase readership. A highly popular model for this kind of reporting was a tabloid called the *National Police Gazette.* It had been appearing since 1845 with only a modicum of success. But when publisher Richard Kyle Fox took it over in 1876, he injected new life into the ailing paper by making crime and scandal its main topics, for, as he contended, the *Gazette* "did not exist for the discussion of great issues. It stood for entertainment, raciness, and readability."[26] To appeal to an even wider audience Fox came up with the idea of special sections devoted to popular theater and sports, particularly the then renegade sport of boxing. In a day when sporting figures and theatrical performers were not so readily recognizable or exposed to the general public, the illustrations that the *Gazette* carried depicting prizefighters as well as baseball and college football players engaged in their respective sports were proudly displayed on the walls of barbershops and saloons around the country.

But to males the daring pictorial content featuring female performers of the burlesque stage in scanty attire and pretty actresses in alluring poses also drew much attention. Anticipating tabloid journalism's propensity for exposing society's more aberrant transgressions were the sensational stories that the *Gazette*'s risqué cover illustrations promoted. Although such coverage was frowned upon by the cultural custodians, its reception revealed a large following that relished reading stories about the unsavory side of human nature. It also hinted at the underground circulation of pornography, which, since the invention of the camera, was more visually prevalent than most people of this era realized.[27]

During the 1880s, innovative New York newspaperman Joseph Pulitzer, whom many would consider the father of the modern American newspaper, turned the *New York World* into the most widely read paper in the city through his special approach to what he thought a newspaper should mean to the mediated vision. The *World,* in fact, was a varied mixture of general news, sensational crime reports, human interest features, and sharply worded editorials on controversial issues that echoed Pulitzer's crusading spirit, all accompanied by voluminous illustrations and cartoons. Promotional stunts were another ploy of Pulitzer to boost the circulation of his paper, of which the most famous was the globe-circling feat of reporter Nelly Bly in 1890. Assigned to undercut the eighty days it took Phineas Phogg's balloon to journey around the world in Jules Verne's popular novel, Bly resorted to conventional modes of travel and accomplished her goal with a week to spare. Not only did Pulitzer sell more papers to the thousands caught up in the stunt's day-to-day reportage, Bly struck a blow for both serialized reporting and feminism, not to mention the symbolic significance of her achievement that, in the eyes of the mediated vision, helped transform the world into a much smaller place than it had been.

As his flair for promotion revealed, Pulitzer, an immigrant himself, had the interests at heart of ordinary city folk striving to meet the challenges of life in an urban environment, and a large part of his paper's mission was designed to help them realize this end. The Sunday paper's supplement, for example, "was filled with light, heavily illustrated material implicitly instructive in urban mores." As such, it performed "a critical acculturating function for an overflowing polyglot population that had turned New York into the most dynamic, diverse, and socially complex metropolis on earth."[28] The inclusion of daily escapist diversions also played an important role in this process.

To Pulitzer, the developing form of the comic strip, which would become the American newspaper's most popular and enduring feature, had a dynamic daily entertainment appeal that afforded a newspaper increased sales potential. But when his formidable competitor William Randolph Hearst bought the *New York Journal* in 1895, the stage was set for the cutthroat circulation wars between the two, in which the comic strip was to play a major part. That Hearst was as visually-minded a publisher as Pulitzer was demonstrated in his introduction of the Sunday comics section in 1896 as yet another way to sell more papers. Although Pulitzer had initiated the first color cartoon page as early as 1894, Hearst sought to outdo him by producing an entire Sunday comics supplement of such a variety of colors it would, in his words, "make the rainbow look like a lead pipe." Then, when he lured some of Pulitzer's more talented artists to the *Journal* with the promise of higher salaries, the war between the two was on in earnest.

The newspaper comic strip was so called because of its depiction of a comical incident in a sequence of panels spaced across but sometimes down a page. The popular humor magazines that started up in the 1880s—*Puck, Judge,* and the original *Life*—had shown how the follies of everyday life depicted in the single-panel cartoons of A. B. Frost, T. S. Sullivant, and Charles Dana Gibson could involve the viewer in a theatrical manner. Toward this same end, both Pulitzer and Hearst acquired stables of cartoonists who experimented with new narrative conventions that would define the comic strip as a uniquely American art form. Foremost among its early innovators were Richard F. Outcault, Rudolph Dirks, and Frederick B. Opper, whose visually fantasized worlds would have significant impact on the mediated culture. While their initial work in this fledgling form showed the humorous influence of immigrant culture and the ethnic comedy of vaudeville, it also revealed an aesthetic characteristic that set the comics apart from other art forms. It is what comic-art authority Robert C. Harvey terms "a blend of word and picture" that works uniquely "together to achieve a narrative purpose."[29]

Before moving to Hearst's *Journal*, Outcault had created a panel feature in 1895 for the *World* called *Hogan's Alley*, starring a streetwise urchin whose yellow-tinted nightshirt earned him the popular name of the Yellow Kid. Ironically, the color also became associated with the kind of sensational journalism that newspapers were publishing at the time.[30] But a main reason Outcault's feature soon became a bona fide hit was its introduction of the first continuing popular character in the comics, a major distinguishing feature of the genre. Indeed, this character's popularity instigated a Yellow Kid mania in which his image was recast in the form of dolls and toys and used commercially to advertise such products as candy, cookies, and chewing gum. Here was the first but certainly not the last time that the familiar image of a comic strip character would function for advertising and franchising purposes.

In 1897, Rudolph Dirks of the *Journal* staff began drawing what would become the longest lasting comic strip of all, *The Katzenjammer Kids*. Its appeal lay in the ethnic comedy influence evident in the brand of Germanic-flavored English spoken by the strip's main characters, particularly that of two thoroughly mischievous boys whose target for their pranks and escapades happens to be anyone around at the time. From a technical perspective, the strip was important for its contribution to the comics' visual conventions, especially in Dirks's clever use of balloon dialogue in the Sunday page's sequential paneling of ongoing blocks of time to dramatize a longer humorous incident. To Dirks's ingenuity in conveying comedy through a visualized form of communication, the narrative conventions of the comic strip owe a great deal.

Opper, the other influential innovator, was the most versatile and prolific artist of this early group in that he was also a political cartoonist as well as a magazine and book illustrator. In 1899 he created his highly popular *Happy Hooligan* strip, whose title character was in the classic literary tradition of the social outcast who defies public convention through his own personal vision of the way things should be. By winding up in the last panel of a Sunday-page sequence as a fall guy or the butt of a joke, Opper's character was a kind of updated Don Quixote, an innocent misunderstood by the world around him—a type soon to be visualized in the movie persona of Charlie Chaplin's Little Tramp.

As a form of creative social expression whose advent resulted from the combination of urbanization, technological advances, and the proliferation of the newspaper, the comic strip would grow steadily as a cultural force due to its ongoing interaction with the mediated vision over the years. With its inherent purpose dictated by the demands of the marketplace and the ever-changing

Artist Rudolph Dirks pioneered the use of balloon dialogue in depicting the antics of his Katzenjammer Kids. In this Sunday-page excerpt, they are obviously preparing to launch another of their devious schemes on an unsuspecting victim. © 1906 *New York Journal*. Author's collection.

outlook of the mediated vision, the comics, in functioning as a mirror of the American social experience, have persisted not only as a visual repository but an indicator of where the mediated culture has been as well as where it is and might be headed.

ILLUSTRATION: THE NEW ART OF MEDIA CULTURE

To win even more customers, both Pulitzer and Hearst were continually experimenting with the illustrated feature stories and popular amusement attractions that made up their Sunday supplements. While the front sections of their newspapers attended to international news and domestic stories of crime, scandal, and political corruption, both publishers knew that readers welcomed the supplement as an escapist respite from the harsh realities of everyday life. Technologically, the time was receptive to such an innovation, too, since the invention of the rotary press had resulted in faster newspaper production and that of the linotype machine in automatic typesetting. By the turn of the century some two thousand daily newspapers existed in urban areas, with a readership of over fifteen million, and clearly Pulitzer and Hearst were out to capture as many as they could of this total's New York component.

For greater eye appeal, both the newspaper and the magazine were now transforming their traditionally austere page appearance into a new kind of visually balanced layout. The halftone photoengraving process and color lithography were significant factors in this transformation. Breaking up long stretches of the printed page with strategically placed illustrations and photographs as well as decorative design in the Art Nouveau manner resulted in a modernist sense of aesthetic appeal. But because of the pervasive emphasis on the image over the word, critics feared that the dominance of the pictorial would detract from the primary intent of the printed matter. Nevertheless, pictorial journalism had arrived, and its enthusiastic reception was caught by Theodore Dreiser's description of Carrie Meeber's anticipation of a press release in the "large decorative theatrical pages" about her debut.[31] Because the demand existed, then, a new profession was born practically overnight—that of the commercial illustrator whose work would appear not only in newspaper/magazine feature articles but in advertising, magazine fiction, and popular novels.

The tradition of graphic illustration rather than the later cartoon style had shaped the great political cartoons of *Puck* founder Joseph Keppler and Thomas Nast, in which the visual power of icons and symbols as political weapons was used to expose corruption in high places. And by evolving hand in hand with advances in print technology, illustration's liberation from the cumbersome woodcut engraving process saw numerous talented artists come to the fore by the 90s in not only the political cartoon but all fields of illustration.

Both Pulitzer and Hearst used the art of illustration as a way to complement the realism of their newspapers' stories, but Hearst also subscribed to its fantasizing power. To exploit the brief Spanish-American conflict, he sent illustrators to Cuba with specific instructions to elaborate on what they saw and even to improve on what they did not see. Although by this time photography was beginning to compete with illustration for ascendancy in pictorial journalism, a preference still lingered for the graphic artists whose personal observations could capture certain nuances that the camera might overlook by its very directness. Accordingly, such notable artists as William J. Glackens and Howard Chander Christy were contracted by leading magazines to record their visual impressions of the war.

Though reputable painters regarded illustration as a lesser undertaking, those attuned to the illustrator's sense of reality had more appeal to the mediated vision. To it, the representational vision of Winslow Homer's outdoor paintings and Thomas Eakins's sporting scenes were considered more acceptable as art than the kind soon to appear in the modernist, abstract manner. In particular, the appeal of Eakins's photographic attention to detail revealed the influence that the camera must have had on his attempt to raise the transient moment to a lasting place in the collective memory.

During this time the undisputed master of magazine and book illustration in the vein of romantic realism was Howard Pyle. When his classic illustrations for *The Merry Adventures of Robin Hood* appeared in 1883, Pyle's highly crafted manner represented a big step toward elevating illustration to the level of fine art. Pyle's renditions of old-world subject matter also made him a natural to illustrate classic American fiction. Exhibiting a painstaking attention to historical detail in dramatizing key scenes of a narrative's action, his style would have a strong influence on other illustrators who focused on the dramatic highlights of a story line. Numerous artists built their reputations on such an ability, for example, E. W. Kemble in *Huckleberry Finn,* both Kemble and A. B. Frost in collections of Uncle Remus stories, and W. W. Denslow in *The Wizard of Oz.* Fiction directed primarily at an adult audience also profited from the skills of artists like William A. Rogers, who illustrated *A Hazard of New Fortunes.* In fact, print media historian Frank Luther Mott has noted that "many best sellers have owed much of their popularity to pictures which were integral to the text."[32]

During this era of the celebrity illustrator, when an artist's signature functioned as an iconic symbol, the one celebrated above all others was Charles Dana Gibson, mainly because his works were so socially representative of turn of the century America. In his drawings of beautiful, stylishly coiffured women and handsome, athletic-looking men, Gibson was the self-appointed arbiter of fashion for a whole generation. His daringly independent Gibson

Girl playing tennis, cycling, and cavorting at the seashore, as well as his well-dressed, clean-shaven men, demonstrated that for the mediated vision even fashion could function as a fantasized form of escape. In capturing the imagination of the country as few such fads ever had, the Gibson Girl was a visual phenomenon that attested to both her creator's illustrative powers and the dominance of a spreading mediated culture in making such an image universally recognizable. Thus, from the 1890s on into the new century her ethereally beautiful, self-assured face appeared on such everyday products as tablecloths, china, tiles, calendars, and even wallpaper.

Gibson was also instrumental in visualizing another facet of social life—the ostentatious manners of the well-to-do with whom he himself associated. Indeed, his satirical insights into the rich and famous lifestyle revealed a great deal about the social mores of the time. Toward this end no one could handle a pen as expertly as Gibson, although many attempted to emulate the clean-flowing lines of his cross-hatching and shading technique. Gibson's inimitable style was not only evident in his drawings of the Gibson Girl, but also another reason for her popularity.

The main disseminator of the art of illustration was the popular magazine to which Gibson and contemporaries like Harrison Fisher and Frederic Remington were contributing on a regular basis. When George Horace Lorimer was appointed editor of the *Saturday Evening Post* in 1898, one of the great editorial traditions of both American magazine history and illustration got underway. Practicing an autocratic management style that would maintain the *Post*'s conservative editorial policies and publishing standards for thirty-eight years, Lorimer, as a champion of big business and progress, was staunchly Republican in his political outlook but not averse to celebrating the nation's past in a highly nostalgic way. Accordingly, the *Post*'s stories and articles reverberated with the old-time values Lorimer deemed to have made America great. His posture was exemplified in the magazine's iconographic cover art that exalted the familiar sights and scenes of American life—those images in particular of the small-town/rural past that first-generation city dwellers fondly remembered. If the commercial purpose of a magazine cover is to inform the customer what the magazine itself is about, then the *Post* instituted a cover tradition that not only carried out this function, but also presented the nation an ongoing, pervasive cultural image of itself.

Other popular magazines, notably *Collier's Weekly,* adhered to similar cover standards, as from the close of the nineteenth century to well on into the twentieth, many of America's most talented illustrators would achieve fame due to their cover art for mass-circulated magazines. Through a vision that blurred fact and fantasy, the cover illustrator produced art that perpetuated many of the mediated culture's most pervasive myths and character types: the idyllic scene of pastoral or small-town life, the ceremonial tableau to commemorate a holiday, such stock figures of the American West as the

noble Indian and the rough-hewn cowboy, and, most often, female characterizations idealizing the beautiful American girl that Florenz Ziegfeld and
Hollywood would exploit in a few years. Before the movies, in fact, "the great
illustrators were the creators of the most consistently exciting visual experience available to the public, and their fame had no parallel in [later] graphic
arts."[33] Fittingly, the first movie production of *Huckleberry Finn* in 1919
would rely on the character illustrations that E. W. Kemble had done in the
novel as models for the film version.

THE TRANSFORMATION OF SPORTS INTO MEDIATED SPECTACLE

In the early years of the twentieth century the covers of the *Saturday
Evening Post* began to reflect the country's growing interest in organized
sports and leisure activities. Concurrent with this development, the United
States of the 1890s had evolved into a melting-pot consumer culture in
which the mediated vision began to perceive leisure time as a commodity of
consumption itself. Not only were the entertainment venues of vaudeville,
popular theater, and the light musical promoting themselves as consumer
products, but the sporting activities of professional baseball, boxing, horse
racing, and college football were also vying for public attention. The marketing of sporting events, most prominently in large urban areas, responded
to a growing leisure-oriented spectatorship, revealing that the country's
indigenous work ethic was beginning to give way to a new conception of
play as an important adjunct to one's lifestyle, despite lingering puritanical
inhibitions.

The expanding interest in organized athletics during the urbanization and
industrialization of America was enhanced by the appearance of athletic
leagues and associations, in particular those involving the big-city baseball
teams of the Northeast and the Midwest. If the wealthy had their athletic
clubs' elitist activities in which to indulge themselves, the working-class city
dwellers now had their own baseball teams to identify with. They, in fact, accounted in large part for the growth of spectatorship in professional sport. It,
in turn, was enhanced by the spacious ballparks that fans attended by way
of a city's expanded transportation system. As a new kind of business, the
National League had begun baseball play as early as 1876. Then, with the
coming of the rival American League in 1901, one of the country's most
revered sporting events would start up in 1903—the World Series, an annual
contest between the two league champions to decide the world championship
of baseball. As a sport that was fondly referred to as the National Pastime,
the fans' devotion to a team also contributed to a new collective spirit dedicated to winning and a sense of pride in the place the team represented. It

was a feeling that had extended as well to the increasingly popular amateur sport of college football.

By the 90s the Big Game encounters between the Eastern schools were attracting spectators in the multithousands, many of whom looked upon a football game as not just a sporting event but an exciting social occasion, to which the presence of many fashionably dressed young women attested. Even the fact that football was enduring a great deal of criticism in the yellow press due to its brutal style of play was hardly a deterrent to its popularity. In fact, the game continued to condition the public, especially youth, to a highly glamorized social image of college life, dramatized in popular fiction, on the stage, and soon in the movies. Many an idealistic young male was introduced to college football as not only a socialization agent but a formalized rite of manhood contributing to the mediated culture's conception of sports participation as a character building experience.

The outcomes of both football and baseball games played away from home as well as the results of horse races and boxing matches could be learned through telegraph reception in saloons and pool halls. But it was in the daily newspaper sports page that loyal fans found the bulk of their information about the day's leading sporting events. In the 1880s Joseph Pulitzer's *New York World* had become the first newspaper with a department assigned to the gathering of sporting news. But in 1895 William Randolph Hearst's *New York Journal* followed up on the *National Police Gazette*'s pioneering efforts and published an entire section dedicated to sports. Though the *Sporting News* had started out as a baseball news tabloid in 1886, by the 90s the growing popularity of college football demanded expanded coverage of this sport, which the New York papers also responded to in their reportage of the big Ivy League games.

The growth of spectatorship also resulted in the appearance of a new celebrity type and, ultimately, a new kind of cult worship. The mass adulation of such sports heroes as boxer James J. Corbett, who defeated John L. Sullivan in 1892 to win the world's heavyweight championship, and baseball player Honus Wagner, one of the game's first great players, was made possible through the publicity of their exploits reported in newspapers and popular magazines. In addition, the image of the athlete in action in the illustrations of Winslow Homer, A. B. Frost, and Frederic Remington helped canonize the American athlete as a popular heroic type. Also the color portraits on collectible cards that were packaged with cigarettes and other popular consumer items helped idealize the image of the baseball player. The growing realization that sport was a form of entertainment, and as such performed an escapist function, was underscored by those athletes who capitalized on their celebrity status to advertise consumer products, thus establishing the precedent for many a future athlete to promote his image by selling it.

Although the game of basketball was introduced as an amateur team sport in 1892, it would take a back seat to college football well on into the twentieth century. But with the beginning of the modern Olympic Games in Athens, Greece, in 1896, amateur athletics formulated a showcase for the world to witness their achievements at four-year intervals. While American collegians dominated the 1896 Olympics, winning eleven gold medals, the Games had a long way to go to become the glamorous, highly nationalized spectacle of later years.

During the coming century all forms of organized sport, as they were made more visually appealing through technological advances, would be increasingly perceived as entertainment, affording the mediated vision an escapist refuge from everyday life. Appropriately, a book about sport's visual appeal has observed: "Sport, in all its endless variety, is always something to be seen. It is magic to the eye. It lingers in the life-long treasury of the vision."[34]

THE LURE OF TRAVEL AND THE ALLURE OF PUBLIC AMUSEMENTS

By the late 90s a growing middle class was displaying its receptiveness to opportunities to participate in leisure pursuits. Even cross-gender activities were being popularized in the person of the outdoor girl, as in the example of the Gibson Girl, and in the mass-circulated magazines, particularly in the specialized leisure periodical *Outing*. The persistence of the lure of the West helped transform the great outdoors into a highly romanticized place where one could escape the city for the restorative powers of nature through such activities as hiking, camping, fishing, hunting, and cycling. Soon, the coming of the motor car would offer another, more mobile opportunity to explore the attractions of nature. But the railroad was the way most people traveled, and for those families who could afford it a whole summer vacation could be planned around stays at the seashore, a lake resort, or mountain retreat.

In 1872, the opening of Yellowstone National Park, the country's first such venue and a model for those to follow, represented both a shrine to nature and the West and a direct way for the mediated vision to reconnect with the adventurous spirit it engendered. There was also the more commercialized spectacle of the traditional honeymoon mecca of Niagara Falls in the East, where tourists discovered that only the word "sublime" was adequate enough to describe their reaction to seeing it. By this time, the ongoing expansion of the railroad system and its contribution to tourism resulted in sightseeing pilgrimages to these scenic wonders becoming the fashion.

For most, the main reason for putting leisure time to inspirational use was to escape the realities of urban alienation and cultivate a surer sense of self. New York City, in fact, by recognizing the need for an outlet to allow direct communion with nature, had been grooming Central Park since the late 1850s as a pastoral retreat, offering the solace and tranquility of nature amid city turmoil. By the 90s, under the discerning eye of landscape designer Frederick Law Olmsted, it had developed into a revered refuge, a kind of playground for the cultivation of escapism. As such, it was a model for other cities to emulate.

For the wealthy, of course, there were the leisure pursuits that only an un-limited expense account could afford: booking a cruise to Europe on an ocean liner, participating in an African safari hunt, yachting, and maintaining sea-sonal stays at their residences in Newport and other locales. This was also the day of the great grand dame hotels located in the scenic areas of Mack-inac Island, the Southern mountains, and California. And with the West opening up to travel, the rich made a fetish of taking excursions in their or-nate Pullman palace cars, traveling in antiseptic comfort while taking their conventional social customs with them. Unless they were avid sportsmen looking to engage in the ritual of the hunt, they shunned direct contact with the natural environment, preferring to observe it from afar with the aid of a guide book. As a reporter commented in 1897, the well-to-do came to the fashionable resorts "not to worship nature, but to see and be seen by their kind."[35] But underneath the cultural veneer, despite the elitist propensity to showcase its standards of taste, the urge to identify with nature's healing balm still persisted, bonding all classes. It was the mediated vision's natural de-sire to return to something basic and essential, an elemental experience that urban life, whether on the working-class, middle-class, or socially elite lev-els, was blinding its citizens to.

The traveling circus, with its emphasis on the appeal of exotic animal life, had a long history of bringing the wonders of nature to the people, whether in an urban, small-town, or rural setting. After the Civil War, when the ex-pansion of the railroad made this form of entertainment more accessible to the masses, a number of opportunistic entrepreneurs capitalized on the in-trinsic appeal of the circus as not only an extension of theater but, in its uni-versal appeal, the purest form of escapist entertainment. It in turn would have a pervasive influence on other forms of amusements in the domain of a grow-ing mediated culture.

In America the circus's modern history began with the bold entrepreneur-ship of P. T. Barnum, the "Father of American Show Business." In 1874 he had branched out from his dime museum enterprise to incorporate many of his ballyhooed attractions into the traditional circus format. Always one for spectacle and the unusual, whether humbug or the real thing, Barnum ex-panded the single ring European model to two rings, creating a greater visual demand on the spectator but resulting in a more exciting viewing experience. Even the freaks and oddities of Barnum's dime museum cropped up in a sideshow adjunct that would become a circus and carnival fixture. Barnum attributed the overall success of his circus to his inherent feeling that he himself was one of the people and as such understood their feelings, desires, tastes, and escapist needs. As a result, P. T. Barnum became the first great impresario to respond to the collective escapist wishes of both child and adult alike.

After consolidating with British circus magnate James Bailey, the Barnum and Bailey Circus, now boasting three mammoth rings, debuted in New York in 1881, billing itself as "The Greatest Show on Earth." This was only the beginning of yet another period in which Barnum demonstrated his showmanship flair for luring customers to the Big Top. Undoubtedly his greatest promotional stunt was exhibiting the giant elephant Jumbo. Twelve feet in height and weighing seven tons, Jumbo was that rare attraction who drew thousands of the curious to view him. Indeed, his popularity was such that his name contributed a new word to the American language.

Although Barnum passed away in 1892, the practice of a circus publicizing itself around a featured attraction lived on after him, especially after the Ringling Brothers bought into the circus and billed it as "The World's Greatest Show." No matter what it was called, though, to the mediated vision there had never been anything like the traveling circus, due mainly to its fantasized impact on both young and old. For those who were around during its golden age of the late nineteenth century on into the early part of the twentieth, many fond memories would be retained of the colorful billboard posters that announced the dates of the circus's coming and the lavish street parades that occasioned its arrival.

However, it was the amusement park of the late 90s, just beginning to locate near large metropolitan areas, that would compete with the circus and ultimately contribute to its decline. As direct heirs of the Midway Plaisance, these parks were harbingers of the new role that leisure was starting to play in mediated culture. During this time Coney Island's Steeplechase Park was attracting thousands of pleasure-bent visitors from the city to a fantasized realm of mechanized rides and individualized entertainment attractions. As the incarnation of a commercialized dream world, such a place promised city dwellers a potpourri of opportunities to indulge themselves in the rites of pure escapism.

The American amusement park, in setting out to entertain on a grand scale, also offered the masses a welcome alternative to the genteel culture's emphasis on morally uplifting experiences, mainly through the social option of meeting people of kindred interests, especially members of the opposite sex. In an atmosphere of relaxed proprieties the park visitor, whether longtime city resident or newly arrived immigrant, could shun conventional behavior between the sexes for a more uninhibited, laidback lifestyle. By letting one's self go in such a liberated milieu, then, a visitor was mesmerized into the unique role of performing as both a spectator and a participant. Projecting a spirit similar to that of its alter ego—the Midway Plaisance with its earthy elements of beer garden, dance hall, and circus sideshow—the updated attractions of Steeplechase Park clearly demonstrated that amusement for amusement's sake was becoming socially institutionalized. In this process, the amusement park and its heterogeneous audience formulated a subculture whose receptive attitude toward play was a social indicator of things to come. And with the continuing expansion of the interurban transportation system, every large city of the time desired access to a park at some point on a trolley line.

Of the many novel features of the Chicago Exposition that the amusement park exploited, electrical technology was the most significant due to its visual power to fantasize the collective eye of visitors. As prime examples, the dream worlds of entrepreneur George C. Tilyou's Steeplechase Park and, later, Luna Park, incarnated the grandiose and titillating in a veritable orgy of enchanting color and lavish decor. But it was the quarter-million electric lights glowing at night that transformed Steeplechase into a more exciting make-believe experience. Not to be outdone, Tilyou's competitor, the appropriately named Dreamland, would open its doors in 1903 with an astounding aggregate of a million lights to turn night into day. Such fantasized showplaces incited a highly impressed visitor to comment that the Coney Island excursion was the ultimate escape for the harried city dweller—an "escape . . . from the world of What-we-have-to-do into the world of What-we-would-like-to-do."[36]

As a result of the mediated culture's ongoing gravitation toward commercialized amusement at this time and its impact on the work ethic's traditional role in the American value system, the concept of play or leisure time and what to do with it would become a significant social issue in the new century. In breaking away from puritanical constraints, the mediated vision would begin to view the world not so much as a place of trial and tribulation, but as one of infinite possibilities where one could realize self-fulfillment as much through play as work.

THE SOCIOCULTURAL LEGACY OF THE 1890s

Even though the 1890s was a time of sociocultural transition resulting from the interaction of numerous complex factors, the era was generally optimistic despite the ongoing conflict between labor and capital and periodic economic depression that threatened to undermine progress. Paradoxically, the fin de siècle mood allowed materialistic and spiritual values to coexist and formulate a new way of viewing the world—one in which such seemingly contradictory elements as work and play could complement each other. Thus this outlook accommodated the polarities of monopolistic practices and free trade, socialism and individualism, religious skepticism and fundamentalism, isolationism and nationalism/imperialism, and, of course, elite culture and popular culture. The gradual merging of these two entities would lead to hybrid forms of the mediated culture that charted controversial new directions by the second half of the twentieth century.

But if there was any lingering doubt in the 90s about the future of America's role in world affairs, the sensationalized news coverage of the brief but decisive Spanish-American War helped dispel it. In prophetically closing out the nineteenth century, the outcome of this encounter underscored the imperialistic notions spawned by the great fairs of the time. In looking ahead to its initially reluctant role as a world power, one that was to be realized by the time of World War I, the country's confidence was bolstered by its astounding growth in industry and technology, an inherent missionary zeal, and the naturally competitive drive of social Darwinism. As a result, most Americans began to accept what now appeared to be the nation's divine destiny as a world leader. In this light, then, the nation's imperialistic expansion into the South Pacific (Hawaii), the Caribbean (Cuba and Puerto Rico), and the Philippines seemed wholly justified to most citizens.

In conditioning Americans to a new vision of themselves before the world, this global consciousness broadened the horizons of the mediated vision, thus enhancing the development of a media culture that would expand worldwide during the new century. But paradoxically the evolving mediated vision would prompt the individual to look at the world not so much in a cosmopolitan sense as in an increasingly introspective manner—in effect, a personally fantasized way in order to shape experience in terms of one's expectations of it. Appropriately, Theodore Dreiser closes out *Sister Carrie* with an authorial observation about his now socially successful but still daydreaming heroine: "Though often disillusioned, she was still waiting for that halcyon day when she would be led forth among dreams become real. . . . It was forever to be the pursuit of that radiance of delight which tints the distant hilltops of the world."[37]

In preparing the way for the twentieth century, the sociocultural contradictions of the 1890s that fomented pressing new demands on the individual induced the American people to continue pursuing Carrie Meeber's "radiance of delight." It was a vision at once escapist and removed from the harsh realities of life—a mediated vision, in fact, in which personal dreams could be realized, if not in actual fulfillment, then vicariously through one's relationship with the escapist forms of mediated culture. However, it was a perspective that would keep adapting itself to the changing social behavior of the new century. Indeed, by its second half, reality itself would be subjected to the fantasizing power of an ever-evolving media-made culture.

2

1900–1913—Introducing the Mediated Vision
to New Ways of Seeing

> The nickelodeon is tapping an entirely new stratum
> of people, is developing into theatergoers a section
> of population that formerly knew and cared little
> about the drama as a fact of life.
> —*The Saturday Evening Post*

THE WORLD OF THEODORE DREISER'S *SISTER CARRIE*, WITH ITS VIVID PICTURE
of urban lifestyle around 1900, would soon undergo many changes. And
women would play a big role in this transition by countering society's rigid
constraints on them. Though working-class women were laboring in facto-
ries and as shopgirls for menial wages, the better educated were functioning as school teachers, nurses, and librarians. As far as the placement of
women in the business workplace was concerned, the coming of the typewriter in the 1870s had been a significant factor in employing them in
secretarial positions to facilitate office routine, mainly because most self-
respecting businessmen would have nothing to do with this newfangled
device. By the turn of the century, then, women were taking their place in
what was previously looked upon as predominantly a man's world. Thus, the
Gibson Girl's self-assertive air was real enough to establish the social image for many a small-town girl of Carrie Meeber's stripe to emulate. Seemingly oblivious to the time's conservative dictates that sought to preserve
gender distinctions, Charles Dana Gibson's scenes of pretty girls playing
golf or showing up at the seashore in the modest swimwear of the day not
only point this out but reveal changing attitudes toward the social function
of women's casual attire.

By 1913, then, the social image of women as something more than that of
overly idealized homemakers was beginning to manifest itself, and a more
tolerant outlook toward the changes in recreational fashions had a lot to do
with this transformation. Within the province of the mediated culture these
changes "would lead to a sweeping reassessment of the ways in which cos-

By depicting his Gibson Girl in sporting activities and at the seashore in the latest swimwear, Charles Dana Gibson promoted her as a sign of young women's growing air of independent social expression in this era. © 1900 C. D. Gibson.

tume was capable of eroticizing . . . parts of the human anatomy that had never before been considered fair game for public viewing."[1]

While most middle-class women of the early 1900s were still expected to know their place in the social setting as well as their domestic role, more Carrie Meebers, looking for jobs and romance, were arriving on the urban scene all the time. By now, too, many of them were exhibiting the self-confident aura that their Gibson Girl fashions promoted. In contrast to the buxsom appearance of a Lillian Russell in the 1890s, the Gibson Girl's slender counterpart was now appearing on the Broadway stage, either in the form of Evelyn

Nesbit performing in the musical comedy *Florodora* or actress Ethel Barrymore debuting in Clyde Fitch's popular social comedy, *Captain Jinks of the Horse Marines*. As variations on the Gibson Girl type, many dramatic roles revealed her as a social climber well aware of her good looks as an influential force through which she could control the men in her life. The conflict between conventional male superiority and the female's newfound social expression was also a staple of popular fiction, though the showgirl character was often depicted as a gold digger or kept woman. Ironically, Carrie Meeber, who had started out highly dependent on the men in her life, winds up a successful stage personality with an independent identity, though not yet free from her illusions about life.

In the real-life American girl's forceful role in the feminization of society many men saw a dire threat to their social sovereignty. When Theodore Roosevelt assumed the presidency in 1901, his vivacious, outgoing daughter Alice became the exemplar/role model of the New Woman who presaged the image of the 1920s' flapper—the college-age girl who dared to dance until the wee hours, smoke cigarettes, imbibe alcohol, and even engage in some heavy petting. The quarter century encompassing the years 1900–1925 would see great social change but hardly any more revolutionary than in women's dress and social behavior, the first visual evidence of which the mediated vision began to witness during the years 1900–1913.

Progressivism's Reformist Mission

During this period of social crusade when women involved in the growing feminist movement openly demonstrated for their cause, the Progressive politics of the new century revealed the nation's social conscience as growing more sensitive to the need for reform, particularly in the areas of labor conditions, the plight of the poor, and, although grudgingly, women's rights. In the mood of the times, too, fiction and nonfiction became expressive modes for the investigative findings of those who dared to document what they saw wrong with the American capitalistic system. Their writings, in fact, initiated a trend toward a no holds barred depiction of agrarian, labor, and social problems, the kind of journalism that President Theodore Roosevelt labeled "muckraker" reportage. Similar in intent were naturalistic novels like Frank Norris's *The Octopus* (1901), the first part of a trilogy dealing with a major concern of Populist politics—the wheat farmers' fight with the railroad—and Upton Sinclair's *The Jungle* (1906), which exposed the multiple problems created by urbanization and industrialization—slums, exploitation of the working class, and a general decline in morals. Documentary attention to these problems was presented to the public in Lincoln Steffens's *The Shame of the Cities* (1904) and earlier in the photography of Jacob Riis's *How the Other Half Lives* (1890), both grimly candid renderings of life in the urban ghetto. Lewis Hines's photos, which invaded the province of industry to picture, among other things, the evils of child labor, were also in this tradition. The exposé of these problem areas in both print and photography helped undermine the mediated culture's idealized concept of the American Dream by revealing the wide economic gulf that existed between rich and poor in American society.

Though the lifestyles of the wealthy ranged from the conservative, philanthropic manner of Pittsburgh steel magnate Andrew Carnegie to the playboy excesses of *New York Herald* publisher James Gordon Bennett, they all served a similar purpose in informing the mediated vision of what boundless wealth could do for a person. With their multiroomed mansions, plush Pullman cars, genteel sporting activities like the annual tennis tournament at Newport, the rich had created an escapist world all their own. Whether riding the Overland Limited from Chicago to California, whose rails ironically followed the rugged pioneer trails of the old West, or leisurely sailing on an ocean liner from New York to Europe, they were star performers on an outsized stage that compelled them to dramatize their fabulous wealth.

Although the wealthy rationalized their abundance of riches as either a reward for their strong personal motivation to succeed or a sign of God's favor toward the dedication of their wealth to social progress, many reformists viewed the goals of men like John D. Rockefeller and Cornelius Vanderbilt as the most extreme form of social Darwinism, labeling them "Robber Barons" in their attempt to eliminate competition to gain monopolistic control. From such a perspective, Horatio Alger's idealistic version of the American success story saw itself contradicted by the self-aggrandizing methods and cutthroat competition of turn of the century capitalists.

An urban issue generally ignored by Progressive politics was that of race, even as a swelling number of southern blacks continued to filter into northern cities looking for jobs and a better life. But African American civil rights concerns were articulated in the forceful postures of two black leaders. While Booker T. Washington proposed working within the framework of the existing social order for progress, W. E. B. DuBois was more vindictive toward the system in assessing the black experience in America as a kind of "double-consciousness" comprised of "two unreconciled strivings" urging blacks "to be both a Negro and an American."[2] Ironically, this perception inspired blacks to transcend the lingering stereotyped image of late nineteenth-century minstrelsy, mainly through their musical contributions. As a music of contraries, African American jazz, emanating from the improvisational style of Dixieland, became both a refuge and a natural outlet of creative expression—both an escape from imposed social conditions and an implicit statement about their plight. As such, it would resound both culturally and socially throughout the twentieth century.

Although the nation had a population of some seventy-six million in 1900, most Americans still lived in small towns and rural areas—the kind of culturally bleak atmosphere that had driven Carrie Meeber to look for a more fulfilling life in the city. If small-town/rural people lacked the opportunities a big city offered, they at least enjoyed a stronger sense of community as opposed to the social alienation of urban life. But, as Frank Norris depicted, problems also existed within the serenity of the idealized pastoral scene of the American farm; and the ideology of Populism, which centered on the concerns of agrarian America engendered by the forces of industrialization, sought to counter them through a democratic emphasis on the will of the people.

Concurrently, the mediated vision's growing disenchantment with the city and its failure to provide the better life it had promised generated an escapist desire to seek fulfillment through outdoor activities. Teddy Roosevelt's philosophy of the strenuous life, which he practiced not only in word, as his speeches and writings attest, but in deed as a hunter-sportsman, typified his resolve to revive frontier values and their challenges to individualism. This dynamic personality, whom the *Saturday Evening Post* named the "Man of the Decade" (1901–10), was of such individualistic mold that his active life and physical bearing made him a favorite subject of political cartoonists and, in the eyes of the mediated vision, an optimistic symbol of the time. As an advocate of physically demanding sports like boxing and football, Roosevelt defended them as activities essential to maintaining a code of manliness to curb the spread of feminization, the signs of which he undoubtedly detected in the forceful air of his own daughter. Espousing both a scholarly and a nostalgic interest in the old West in his prolific writings as well as active involvement in its attractions, Roosevelt contributed a great deal to the cause of conservation by promoting the West as an American sanctuary where one could find not only escape but self-renewal. Teddy Roosevelt, in fact, helped transform the myth of the West into purposeful escapism.

For city dwellers who lacked the means to travel to the great natural park sites of the West, urban planners were compensating by bringing the natural environment to the city. Toward this end, Central Park designer Frederick Law Olmsted was called on by the fast growing cities of Philadelphia, Boston, and Detroit to help create their own park systems. In helping institutionalize the municipal park as a communal retreat from urban isolation, Olmsted displayed his mastery of merging landscape and vegetation to create an escapist visual experience designed to rejuvenate the youthful spirit of play.[3]

THE VISUAL IMPACT OF NEW MODES OF TRAVEL

Although the electric-powered trolley had replaced the horse-drawn car, the New York subway system made its debut in 1904 as a much more efficient mode of rapid mass transportation. But it was the automobile, just starting to come into its own at this time, that would have the most far-ranging effect on the personal mobility of both city residents and small-town/rural people. If any one person was the living embodiment of the self-made Alger hero, it was Henry Ford, who in 1903 established the Ford Motor Company and with its product revolutionized the social patterns of the American people and the way the mediated vision perceived the world around it. Not long after the first Model T motor cars rolled off the production line in 1910, these black "tin lizzies," as they were fondly called, were showing up in every rural outpost, town, and city across the country. In fact, the implementation of Ford's moving assembly line in 1913 and its more efficient means of mass production resulted in a vehicle that the average man could afford, as opposed to the high-priced luxury chariots of the wealthy. The upshot of Ford's contribution to a steadily improving economy was a higher living standard that bolstered faith in the American way of capitalism.

With access to a more personalized mode of travel, then, automobile owners were afforded a unique mobile viewpoint that "altered the way [they] perceived the environment and changed man's very image of himself."[4] No longer would the world be discerned as the static place that had been so wondrously idealized in nineteenth-century nature painting. It was now evolving into a more dynamic, even cinematic place, seemingly in continuous motion, making it difficult to focus on a definite point of perception. Soon, the modernist artist would attempt to express a similar kind of viewpoint in abstract painting. Railroad travel had foreshadowed such a perspective, as intimated in W. D. Howells's *A Hazard of New Fortunes* when train passenger Basil March, in a moment of reflection, remarks to his wife: "Do you see how the foreground next the train rushes from us and the background keeps abreast of us, while the middle distance seems stationary? I don't think I ever noticed that effect before. There ought to be something literary in it; retreating past, and advancing future, and deceitfully permanent present."[5]

But at this time there was no established road system beyond the cities and towns that a motorist could take to, and only the most intrepid driver dared to confront the untested terrain that lay in the hinterlands. Not until the 1920s would far-ranging paved highways become available.

The most revolutionary way of seeing in motion was about to materialize in the airplane's bird's-eye view. Ironically, though, when the Wright brothers engineered their first brief flight of a controlled, heavier-than-air machine in 1903, the event was considered by most as nothing more than a passing fancy, hardly worth newspaper coverage. Soon, though, the skeptics would see the airplane prove its worth not only as a means of rapid transportation but as an instrument of warfare.

THE EMERGENCE OF SENSATIONAL JOURNALISM
AND ITS PICTORIAL APPEAL

By 1904, the *Saturday Evening Post* had become the country's best-selling magazine. With its appealing covers, many of which were adorned with the fashionable young women of Harrison Fisher or the rosy cheeked children and handsome athletes of J. C. Leyendecker, the *Post* published what its authoritative editor sensed its readership was primarily interested in. Thus, George Horace Lorimer saw to it that business success stories were among his magazine's most popular features. He justified this end by asserting that "American life is business . . . a big, active drama of romance and achievement."[6] Even though the success story, either as fiction or biography, was an urban-inspired myth that grew out of the industrialization of America, the mediated vision's inherent loyalty to the values of small-town/rural life continued to be reflected in the *Post*'s pervasive nostalgia for the country's fading pastoral past.

Like the *Post*, most magazines addressed to a wide audience avoided any harsh criticism of the American way to publish articles and stories that enshrined it. In abiding by the era's genteel standards, they generally shunned controversial themes and sensational subject matter to appease readers' desire for escapism through the fantasy of historical romance or an Alger-like rapport with the American success story, whether in business or entertainment. But things were happening that even conventional journalism found hard to ignore, in particular, what became known as the celebrity scandal.

In 1906, the print media exploited a sensational murder trial that had enough scandalous ingredients to keep the public intrigued long after its drama had been played out. The principals included wealthy Pittsburgh heir Harry K. Thaw, beautiful showgirl/model Evelyn Nesbit, and renowned New York architect Stanford White. While Thaw had never accomplished anything more notable than to build a playboy reputation for himself, White's architectural achievements were of such magnitude that they had helped change the face of New York City. One of his edifices, the new Madison Square Garden, boasted a roof-garden theater that, ironically, provided the setting for what the press then called the "Crime of the Century."

When Thaw discovered that White had carried on an earlier affair with his new wife Evelyn Nesbit, his extremely jealous nature prompted him to fatally shoot White as he witnessed a musical production on the Garden roof. In 1893 the trial of one Lizzie Borden, accused of the axe murders of her step-mother and father, had made sensational coverage. But those players were distinct unknowns compared to the social standing of these latest performers. As a result, the press had a field day reporting the sordid details that came out during the trial, which, of course, were accompanied by pertinent illustrations and candid photographs.

Thus, the modern day of tabloid journalism had arrived, characterized by its innate bent for lurid details to captivate readers. As the Thaw trial revealed, criminal acts were even more fascinating to the mediated vision when they involved well-known individuals of society—those people whose wealth and celebrity status made the repercussions of any kind of aberrant goings-on that much more entertaining.[7]

Other sensational news events that the press was compelled to play up in a big way were great natural disasters like the devastating San Francisco earthquake in 1906. But the most momentous calamity of this time was the tragic sinking of the "unsinkable" luxury liner *Titanic* on her maiden voyage in 1912. Shipbuilding experts had contended that the ship's watertight compartments could withstand any amount of flooding without endangerment, but it was the lethal damage of an iceberg that disproved their contention. With a loss of more than fifteen hundred lives, the tragedy of the *Titanic* was further compounded by the number of reputable people among them. All told, the sinking of the *Titanic* was a disaster of such magnitude that it would continue to haunt the mediated culture throughout the century, as attested to by the volume of articles, books, and visual media productions it generated. It also marked the beginnings of a decline in the mediated vision's inherently optimistic view of life. Now, with the seemingly favored of the world just as likely to become victims of chance as anyone, doubt in the divine scheme of things became a real issue.

Concurrently, the newspapers' growing pictorial attention to sensational subject matter helped create a new kind of escapist entertainment by allowing the mediated vision to relate directly to a real-life event while distancing itself from it. But another more mundane form of pictorial expression was starting to impress itself on the mediated vision's natural inclination toward visually induced escapism during these years—the newspaper comic strip.

The Developing Art of Newspaper Comics

With the expansion of the syndication system for distributing newspaper comics, among the first cartoonists to capitalize on it was Harry "Bud" Fisher, who created one of the most popular and longest lasting comic strips, *Mutt and Jeff.* Starting out in 1907 as a daily strip appearing on the sports page of the *San Francisco Chronicle,* where it offered horse-race touts, *Mr. A. Mutt* began to build a wider following after the title character was paired with a top-hatted naif named Jeff in 1908. Vaudeville and burlesque comedy fans had little difficulty recognizing the prime source of Fisher's humor, and they reveled in it. As a foil to Mutt's schemes and plots to make his mark in life, Jeff was an innocent who seemingly lived in a world to which only he was privy, much to the exasperation of Mutt. Not only did syndication bring greater national recognition to *Mutt and Jeff,* it made Bud Fisher a very rich man, whose flamboyant lifestyle promoted the image of the cartoonist as celebrity. As a progenitor of the daily strip, Fisher was also one of the first newspaper cartoonists who conditioned readers to follow the daily happenings in the life of a favorite character or characters. It was in the popularity of a strip like *Mutt and Jeff,* then, that newspaper publishers discovered a natural bonanza to help sell their papers.

By 1910 a flood of daily strips was appearing in black and white, but because of the popularity of the Sunday section, color and the so-called "funnies" came to be thought of as inseparable. That rabid competition was a major factor in the success or failure of a newspaper was attested to by the continuing "war" between the *New York Journal* and the *New York World* over the rights to publish *The Katzenjammer Kids.* When its creator, Rudolph Dirks, decided to leave the *Journal* for the *World* in 1912, publisher William Randolph Hearst instigated court proceedings, averring that as the copyright holder his paper was the rightful owner of the strip. Upon settlement Dirks was allowed to continue his feature for his new employer but under a different title—*The Captain and the Kids.* With the original title carried on by Harold Knerr in 1914, readers encountered the unlikely situation of two versions of the same cast of characters whose artwork looked virtually the same.

With its basic conventions established by 1910, then, the standard comic strip focused on an ongoing set of characters who appeared in the enactment of a joke or prank in the daily and the dramatization of a longer comic episode in the Sunday page. In either form the action developed sequentially, relying on balloon dialogue to express speech or the thoughts of a character. The result was a theatrical kind of experience for the reader who, in equating words with pictures, was lured into an escapist world where the artist could "play with time, space and narrative progression in a way that no other art form ever has, not even film."[8]

Thus, this period was a highly experimental one for cartoonists who had the talent to exploit the opportunities available to them. Free from the later space restrictions that would inhibit creative expression, they were inspired to introduce any new concept that might appeal to their audience. And with three or more dailies competing in the larger cities, there was a growing demand for novel ideas that might develop into ongoing features. Accordingly, a myriad of new titles appeared and disappeared during these years as the demand for new comics kept increasing. A survey of one city's newspapers revealed, in fact, more than a doubling of titles over the period from 1900 to 1909 (sixty-five to 165), this despite frequent attacks by the cultural custodians.[9]

One reason their criticism fell mostly on deaf ears was that strips structured around the favorite topics of the family and the mischievous child attracted large followings. After the success of the single-panel escapades of Mickey Dugan, better known as the Yellow Kid, and *The Katzenjammer Kids,* strips focusing on the incorrigible child became legion. R. F. Outcault, who had been lured away from the *World* by Hearst to draw the large-panel scenario of *Hogan's Alley,* went to James Gordon Bennett's *Herald* where in 1902 he created a title character destined for iconic popularity—Buster Brown. Its conception was a role reversal from that of the back-alley Yellow Kid in that the fashionably dressed Buster came from an upper-class background. Though Buster was well versed in the art of plotting a scheme or prank, the strip's final panel, apparently due to the moral expectations of the day, always showed Buster in a penitent mood, resolving to do better in the future. As another hit for Outcault, *Buster Brown*'s popularity continued unabated, becoming one of the most enduring mass-media characters ever created. Following up on his merchandising success with the Yellow Kid, Outcault licensed Buster and his dog to promote a variety of consumer items. Like its predecessor, the Buster Brown character also inspired a Broadway musical production. Thus, the comic strip, in displaying a natural affinity to relate to other cultural forms, obviously had a great deal more to offer than just its daily obligation to sell newspapers.

Experimentation also saw fantasy become a popular theme in comic strip creativity from 1905 to around 1915. Much of it was only of passing interest, but some was so highly innovative it would command lasting appeal. In this vein, a Sunday feature began appearing in 1905 that would demonstrate the artistic heights that the comic strip format could achieve in the hands of a brilliant innovator. Winsor McCay's *Little Nemo in Slumberland* was a weekly tour de force in technical virtuosity, cinematic technique, and psychological import—all elements that through the atmospheric control of color merged in a stunning visual experience for the viewer. In fact, this strip is still considered by aficionados as among the greatest achievements of comic strip art.[10]

The most significant visual characteristic of McCay's art, mainly because it foreshadowed the technical devices of film, was his way of controlling the strip's action. In fact, many of the cinematic sequences presaged the wild chase scenes of the silent film comedies. Actually, McCay's creative versatility seemed to know no bounds as his contribution to the graphics of the comic strip extended from *Dreams of a Rarebit Fiend,* whose preoccupation with the dream as nightmare made it a precursor of *Nemo,* to the animated cartoon, which he pioneered long before the advent of the Fleischers and the Disney dynasty. By employing what would become the movie conventions of

His Buster Brown character resulted in numerous merchandising windfalls for creator R. F. Outcault, presaging the good fortune that would befall later artists who created popular mediated icons. Author's collection.

the long shot, the close-up, and the oblique angle to emphasize point of view, McCay demonstrated a natural understanding of the relationship between the developing art of the comic strip and the emerging technique of the movie camera. For the mediated vision the upshot of McCay's vision was to be transported to a fantasy world where the conflict between dream and reality found release in fanciful scenes of awesome beauty and design.[11]

If Winsor McCay's art resulted in a brilliantly fantasized world that helped turn the lowly comic strip into an art form, then the developing art of George McManus would do the same for the mundane world of the family-strip genre, proving that most any kind of subject matter could appeal when treated by a skilled artist. In *Bringing Up Father,* which started out in 1913, the mediated vision's sensitivity to an older, more familiar way of life being threatened by a fast-changing world found a comic correlation in McManus's contrapuntal characterizations of newly rich married couple Maggie and Jiggs— she the perennial social climber and he seeking to maintain his ingrained social habits with his old saloon cronies. This prototype of the radio situation comedy presented McManus the latitude to satirize the excesses of the American social scene over a forty-year span. And as his style matured during this time, fans were treated to a showcase of visual delights: the fine-line Art Deco design of interior scenes, including rococo-styled furnishings, and urban architectural perspectives that rivaled those of McCay.

Another first appeared in 1912 in Cliff Sterrett's family strip, *Polly and Her Pals,* which featured a single, independent young woman who was both heir to the Gibson Girl and precursor of the 1920s' flapper. Like popular fiction, the comics were beginning to reflect the changing social roles of women, and Sterrett's title character Polly Perkins was in the self-assertive mold of the New Woman. But the thing that stood out about *Polly* in its overall run of forty-six years was the unique graphics style its creator cultivated. In fact, by the late 1920s Sterrett's abstract manner clearly revealed the influence of Cubism, a force in modern art that dated from the work of Picasso and other artists around 1908. The movement was so avant-garde that hardly anyone would have thought a newspaper cartoonist audacious enough to relate to it. But Sterrett's growing reliance on an abstract style played an integral role in acclimating the mediated vision to the function of surreal art in setting mood and atmosphere. As the modernist trend in art had found interpretation in Winsor McCay's Art Nouveau stylings and later George McManus's debt to Art Deco, so Cliff Sterrett's evolving abstract technique revealed a popular media-made form as a significant force in helping blur elitist and mass tastes.

A strip that might have had an even greater influence in sensitizing the mediated vision to modern art as a new force in American culture was George Herriman's *Krazy Kat.* But during its run from 1913 to 1944 it never attracted the wide following of other long-run comics. Its singular, esoteric manner of presenting a never ending plot through the love-hate triangular relationship of Herriman's cat, mouse, and dog characterizations restricted it to a small audience, as attested to by its appearance in only thirty-five papers by Herriman's death in 1944. Transcending the restrictions of space and time, the strip's humor emanated from the characters' colorful wordplay exchanges in the continuously shifting surrealistic environs of an imaginary community in the Southwest. To fully appreciate *Krazy Kat,* though, readers discovered that they had to pay close attention to its linguistic nuances and poetic flights, an unexpected demand from so ephemeral a form as the comic strip.[12]

A popular format of this era was the panel cartoon produced by newspaper and magazine artists who focused on sports, politics, and humorous situations of social relevance. Although sports photography was coming into vogue at this time, it was the cartoonist who had the visual advantage in staging the heroic or satirical side of sports. The demand was such that many fledgling cartoonists who would go on to bigger things got their start in this arena. A real master of the field was Thomas A. Dorgan, who signed his work simply as "Tad."[13] Among his most popular panel series was *Indoor Sports,* which depicted the interaction between those who engaged in activities like poker and billiards along with the reaction of kibitzers. Spiced up with the earthy argot of the sporting scene and the street, or what Tad termed "slanguage," this series was a satirical dissection of middle-class social behavior, reinforcing the image of the cartoonist as a keen observer of the nation's changing social scene.

Naturally, the perspectives of a number of editorial cartoonists were tempered by the social issues of Progressive politics. In the tradition of the cartoon as a weapon to warn of political corruption and social injustices, Winsor McCay produced meticulously detailed illustrations for the Hearst papers that came across primarily as moral allegories, devoid of the satirical humor that characterized the output of contemporaries Homer Davenport, John T. McCutcheon, and Eugene Zimmerman, who signed his work "Zim."

While illustration for advertising and magazine fiction provided an outlet for many women artists, not a few tried their hand at drawing panel cartoons and comic strips. Prominent among them were Fanny Cory, Grace Drayton, who originated the Campbell Kids advertisements for the soup company, and Rose O'Neill. In 1909 O'Neill created a panel feature that was in keeping with this era's fantasy tradition—*The Kewpies.* Her highly stylized depiction of these cuddly little Cupid-like characters who dwelled in an idealized world of peace and goodwill proved so popular that the merchandising of them as dolls and toys made her more famous than her art had. But like her male contemporaries who introduced elitist art styles into the democratic sphere of the comics, Rose O'Neill professed no less a purpose in her work.[14]

During this highly productive period of the comics, their aesthetics were forged by a commercial milieu in which cartoonists responded directly to the mediated vision's escapist fancies to gain a loyal following. According to

By the 1930s the artwork of Cliff Sterrett's *Polly and Her Pals* had evolved into an abstract style like that shown here. © 1932, International Feature Service, Inc. Author's collection.

comics historian Judith O'Sullivan, comic strip artists, by diurnally recording their "personal social vision while making their work comprehensible to a wide public," bequeathed a unique way of viewing twentieth-century social history.[15] Because the commercial motivation of comic strip art inspired it to stay in tune with the evolving interests of the mediated vision, it would persist as a social mirror of its times' preoccupations. Through their natural affinity to cross over into other creative forms, the comics would also influence many areas within the spectrum of mediated culture: popular songs in the format of sheet music and recordings, animation/movies, toys, games, and even fashion styles. Often overlooked is their impact on the American language. Not only did the comics introduce readers to the slang and fads of an era, they functioned as a democratic educational aid for children and semiliterate adults.

THE MOVIES IN THE DAYS OF THE NICKELODEON

During the time when newspaper comics were developing a visual language of their own, movie speculators were beginning to realize the commercial possibilities of Thomas Edison's invention, the Vitascope. Earlier, in 1894, the introduction of the Kinetoscope in New York had customers lining up in amusement arcades to peer into this exciting new device. For the price of a penny, one could witness the illusion of everyday life in motion, usually in the form of such mundane events as parades, trains pulling into a station, or bathers cavorting at the seashore. Naturally, the novelty of this kind of fare soon wore off. But in 1896, Edison's demonstration of his Vitascope at a New York vaudeville theater where it offered an audience large-screen viewing paved the way for the "store-front" theaters that began showing motion pictures as a shared experience. Popularly known as nickelodeons, the term was supposedly coined in 1905 after the admission price set by a Pittsburgh exhibitor, who was among the first to open a theater for the express purpose of showing motion or moving pictures, soon called simply "movies." By 1909 the nickelodeon craze was developing into a national industry with thousands of theaters catering to fascinated moviegoers across the country.

As both a form of cheap entertainment and a temporary escape from real-life concerns, the movies had a strong appeal to the working class, among whom were many immigrants who, untutored in the dominant language of their new country, found that film could help them adjust to the intricacies of English through the correlation of image and subtitle. The real challenge to exhibitors lay in attracting the more lucrative patronage of middle-class, white collar customers. As early as 1908 vaudeville entrepreneur Marcus Loew, who was branching out into film exhibition, sensed the appeal that a more wholesome viewing environment would present. Thus, his leasing of some unprofitable New York theaters and converting them into outlets for the exclusive showing of movies foreshadowed the fabulous movie palaces of the 1920s. As a commercial undertaking from the start, then, the movies originated the basic system for their distribution and exhibition in the nickelodeon network of the teen years. Realizing the wide-open opportunities for making money in this promising new venture, future Hollywood movie moguls William Fox, Carl Laemmle, and Adolph Zukor started out as exhibitors but soon found their proper niche in production.

During this time, the creative side of the business, in which the new profession of film director played a key role, was trying to decide on the kind of subject matter in which its growing audience's interest primarily lay. The camera's obvious role in recording significant sporting and political events as well as the tragic impact of natural disasters was popular enough to result in the first weekly newsreel produced by Pathé in 1911. This early attempt at on-the-spot film reportage helped condition the mediated vision to "news" as entertainment, and its historical import would prove invaluable in providing a visual record of the likenesses of well-known figures of the time as well as revealing the fashions, fads, and social behavior of those times. But, as filmmakers discovered, the real future of the movies did not lie in the recording of nonfiction events.

During this era, in fact, certain pioneers of the moviemaking business were obtaining a valuable education experimenting with not only *what* moviegoers might want to see on the movie screen but, most importantly, with *how* they might want to see it. In 1903 an Edison employee, Edwin S. Porter, produced the most widely distributed film of the early nickelodeon era—*The Great Train Robbery.* It also became the most influential film up to that time in developing a cinematic style for the one-reel film of eight to twelve minutes in length, considered standard at that time. One reason for this film's immense popularity was the dramatic elements it derived from the myth of the old West. Numerous illustrators of popular magazine fiction during the late nineteenth century had helped establish the pervasive image of the West as a land of eternal conflict between cowboys, Indians, and outlaws. Now it was the movies' turn to visualize its version of the Western myth.

By incorporating dime novel elements of the legend into *The Great Train Robbery,* Porter created the first film that told a story with sufficient suspense to hold an audience's interest throughout its viewing. Technically, Porter's revolutionary editing of dissolves and scene transitions was rudimentary enough for his film to suffice as a guide book for others to follow in making a fictively inspired film. Transcending the conventions of the stage by allowing the camera to tell the story, Porter introduced the mediated vision to a new way of visualizing dramatic experience. And even though his was a formulaic interpretation, its appeal would be of sufficient import to generate infinite variations on the Western theme.[16]

Among the early directors who helped film narrative find itself as a receptive medium to dramatize the fantasies and dreams of the mediated vision was Thomas H. Ince. Realizing his shortcomings as an actor, he decided he was better suited as a director. It was a wise decision, as he began to make his mark in 1912 with a two-reel film about the old West titled *War on the Plains.* Heightening its realism through an on-site setting was only one sign of Ince's dynamic plans for making movies, first as a director and then a producer. The very next year found him experimenting with multiple cameras to capture the up-close action of the combat scenes in *The Battle of Gettysburg,* a technical innovation that would warrant special attention from a young director named David Wark Griffith.

In 1907, Griffith also started out on what he thought would be an acting career. But after a brief stint under director Edwin Porter, the next year saw him directing his first film for the New York-based Biograph Company, a melodrama in the fashion of the time. But Griffith found himself equally at home in any film genre, and during his time at Biograph he honed his craft in well over four hundred films from comedies to adaptations of the classics. Many of his productions revealed an imaginativeness of scope and invention that foreshadowed his later contributions to the refinement of film technique.

Heeding the camera's capability to move directionally with the flow of the action, Griffith employed ways to free the screen from static stage conventions and build dramatic suspense by highlighting points in a film's narrative through close-ups, mood lighting, and parallel editing. Like Ince, too, Griffith sought to enhance realism by filming on location, as he did in the prototypal gangster film, *The Musketeers of Pig Alley,* shot on the streets of New York City in 1912. At this early stage of his career, he was experimenting with an intuitive feel for what the camera was capable of in terms of what he thought an audience should expect from it.

The demand for filmed stories with bountiful action in a realistic setting grew steadily, as evidenced by the production output of three Eastern companies that had been making one-reel movies since the late 1890s: Edison, Biograph, and Vitagraph. To enhance this end, some independent companies had been taking seasonal treks since 1907 to California to film under better weather conditions. By 1910, many of them were considering this area as a permanent location since it was so conducive to year-round on-site filming. Soon after their arrival in 1912, independent producers Carl Laemmle and Adolph Zukor planted the seeds for their major corporations, Universal and Paramount studios, in a remote area of Los Angeles called Hollywood.

A misconception resulting from the popular reception of *The Great Train Robbery* was that an audience's span of attention for a filmed narrative was limited to one reel of no more than fifteen minutes. Griffith, among the first to advocate the feature film of four reels or more, contended that, like a novel, the length of a film depended on how well the story line could hold a viewer's interest. A major reason he would leave Biograph was the company's ban on making longer films. But by 1913 the trend toward longer films was in full swing as feature productions of four to five or more reels began to appear regularly, much to the delight of moviegoers who now had access to classic works that in their original print form were too culturally remote for popular consumption. Now even the popular theater began to abandon its productions for the more lucrative returns from regular showings of four-reel feature films to family audiences that by 1913 were becoming accustomed to spending time at the movies. By this time, then, the mediated vision had begun to realize its most appealing and accessible ritual of escapism in the first half of the century—going to the movies.

In 1909 another would-be actor named Mikell Sinnott joined the Biograph Company, where under the stage name of Mack Sennett he discovered his real talent lay in directing and helping develop the slapstick comedy genre. In fact, under his direction the silent comedy short became such a program favorite that by the 1920s it would be critically acclaimed as an art form unto itself. To achieve this honor, it took a great deal of experimentation during the early days of Sennett's Keystone Film Company, formed in California in 1912. Featuring the zany escapades of Chester Conklin and the wild chase scenes of the Keystone Kops, the early shorts were spiced up by Sennett's Bathing Beauties, whose members included Gloria Swanson and Mabel Normand. To maintain a comedic atmosphere of antic action in his films, Sennett also recruited such uniquely talented performers as Ford Sterling, Ben Turpin, Roscoe "Fatty" Arbuckle, and a young Charlie Chaplin, just starting out on his illustrious film career. By engaging them in a fast-paced brand of pie-in-the-face pratfall comedy of fascinating visual appeal, Sennett introduced the mediated vision to a slapstick version of pure escapism.

In time, the players who performed in the movies began to win a dedicated following, mainly from those fans looking to see more of a favorite performer in a future film. When Mary Pickford and Mabel Normand were recruited by Biograph in 1909, the seeds for the "movie star" fan tradition were planted, as these two—Pickford in melodrama and Normand in comedy—were soon ranked among the most popular personalities in the movies. D. W. Griffith displayed his flair for recognizing star potential when he signed sisters Lillian and Dorothy Gish in 1912. All four of these women would command such a widespread following that in the pantheon of the mediated vision they became idolized celebrities.

Not until producers themselves realized that certain performers' film presence helped sell a movie did the star system really come on in a big way. After Florence Lawrence signed with Biograph in 1908, her roles as an anonymous player were popular enough for her to be billed as "The Biograph Girl." But when she joined Carl Laemmle's independent production company in 1909, he started publicizing her actual name to keep drawing fans to her films. The upshot of this action was the creation of the first movie "star" and, of course, Hollywood's promotional role in sensitizing the mediated vision to a new kind of celebrity ethos. This latest trend in the growing fascination with the careers and intimate activities of personalities in the entertainment field would soon lead to mythic implications.[17]

EXPERIMENTATION IN THE ANIMATED CARTOON
AND OTHER CINEMATIC DEVELOPMENTS

Even before the appearance of the animated cartoon, a number of popular comic strip characters like Happy Hooligan and Buster Brown were being transcribed to the screen in live-action features. These films, by capitalizing on the mediated vision's fascination with the fantasized world of the comic strip, initiated a long and prosperous relationship between the movies and the comics. If the technology for animation had been in place by the turn of the century, comic strip characters would surely have been appearing earlier in animated cartoons. But despite the astronomical number of drawings that had to be produced to create the illusion of motion, many thought that single-framing photography would provide the only practical way to develop an animation system.

The earliest successful attempt at creating a full-blown animated cartoon was undertaken in 1911 by Winsor McCay in a production of his comic strip *Little Nemo*. Though it would be comprised of more than four thousand drawings, McCay possessed the appropriate disposition to complete such a task, having been a compulsive drawer all his life. After further experimentation, he introduced the prototypal animated cartoon personality in 1914 in the title character of *Gertie the Dinosaur*. Gertie, in fact, was created to complement the popular lightning-sketch vaudeville turn he had been performing since 1906. This drawing technique enabled a skilled artist like McCay to entertain an audience through impromptu chalk drawings done so rapidly they generated the illusion of motion. With Gertie's film role as an integral part of his act, McCay led onlookers to believe that he and the character were actually interacting in a live-action manner. Endowed with a personality all her own, Gertie's character looked ahead to the anthropomorphic animals soon to be created by the developers of modern animation. Even in its silent mode, the animated cartoon suspended disbelief by dramatizing an escapist realm that appealed to both children and adults—a fantasized world limited only by the animator's imagination.[18]

Although a great deal of experimentation with synchronized sound was going on in early cinema, its ultimate integration into film would have to await the advent of the "talking" film in the late 1920s. Consequently, the subtitle was essential for moviegoers to follow the narrative transitions of a silent film, but as they became conditioned to anticipating characters' actions, it was utilized more sparingly. As a film critic noted in 1913: "People get used to reading pictures. There is a grammar of pantomime which is easily learned by a little practice."[19]

If the early movies were mostly devoid of color, their major medium of publicity more than made up for this lack. The gaudily colored, highly stylized lithograph poster that appeared on the sides of buildings and fences and at

WINSOR McCAY

Creator of Little Nemo, Dreams
of a Rarebit Fiend and Other
Newspaper Cartoons

AND HIS WONDERFUL
TRAINED DINOSAURUS

GERTIE SHE'S A SCREAM

SHE EATS, DRINKS AND
BREATHES! SHE LAUGHS
AND CRIES! DANCES
THE TANGO, ANSWERS
QUESTIONS AND OBEYS
EVERY COMMAND!—
YET, SHE LIVED
MILLIONS OF YEARS
BEFORE MAN IN-
HABITED THIS
EARTH AND
HAS NEVER
BEEN SEEN
SINCE!!

ACCORDING TO
SCIENCE
THIS MONSTER
ONCE RULED
THIS PLANET.—
SKELETONS NOW
BEING UNEARTHED
MEASURING FROM
90ft TO 160ft.
IN LENGTH.—
AN ELEPHANT
SHOULD BE A
MOUSE BESIDE
GERTIE

THE GREATEST ANIMAL ACT IN THE WORLD !!!

Winsor McCay's *Gertie the Dinosaur*, created in 1914, antedated all the anthropomorphic animated film characters with unique personalities. Author's collection.

the entrances to theaters was an eye-enticing celebration of the movies' fantasy appeal. With the coming of the fiction film and the need to highlight its story content, still photographs, the forerunner of the eleven-by-fourteen-inch lobby card that pictured a film's dramatic highpoints, made their appearance as an inducement to paying customers. Then, by utilizing the lithographic process of poster art that advertised circuses, Wild West shows, and popular stage melodramas, the movies discovered their most visually commercial way to promote a film as well as contribute to the escapist mythology of Hollywood. The overall effect of such graphics was to inform a potential patron that his or her investment in a ticket would be well rewarded.

In spite of the generally positive reception of the movies, there were those who attacked them as a threatening menace to society, mainly to the morals of its youth. Accordingly, the moralists lumped movie theaters with the other so-called pitfalls of urban life: the saloon, the dance hall, and the burlesque show. Although a national board of censorship for exhibition had been established in 1909, movie producers recognized early on that sensationalism would sell, and though the professed intent of the exploitation film was to educate as well as entertain, it was soundly criticized by the cultural custodians. For example, they saw few, if any, redeeming elements in two 1913 films, *Traffic in Souls,* which dealt with white slavery, and *Slaves of Morphine,* which was about drug addiction. To transcend the problems of the day that the mediated vision was expected to ignore but was increasingly exposed to, most movies strived to create an alternative world of make-believe that would appeal to the widest possible audience.

By 1913, then, the movies were on their way to achieving their status as the dominant entertainment form of the mediated culture. From its humble origins as something of a novelty, the silent film, in the space of only about fifteen years, had laid the foundation for a universal visual language that people could intimately identify with. It was an achievement that during the years to come would expand the horizons of the mediated vision by introducing it to subject matter that previously it could only hear or read about. As a unique collaborative operation between producers, directors, actors, writers, and technicians, the making of movies became a highly complex enterprise. As such, it was unique as a visually creative form in allowing for a human interaction with technology. Ironically, this unlikely alliance would result in a new art form but one that, as a communally shared experience, allowed an audience to view images not only larger than life but seemingly more real than life. By creating a fantasized milieu in which universal daydreams could be both shared and hopefully realized, then, the movies fostered the development of a special mythology, but one that would continue to derive its inherent inspiration from the evolving escapist moods of the mediated vision.[20]

ADVERTISING'S CELEBRATION OF THE CONSUMER PRODUCT

As the Hollywood movie became a mass-mediated consumer commodity of the studios in their production of more movies than moviegoers could view in a week's time, so the corporate world of business/industry had begun to produce more goods than consumers were interested in buying. To respond to this unique quandary, an increased visual emphasis on more sophisticated, psychological methods of advertising was employed, particularly in popular magazines, some of which by 1900 carried advertising exceeding one hundred pages an issue. As it did for the lithograph poster, color also added a great deal to the seductive quality of a magazine ad's appearance.

By 1910, advertising agencies, in order to test and validate the demand for a new product, were gathering nationwide marketing data to determine consumer wants and buying habits. Mindful of such scientific research as well as the profits to be made from the promotional tactics resulting from it, the *Saturday Evening Post,* whose wide circulation assured highly profitable rates, became an aggressive leader in securing the sale of advertising space. Its large pages, of course, were tailor-made for the kind of display ad that dramatized the escapist dreams of the mediated vision.

In addition to the general interest magazines, numerous special interest periodicals started up in this era, all of them looking to reap the benefits from promoting products directed at a select audience. But it was the traditional women's magazines designed for the largest "specialized" audience of all that looked to garner the lion's share of advertising profits. By this time, keeping up with the seasonal change in fashions had become a major interest of middle-class women, and the ads in the magazines they subscribed to were a reliable means of being updated on the latest styles. As homemakers, too, they were natural targets for the advertising of household appliances and aids to the preparation of food as well as ready-prepared packaged and canned foods which were flooding the display ads of magazines. As managers of their households, women were also amenable to advertisements promoting a product conducive to their family's health, such as cereals, dental aids, and, before they were outlawed, patent medicines.

One magazine actually helped bring about an end to the exaggerated claims of the patent medicine cure-all product. Although the *Ladies' Home Journal* began refusing such advertising as early as 1892, it was the investigative series carried by *Collier's Weekly* in 1906, along with Upton Sinclair's classic muckraking novel *The Jungle* the same year, that was instrumental in ensuring the passage of the Pure Food and Drug Act of 1906. While advertising alcoholic beverages was generally frowned upon, tobacco was now being widely promoted, as cigarette smoking, just starting out on its controversial status as an escapist social habit, began to catch on in a big way.

Under the guise of brand names, tobacco and other packaged or bagged and canned goods continued to promote themselves as the best of their kind. In time the more durable of these products' commercial symbols engendered by the American system of advertising would become as familiar as old friends to the mediated vision. In their evocation of a product's quality, something of an intimate bond developed between product and consumer. During the early years of the century, for example, such consumer icons as the Victrola record player, the Kodak camera, and General Electric appliances were becoming a significant part of the visual experience of being an American.

In 1912 the standard twenty-four-sheet billboard poster (twelve-by-twenty-five feet) that first appeared in an urban setting was not only the largest print space yet available for promoting a product's merits, it was also an omen of the automobile industry's growth when such advertising would become a highway fixture. New York City, with its burgeoning population, continued to be a natural site for eye-catching, innovative kinds of electrified promotion. One of the most spectacular appeared in 1913—the gigantic (two hundred feet long by fifty feet high) Wrigley's chewing gum sign in Times Square, a showpiece of electronic wizardry that elevated its product from the commonplace to renowned import. It was a sign of even more spectacular things to come, especially when the celebrity entertainer would play a key role in promoting a product.[21]

The Celebrity Culture of Live Entertainment

By the beginning of the twentieth century the professional entertainer had achieved a more culturally acceptable image, mainly in the larger cities where puritanical constraints and social taboos were less pronounced than in the towns and rural communities of the hinterland. With the urban impulse a dynamic force in the development of mass entertainment—as evidenced by the rise of the silent film—vaudeville and both dramatic and musical theater also mirrored the mediated vision's acclimation to social change in the face of a fading Victorian consciousness. Although the rapid growth of the film industry would soon be making inroads into both vaudeville and theater audiences, the opening of Broadway's Palace Theater in 1913 was a monument to the general belief that the vaudeville tradition would be ongoing.

The popularity of vaudeville during this time was mainly attributable to its large variety of fast-moving turns extending from the crowd appeal of baggy-pants comics to heralded women entertainers. Although vaudeville had striven to maintain its wholesome family entertainment image since the early days of Tony Pastor, a degree of laxity had begun to creep into its programming. The erotically explosive energy of Eva Tanguay's dancing/singing performances, for example, never failed to excite audiences as well as arouse the ire of not a few bluenoses. Scoffing at convention, she projected a liberated sexuality that induced the mediated vision into a more permissive attitude toward her kind of entertainment. In 1911 Eva's spiritual sister, Mae West, made her first appearance in vaudeville at the age of eighteen. It would be her apprenticeship for developing the sex symbol image of her later stage and screen roles. A number of other women personalities like Nora Bayes, Marilyn Miller, Sophie Tucker, and Fanny Brice also helped transform the conventional image of women entertainers into one of unique media appeal.

The predominantly male province of stand-up comedy in both vaudeville and burlesque proved to be a training ground for numerous comedians who would go on to star on radio and in the movies, among them, Ed Wynn and Eddie Cantor. Emanating from the melting pot of the urban population's ethnic groups, a dominant strain in American satirical humor found its theatrical niche at this time. Although its racist tone would be frowned on later, vaudeville drew very few objections to its programming, for as the most publicly accessible form of live entertainment, it had a great deal to offer its largely middle-class white audience.

Among the most anticipated of vaudeville's attractions were the visually challenging, or visually deceiving, performances of magicians and illusionists. By playing on an audience's fascination with the improbable, such performers as Howard Thurston, Harry Blackstone, and Harry Kellar drew large followings. Of the three, Blackstone was the greatest showman, surrounding himself with a bevy of attractive female attendants while performing his specialty of Indian rope tricks. But it was Kellar who, in defying the laws of the physical world as an escape artist, had the biggest influence on a young man who would become the master showman of them all—Harry Houdini.

Upon reading about the feats of French magician Robert Houdin, Erich Weiss changed his name to Harry Houdini and a legend was born. Realizing that much of Kellar's appeal derived from an audience's involvement with his acts, Houdini publicized many of his exploits in advance to invite the skeptics. But in the art of escaping from handcuffs, chains, and straitjackets Houdini had no peer, as he amazed onlookers everywhere he appeared. The image of Houdini shackled by chains and locks of every description and complexity, yet managing to escape miraculously from any perilous predicament, lent him an heroic aura of seeming invincibility. To the public, too, there was something symbolic in his uncanny escape ability, almost as though he were overcoming the modernist forces of technology that were beginning to dominate urban life at this time.

By 1901, New York City and its forty-one playhouses represented the country's number one theater city, but their offerings' predominantly melodramatic themes were beginning to give way to the realism that was now a dominant force in fiction. An example of the growing symbiotic relationship between popular fiction and the stage was the 1904 dramatization of Owen Wister's best-selling novel *The Virginian* (1902), with Dustin Farnum in the title role. Perhaps the most representative play to express the clash between Eastern values and those of the frontier was William Vaughn Moody's ambiguously titled *The Great Divide* in 1906. Envisioning life from the traditional perspective of the mediated vision, Moody urged a return to the old-time values that an evolving consumer society was eroding. On the other hand, Israel Zangwill's *The Melting-Pot* (1909) looked ahead to an idealized future when all ethnic groups would be fused into a new national identity.

Signs that the American theater, under the influence of European drama, was leaning toward portraying life more honestly and realistically had been appearing since the 1890s. Paradoxically, dramatic realism was laying the foundation for a type of escapism which enabled the mediated vision to forget temporarily the problems of the real world to identify with those of the actors on stage. Other than David Belasco in his innovative staging effects, the most influential dramatist to lead American drama toward a new sense of realism was Clyde Fitch, who combined a sure feel for craftsmanship with a daring vision for his time. Before Fitch it was considered strictly taboo to dramatize, or even imply, anything to do with sex. That the moralists were still very much around in 1900 was evident when Olga Nethersole, the star of Fitch's *Sapho,* was arrested after appearing in the most explicit love scenes ever seen on the New York stage. Although she was acquitted, so much publicity accrued from Nethersole's trial that *Sapho* was revived before sold-out audiences.

Even though the bars were lowering, any sign of indecency on stage was still sufficient to bring down the wrath of social censure. Proactive in this cause was self-appointed vice crusader and guardian of public morals Anthony Comstock, who, in his unexcelled zeal, once boasted that he had "destroyed 160 tons of obscene literature."[22] In his concerted efforts to shield the mediated vision from what he thought it should not see, Comstock mainly targeted sex, both explicit and implied, even trying to outlaw the performance of George Bernard Shaw's *Mrs. Warren's Profession* in 1905 because of its references to prostitution.

But Clyde Fitch crafted plays of more modernist bent than *Sapho,* which he had based on a mediocre French novel. Though Fitch wrote and produced thirty-six original plays over a period of twenty years, *The City,* due to its then shocking language and references to drug use and even incest, is considered a groundbreaking play in American drama. As another step toward undermining the mediated vision's fantasized views of urban life, Fitch portrayed the psychological problems and moral decay of a family recently moved to the big city, foreshadowing the modernist themes of Eugene O'Neill. As still another harbinger of things to come, 1910, the year after Fitch's death, saw American plays on Broadway outproduce European plays for the first time.

With traveling tent shows staging theatrical productions mainly in the Midwest and the South in the early twentieth century, their repertoire often treated its patrons to a nightly change of bills for a week or more, depending on audience reception. Before the coming of the movies, the social impact of tent productions on entertainment deprived rural folk was considerable, especially in its fantasized response to their escapist desires that revealed other beckoning worlds beyond their own.

The most acclaimed theatrical form to come into its own during this era was the musical comedy, particularly the kind produced by a former vaudeville performer named George M. Cohan. In 1901 he began drawing on his vaudeville experience as the basis for a new type of musical comedy, resulting in 1904 in his first major production, *Little Johnny Jones.* In this show Cohan's spirited music and dynamic dance style captured the energetic pace of urban life as it was particularized in New York City during the early years of the new century. In fact, Cohan's musical output was a barometer of this exciting social milieu. Countering those who espoused an anti-urban mindset, he ignored the city's social ills to champion it as a symbol of American progress and opportunity, a place where the personal goals of the mediated vision could be fulfilled. The hit songs of Cohan's productions were testimonials to both his patriotic fervor and his belief that the spirit of the city represented democracy in action. Both *Little Johnny Jones* and *George Washington, Jr.* (1906) offered songs that in echoing patriotism and the modern temper were popular enough to become perennial favorites as, for example, "Yankee Doodle Boy," "You're a Grand Old Flag," and "Give My Regards to Broadway." But Cohan's real contribution to the development of the American stage musical was in the artistic unity he created through the integration of music, choreography, and story line, an alliance that anticipated the momentous achievement of *Show Boat* in 1927. Also, in composing some of the era's greatest song hits, Cohan enriched a long-standing tradition—the reputation of the Broadway musical as a bountiful source of appealing songs that would enjoy crossover popularity in other entertainment forms of the evolving mediated culture.

That African American music was making an impression on the mediated culture was epitomized in the career of the talented Bert Williams, who demonstrated that he was versatile enough as a comic, dancer, and singer to transcend the racist stereotype of the coon song. Expressing a dominant blues theme of black music—the individual down on his luck and up against hard times, Williams's songs were so well received that Victor signed him as the first black recording artist. In 1903 he and partner George Walker wrote, produced, and starred in *In Dahomey,* the first all-black Broadway musical with an African setting. Although the black musical would fade after 1913, not to reappear until the 1920s, Williams became a ten-year headliner in Florenz Ziegfeld's *Follies,* beginning in 1910. There, his talent for pantomime and comedy routines with Leon Errol convinced a prejudiced public there really was a place for the black entertainer in the pantheon of show business greats.

What George M. Cohan did for musical comedy Florenz Ziegfeld would do for the musical revue. As an annual event from 1907 until 1927, after which it was revived intermittently, the *Follies'* fast-paced program of specialty acts, comedy routines, and promenades of beautiful chorus girls set the highest production standards for musical theater. Combining the venues of glorified burlesque and sophisticated vaudeville, its revue format was thematically organized around topical humor and the high-fashion display of feminine beauty—all staged amid lavish sets of eye-dazzling color and musical numbers of wide-ranging appeal, from the romantic ballad to the latest ragtime hit. Even though Ziegfeld dressed his showgirls in revealing, exotic costumery, his placement of them in glittering, flamboyant sets cajoled patrons into believing that the nudity displayed in a Ziegfeld production was not only respectable but morally acceptable.

In justifying his major objective of glorifying the American girl, Ziegfeld once commented: "For beauty of face and form, for magnetism of personality, for grace and talent and intelligence, the American chorus girl stands in a class by herself. . . . The American girl is the most beautiful girl in the world."[23] And in marked contrast to the nineteenth-century physical ideal of the plump female performer, his was a refreshing new image of the showgirl, even in her very posture and walk. Though racist in attitude, Ziegfeld's Caucasian standards of the ideal American girl set the tone for her appearance during the first half of the century in advertising, fashion shows, and beauty contests, as well as various forms of the mediated culture, most notably the movies, and, by extension, these forms' effect on the mediated vision's conception of the American girl as sex symbol.

An important factor that gave the *Follies* its trademark opulence was the hiring of Joseph Urban in 1915 to design the production sets. Urban, whose talent for design extended from his sets for the Metropolitan Opera to ultimately those he did for the movies, drew on the pointillage technique of the Impressionists and the modernist stylings of Art Nouveau to create sets that involved audiences in an overwhelming visual experience. The combination of Urban's set designs and Ziegfeld's flair for staging his alluring beauties within them not only aroused the erotic fantasies of males in the audience, it inspired untold numbers of young women (and certainly many matrons longing for their lost youth) to identify with the glamorous world of the Ziegfeld girl.

MUSICAL THEATER'S INFLUENCE ON NEW DANCE STYLES

There were those, however, who saw the nudity displayed so boldly in the *Follies* as yet another sign of the pervasive breakdown in morals. Nowhere was this situation more evident, they felt, than in the dance mania cropping up in the urban centers of the country. By 1910, as a burgeoning number of Southern blacks settled in the Harlem section of New York City, their physically exciting kind of music began to attract an enthusiastic white following. In 1913 they were taking in a revue called *Darktown Follies* in which a syncopated dance routine called "Balling the Jack" was featured. Its uninhibited style and others like it that had been introduced in black musical revues fomented a dance craze that would last on into the 1920s. Suggesting their animalistic manner of expression through such names as the grizzly bear, turkey trot, bunny hug, and the fox trot, the new dance steps offered couples the opportunity to break away from Victorian gentility on the dance floor and present themselves in a spontaneous, self-promotional way. The effects on social behavior, especially that of young women, were revolutionary. To accommodate the demands of a fast-paced dance beat, their dresses became less restrictive and shorter. And since participation in the new dances placed them in the social eye, there was a big increase in the sale of cosmetics, whose use helped to model themselves after the idealized image of the Ziegfeld girl—daringly independent and, above all, sexually attractive. As expected, their new-found social style was not taken lightly by the guardians of social mores who found such behavior shocking and repulsive.[24]

To counteract any negative attitude toward ballroom dancing and lend it an air of respectability, the team of Vernon and Irene Castle set out to transform popular dance steps into socially accepted rites. Also, by inventing new steps like the Castle Rock or introducing such imported styles as the tango, they turned ballroom dancing into a combined expression of both its liberating and constraining elements, thus helping dignify its erotic movements. Ultimately, Irene, as a feminist who promoted dancing as a healthy social expression of the liberated woman, and Vernon, who brought sophistication to the male's role as her partner, generated a dance phenomenon that would have widespread social import. Participating in a popular new dance step satisfied both the primitive instincts of the libido and the cultural rules of the social order, helping free the mediated culture from its obeisance to past customs governing dancing as a social activity.

PRODUCING AND PROMOTING THE MUSIC OF THE MEDIATED CULTURE

While the music of Tin Pan Alley had been created primarily for the stage and the sheet-music business, the spreading popularity of the phonograph was demanding a continuous output of recorded Tin Pan Alley songs to satisfy the ever-evolving, capricious nature of the mediated culture, especially in the wake of the proliferating dance craze. Earlier, in 1901, the merger of the Berliner Gramophone Company and the Consolidated Talking Machine Company resulted in the country's most prominent phonograph/recording corporation—the Victor Talking Machine Company, as it was then known.[25]

Thus, the invention Thomas Edison initially thought would serve mainly as a device for dictation and recording famous personalities' voices had now become a mass-made medium for the playing of sentimental ballads, patriotic marches, ragtime numbers, coon songs, and most any kind of novelty number that appealed to popular taste. But when Enrico Caruso, the best-known operatic singer in the world, started recording on Victor's expensive Red Seal line in 1902, his voice not only accorded the phonograph player something of an elitist distinction, it marked the first time that a medium of mass communication helped override the demarcation between elitist taste and the popular.

In 1906 the Victrola appeared, the first record player with its amplifier horn enclosed in a cabinet and the turntable and tone arm covered by a lid, and with it the Victor Company clearly took the sales lead in the industry. Magazine advertising reflected the corporate pride in Victor's new product by promoting it as an essential household piece of furniture. Colorfully illustrated ads carried tag lines like "After dinner, introduce your guests to the world's greatest artists" and "Dancing is delightful to the music of the Victrola." In this latter pitch Victor revealed that by 1910 its goals were no different from those of other companies in cashing in on the current dance mania.

To meet this demand, the recording industry turned its attention to producing a plethora of tunes geared to either a syncopated ragtime beat or the two-step rhythm of the fox trot, sending it on the way to becoming the most popular dance step in social history. The upshot of the recording companies' new market enabled couples to dance most anywhere—at a social club, a recreation hall, a school gymnasium, and, of course, in the home. Here was further evidence of the mediated culture's propensity for merging the escapist needs of all social classes, providing an opportunity for those of lower estate to emulate the lifestyle of socialites who contracted live orchestras to play dance music for their lavish balls.

Around 1900, when the business interests of popular music moved further uptown from New York's Union Square to 28th Street, the opportunities for increased profits from the sales of popular music mushroomed. But with this relocation, the term "Tin Pan Alley" became more associated with a certain style of music rather than the place of its production. Although the phonograph recording was competing for attention, the parlor piano's sheet music was still central to the home life of many turn of the century families, particularly urban families of modest means and those in isolated rural areas. One of the last expressions of family togetherness in the twentieth century occurred when household members gathered around a piano for a sing-along.

During this era, then, the piano, the phonograph, and the dance phenomenon combined to make music publishing a very lucrative business in which over one hundred songs each sold more than one million copies of sheet music. Many of these hits were composed in the traditional mode of the romantic ballad, for example, "Meet Me Tonight in Dreamland" (1909), while numerous others were inspired by the topical and technological interests of the time, as "Meet Me in St. Louis, Louis" was by the 1904 St. Louis World's Fair and "In My Merry Oldsmobile" (1905) by the automobile. In fact, any new invention of note, such as the movies and the airplane, could be expected to trigger a number of novelty songs whose colorfully illustrated sheet music covers were designed to catch the mediated vision's fancy.[26]

During this time, department stores were hiring singers and pianists to perform such songs in their sheet music sections. In 1911, for example, Woolworth's five-and-dime stores, now a chain of over six hundred outlets, were selling sheet music for ten cents a copy to thousands of customers. But the surest way for a song to become a hit was for a well-known entertainer to sing it. The upshot of this effort might be a listing in the popularity chart that *Billboard* magazine began publishing in 1913, a feature that proved a boon to both sheet music sales and the recording business.

Al Jolson, who generated an appealing aura of showmanship that endeared him to audiences, was the prototype of this new kind of entertainer with the power to make a big hit out of a song. As such, he was a major target of the song pluggers. After attracting attention in 1911 as the quintessential black face singer, he maintained a solid rapport with his fans over a twenty-year period, during which he was billed as "The World's Greatest Entertainer." His female counterpart was the buxsom Sophie Tucker, who sang audience favorites like "Some of These Days" and "St. Louis Blues" with an uninhibited syncopated beat. Like Jolson, Tucker often performed in black face and recorded coon songs that were either written by black composers or inspired by the African American lifestyle. The close relationship that Sophie Tucker and Al Jolson had with their fans set an entertainment tradition that would last throughout the century—that of the headline performer whose personality radiates a magnetic image in the eyes of the mediated vision.

By intuitively realizing the kind of song the public might identify with, the major contributors to the success of a Tin Pan Alley tune were really the composers themselves. Many successful songwriters, as well as their publishers, were either recent immigrants or just one generation away from the old country. Paradoxically, they were outsiders who became insiders through assimilating the basic values of the American experience and then interpreting them in a fresh way that resulted in songs of wide appeal. A young Jew named Israel Baline, who changed his name to Irving Berlin, was the leading example of this kind of songwriter. Although he was untrained in music composition and performance, he instinctively knew what his fellow citizens, established or newly arrived, were looking for in a song. As a result, he would turn out hundreds of the most popular songs ever composed by any song-writer. Although he was most adept at the romantic ballad, his most popular song of this era was "Alexander's Ragtime Band" (1911), a prime example of Tin Pan Alley's practice of transforming black musical forms into an accept-able cultural expression for white audiences. The popularity of Berlin's songs was greatly enhanced by the dance bands and honky-tonk pianists who per-formed them in cafés and saloons, but many unauthorized performances re-sulted in a copyright problem that Berlin and his fellow composers soon moved to resolve.

The most prominent figure in this movement was Victor Herbert, another immigrant whose music in the tradition of the European light opera or op-eretta had made a name for him in American theater. That such musical pro-ductions were still popular was evidenced by the overwhelming reception of Franz Lehar's *The Merry Widow* in 1907, inspiring Herbert's faith in the op-eretta's popular appeal in the spectrum of mediated culture. The production of *The Wizard of Oz* as a musical in 1903 probably influenced his delightful *Babes in Toyland* of the same year, while the crossover practice of convert-ing one form of creative expression into another inspired his staging of Win-sor McCay's *Little Nemo in Slumberland* as a musical in 1908. Herbert was at his best, though, in a production like *Naughty Marietta* (1910), paving the way for the colorful musicals of Rudolph Friml and Sigmund Romberg, who, along with Herbert, composed some of the great standards of American pop-ular music.

By this time, even gospel music had taken on some Tin Pan Alley charac-teristics, mainly in its personalized emotional tone. While the Negro spiri-tual was being transformed into the black church's version of gospel music, gospel song composers were attempting to bridge the gap between the tradi-tional hymns of the established church and compellingly emotional songs like "Amazing Grace," which first came on the revival scene in 1910. Those gospel musicians who were the first to record their music anticipated a vi-able way to spread the message of fundamentalist Christianity through the wider congregation of radio, a sign of things to come in what came to be called the "electronic church."

Whether religiously or secularly inspired, popular music was communally addressed to a broad audience; yet it spoke to each listener in a uniquely pri-vate way, which is why such music could be reminiscent of the time that pro-duced it. Even though a certain type of popular music could pass out of fash-ion, it may resurface on occasion and gain renewed popularity, as musical styles would in later film soundtracks intended to capture the remote atmos-phere of an era. Ragtime was certainly the dominant musical sound of the years 1900–1913, and although it was originally intended to be performed instrumentally, its syncopated beat had an unprecedented influence on the way certain songs were performed, as the styles of Al Jolson and Sophie Tucker demonstrated. Overall, ragtime generated a happy, volatile sound that echoed the optimistic temper of an urbanized nation awakening to its latent greatness. Its flamboyant style was mirrored in the visual fancifulness of sheet music cover art—a veritable explosion of colorful lithographs in the Art Nouveau manner. In spite of this era's ongoing debate in the press and attacks from the pulpit concerning its social evils, ragtime's future influence as jazz was assured, in particular on those composers and musicians of the dominant white culture who would absorb its substance and transform it into hybrid musical stylings of great escapist appeal to the mediated vision.

THE GROWING LITERARY DIVERSITY OF THE MEDIATED CULTURE

By 1911 and the publication of Theodore Dreiser's *Jennie Gerhardt,* as well as the reissuance of *Sister Carrie* in 1912, Victorian standards were deferring to a more tolerant attitude toward stories about well-meaning young women who fall prey to the seductive illusions of a mediated culture. Such an outlook was congruent with the Progressive mission to strip away any signs of hypocrisy to expose corruption. Now, serious women writers, under the sway of realism, were examining the social concerns of American life more fearlessly. Edith Wharton's *The House of Mirth* (1905), for example, painted a satirical picture of New York society's code of conventional behavior in the late nineteenth century. Ellen Glasgow, in one of her best novels, *Virginia* (1913), deglamorized the aristocratic tradition of the old South during its troubled Reconstruction era. But Mary Johnston, another writer from Virginia, revealed that the historical romance still retained its popularity by reviving antebellum ideals in *To Have and to Hold* (1900). And during this problematic period, the majority of best-selling novels were, in the escapist vein of Johnston's, geared to romantic, sentimental, and nostalgic themes. As a result, historical novels that depicted the past as eminently more interesting than the present were always somewhere among the top ten best sellers during the years 1900–1910.

Among the other more popular fiction writers of this era was Harold Bell Wright, whose success can be attributed to two main factors: his sentimental approach to revitalizing the faltering Christianity of his day and the mass-mediated promotion of his books in full-page display ads in big-city newspapers that helped his books achieve their status as best sellers. In the fast-moving urban society of the early twentieth century, fraught with the social problems that industrialization and a burgeoning population had fomented, the established Church was having a difficult time adjusting its traditional theology to the mediated distractions of modern life. As a result,

Wright, who was an ordained minister, was compelled to use his novels to "preach" sermons on the vital place of Christian values in such a milieu. Accordingly, *The Shepherd of the Hills* (1907), Wright's first popular success, stands out as a prime example of his ability to allegorize the experiences of a disenchanted minister who retreats from his big-city pastorate to relocate in an isolated area in the Ozark Mountains where he seeks the true meaning of Christianity among its people. In this and other best-selling novels like *The Calling of Dan McGrew* (1909) and *The Winning of Barbara Worth* (1911), Harold Bell Wright spoke to his readers as no other writer of his time did, presenting them with the kind of fiction he felt they needed for spiritual succor.

Much sentimental fiction that came to the fore during this era was written from a woman's perspective and naturally dominated by female characters. One of the most popular was *Mrs. Wiggs of the Cabbage Patch* (1901), in which Alice Hegan Rice focuses on a widowed, indigent mother's courageous but humorous outlook in confronting an ongoing series of hardships raising her children, a situation that anticipated the radio soap opera of a later day. This novel's future success as a crossover (play in 1904, silent film, and two sound versions in 1934 and 1942), was emulated by Kate Douglas Wiggins's *Rebecca of Sunnybrook Farm* (1903).[27] In its appealing melodramatic plot, young Rebecca, as the daughter of poor parents, is sent to live with relatives who are in a better position to afford her an education and the opportunity to get ahead in life—essential ingredients for this kind of fiction and a valid reason for its popularity.

The most successful writer in the tradition of the adolescent girl protagonist was Gene (Geneva) Stratton Porter. Over a period of twelve years she produced a total of five best sellers, rivaling the rankings of Winston Churchill's historical fiction. In reverting to youthful eyes to recall the wildlife of the fields and woods of her Indiana girlhood, Porter drew on her intense love of nature to charge her writing with a strong visual sense of the way things were. As such it was especially admired by older women readers looking to relive their youth.

But a highly popular writer who took a naturalistic approach to interpreting nature's downside was Jack London, whose stories were appreciated on both a narrative as well as a philosophical level. In his most famous novel, *The Call of the Wild* (1903), he drew on the rugged setting of the Alaskan Klondike to tell the story of a dog's struggle against the unrelenting forces of nature. As such, it was praised as one of the best dog stories ever written, charged with a narrative power that admirably succeeds in humanizing Buck the dog as the story's central character. But in a deeper sense, *The Call of the Wild* reveals the naturalistic literary influence of this period that transforms it into an allegory of mankind's primeval roots and fatalistic plight in a Darwinian universe. Little wonder, then, that most readers of this time chose to ignore the tale's bleak picture of existence to relish instead its adventure elements.

Yet during this era of outward confidence that masked a growing inner uneasiness, London's philosophical stance was right for the times, affirming the necessity to rely on an inner will to confront the indifference of nature or fate and the uncertainties of existence, as his best novel *The Sea-Wolf* (1904) asserts. Ironically, London's self-indulgent lifestyle belied the Nietzschean philosophy he expressed in his fiction. As chronicled in the autobiographical *Martin Eden* (1909), his tempestuous life introduced the mediated vision to the American writer as a hard-drinking, contentious rebel against conventional mores—the kind of media image later embodied in the celebrated writing career of Ernest Hemingway.

Jack London may have extended the strong-willed frontier hero of the American West to the Klondike, but it was Owen Wister's *The Virginian* (1902) that formally conceptualized the myth of the West in terms of its key character types. In fact, this novel provided the paradigm text for not only the Western fiction that followed but also the Western film. A major reason for its universal appeal was the title character. As a forceful symbol of Western justice, he established the model for a more self-reliant image of the fictionalized cowboy, particularly in the gun play and confrontational scenes that became so much a part of the genre. This end was visually reinforced when matinee idol Dustin Farnum would be signed to reprise his stage role in the 1914 silent film.

Among the most popular and prolific contributors to this genre was Zane Grey, whose first successful novel, *The Spirit of the Border,* appeared in 1906. By the time of *Riders of the Purple Sage* in 1912, Grey's reputation as one of the most revered Western novelists of all time was assured. Zane Grey's West may have been a fantasy world that modified historical realities, but his vivid description of its natural scene, as Grey himself knew it from firsthand observation, lent a high degree of authenticity to his writing. It was a visual quality that was highly attractive to the movie people, who would continue to make films of his works in both the silent and sound eras.[28]

The mythical West of fiction and film, in dramatizing a theme of universal appeal—the basic conflict between good and evil—necessarily resorted to violence to effect dramatic resolution. Its concept of justice embodied in the cowboy character also found an urban counterpart in the modern detective hero whose fictional makeup was comprised of both the vigilante and outlaw elements of the old West. Although Edgar Allan Poe had invented the detective hero, Arthur Conan Doyle's Victorian sleuth Sherlock Holmes established the popular image of the detective who relies as much on intuition as deductive reasoning to solve a crime. Indeed, Holmes's characterization was so influential that until the 1930s it persisted as *the* model for the American detective hero. The first best-selling detective-mystery novel in America,

Doyle's *The Hound of the Baskervilles* (1902), set the pattern for this kind of fiction by focusing on the puzzle of who might have committed a criminal act, or a series of them, and in the end providing a solution.

The popular literary character of this era who operated as an urban detective was Arthur B. Reeve's Craig Kennedy, a New York college professor, who utilized the scientific method in his stories of criminal investigation. Soon, a flood of such stories were appearing, as urbanization's role in spawning crime would prove to be a major factor in the emergence of the American detective hero in the late 1920s.

If ever there was a medium that catered to the mediated vision's propensity for fantasizing real life, it was the pulp magazine. Toward this end, detective-mystery fiction was just one of many genres to find a welcome home in the pulps. In 1903 the publishing house of Street & Smith jumped on the pulp bandwagon with *The Popular Magazine*. Concentrating on tales of action and adventure, it was a direct imitation of Frank Munsey's pioneering *Argosy* and its first outright competitor. Subsequently, numerous other publishers, aware of bountiful profits to be made, produced their own versions of this upstart medium's dedication to fantasy and escapism.

By 1912, pulp editors, in their zeal to attract more readers through even more appealing stories, had come up with what pulp historian Leo Server calls "the definitive pulp story—larger than life, lucidly written, plot driven, with strong characters and lots of action, preferably violent."[29] Frank Munsey, who was facing tough competition from all sides by now, countered in 1912 when he published the first novel of Edgar Rice Burroughs in his *All-Story Magazine*. Not only did *Under the Moons of Mars* fit the pulp formula, it was sufficiently original to anticipate fantasy adventure and science fiction as exciting new modes of escapist release. *All-Story* had first appeared in 1905 with the first three-color action oriented cover as well as plot related interior illustrations, thereby setting a standard for other pulps to emulate. But with the publication of Burroughs's premier story, Munsey had established another standard for the kind of fiction whose celebrated author's name alone would be sufficient to sell a magazine in which his work appeared.

Ironically, Burroughs's career as one of the most widely read authors of all time had a curiously belated start. As an uninspired businessman given more to daydreaming than selling a product, he put his story-telling instincts to work in his mid thirties, and *Under the Moons of Mars* was the result. (The later book version was titled *A Princess of Mars*.) It was the beginning of a lifelong writing career in which Burroughs combined his knowledge of history and anthropology with a wide-ranging imagination to create a fantasy world all his own. Because of this power to summon up highly exotic realms from a fertile imagination, his stories of alien worlds and lost civilizations would reveal an intermingling of romanticism and realism, a blurring of fantasy and reality that created a new kind of escapist experience for the mediated vision.

However, it was another mythical hero who would far outshine the exploits of the space-defying John Carter of the Martian stories. In 1912, *All-Story*'s publication of *Tarzan of the Apes* introduced Burroughs's most famous character, through which the extension of the Frontier's mythic space to the African jungle would receive its most spectacular treatment. Not only did the story of Tarzan as an individual conditioned by the demands and rigors of a primitive environment establish the genre of the jungle tale, it presented the mediated vision with a new perspective on the relationship between the constraints and demands of a modern lifestyle and the desire to live more naturally and freely. Even renowned writer Gore Vidal has admitted to a respect for the Burroughs canon, especially the early Tarzan novels, by calling him "the master of American daydreamers."[30]

Juvenile fiction that instructed as it entertained was still highly esteemed during this time. One book that became an immediate classic was L. Frank Baum's *The Wonderful Wizard of Oz* (1900). As the first of fifteen books he would write about his magical fairyland, Baum declared in his introduction that his story "aspires to be a modernized fairy tale, in which the wonderment and joy are retained and the heartaches and nightmares are left out."[31] But Baum contradicted himself, for the story contains several nightmarish episodes that conspire against Dorothy Gale's attempts to find a way back home. That her persistence pays off in the end is the moral of the story. While W. W. Denslow's illustrations, characterized by his blend of color with Art Nouveau detail, lent the first book in the Oz series a charm all its own, those of John R. Neill's in the later books helped personalize the varied lineup of colorful characters who popped up here and there. The inimitable styles of both artists charged the Baum stories' settings and their characterizations with a visual enchantment that would continue to fascinate generations of children. Their art, in fact, inspired the models for dramatized interpretations. In addition to the 1903 Broadway musical version, which had an amazingly long run despite its distortions of the original plot, silent film productions appeared in 1910 and 1924, looking ahead to the classic 1939 sound version.

During this time, too, young girl readers were being avidly courted by the Stratemeyer Syndicate through a number of publishing houses, such as New York's Grosset & Dunlap, which promoted a diverse line of series books. Reflecting the growing feminist mood, they were structured around self-reliant female characters whose adventures took them far a field to test their new-found resourcefulness. Among the most popular, for example, was the Moving Picture Girls series, inspired by the movie mania of the time and authored by the house name of Laura Lee Hope.

While a wide variety of series books for boys appeared that dealt with just about every conceivable area of interest to them, the subject of athletics had grown increasingly popular as organized school sports caught on with youths nationwide. The continuing appeal of Frank Merriwell was a major reason, since his creator Gilbert Patton was still turning out his stories and other sports series books under his real or pen name of Burt L. Standish. But the most popular series character created by the Stratemeyer fiction factory was not an athlete but an inventor. Beginning in 1910 with *Tom Swift and His Motor-Cycle* and on until the late 1930s, a total of nearly forty books would appear in the original series. In them Tom always came up with a new invention that appealed to his readers' growing fascination with technology. The motorcycle was a good choice to start off with since it was a recent invention whose personally mechanized mode of travel promised exciting adventure. Thus the Tom Swift stories, under the house name of Victor Appleton, transformed the highly fanciful inventions in the Frank Reade tales of an earlier generation into technological achievements of a more practical bent. To complicate their fast-paced plots a variety of villainous types appeared on the scene to foil Tom's plans, maintaining interest through the juvenile series' convention of a suspenseful chapter ending to keep readers turning pages.

The upshot of Edward Stratemeyer's staff of hack writers and their response to youth's escapist interests was that between 1900 and 1930, the year of Stratemeyer's death, his syndicate would churn out more than thirteen hundred novels in 125 different series. These years, in fact, represent the golden age of the series book, not to fade until the superhero comic book, sound movie serial, and B-movie series heroes would offer more immediate visual distractions to the reading habits of American youth.

To meet the demand of young and old who found reading fiction a favorite form of relaxation during these years, all the popular magazines published both short and serialized stories of established authors and those of promising new writers, some of whom would soon become better known. Among this group was William Sydney Porter, who wrote his short stories under the pen name of O. Henry. Settling in New York City in 1902, he displayed a unique talent for turning out down-to-earth stories about the trials and tribulations of ordinary people, mainly in an urban setting. Tempered by the polarities of the mediated culture, these were the dreamers and schemers who, in general, were not too far removed from their small-town/rural backgrounds or life in the old country. O. Henry's contribution to the American short story form was the surprise, ironic closure—what came to be termed and widely imitated as the "twist ending." His stories, which quickly became anthology favorites, were first collected in *The Four Million* (1906), whose title referred to the population of New York City at the time. It was an immediate best seller, attesting to the author's natural affinity for relating to the everyday concerns of the mediated vision.

Compared to the popularity of magazine fiction, the genre of poetry was not nearly as fortunate. When Harriet Monroe founded *Poetry: A Magazine of Verse* in 1912, a major goal of hers was to make poetry more accessible to the general public. The first issue editorialized that the popular magazines had generally ignored publishing serious poetry because they had acceded to the whimsical desires of "a public which buys [the magazines] not for their verse but for their stories, pictures, journalism, rarely for their literature, even in prose."[32]

A widely popular poet of this time was Robert Service, whose colorful Klondike characters depicted in *The Spell of the Yukon and Other Verses* (1907) made it a best seller, a publishing rarity for a book of poetry. The sentimental poem was also highly favored during this time, and its potential as a Tin Pan Alley song saw many appear as sheet music for the parlor piano. Among the most popular poems of this type set to music was Joyce Kilmer's religiously inspired "Trees." If "only God [could] make a tree," as the lyric emotes, there appeared to be plenty of poets around like Kilmer who could "make" a sentimental poem that appealed to the mediated vision.

DIVERSIFYING THE VENUES OF PUBLIC AMUSEMENT

By the early 1900s dozens of small circuses were traveling the land by railroad, with their greatly anticipated arrival at specified locations announced by the usual colorful posters and billboards. In 1907 the merger of the Ringling Brothers circus with Barnum and Bailey helped assure this mammoth enterprise's ongoing predominance and profitability at the expense of the smaller ones. But during this time all circus operations strived to uncover new ways to compete with the spreading popularity of the amusement parks located near large metropolitan areas.

In 1903 amusement park developer Frederic Thompson opened up another of Coney Island's fun centers called Luna Park, fittingly named after a featured attraction that promised a fantasized trip to the moon. That same year saw the million lights of Dreamland lit up to compete with Steeplechase and Luna Parks. Of the three, though Luna had come up with the most visually appealing amusement formula to attract the thousands of city folk who frequented Coney Island at this time. As another entrepreneur attuned to the mediated vision's escapist wishes, Fred Thompson capitalized on his theory that people came to amusement parks to satisfy the illusion that life should be better than it is. Thus he envisioned Luna Park as a "grown-up toy shop" where visitors were challenged to create their own personal show by laughing at themselves and others.

A major factor in the communal appeal of the amusement park lay in its special attention to mechanizing the escapist desires of the mediated vision. According to Thompson, his thrill rides were "a natural result of the American love of speed. Just as we prefer the fastest trains, the most powerful motorcars, the speediest steamships and the fastest horses, so we like best the amusement rides which furnish the biggest thrill."[33] For children this experience was best captured in the innocent aura of the musical carousel's fantasized horse ride, but for adults it was in the stomach-churning descent of the roller coaster ride. While the carousel helped establish a nostalgic bond with its riders' childhood, the roller coaster, by terrifying as it pleased, charged the immediate moment with a sense of exhilaration its passengers could experience nowhere else.

By the new century's second decade, the Midway Plaisance prototype was being recast in a multitude of other urban parks boasting a wide variety of thrill rides, sideshow attractions, and penny arcades. They also publicized events as varied as fireworks displays, band concerts, and daredevil stunts. In creating an escapist approach to leisure time as justified self-indulgence, the amusement park embodied a democratic ethos through the opportunity it presented the visitor to be one's self in a magically-charged realm where time itself seemed to stand still.

During this era, too, the great Chicago fair of 1893 bequeathed its vision of technological progress and America's imperialist destiny to a number of thematically organized expositions that extolled the nation's cultural and technological achievements. In 1901 the Pan-American Exposition in Buffalo was laid out around its 375-foot Electric Tower that dominated both the fair's day and night scenes. As though to ensure international unity and peace, the Buffalo exposition advanced the notion that the United States was divinely appointed to carry out this noble mission. That there was dissatisfaction with the existing system appeared in the person of a deranged anarchist who fatally shot President William McKinley during an official visit to the fair. The stage was now set for the most imperialistic president up to that time to take office—Theodore Roosevelt.

In 1904 the most grandiose fair the world had seen up to that time was staged in St. Louis—the Louisiana Purchase Exposition commemorating the centennial celebration of Thomas Jefferson's bold venture. It made the most of an expansive domain to showcase the latest technological and cultural achievements that presaged a utopian future. The gasoline-fueled automobile had been exhibited first at the Buffalo fair, but the St. Louis Exposition did it one better by displaying what was then referred to as an airship or aeroplane. Though some visionaries saw air travel as resulting in a world in which both the geographical and sociocultural distances between nations would be diminished, cultural differences were still being recognized, as the fairs' ethnic villages demonstrated. These anthropological exhibits, which unwittingly perpetuated the racist posture of the larger society, were considered "integral components [that] reflected the growing efforts by the upper classes, threatened by class conflict at every turn, to influence the content of popular culture" and, by extension, their own sociocultural perspective.[34]

With the American frontier now closed, other fairs of this era promoted the imperative to look further westward, as exemplified by the theme of the 1905 American Pacific Exposition and Oriental Fair at Portland, Oregon. In 1907 Teddy Roosevelt concurred with this outlook when he drew on the backdrop of the Tercentenary Exposition commemorating the first English settlement at Jamestown, Virginia, as the pretext for sending sixteen battleships from nearby Hampton Roads on an around-the-world cruise. It was both a good-will tour and a show of the nation's growth as a naval power. In bolstering Roosevelt's foreign policy as well as the patriotic fervor of the mediated vision, his Great White Fleet returned fourteen months later, having shown the world America's deserved ranking as an international naval power.

FUTURE IMPLICATIONS OF SPECTATOR SPORTS AND PERSONAL LEISURE

While the professional sports of baseball and boxing helped nationalize interest in athletic competition during this time, amateur sport took on an international flavor. The second and third modern Olympics, again dominated by American athletes, were held in Paris (1900) and in St. Louis (1904), both organized in cooperation with the world's fairs conducted in these respective cities. London, the host for the 1908 competition, saw women, whose day in the athletic sun lay some years ahead, competing on a limited basis in such events as archery and lawn tennis. The biggest and best Olympic Games to date were held in Stockholm in 1912, attracting four thousand athletes from twenty-eight countries. Here, Jim Thorpe's achievements in track and field saw him acclaimed as the greatest all-round American athlete ever. His efforts also transformed him into a media-made image of legendary proportions.

Tennis, like golf, maintained its social status as an upper-class sport, accessible to those who held membership in the country/athletic clubs of the time. But the game took on broader significance in 1900 with the inauguration of the international Davis Cup championship. This event, which helped promote tennis as a spectator sport, would see it become more democratized over the years. Golf would also open up opportunities for middle-class participation due to the availability of more leisure time. But with communal space at a premium for such individualized activities in the large urban areas, organized team sports came to the fore as a surrogate escapist experience for spectators who began to involve themselves in "playing" a game by identifying with its players.

The game that did the most to attract a spectatorship and a national following during these years was professional baseball. With teams entrenched in the fast-growing cities of the East and Midwest, baseball spawned fans who espoused a manic obsession for the game. As early as the first World Series in 1903, won by the Boston Red Sox over the Pittsburgh Pirates, fan interest was high enough to turn each game into a sellout.

Though baseball was becoming the nation's most statistically referential sport through which the achievements of its players would be measured against all those who had preceded them, it reflected changing social attitudes toward sports as a business and players as paid performers, in effect epitomizing the problems between management and labor at the time. But most fans hardly cared about or even thought of the game as a mirror of a capitalist society. To them, baseball was a welcome escape, a communal refuge from everyday cares and concerns, and as such it was *the* game of the mediated culture.

Ironically, at a time when the dominant system barred blacks from participation in professional team sports, organized athletics served to reinforce the power of social class and contribute to the racial injustices of the American system. While blacks would organize their own baseball leagues that fielded many highly talented players, they had a long way to go to make an impact on institutionalized team sports, both professional and amateur. A more likely way for a black athlete to find fame during this racially divided period was through the renegade sport of boxing. And the most notable as well as notorious boxer to do so was Jack Johnson, the first black champion. His attraction to fast cars, high living, and white women resulted in such a negative image in the eyes of the media and general populace that in 1910 Jim Jeffries, undefeated heavyweight champion, was coaxed out of retirement to fight the controversial Johnson in Reno, Nevada. As something of a media circus, the match was of such symbolic racial import that Jeffries was billed as "The Great White Hope." However, Johnson's victory predictably resulted in intensifying race problems in the country.

As national interest in athletes and their accomplishments soared, urban newspapers, with the big New York papers as models, continued to expand their coverage. Competing for sporting news with such weekly publications as the *National Police Gazette* and *Frank Leslie's Illustrated Magazine,* newspapers and magazines were now supplementing their reports with photographs as well as illustrations that provided readers a more immediate identification with a sporting event. This appealing visual feature, along with the compilation of statistics, made athletic achievement (and failure) among the most discussed topics of American males.

Sports journalism, particularly that of the New York newspapers, also played a key role in creating a public spectacle out of college football by focusing on the game as it was played in the East, where it drew the largest crowds at the time.[35] As football began to spread nationally, its popularity was enhanced in 1902 when Michigan defeated Stanford in a postseason game played in southern California—the prototype of the annual Rose Bowl game that would be initiated in 1916. With the advent of the intersectional game and the great football stadiums, sport as mediated spectacle had truly arrived. To fans and devoted alumni, college football stood for tradition, and tradition meant allegiance to both past success and the area or community the school represented.

Although Big Game heroics were extensively covered each fall by the new profession of sports reporting, another more ominous, darker side to football was generating a large amount of coverage in the form of investigative journalism. In the aftermath of numerous injuries and fatalities incurred by players since before the turn of the century, *McClure's* carried a two-part condemnation of the game in 1905 that spurred President Roosevelt to call for remedial changes in its barbaric style of play, lest the game be abolished. In 1906, after much deliberation by a national committee (forerunner of the National Collegiate Athletic Association), the forward pass and certain significant rule changes designed to open up the game were adopted. The upshot of these decisions was football's transformation into its modern form by 1912, which not only made it a safer game for the player but a more visually exciting game for the spectator than that controlled by the mass-momentum play of earlier years.

The threat of injury and even death haunted another rising sport during this time. The novelty of the gas-powered vehicle's potential for personal mobility had hardly worn off before speculators were capitalizing on the American fascination with speed by staging stuntcar exhibitions. This obsession cut across the entire spectrum of the mediated vision, as a car-racing historian has observed: "The spectacles of speed began with individual barnstormers and stunt artists whose solitary performances were as thrilling to city folks as they were to yokels."[36] Soon, though, it was head-to-head racing that offered the ultimate in thrills for fans of this sport, and in 1903, when Barney Oldfield broke the mile-a-minute barrier on a dirt track, he dramatically demonstrated the potential of mechanized speed to generate spectator appeal. Although the banked wooden-board track, utilized in bicycle and motorcycle racing, provided the standard course for many of the early races, auto racing pioneer Carl Fisher had an eye toward the future when he constructed his brick-based Indianapolis Motor Speedway in 1908. In follow-up to the popularity of a prototypal race in 1909, the "Indy 500" became an annual event in 1911 and with it the establishment of technology as sport. For the devotees of a sport so new it would be some time before it created its own mythology, the design of the mass-produced automobile itself would grow more like that of a racer and inspire a surrogate racing experience of its own.

During these years, popular fiction's glorification of sport's heroic ideal and the mass-mediated images of real-life athletes contributed to the myth that involvement in sports was a moral experience that developed character and leadership. The idealized example of baseball pitcher Christy Mathewson on

field and off made him, in the eyes of admiring youth, the real-life personification of Frank Merriwell. If other baseball players, such as Ty Cobb, were
not as antiseptically heroic, they did come across as popular celebrity types,
thanks to the newspaper and magazine stories about them. Regardless of an
athlete's social reputation, though, the mediated vision's outlook on athletic
achievement as symbolic of the American way of success would assure the
champion athlete an honored place in its pantheon of heroic achievers.

While participation in organized athletics was being touted as an important
way to socialize youth into the values of the American capitalist system, the
growing emphasis on both participatory and spectator sports was coming under attack, particularly by outdoor enthusiasts. For example, Ernest Thompson Seton, founder of the Woodcraft Society, saw organized sports as blinding
the masses to what he called the "natural realities," lamenting that the closest most city people got to nature was the trolley ride to a baseball park. As
though to counter any negative views on the passive role of sports spectatorship, a 1913 magazine article interpreted the widespread fan interest in sport
in a positive light, seeing it as a "symbolic expression of people's values."[37]
For its time this was a unique assessment that would be expanded upon in the
thinking of later cultural historians and sociologists. As the mythology of
American sport was woven into the fabric of a society in which the heroic ideal
was held in high regard, the mediated vision would look increasingly to the
past where this virtue was enshrined in sport tradition, particularly as organized sports became more professionalized and commercialized.

MODERNIST WAYS OF SEEING IN THE ARTS

Although well-known illustrators were enhancing their reputations by drawing for the magazines and books that catered to escapist fiction's blend of fantasy and realism, a group of artists appeared in this era who were not as commercially motivated, even though they supported themselves in part through
newspaper/magazine illustration. Their work, in fact, revealed a whole new
approach to art in its realistic depiction of urban life. These were the daring
young artists who had migrated from Philadelphia to New York in the late
1890s—William Glackens, George Luks, Everett Shinn, and John Sloan. By
1904 Sloan was painting the teeming day-and-night street life of the New
York City scene, subject matter that most critics of the time considered un-
suitable for art. In depicting people in ordinary or even squalid surround-
ings, Sloan's art, as the naturalistic fiction of his contemporaries was doing,
intimated that environment was a strong social force in people's lives. Similarly, his work echoed the seemingly lost goal of the American Dream in its
underlying intent to "express a wish for some larger individual fulfillment,
for a more splendid existence than the crushing real world offers."[38]

Although Sloan's group, along with art teacher Robert Henri and three other artists, banded in 1908 as the Eight Independent Painters, the negative critical reaction to their first exhibit labeled them "apostles of ugliness" and their work as products of the "Ashcan School." Nevertheless, the adamant posture of the Eight infused American art with a new spirit by demonstrating that commonplace subject matter was worthy of the artist's special feeling for it. Thus, by charging their work with the vitality of urban life—really those things inspired by the evolving perspective of the mediated vision—the Eight became heralds of the American modernist movement by countering the arts' formalist allegiance to the idea of beauty. While they were a long way from emulating the abstract manner that many artists would adapt to, their output manifested a modernist temperament through the shock effect of its unlikely subject matter—immigrant lifestyles, popular entertainment venues, consumerism's impact, changing gender roles—in short, all the modernizing trends that were transforming the urban scene in the century's early years.

But abstract art, in portraying nonrepresentational visions, would not find too warm a reception in the mediated culture at this time. One who played a significant role in promoting modernist concepts was Alfred Stieglitz, who championed their cause not only in painting and sculpture but in the relatively new art form of photography. In 1906, to promulgate his ideas, he and fellow photographer Edward Steichen opened the Little Gallery of the Photo-Secession in New York where they exhibited the latest examples of the modern spirit in the arts, including photography.[39] Stieglitz's theory of photographic art posited the camera as an "instrument of revelation" through which artistic truths hidden from the eye could be revealed. As though to reinforce his posture against the common notion of the camera as a direct recorder of human experience and the milieu in which it takes place, Stieglitz had founded *Camera Work*, the first publication to propagate modernist criticism of the visual arts. It was, in a sense, Stieglitz's counterattack on those who faulted modern art's failure to communicate directly to the public. According to him, one had no basis to inquire about "what cannot be communicated in words. If the artist could describe in words what he does, then he would never have created it."[40] Stieglitz's radical rejection of the explicit illustrative style of the popular print media was only a prelude to what was to come.

The setting of the revolutionary Post-Impressionist Show in New York City's National Guard Armory in 1913 turned out to be pointedly symbolic of the cultural war that ensued between the defenders of abstract art and those who saw it as a hoax. For the first time in America, modern art dared to confront a public whose artistic sensibility had been cultivated by the commercial output of artists like Charles Dana Gibson and J. C. Leyendecker. Exhibiting both the works of European and American artists, the Armory

Show generated enough notoriety to attract a large number of visitors, many of whom were more seekers after sensation than admirers of art. To many the reaction to Marcel Duchamps's "Nude Descending a Staircase" was most representative of the general attitude toward the show, summed up in a critic's description of the painting as an "explosion in a shingle factory." Only a few seriously considered Duchamps's shocking technique as a new way of seeing in the visual arts. Ironically, American artists who exhibited in the Armory Show—Stuart Davis, John Marin, Charles Sheeler, and Joseph Stella—would go on to critical acclaim and find their works displayed in the modern art museums established to commemorate theirs and other artists' efforts. By then the mediated vision would start to see the shock of the new wearing thin.

In the same year as the Armory Show, Igor Stravinsky's ballet *The Rite of Spring* created a furor of its own at its first presentation in Paris. This latest of his works, marked by the dissonance and irregular rhythms of the modernist sound, saw its audience repelled by a seemingly outright affront to the consonant sound of conventional music. But Stravinsky and other composers of the modernist bent were contributing to a new musical sensibility that demanded an adjustment of the ear to appreciate a visually inspired music intended to create and project moods. Also contributing to this new sense of musical ambiance were elements of African American jazz that were being incorporated into both traditional modes and new formats. Claude Debussy revealed its influence in his *Golliwog's Cakewalk* as did Stravinsky in *Ragtime* and *Piano-Rag-Music* and Kurt Weill in *The Three-Penny Opera*. The arts, once strictly reserved for elitist connoisseurship, were now showing signs of interrelating with the output of mass culture, revealing that both elite and popular creative expression had something of relevance to offer each other—and ultimately the mediated culture.

AN END TO INNOCENCE: FOREBODINGS FOR THE MEDIATED CULTURE

The years 1900–1913 represent a time when intellectual, political, economic, and technological forces were making the world over into a place that would never again be the same. The great monarchial powers of the nineteenth century were fading in authority, momentously symbolized by Queen Victoria's death in 1901, and with it the passing of a way of life. Other significant uncertainties evolved from revolutionary intellectual developments: the Darwinian theory of evolution that had undermined theological thought and religious certitude in the late nineteenth century, Albert Einstein's reinterpretation of the physical world and its relationship to the cosmos at the new century's beginning, and Sigmund Freud's pronouncements about the inner world of the subconscious self and sexuality as important keys to unlocking the mysteries of human behavior. Daring to explicate and expand on his theories, a new field of study branched off from philosophy and called itself psychology. And to help relieve the anxieties created by the fast-paced lifestyle of an urban society, a new kind of doctor appeared—the psychiatrist, who would play a dominant remedial role in assisting those undone by the nerve-wracking stress and demands of modern living.[41] The mediated vision had begun to see that along with the benefits of a higher standard of living there was another kind of price to pay in the process of getting and spending.

In revolt from such a milieu was the aura of intellectual ferment and social dissent cultivated by a sector in the lower Manhattan area of New York known as Greenwich Village. The Bohemian rebels arriving there around 1910 were generally of college age and from another part of the country where the traditional values of Carrie Meeber's small-town background had been perpetuated. For those who desired to escape such a culturally dormant way of life and subscribe to radical, unconventional ideas about the arts and social reform, the Village was a mecca-like refuge where one's personal beliefs and attitudes could be expressed not only in conversation but in dress and behavior. Indeed, the Villager of this time was the prototype of the insurgent, self-referential iconoclasts who would create a strong social image for themselves in the years ahead.[42]

In 1912, arts connoisseur Mabel Dodge, recently returned from a ten-year sojourn in Europe, opened up her home in the Village's Washington Square as a gathering place for those who thrived on open forums devoted to modernist themes in literature and the arts as well as controversial social issues. After her years in Italy, Dodge had become strongly attracted to the avant-garde artists, writers, would-be social reformers, journalists, and even the pretenders that this kind of coterie always seemed to attract. A number of these new Villagers were young women from the hinterlands who, in contrast to Carrie Meeber, were becoming more outward going in their social behavior and eagerness to experiment with a liberated lifestyle. Not a few were products of the proliferating women's colleges of the time, and as outspoken advocates of women's rights, they openly drank, smoked, and flaunted their newfound sexual freedom after the manner of their role models—anarchist Emma Goldman, ballet dancer Isadora Duncan, and birth control proponent Margaret Sanger.

Thus, at Mabel Dodge's salon one encountered a varied cross-section of counterculture types heatedly discussing such subversive topics as Freudian sexual theories, birth control, free love, and Marxist socialism. Although opinions were varied, most were generally unified in their stand on issues of social reform or modernist attitudes toward the arts. Deriding the *Saturday Evening Post*'s portrayal of the capitalist as culture hero, the Village intelligentsia were incited by the forceful stand of the ebullient John Reed, who defended his socialist leanings by writing for *The Masses* and asserting that capitalism had duped the American people into a form of slavery. Thus, in this controversial but highly creative atmosphere, the Village Bohemian established the modernist image and free-spirited lifestyle of the kind of rebellious individual who would become engaged in counterculture movements throughout the new century.

To another notable idealist in this mold, New York City's growing pluralistic society during the years 1900–1913 presaged a socialist future. In 1911 Randolph Bourne wrote of the "mysterious power of the city which sucks out the life of the countryside, which welds individuals into a co-operative life . . . does it not suggest the stirrings of a new civilization, socialized and purified? In this garish, vulgar, primitive flow of Broadway are not new gods being born?"[43]

But during the coming expansive era of the twentieth century, this "new civilization" would counter the Bolshevik challenge to assume the unlikely but destined role of a world leader and, in so doing, realize that the "new gods being born" were of the American ethos—particularly those inspired by the increasingly egalitarian perspective of a visually oriented media-made culture that would take on international import in the years 1914–29.

3

1914–1929—Fantasizing the Promise
of a Consumer Society

Radio entered peoples' daily lives in an immediate and
intimate manner. In its content and financial organization,
commercial radio was part of a larger notion, the promotion
of a consumer society.
—*Passing Parade: A History of Popular Culture*
in the Twentieth Century

THIS ERA WAS NOT ONLY A TIME OF MOMENTOUS CHANGE FOR THE UNITED States but for the world as well, as events developed that would shape the course of the twentieth century. While at first the complex political situation that precipitated a war in Europe seemed too distant and unrelated to American concerns, a series of unexpected events brought the war closer to American shores, beginning in 1915 with the sinking of the luxury liner *Lusitania* by a German submarine. The loss of over one thousand lives, of which 128 were American, played a big part in the country's retreat from an isolationist stance to heed President Woodrow Wilson's idealistic justification for entering the war in 1917—"to make the world safe for democracy." Even as a late participant, the United States, through its contribution of manpower and matériel, helped bring World War I to an end in 1918 and achieve the status of a recognized world power.

Once the country got behind the war effort, the patriotic fervor of the American people knew no bounds, especially when propaganda messages warned that their way of life was at stake. Colorful posters beseeching the country to mobilize and support the Liberty Bond drives seemingly popped up wherever there was accessible space to mount them. When the armed forces started mobilizing in earnest, one poster's graphic image and message, James Montgomery Flagg's portrait of a deadly serious Uncle Sam pointing his finger and declaring, "I Want You," was so visually effective it claimed many enlistees on the spot. Due to the shortage of manpower, then, many women volunteered for assembly line work, a role that would enhance their growing sense of social independence. Moreover, the demands of magazine, newspaper, and billboard advertising insisted on the worth of personal sacrifice to aid in the war effort.

It was no time to be a slacker, and the mediated force that promoted dedication to the war effort more emotionally than any other was the hundreds of inspirational songs turned out by Tin Pan Alley. As the national mood grew more militant, the songs of patriotic fervor mirrored the trend. On U.S. entry into the war in 1917 the song that caught the spirit of dedicated involvement more fervently than any other was George M. Cohan's stirring "Over There." Its huge popularity was evidenced by the sale of over two million copies of sheet music and over one million recordings.

ROMANCING THE ROAD: THE MEDIATED VISION AND THE LURE OF TRAVEL

The year 1914, the same year the war broke out in Europe, was a triumphant one for labor, as Henry Ford instituted the audacious policy of paying his automotive workers five dollars for an eight-hour day. By raising wages and cutting the price of his Tin Lizzies, Ford looked to give the public more buying power. In spite of its critics, his plan ultimately paid off by the 1920s when, with the price tag of a Model T in reach of most everyone, Ford achieved the capitalist dream of making more profits through more efficient production methods. Statistics also substantiated that the peoples' dream of owning an automobile was rapidly being realized. While in 1915 there were less than two and a half million registered cars in the country, by 1929 over twenty-six million owners were registered. As a symbol of personal freedom and status to the mediated vision, the automobile would soon obviate the idealistic intent Ford had envisioned for it—as a way for a man "to enjoy with his family the blessing of hours of pleasure in God's great open spaces."[1]

But due to the lack of navigable roads in the early years of the century, the experience of driving a motor vehicle in the "great open spaces" could be a challenging, unnerving adventure, sufficient to discourage most car owners from venturing too far from their home base.[2] Although the proposal for a cross-country highway looked ahead to the kind of safe roads needed to accommodate motorists, it wasn't until the passage of the Federal Highway Act of 1921 that the construction of a national network of good roads was assured. By the mid 1920s, motor travel became a much less forbidding venture.

As a consequence of the growing ease with which the automobile made it possible to satisfy the escapist desire to be most any place else and pursue new leisure outlets, traffic grew thicker and more hazardous. And in spite of concerted efforts to promote safety and regulate driving speed, the accident/death toll increased alarmingly, due largely to those who equated speed with the personal freedom afforded in driving a car.

Technological advances, of course, played an instrumental role in promoting a car's appeal to the public. When sales faltered in 1926, General Motors's Alfred Sloan came up with the visual enticement of merging technology and fashion through an annual change in styling with color promoted as a prime sales feature. By the late twenties, the major competing companies—Ford, General Motors, and Chrysler—were advertising a variety of features as, for example, the self-starter, the detachable tire, and the closed car. In the eyes of the mediated vision this latter modification transformed the automobile into a veritable house on wheels designed to accomplish a variety of recreational ends. Not surprisingly, for many daring young couples this recreational side of the closed car invited sexual experimentation.

Because early automobile travel was limited to local areas, most people still traveled by railroad in a network that covered 245,000 miles in its peak year of 1916. Even in the smallest towns the escapist horizons of the mediated vision were broadened with the arrival of railway service. In fact, by the 1920s Carrie Meeber's symbolic ride to the big city was being replicated by thousands of young women in search of jobs and romance. Although the nation still seemed geographically immense to both the train and automobile traveler, the time zone differences of transcontinental railway travel, access to long-distance telephone service in 1915, and the opening of the cross-country Lincoln Highway in the 20s contributed to a new concept of time's relationship to place and a pervasive understanding that indeed the country was becoming smaller.

SELLING THE AMERICAN DREAM
AS A CONSUMER PRODUCT

During this era, no advertising appeared more appealing to the mediated vision than that for automobiles. Consequently, their promotion in popular magazines, along with that for the accessories needed to maintain them, predominated. Ranging from the everyman models of Ford and his GM competitor Chevrolet to the rich man's Pierce-Arrow, the automobile was so highly coveted that it practically sold itself. A major reason for its marketing success was that automobile advertising functioned as a visual reminder to the mediated vision of what the achievement of the American Dream must be like. It was a concept epitomized in the magazine ads' well-dressed, socially active people of high estate either riding in or stepping into their Essex or Winton. Even though Ford promoted his cars to suit the pocketbook of the middle class, the overly idealized advertising of the elite manufacturing companies went a long way toward informing the mediated vision that the good life was in reach of everyone through owning an automobile.

New directions taken by business and industry during this time also demanded new ways to promote their products in a growing consumer culture. The increased efficiency of the railway system, in allowing for faster handling and large distribution of freight, helped stimulate the expansion of the chain store throughout the land and nationalize its approach to marketing. By 1924, well over eleven thousand A&P grocery stores (originally known as the Great Atlantic & Pacific Tea Company) were selling their products at a cut rate. In marked contrast to shopping at the traditional corner grocery store where a customer had the clerk fill a ready-made list of items, patrons of these prototypal supermarkets could choose packaged and canned goods from eye-level shelves situated in a series of aisles or on display stands. In such a showplace of merchandise as spectacle, somewhat after the department store system, shoppers were cajoled into testing their visual familiarity with a large array of competing trademark logos on colorful packages and cans designed to sensitize the mediated vision to the brand name as a sign of quality.

A major breakthrough that enhanced the sales of these stores' cold-storage items was the coming of that most integral of all household appliances—the electric refrigerator. For those who could afford one, it supplanted the "ice box" and the troublesome task of emptying the melted water produced by a home-delivered block of ice. The necessity of not only the refrigerator but other appliances in the day-to-day functioning of the household was being widely promoted in the 1920s through such up-and-coming brand names as General Electric and Westinghouse, whose product ads visualized a higher quality of life for a burgeoning middle class.

While radio during the 1920s was developing its advertising techniques, the popular magazines continued to be the major medium through which readers were visually informed of the vast array of consumer products flooding the market at this time. Thus, a major mission of the business-minded publishers of the *Saturday Evening Post* and the *Ladies' Home Journal* was to condition the mediated culture to the meaning and promise of consumer advertising in American life—that a higher standard of living could be attained through the acquisition of the desirable things their ads promoted. In the process, these publications enjoyed high profitability, for as circulation increased so did advertising revenue. By 1922, the *Post,* for example, was selling over two million copies an issue, reflecting a 78 percent increase in advertising revenue over the twenty years since 1902. Though the old familiar products were still mounting their campaigns, their ads adjusted their messages to changing lifestyles to attract new customers.

Because women comprised a large readership of magazines, the bulk of advertising was naturally aimed at their personal interests, particularly fashion, cosmetics, and homemaking. By the 1920s, the flapper look of bobbed hair, short dresses, and makeup accessories of lipstick and rouge was setting the fashion tone for a variety of colorful display ads appearing in both the women's and general interest magazines. Also, as women started to express themselves in accordance with the freer lifestyle that the more lax mores of the times permitted, magazines ran socially conscious ads suggesting ways to resolve the kinds of problems that might adversely affect interpersonal relationships, such as bad breath, irregularity, and personal hygiene and appearance. According to these ads' illustrated minidramas of supposedly real-life situations, the answer to such problems came in the pitches of a variety of soaps, toothpastes, deodorants, and mouthwash. Men as well as women, especially those looking to succeed on the job, were depicted as well on their way to the top after discovering the effectiveness of any one of these products. Throughout the 1920s the mediated public's desire for career success and its attendant good life, as well as lasting romantic relationships, inspired much of advertising's social focus on life's little personal failures and how they could be overcome through consumer awareness.[3]

By this time, too, most magazine advertising reflected the social level of the readership it was aimed at. While mainstream magazines addressed the interests and concerns of the middle class, a popular pulp magazine like *Argosy* carried ads that appealed to readers of lower estate but who were no less desirous of improving their lot in life. Lacking the display emphasis of the slicks, most pulp ads were brief and to the point, offering jobs in sales, plans for quick riches, bodybuilding programs, cures for physical ailments, advice books on sexual problems, and a variety of novelty items. Clearly, American magazine advertising, in addressing the fantasy and escapist desires of its targeted audience, was visually motivated to capitalize on the dreams of many hopefuls seeking to improve their lot in life.[4]

Because cigarettes had become so popular with the military in the war, by the 20s names like Camel, Chesterfield, and Lucky Strike established themselves as favorite brands among smokers. By this time, too, Chesterfield was suggesting in its advertising that it was socially acceptable for women to smoke. Recognizing the persuasive power of personal endorsements by celebrity types, cigarette companies R. J. Reynolds and American Tobacco relied on the visual power of such advertising to overcome social taboo as well as attacks from the medical profession. A more subtle form of advertising showed up in the mediated culture venues of fiction and the movies, which revealed the smoking habit as associated with personal assertiveness, success, and a glamorous, socially proper lifestyle. Though it was a relatively cheap habit to indulge in at this time, smoking as a questionable escapist outlet from the pressures of modern living would fall prey to increasing taxation and persistent inquiry into its harmful physical effects.

Due mainly to the upsurge in automobile traffic in the 1920s, the framed billboard format had largely supplanted the poster as a common roadside advertising fixture. By synthesizing an appropriate image with color and minimal wording in the stylized graphic design that characterized this era, the billboard ad projected a succinct message, as well it should, to cars negotiating urban traffic or speeding down a busy highway. Other signage of much lesser size and distinction popped up most anywhere along a rural road, in particular that for gasoline/automotive products, tourist attractions, and diners. But the spreading, largely unregulated appearance of urban commercial signage still incited certain concerned groups.[5] On the other hand, the new electronic messages that lit up the urban night had onlookers marveling at the flamboyant art of modern consumerism. Whether promoting a soft drink or identifying a movie theater or restaurant, these colorful, eye-catching inducements to buying seemed to symbolize American consumerism's surging confidence.

In the teen years, world's fair enterprises were still functioning as glorified advertisements for the American way of life and its accomplishments. To celebrate the opening of the Panama Canal in 1914 as well as to promote the wonders of technology that had made its completion possible, fairs were held in San Francisco in 1915 (the Panama-Pacific International Exposition) and San Diego in 1915–16 (the Panama-California Exposition). While both catered to an increased emphasis on popular entertainment and amusements, they were more intent on exhibiting examples of technological triumph that were transforming America into a world leader. In fact, San Francisco's replica of Henry Ford's assembly line turning out his Model T was a clear-cut demonstration of the technological know-how that had brought the U.S. to the forefront among industrialized nations. Another sign of coming world leadership was taking place in film production, as represented by the San Francisco fair's popular movie concessions that offered short documentary-type films on a variety of topics. Rising film director D. W. Griffith, who was a visitor to the fair, would have readily endorsed the notion that the films shown there were helping introduce the mediated vision to the movies "as a powerful medium for shaping cultural values under the aegis of entertainment."[6] However, in this the year of his greatest film triumph, Griffith would make his name in a film genre of more popular acceptance than the documentary—the fictional narrative of epic dimensions.

THE IMPACT OF THE SILENT FILM
ON THE MEDIATED CULTURE

The year 1914 saw the beginning of the golden age of the silent film, which by the end of World War I was the mediated vision's most popular medium of escapist entertainment. During the war, the movies also demonstrated how they could help inspire patriotic fervor by featuring its big stars in at least one film based on the conflict, for example, Mary Pickford in *The Little Amer-*

ican, Lillian Gish in *Hearts of the World* (both 1917), and Charlie Chaplin in *Shoulder Arms* (1918).[7]

It was during this era that film producers realized the real future of the movies lay in the production of narrative films. Jesse L. Lasky had set a precedent for such an enterprise when he established his own company in 1913 to produce widely promoted features like *The Squaw Man.* In 1916 his merger with Adolph Zukor's Famous Players Company and the absorption of a company named Paramount provided the groundwork for a major studio. But with the big studios of the future in a developmental stage, the company that outproduced its competitors during this time was the Triangle Film Corporation, formed in 1915 as an alliance between the studios of D. W. Griffith, Mack Sennett, and Thomas Ince. In this arrangement each producer/director practiced his own special approach to the kind of movies he felt the public wanted to see, in effect conditioning the mediated vision to anticipate the "brand" of film entertainment it could expect from each of these filmmakers.

As a producer/director, Ince was much more organized in his methods than the other two members of the company. Whereas Griffith might be moved to improvise on a script, which Sennett did most of the time in his madcap comedies, Ince's wont was to visualize beforehand how a particular scene should look to the viewer. Subsequently, in his production system, fully edited scripts with special instructions for filming specific scenes were assigned to subdirectors under his strict supervision. To Ince the studio system was a cooperative enterprise—from producer through director to actor. It was a Hollywood production style that would endure until the 1950s when a new corporate approach to making movies would come into being.

To star in his realistic Westerns, Ince signed the stage-trained actor William S. Hart to cultivate the image of a strong-willed, rugged gunfighter. Performing in films whose characterizations and tight dramatic structure anticipated the adult Western, Hart was an exemplar of the "good badman," an image later cowboy stars who relied on violence to right a wrong would adapt to changing tastes.

Hart's career as a movie actor and director was inspired by his desire to re-create the vision of the West he had known as a boy living on the prairie. Disturbed by the modernist ways that were undermining the values of the West's past, Hart saw this area "as the last bastion of all those virtues he had once believed in, and the older he got the more he became convinced that it was really like that. . . . If there was an evil in the West, it was the future— all those forces which threatened the world."[8] As the prototypal movie cowboy whose self-reliance helps him overcome any devious plot afoot, Hart's character was representative of the time's values as the mediated vision saw them. Thus, his screen character functioned as the visual equivalent of Progressivism's stand against those who abused and misused the privilege of power or position. From *Hell's Hinges* (1915), a compelling moral fable about the power of good overcoming evil—the traditional adversarial elements of the Western film—to his epic Western *Tumbleweeds* (1925), Hart refused to sell out to the sensational elements of showmanship, which to most audiences meant unadulterated action for the sake of action. He was content to leave all that vulgar exhibitionism to the flamboyant Tom Mix and others of similar stripe.

By the early 20s a decline in the popularity of Hart's serious approach to the Western genre presented Mix the opportunity to forge a highly fantasized but no less dedicated hero who chased after Western outlaws. With his flashy outfit that set the style for the new movie cowboy, an acrobatic ability to perform his own stunts, and the tricks of his "Wonder Horse" Tony, Mix came up with a winning combination that appealed to young and old. As a result of his entertaining approach to the mediated vision's conception of the mythical West, Mix soon found fame and riches. By 1929, when he dropped out of the movies to become the star attraction of a traveling circus, many other popular cowboy stars were riding the range of a fantasized West that Mix helped create. Most of the silent Westerns like Mix's were designed to be nothing more than pure entertainment—escapist fables derived from a pervasive myth that addressed the dreams of the mediated vision in an endless stream of variations on a theme.

Prior to Hart's *Tumbleweeds*, though, two other pioneering directors had demonstrated how the Western could conform to the epic format. James Cruze's *The Covered Wagon* (1923), based on Emerson Hough's novel, was filmed in an on-site setting that helped audiences visualize how challenging life must have been for the pioneers who headed west in the 1840s. The theme of taming the West was also implicit in John Ford's *The Iron Horse* (1924), which dramatized the story of constructing the first transcontinental railroad in the 1860s. Ford's emphasis on the sweep of the western landscape as a backdrop and his special way of controlling the camera to project it and the film's action scenes foreshadowed his and other directors' later Westerns of epic dimensions.

Even before Triangle began distributing Mack Sennett's films, he had created a brand of comedy that thrived in a milieu of social anarchy, sight gags, and wild chase scenes. His theory of highly exaggerated but well-timed action as the key to comedic effect appeared to work well, too, as moviegoers seemed never to get enough of Sennett's zany, two-reel escapades, many of which were shot outdoors, with actors improvising comic bits on the spot.

Integral to the success of these madcap movie misadventures, of course, was the talented team of clowns whose faces had become delightfully familiar to moviegoers by this time. In addition to those cited earlier were now such stalwarts as Mack Swain, Al St. John, and Bobby Dunn. The upshot of their inspired antics was Sennett's richest period, lasting from 1914 into the 1920s. During this time, audiences saw his slapstick clowns at their most riotous, engaging in frantically paced car chases, cliff-hanging predicaments, or disrupted social gatherings in which an assortment of vengeance-bent revelers throw crockery and custard pies or dash haphazardly about into every kind of obstacle. Such unabandoned action as the hallmark of Sennett's social iconoclasm apparently drew its basic inspiration from the frenzied pace of modern life itself. If the world was such an unpredictable, chaotic place, as Sennett's comedies seemed to imply, then why not laugh at its follies and absurdities.

Of all Sennett's achievements as the silent film's King of Comedy, among his greatest was providing a training ground for those who went on to film stardom, in particular Charlie Chaplin. Not long after Chaplin, fresh off the vaudeville circuit, arrived in California in 1913, he became a key player in turning Hollywood, then an isolated suburb of Los Angeles, into the movie capitol of the world. Readily adjusting to film, Chaplin began to make his mark appearing in a series of slapstick comedies at Keystone. His most noteworthy work for Sennett, though, came in 1914 when he teamed up with Mabel Normand and Marie Dressler in the first feature-length comedy—*Tillie's Punctured Romance*. The ideal cinematic relationship of these three proved to the skeptics that a multireel comedy could hold the ongoing attention of an audience.

In rising to the roles of director and producer of his own films, Chaplin used his growing mastery of comedy as a selling point, starting in 1915 when he resigned his $150 weekly salary at Sennett's studio to sign with the Essanay Company for the lucrative sum of $1,250 a week. There in *The Tramp* (1915) he began to cultivate his persona of the little man against the world. But not until he signed with Mutual a year later did his style start to reveal more pathos than knockabout. By this time, too, he was making the phenomenal salary of ten thousand dollars a week. Then, when he contracted with First National in 1917 to make eight films in eighteen months for one million dollars, the day of the fabulously wealthy movie star had truly arrived.

Ironically, producers had initially sought to suppress the "star" system with its inclination toward higher salaries. But with the growth of the studio system and the competition for screen personalities of magnetic appeal, the movie moguls now conceded that these fantasized faces were what sold the pictures they made, creating a growing base of fans that would assure even higher profits. Indeed, the moviegoers themselves had become the barometers of taste, influencing the moviemakers as to whom they wanted to see on the screen and in what kind of role. In effect, the mediated vision had gone to the movies and made its presence known on a grand scale.

The art of Chaplin's silent films was never so esoteric that it failed to communicate with both juvenile and working-class audiences as well as more

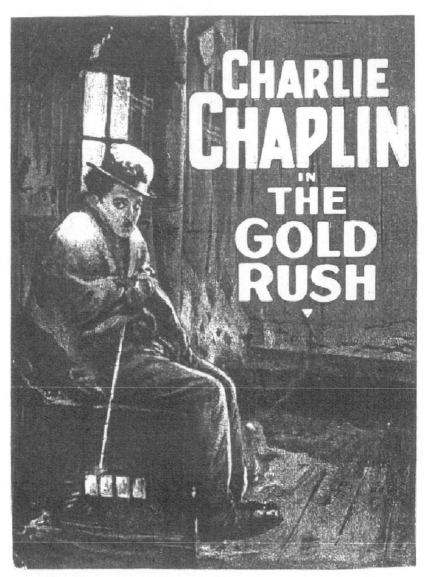

In a highly popular feature film like *The Gold Rush* (United Artists, 1925), Charlie Chaplin was at the top of his form as the master of silent film comedy. Author's collection.

sophisticated moviegoers. They recognized in Chaplin's sensibility a universal bond with everyman's heroic attempt to transcend life's harsh realities, as his character does in such silent film classics as *The Kid* (1921), *The Gold Rush* (1925), and *The Circus* (1928). Derivative of the trials, tribulations, and occasional triumphs of the common man, the film persona of the Little Tramp soon became a visual icon of universal appeal.[9] Within a few years of its first appearance, in fact, practically everyone, and not just moviegoers, could identify the mediated image of the little man of the ill-fitting clothes, derby, cane, and uniquely funny walk. Marketable dolls, toys, and games capitalized on the character's appeal, as did the comic strip and the animated cartoon. As early as 1919, Chaplin's film image had also been so well received by the critics that New York's Rialto Theater presented a "Chaplin Revival," the first of many to appreciate his films in both a popular and cultural sense.[10]

Like Charlie Chaplin, the most successful film comedians rejected the narrative constraints of the two-reeler for the expansiveness of the feature film, developing individualized personalities in it that moviegoers readily identified with. In contrast to Chaplin's reticent Tramp, Harold Lloyd created an ambitious social-climbing character who was endowed with a bumbling yet sincere manner that somehow got him through his challenging ordeals. Since his middle-class values were those of most moviegoers, his Alger-like but near calamitous endeavors to achieve a personal goal made Lloyd's character a comedic favorite of the time. Following his apprenticeship at the Mack Sennett studio, Lloyd began to realize his film persona in 1917 in the bespectacled Lonesome Luke character he played for Hal Roach, the other silent film comedy master who gave the world Laurel and Hardy and the Little Rascals. By the time of Lloyd's feature films, beginning in 1921, his character had become so obsessed with proving himself socially and romantically that even the most dire misfortune or perilous predicament could not impede his efforts to win over a reluctant girlfriend, become the campus football hero, or earn a job promotion.

Lloyd played this popular character in roles that ranged from the well-meaning but naive small-town type, as in *Grandma's Boy* (1922), *Girl Shy* (1924), and *The Freshman* (1925), to that of an upwardly mobile young man in *Safety Last* (1923) and *Speedy* (1928). His films with urban settings, in their depiction of the products of modern technology as significant obstacles to be dealt with, were seemingly inspired by his character's attempt to adjust to the rapid pace of city life. Moviegoers, in escaping from their own problems in the day-to-day demands of urban life in the 1920s, undoubtedly felt a cathartic identity with the predicaments of Lloyd's struggling character. And no matter how problematic his situation, whether dangling from the side of a building high above the city streets or involved in one of his seemingly wild but well choreographed vehicular chases, the stubbornly determined, studious looking young man in the dark-rimmed glasses always came through in the end.

Whereas the problems of Chaplin and Lloyd were but temporary setbacks to a positive outcome, Buster Keaton presented a stoically determined character constantly challenged by the indifferent caprices of fate, whether in the guise of institutional or natural forces. After serving as a stock character under Mack Sennett, Keaton went on to mold his own unique screen persona in a series of brilliant comedy shorts in the early twenties but more definitively in the dozen feature films he made from 1923 to 1928. In such classics, for example, as *The Navigator* and *Sherlock Jr.* (both 1924), *The General* (1926), and *Steamboat Bill Jr.* (1928), audiences were treated to story lines featuring startling sight gags and action/chase sequences in which the deadpan Keaton character remained a stoic party of one against the forces mounted against him. To underscore his comically impassive way of confronting the fatalistic side of the human condition, Keaton drew on his own natural abilities as a dramatic countermeasure, especially in scenes whose visual effects were dependent on his athleticism, at which he was more adept than any other silent film comic.

Ironically, a number of the time's film comics, such as Stan Laurel and Oliver Hardy, Charley Chase, Edgar Kennedy, and Will Rogers, would find greater popularity in the sound era while Chaplin, Lloyd, and Keaton discovered such a transition to be a difficult process. Chaplin, in fact, would hold off implementing sound in his films until the 1940s. Even so, the silent film comics demonstrated that their success mainly depended on how well they appealed to the widest possible audience—that is, an audience whose standards of entertainment were set by the evolving social values of a mediated culture. Laughter as escapism, of course, was the primary intent of silent film comedy, and to moviegoers it was a natural antidote to their own problems, at least momentarily as the problems endured by the comics on screen superseded those of the audience, turning laughter into therapeutic medicine.

During the years 1915–22, the third member of the Triangle Corporation, D.W. Griffith, introduced a cinematic language that turned filmed drama into a viewing experience quite apart from that of the stage. Although a number of pioneer film directors had also experimented with such innovations as close-ups, dissolves, unique camera angles, and cut-away editing to help build suspense, Griffith kept improving on the use of these devices from the days of his Biograph films until he felt prepared to incorporate them into a feature film of the stature of *The Birth of a Nation.*

Realizing that much of the legitimate stage's action was hardly essential to the dramatic moment, Griffith had the camera focus only on action integral to narrative development. He also determined that the close-up, which early critics had derided as unnatural due to its overblown image of a face or scene, could play a key role in suggesting the psychological undercurrents of a story by emphasizing facial expression as opposed to the melodramatic stage gesture. The upshot of Griffith's cinematic use of the camera would be a new visual language, offering key insights into how film should tell a story.

To intercede between the growing appeal of the visually sensational or vulgar and what he thought the screen should reveal to an audience, Griffith drew on the conservative values and religious faith of his native South, which by this time were being undermined by the spread of modernist thought. Thus, Griffith saw the function of a film director as akin to that of a missionary—a role no less important than a minister's in inspiring moviegoers through the moral lessons that could be transcribed to the screen. For example, in the biblically inspired *Judith of Bethulia* (1914), which effectively experimented with the technique of montage in conveying its message, Griffith was on the threshold of demonstrating to the world that the bigger the subject, the more latitude could be taken to create spectacle as an enhancement to message.

When *The Birth of a Nation* opened in New York on the evening of 2 March 1915, the Liberty Theater audience soon found itself emotionally overwhelmed by this twelve-reel production that lasted nearly three hours. Though the dramatic highpoints of the story were complemented by a stirring symphonic score performed by a full orchestra, it was the epic sweep of Griffith's vision that incited the audience's visual reaction to the most innovative use of the camera's eye up to that time. In fact, a *New York Times* reviewer saw the film as "an impressive new illustration of the scope of the motion picture camera."[11]

To depict his story line's inherent drama, Griffith, ably assisted by his perceptive cameraman Billy Bitzer, pulled out all the stops to portray the ravages of the Civil War and the ensuing hardships of the South's Reconstruction period. Battle scenes were seen in panoramic long shots as well as graphic close-ups, while all known filming devices were employed throughout the film, in particular the split and even triple-split screen. Thus, the film's battle scenes of what appeared to be actual combat, as opposed to the stylized semblance of a mock tableau, impressed critics who realized that here was the "first truly modern film, in which all the technical and stylistic advances of the cinema's first decade were . . . combined."[12] To the mediated vision, then, this film momentously revealed how a time and place from the past could be brought to life to create a viewing experience that was both realistic and entertaining.

But not all audiences were sympathetic toward Griffith's attempt to glorify the South's lost cause, as to them his vision evinced a racist posture. *The Birth of a Nation*'s inspirational source was Thomas Dixon's polemical 1904 novel *The Clansman,* which extolled the Ku Klux Klan's violent vigilantism to purge a destitute South of profiteering carpetbaggers, especially blacks. Consequently, some areas considered the film's racist perspective so rabid that they banned its showing. Social and political implications aside, though,

Griffith's monumental film came to be judged mainly for its technical impact, tempering critics' and moviegoers' realization that movies could provide something more than pure escapism.

That *The Birth of a Nation* helped establish narrative film as an art form was evidenced in the same year it appeared by the publication of poet Vachel Lindsay's *The Art of the Moving Picture.* In attempting to justify a critical basis for analyzing film, Lindsay contended that "the photoplay cuts deeper into some stratifications of society than the newspaper or the book have ever done."[13] Because of this capability, then, he further asserted that the function of film criticism is to reveal how the movies abide by their own set of aesthetic rules in liberating literary narrative from the constraints of print. By opening up new ways to explore human experience, the movies, Lindsay predicted, would show "the entire American population its own face in the Mirror of the [movie] Screen."[14]

The Birth of a Nation was such a supreme film triumph for its day that, by comparison, Griffith's later films seem anticlimactic, even the overly ambitious *Intolerance* (1916). While its scenes of lavish spectacle were eye-boggling, the incoherence of the film's multilayered story line was clearly its major weakness. From a technical standpoint, though, *Intolerance* had a great deal to offer. The mass-action scenes within the grandiose scale of the Babylonian set were unprecedented visual achievements that undoubtedly influenced a young Cecil B. DeMille, who was developing his own theory of filming epic spectacle at this time.

In Griffith's attempt to use film as a medium for inspirational uplift, other productions like *Broken Blossoms* (1919), *Way Down East* (1920), and *Orphans of the Storm* (1922) revealed his fondness for placing sentimental subject matter in a harshly realistic atmosphere. But judging from the influence his overall method had on the filmmaking process as well as its indoctrination of the mediated vision into a new way of relating to dramatic action, D. W. Griffith's real legacy to the future of narrative film was in awakening it to its unlimited potential as both an entertainment and an art form.

Like Griffith, whose achievement commanded international attention, many European directors were dedicated to film as a dramatic form of sociocultural as well as artistic implications. Though German film's expressionistic style became internationally influential during this time, the devastating economic impact that World War I had on European film production gave Hollywood a lead it would never relinquish. Fortunately for the American film industry, too, the uncertain business climate of the postwar European scene prompted some of its most talented directors to head for Hollywood, where they brought a fresh, creative eye to making American films.

However, when the Austrian-born Eric von Stroheim began directing American films during this time, he soon became a highly controversial figure, due mainly to an autocratic manner that alienated him and the studio production heads. Taking a wholly different tact from D. W. Griffith's didactic manner, von Stroheim projected his modern vision of an amoral, decadent society through his uncompromising approach to sexual matters in films like *Blind Husbands* (1919) and *Foolish Wives* (1922). Shocking for its time, his posture indoctrinated audiences into an awareness of the movies' special power to dramatize the transgressive side of the human condition.

Perceiving himself as much an independent artist as a painter or a composer, von Stroheim ignored the producers' prime concerns of time and money in fulfilling his obsession for authenticity in the cinematic process. The most extreme example of this quest was *Greed* (1924), his self-avowed masterpiece, which strove to be an exact visual replication, page by page, of Frank Norris's naturalistic novel *McTeague* (1899). The upshot of his ambitious attempt to document the moral decay of the novel's central characters was a production of forty-two reels that had to be drastically cut to accommodate a normal viewing time. Von Stroheim's flair for atmospheric details obviously ignored an integral rule for film as visual narrative—that in expressing the emotions of human relationships the camera can be more effective for what it leaves out than what it puts in. Nevertheless, von Stroheim's quest for realism was among the strongest influential forces of the silent film era, reminding the mediated vision that reality could be as compellingly entertaining as the most escapist fare.

Cecil B. DeMille's visual powers of film direction were evident right from the start in *The Squaw Man* (1913), a story whose Western locale was utilized so effectively that he was a natural to direct the first screen version of *The Virginian* the following year. DeMille's growing interest in the historical epic also resulted in his first major production, *Joan the Woman* (1916), based on the life of Joan of Arc as a patriotic response to the war in Europe. Then, during the postwar era he made a surprising but timely switch to directing a series of sex comedies and melodramas mirroring the looser morals of the time, as suggested by such ambivalent titles as *Male and Female* and *Why Change Your Wife?* (both 1919).

Psychologically, these films reveal DeMille's inner conflict between a desire to moralize (in that in the end the worth of the social order is upheld) and his fascination with the lure of the flesh. Later, in his silent biblical epics, *The Ten Commandments* (1923) and *King of Kings* (1927), he drew on Griffith-like religious convictions ostensibly to transcend any overt attention to sex and violence that might offend viewers. Thus, in these widely promoted film spectacles that were seemingly inspired by the moral conflicts of changing times, DeMille induced his audiences into feeling spiritually uplifted while vicariously indulging themselves in whatever illicit behavior might appear on screen. His method thus afforded a way to avoid the censor's mandates through the public's acceptance of his biblical films as morality plays.

Although by the 1920s, film directors had achieved the status of movie icons themselves, as the marketing power of Cecil B. DeMille's name credited to a film attested, in the eyes of moviegoers it was the stars who sold the pictures. Their images, spotlighted by the mass media, sparked a national following unprecedented in the annals of American mediated culture. One reason for this development is that many performers were associated with a special talent for playing a particular kind of role that endeared them to fans. Douglas Fairbanks, for example, displayed his flair for physical action and derring-do in the Westerns he made as early as the teen years. By the time of his appearances in *The Mark of Zorro* (1920), *The Three Musketeers,* and *Robin Hood* (both 1921), his career as a swashbuckling, athletic hero was fairly well typed. The highpoint came in *The Thief of Bagdad* (1924) with its spectacular effects never before seen on the screen.

But movie heroism could not exist without villainy, which, of course, had been an essential element of the movies from their beginning, evolving into such stereotyped roles as the Western outlaw, the mad scientist of the serial, the gangster, and, of course, the femme fatale. As early as 1915, Theda Bara had begun to establish the image of the sexually emancipated female in *A Fool There Was,* a profitable production of William Fox's new film company. In what came to be referred to as a "vamp" role (after vampire), she portrayed a sexual opportunist who made the men in her life consummate victims. It was a role that would type all her ensuing performances, in particular the title role of *Cleopatra* (1917). Although the major part of Theda Bara's career was over by 1919, her screen image, which had been manufactured by studio publicists, would live on into the flapper era to influence the sex goddess roles of Clara Bow, Gloria Swanson, and Joan Crawford. She also anticipated the calculating sexuality of European expatriate actresses like Pola Negri, Greta Garbo, and Marlene Dietrich, who were beginning to arrive on the Hollywood scene. The rapid but brief success of Theda Bara attested to the growing power of the Hollywood studio system to take an unknown ingénue and transform her into an exotic image of mass-mediated appeal.

That the mediated vision was gradually being subjected to sexual sensationalism can be observed in the film career of Gloria Swanson. After starting out on Mack Sennett's comedy lot, she capitalized on the training she had acquired in Cecil B. DeMille's morally ambivalent films about the problems of American-styled marriages to play the title role prostitute in *Sadie Thompson* (1928). Other stars' roles responded to the "flaming youth" temper of the twenties, centering on uninhibited social behavior like that of Clara Bow in *It* (1927), whose blunt title suggested her sexual magnetism, and Joan Crawford's designing ways to capture a husband in *Our Dancing Daughters* (1928). In this film, Crawford, wearing bobbed hair beneath a helmet-like cloche and knee-length dresses that complemented the then fashionable flat-chested look of a boyish figure, was the visual personification of the flapper.

By enhancing her sexuality with a liberal application of lipstick and rouge, she also symbolized the fact that the New Woman had finally liberated herself from Victorian constraints. Acceptance of certain stars performing in transgressive roles was evident in *Flesh and the Devil* (1926), which featured a torrid romance between two of the day's biggest sex symbols, Greta Garbo and John Gilbert. In this more liberal atmosphere, then, sexually oriented themes appeared more frequently in spite of any attempt to regulate them.

Surprisingly but fittingly, a number of films dealing with controversial issues were directed by women, whose feminist mind-set seemed more appropriate to interpret such subject matter. Dorothy Davenport, better known as Mrs. Wallace Reid, made a film about her handsome movie idol husband's fatal addiction to drugs called *Human Wreckage* (1923). Following up on the pioneering work of producer-director Alice Guy-Blaché, a Frenchwoman who had migrated to the U.S. in 1907, Lois Weber wrote, directed, and produced films dealing with such women's concerns as birth control and abortion as early as the teen years. But they were considered too exploitative for the times.

The movies were also exerting their socializing influence on other areas of interest to women, who by now were among their biggest fans. Even before Joan Crawford's arrival, Theda Bara's dark-ringed eye makeup and dyed black hair had demonstrated the power of the movies to initiate grooming and fashion crazes. Accordingly, a little known makeup artist named Max Factor, whose business got in on the ground floor of the movie industry, would soon be offering the cosmetics used by the stars to women fans who desired to cultivate a winning social image. And when Gloria Swanson, Clara Bow, or Joan Crawford appeared on screen wearing an eye-catching outfit and/or a new hairstyle, the entrepreneurs of fashion were quick to recognize the profits to be made in assisting the American woman to make herself over in the image of her favorite movie star. In this intimate relationship between fan and star, the distaff sector of the mediated vision's tendency toward fantasy and escape found full expression. Of course, the underlying motive for women to emulate the styles promoted by the movies was to appear as sexually attractive to the men in their lives as the female stars appeared to their handsome leading men. This goal served to underscore the realization, too, that the image of the male as sex symbol in the movies was also coming into its own in the 1920s.

Although such male film idols of the era as Francis X. Bushman, Wallace Reid, Ramon Navarro, and John Barrymore caused many a feminine heart to flutter, there had never been a star with the pervasive impact of Rudolph Valentino on women moviegoers. Indeed, in the same year he was introduced in *The Four Horsemen of the Apocalypse* (1921), Valentino's role in *The Sheik* catapulted the young Italian-American into an overnight sensation as another example of a movie-made sex symbol. The smoldering good looks he exhibited in this film helped type him for the roles he played in *Blood and Sand* (1922) and *Monsieur Beaucaire* (1924). By 1926 his still growing popularity demanded a sequel to his earlier role as an Arab desert ruler. While *Son of the Sheik* projected his exotically alien image that promised seductive, illicit pleasures to the many women mesmerized by it, this same identity naturally repelled most men, who opted to use the term "sheik" as a sarcastic epithet. Nevertheless, Valentino's premature death in 1926 was promoted as a national event of mourning among his women worshippers, serving to elevate his short career to legendary status. Once again, a larger-than-life image attested to the visual magic of the movies to transfigure ordinary people into mythical symbols in the eyes of the mediated vision.

THE SOCIOCULTURAL IMPACT OF THE STARS' REAL-LIFE PROBLEMS

The fan magazine, having helped perpetuate the movies' mythology through the success stories it published of established as well as rising stars, saw its popularity spread during these years. Addressing a largely female audience, the fan magazine began to focus on its readers' wishes to learn more about their favorite stars' private lives. Initially, *Photoplay*, as the earliest movie fan journal, led the way, combining both glamorous and candid photographs of the most popular stars with a conservative journalistic style that focused on their studio obligations and off-camera social activities. But as the virginal image of Mary Pickford gave way to the flirtatious, seductive manner of a Clara Bow, *Photoplay* and its competitors soon learned that fans were more interested in delving into the stars' real-life concerns and even their personal problems. In observing the human side of the glamorous images it saw on the screen, moviegoers also discovered that things were not as they seemed, especially when certain shocking events came to light that revealed these idealized celebrity types in an all too human light.

During the first half of the twenties the press exploited such revelations as the tragic cases of young actress Olive Thomas who poisoned herself in a Paris hotel in 1920; the comedian Fatty Arbuckle, who was charged with the rape-murder of a starlet in 1921; and comedienne Mabel Normand, who was involved in the unsolved murder of film executive William Desmond Taylor in 1922. Tabloid journalism had a field day publishing these and other stories that exploited Wallace Reid's drug addiction and early death, producer Thomas Ince's unexplained death aboard William Randolph Hearst's yacht in 1924, and Clara Bow's orgiastic revels. Unexpectedly, the print media had found a large audience at once repelled and fascinated by film celebrities' self-indulgent escapades as well as the tragic circumstances that often surrounded them.

To help promote the movies and their stars, Hollywood studios had established public relations departments to keep the media apprised of what they wanted (and did not want) the public to know about the latest movies and their stars. And even though most stories by the movie journalists were favorable toward the stars, the scandals of the early 1920s rocked the public's moral sensibility to the extent that editorialists began to take a more critical attitude toward Hollywood's hedonistic lifestyle. Like some kind of new royalty, movie stars of the time were living it up in a real-life dream world fueled by their astronomical salaries, evoking the epithet "New Babylon" for Hollywood and its profligate ways.

Undoubtedly, though, such sensational copy sold newspapers and magazines, and a natural offshoot of its popularity was the profession of the Hollywood gossip columnist who, in the media-made personas of Hedda Hopper and Louella Parsons, would maintain a powerful influence among the movie people. In keeping the public informed of the stars' latest romances, affairs, and indiscretions, the gossip columnists made the lifestyles of the stars over into a paradoxical kind of fantasy culture that had both its good and bad sides. But in spite of any negative stories that circulated, Hollywood still persisted as an exotic, glamorous place, especially to naive youth in the hinterland dreaming of the beautiful life that awaited them there. To them, Hollywood represented what Chicago and New York had been to Carrie Meeber's generation—a place where personal dreams could be made real. To the disgust of the moralists, though, the movies themselves were reflecting the reckless lifestyle of the Jazz Age through an overt obsession with sex, drugs, and alcohol. They contended that such films were hardly the kind of exemplary fare America's youth ought to be seeing.

By 1916 the National Board had lost sight of its original censorship mission by overlooking the bad films and approving only those it decided were worthy of exhibition. But in 1922 the recently established Motion Picture Producers and Distributors of America (MPPDA), fearful of the movie industry's faltering image, hired former postmaster general Will H. Hays as president to set standards for the studios to abide by and police the morals of the movie industry. But as far as the studios' posture toward subject matter was concerned, they were still pretty much left to their own devices as long as their films showed virtue rewarded and sin punished in the end. A more restrictive effort at censorship would not arrive until the 1930s.

HOLLYWOOD'S RESPONSE TO THE COMPETITION OF RADIO

By 1925 a new mass medium was making its presence known as a potential threat to the film industry, since those who owned a radio had access to free entertainment. As though to flaunt its visual primacy over an aural medium, Hollywood produced a plethora of films in every kind of genre—from the most spectacular epic to the most melodramatic weekly serial. While many of these productions were mediocre at best, moviegoers were treated to many of Hollywood's greatest films of the silent era. Among the most critically acclaimed were those with World War I settings, such as *The Big Parade* (1925), *What Price Glory?* (1926), and *Wings* (1927). The same year as director King Vidor's *Big Parade* Fred Niblo's Roman epic *Ben-Hur* appeared. Both were notable for their realistic cinematography, in particular the latter's thrilling chariot race. While Raoul Walsh's *What Price Glory?* mixed the humor of military life with the tragedy of combat, William Wellman's aerial dogfights in *Wings* were realistic enough to help it win the newly inaugurated Academy Award as the year's best picture. But in a more philosophical vein was Vidor's *The Crowd* (1928), which poignantly dramatized how the American Dream persisted as a defiant illusion of middle-class life in the late 1920s. As such, this film was not only a far cry from the usual escapist fare being churned out for a mediated culture's edification and entertainment, but also a sign of the American film's maturation.

Nevertheless, escapist fantasy remained a big attraction to moviegoers, especially that offered by the horror genre during this time. Although it posed a number of cosmetic problems to challenge the imagination of the studio makeup man, some actors were innovative enough to rely on their own ingenious methods to frighten moviegoers. Lon Chaney, in fact, became the silent era's master of disguise in the many films he made, earning himself the uncontested title of Man of a Thousand Faces for his performances in such films as *The Hunchback of Notre Dame* (1923) and *The Phantom of the Opera* (1925). Chaney's roles, which set the visual standard for many such characterizations to follow, established the horror genre as one of the mediated vision's favorites by challenging it to endure the terrifying experience as pure escapism.

As far as the atmospheric mood of the horror film was concerned, it owed a great deal to the German-made films of the 1920s, in particular *The Cabinet of Dr. Caligari* (1921). Although its startling expressionistic sets impressed both American directors and critics, the film's puzzling story line alienated audiences who failed to comprehend its symbolic intent of projecting more of a psychological state of mind than a plot. That it strived to express the mediated vision's conception of the ultimate escapist experience, though, was intimated in critic Alfred B. Kuttner's reaction to the film's overall dramatic effect. He noted that those who saw *Dr. Caligari* found themselves "transported into that sphere where man creates his own imaginative realities as an escape from the realities of life which constantly overwhelm without ever completely satisfying him."[15]

Three other German films also made a significant impression on the style of American directors who would make horror/fantasy films in the future. The title character of *The Golem* (1921) was the model for the coming deluge of man-made monster movies, while F. W. Murnau's *Nosferatu* (1922), the earliest feature-length treatment of the vampire legend, was rife with the sexual symbolism that would characterize the vampire character's modus operandi in later films. The prophetic vision of a future machine state in Fritz Lang's *Metropolis* (1927) offered a sobering viewing experience for those optimistically inclined toward the future's promise. But the film's unique special effects that visualized what urban life in the future might be like placed this film more properly in the new science fiction genre. By comparison, British author A. Conan Doyle's modern rendering of a prehistoric setting in his novel *The Lost World* (1912) inspired Willis O'Brien's innovative stop-motion effects for the 1925 American film version's primeval animal scenes, foreshadowing his spectacular technical achievements in the 1933 fantasy classic, *King Kong*.

Fantasy/adventure fiction, of course, was now the movies' most reliable source for creating a make-believe world that appealed to the mediated vision's escapist desires. Accordingly, in 1918, Edgar Rice Burroughs's *Tarzan of the Apes* was brought to the screen with Elmo Lincoln as the first of a long line to play the lord of the jungle. As a highly romanticized figure who was a natural for the movies, Tarzan would become one of the most popular series characters in film history. In contrast to life in an urbanized society, filmmakers realized there was something especially intriguing about a skimpily attired heroic character holding sway over his primeval environs, and in the ensuing years they would make the most of the mediated vision's fascination with this fable of man reacting to his primal element, producing over forty movies about the jungle-bred hero.

The Tarzan character would also find popularity in the serial or chapter play, which had come into its own by 1914 with the appearance of Pearl White in *The Perils of Pauline*. Generating action for action's sake, each episode saw its intrepid heroine entangled in cliff-hanging predicaments perpetrated by the scheming villains she was forever encountering. As a result, captivated viewers were lured back week after week to see how the daring Pauline escaped her "peril." It was a formula popular enough to become a mainstay of the Saturday matinee program.

While even the most fantasized of film genres like the serial were naturally disposed to reality-based action, another way the movies captivated audiences was through their fabricated settings that ranged from the mundane to the exotic and grandiose. Despite the limited technology of the time, silent-era art directors and set designers strived to create a visual kind of magic that could transport audiences anywhere, real or imagined, as the films cited

Edgar Rice Burroughs's fabulous jungle hero first appeared on the movie screen in 1918, attesting to a growing popularity that would soon extend to other media forms. Author's collection.

above reveal. Their control of fantasized reality was also adept at projecting a psychological aura, as noted in the horror film. The upshot of such efforts was that by the sound era the films produced by such major studios as Metro-Goldwyn-Mayer, Paramount, and Warner Brothers would take on a characteristic look that reflected each studio's production values, a major reason for their audience appeal.

The True-Life Realism of the Documentary Film

Although the movies had evolved primarily as a commercial medium to create visual fiction in response to the mediated vision's desire for pure entertainment, some filmmakers used the medium as a way to introduce viewers to foreign cultures most would never get to see firsthand, in particular those cultures' lifestyles that the great fairs had sought to disparage. To the documentarians the nonfiction film could better educate and entertain than the fairs had by depicting its subjects in their natural habitat.[16]

A true pioneer of this kind of film was a poet of the camera named Robert J. Flaherty, whose vision opened up fresh, new vistas for American moviegoers from a humanized point of view. His first film in this category, an intimate look at Eskimo life called *Nanook of the North* (1922), provided audiences the special insights into reality that only the camera's eye could record. As both a critical and commercial success, the film brought Flaherty immediate fame. By avoiding the more exploitative films produced by the Martin Johnsons, a husband-wife expeditionary team, Flaherty showed his subjects as themselves and not as actors. Impressed by the success of *Nanook*, Paramount sent Flaherty to the South Seas to explore Polynesian culture. The result was *Moana* (1926), which was not as successful as his previous film, even though it was inspired by the same philosophy of the camera. But in this undertaking Flaherty had to endure an irreconcilable conflict between his personal standards of filmmaking and the commercial goals of a Hollywood studio, a situation not uncommon to other idealistic filmmakers confronting the demands of a corporate mentality.

Flaherty's unwillingness to compromise his concept of the documentary film's mission with the commercial demands of Hollywood found an outspoken champion in film critic John Grierson, a pioneer of the documentary form in England. Expounding on a theory inspired by Russian director Sergei Eisenstein, Grierson declaimed film as a receptive medium for attending to serious issues and problems that beset humanity. This posture also posited him as a spokesman for the mediated vision and the fiction film's obligation to inspire it when he wrote in 1926 that the "modern public . . . is coming to depend on the cinema for its deepest imaginative experience." Moreover, he noted that the "modern multitude craves a release from the everyday as all other multitudes did before it. . . . It craves participation in a world where dreams come true, where life is more free."[17] In filming fiction, then, naturalness in expressing a universal theme was extolled by Grierson, who contended that the greatest art is that which conceals any attempt to be art, concluding that "visual story telling is so much an art that it might be the greatest of arts."[18] To John Grierson, humanized realism in both the fiction and documentary films was only just beginning to make its mark.

THE STUDIO MOGULS AND THEIR MOVIE PALACES

To entrepreneurs like William Fox, Carl Laemmle, Marcus Loew, Jack Warner, and Adolph Zukor, who built their fortunes producing and distributing movies during these years, moviemaking was more a business than the so-called art form critics were making of it. In only a decade the movies were paying big dividends to their investors, as by 1919 motion picture production was recognized as a major industry with investment quotes appearing on the New York Stock Exchange. Even the establishment of the Academy of Motion Picture Arts and Sciences in 1927 did little to alter the minds of the movie moguls about the business side of their operations. They saw the publicity role the Academy played as mainly a commercial stimulant to attract more customers to movies. Through their dictatorial style and innate sense of what the mediated vision desired as entertainment, the producers now commanded a factory-like studio system staffed by the best directors, writers, and actors that money could buy. Ever sensitive to any shift in the public mood, they had their companies attuned to the latest fads and follies, making sure that the right stars were selected to attract the widest audience followings.

Attesting to the film producers' natural business sense was the development and expansion of their own systems for distributing and exhibiting their movies. In 1924, Marcus Loew's chain of downtown theaters began to function as the major exhibition outlet for the recently established Metro-Goldwyn-Mayer studio that would become the most illustrious movieproducing corporation of them all. Earlier, in 1919, three of the most idolized stars—Charlie Chaplin, Douglas Fairbanks, and Mary Pickford—and director D. W. Griffith, had pooled their independent company ties to form one of their own to circulate their films—United Artists. With the concurrent growth of the Paramount and Warners studios, the stage was set to introduce the downtown movie palace and its mission of providing a special place for the mediated vision to nurture its dreams.

In 1914, moviehouse pioneer S. L. Rothafel had opened the Strand in New York, a modern-designed theater that served as a model for movie theaters across the country. Rothafel, popularly known in the theatrical business as

Entrepreneur S. M. "Roxy" Rothafel's Roxy Theatre, which opened in 1927, was the epitome of the glamorous movie palace, as this *New York Times* ad asserted. Author's collection.

"Roxy," by declaring his intention to give the public not only what it wanted but "something better," would institute "a new style in motion picture theaters: comfortable seats, thick rugs, elegant lounges, velvet draperies, gilt-and-marble ornamentation—all the trappings of wealth that had previously belonged to a select few in the orchestra of a legitimate theater—and all for twenty-five cents."[19] It was Rothafel's namesake, the Roxy, that incorporated all these things on a grand scale on its opening in 1927. Dubbed the "Cathedral of the Motion Picture," it featured seating for 6,200, elegant decor amid an aura of breathtaking architectural design, and a staff of military-trained attendants to guide patrons to their seats.

Between 1915 and 1945 over four thousand ornately styled movie houses would spring up all over the country, along with innumerable small-town houses and neighborhood theaters in the larger cities that modeled themselves after their more grandiose counterparts. By responding to the escapist dreams of the mediated vision, such communal showplaces changed the leisure habits of entire families, as by 1929 most of the American population was going to the movies on an average of twice a week. It was a highly anticipated ritual that involved moviegoers in both a communal and a private experience of escape into a world of illusion. Thus, the great movie palaces served a dual purpose by creating a milieu of elegance and congeniality where one's immediate fantasies could be indulged while escaping to the other fantasy world projected on the screen.

To promote that world, advertising that appeared in newspapers, magazines, posters, lobby cards, and on twenty-four-sheet billboards also worked their magic, reaching voluminous proportions during these years. To aid movie exhibitors, studios sent out press books weeks in advance, since the life of the large number of movies released at this time was brief. Promotional kits contained a variety of stylized display ads and thematic ideas for an enterprising exhibitor to exploit a film's selling points. Pursuant to trade journal directives, many movie palaces set up spectacular displays on their marquees and facades as well as in their lobbies to ballyhoo major productions. In all its varied forms of expression, movie advertising was directed toward one main goal—to attract paying customers by capitalizing on the escapist susceptibilities of the mediated vision.[20]

THE COMING OF THE SOUND FILM
AND ITS VISUAL IMPACT

By the advent of sound in the late 1920s, the essential ingredients of the Hollywood mythology were all in place—the star system, the studio production and distribution systems, the movie palaces, and the publicity modes. Although the silent film was at the peak of its visual sophistication when the transition to sound began during 1927–28, the shock to studios in transforming to a new way of visualizing dramatic experience was only temporary. As early as 1926, when Warner Brothers began experimenting with a system to synchronize recorded music with its scenario of *Don Juan,* the industry sensed momentous change in the wind. Though the voice of John Barrymore's title role was never heard throughout the film, his actions were accompanied by occasional sound effects and a symphonic score.

Of course, music as a complement to the emotional moods of the silent film was an integral part of the moviegoing experience, as a film's plot was cued to the score of an organ or orchestra in the larger theaters and a piano in the smaller venues. It was the reception of Al Jolson's singing in Warners' *The Jazz Singer* (1927), along with a limited amount of dialogue, that paved the way for the total sound picture. Other studios quickly jumped on the sound bandwagon, but Warners broke ground again in 1928 with the first all-talking picture, a gangster melodrama titled *The Lights of New York.*

Though the transition to sound posed numerous technical problems for existing movie theaters, by the end of 1929 many houses had made the switchover, which paid off handsomely as a record-breaking 110 million fans flocked to movies promoting this exciting innovation. One of them was the first all-talking film to be produced outdoors, the Fox Western *In Old Arizona,* for which Warner Baxter won an Oscar as 1929's best actor. By this time, too, all the vaudeville theaters on Broadway, except the die-hard Palace, were showing talkies, though the big movie palaces also included vaudeville acts in their programs.

The filmmakers themselves also faced some unique problems. Now, screenwriters confronted the challenge of adapting to a new script style that projected the drama of heard dialogue rather than that visually suggested. Despite the suspended microphone's integral role in recording dialogue, audiences' equating a silent star's voice with his or her familiar image took some adjustment. Then there was the problem of some foreign actors' heavy accents failing to come across as expected, and even though many silent-era stars would go on to greater fame in the sound era, others were not so fortunate. A few conservatives still contended that the silent film would always have a life of its own.

It took the musical as the newest film genre to convince moviegoers that sound was here to stay, and the last year of the twenties saw a number of lively musicals released despite the limited technology of the day. Although Warner Brothers' first movie musical, based on Sigmund Romberg's *The Desert Song,* was well-received, film versions of Broadway musicals with American settings like *Good News* and *The Cocoanuts* proved more popular. Warners and MGM even came up with original scores for *Gold Diggers of Broadway*

By 1929 "all-talking" movies were the rage, and *In Old Arizona* (Fox), the first big sound Western, anticipated others in the large-scale mold. Author's collection.

and *Broadway Melody* respectively. The latter film, the prototype of all the many backstage musicals to come, won an Academy Award as 1929's best picture.

The nation may have been humming, whistling, and singing the popular tunes it heard on the radio, but the movies were now assuming the role of the more influential song plugger by contracting with teams of lyricists/composers who would produce many of the most popular songs ever written. Of these, Harry Warren, a talented songwriter for Broadway musicals, came to be called the Father of the Hollywood Musical in a career that began in 1929 with the first of over three hundred songs he composed for seventy-nine movies. The mediated vision, in perceiving the glamorous singers of the movie musical as fantasized figures who brought these songs to life, would see its escapist horizons broadened through this new visual/aural dimension that lasted well into the second half of the century.

Although the silent film developed as a wholly commercial enterprise catering to the escapist fantasies of a mediated culture, its being accorded the distinction of an art form played a big role in the still evolving synthesis of elite and mass tastes. As a mirror of changing times but a recorder of unchanging human emotions, the silent film would extend the cinematic vision it had cultivated on into the sound era, where the movies would become an even stronger visual force in the democratization of American culture.

The Animated Cartoon Breaks New Ground

With movie audiences beginning to look for original cartoon characters created exclusively for the screen, the animation methods of the studios became more systematized, allowing for production on a larger scale. The initial problem, as Winsor McCay had realized, was to find a way to relieve artists of the burdensome process of creating the multiple drawings required to make an animated cartoon. In 1914, John Bray in his New York studio came up with the first major breakthrough when he started animating only the area of a scene that was to move, relying on the use of an opaque celluloid or "cel" for static backgrounds. This method resulted in an assembly line production system with each studio artist assigned a specialized task in the creative process. Another studio in New York, then the center of animation, saw Max Fleischer patent his rotoscope invention in 1917. It was a device through which the illusion of motion could be reconstructed by tracing film footage of real-life action scenes. From this system Fleischer's *Out of the Inkwell* series originated in 1919, combining both live and animated characters in a narrative sequence that starred Ko-Ko the Clown, one of the first continuing characters of the animated cartoon.

The most popular animated character during the 1920s was Felix the Cat, who also arrived on the cartoon scene in 1919. By 1924, creator Otto Messmer and production chief Pat Sullivan had set up an assembly line system to turn out a cartoon every two weeks. They had to, for by the mid 1920s the demand for a Felix cartoon was rivaled only by that for a Charlie Chaplin live comedy. But Felix proved a tough competitor, appearing in a comic strip of his own, in magazine ads that promoted consumer items, as toy and doll spinoffs, and even as the inspiration for a Tin Pan Alley song. By incorporating the continuity character's qualities of familiarity and personality, Felix paved the way for the mediated vision's reception and celebration of the Mickey Mouse character.

Walt Disney, working out of his own Hollywood studio, now began to capitalize on all the technical advances that had then been made in animation. Realizing that the continuity character was the key to the animated cartoon's popularity, Disney produced his version of the live/animated character series with *Alice in Cartoonland* in 1923. In 1926, he came up with Oswald the Rabbit, the short-lived forerunner of Mickey Mouse and all the Disney animal characters that would soon appear. By the mid 1920s, the studios of Disney and Fleischer were experimenting with sound as an essential function of the animated cartoon. As early as 1924 Fleischer had created animated sing-along shorts in sound, but not until 1928 did Disney produce the first sound animated cartoon, *Steamboat Willie,* which introduced the character of Mickey Mouse to the world. The following year saw Disney inaugurate his highly popular *Silly Symphony* cartoon series based on musical themes. With sound now a reality, one wondered if color could be far behind.

In 1916 Winsor McCay created an animated film based on the sinking of the liner *Lusitania* by a German submarine. In arousing public sentiment for entering World War I, this film combined McCay's imagination with the power of animation to recreate this tragic event more poignantly than any newsreel could have portrayed it. More surprisingly, it countered those who contended that the animated cartoon was a medium restricted to filming the insipid antics of comic strip characters. In his later feature-length productions, Walt Disney would dramatically demonstrate how fantasy and realism could be blended into a new kind of insightful viewing experience in which traditional values were interpreted in not only an escapist but a meaningful way.

Although the silent cartoon demanded both sound and color to realize itself fully, its early confinement to strictly visual expression compelled animators to strive for strikingly original effects. The upshot of their efforts helped infuse the animated cartoon with a special kind of magic that, along with advancing technology, would continue to weave a spell over audiences throughout the century, transporting viewers to a transcendent but paradoxical world that was at once humanized and supernatural. In the 1930s–40s, this kind of escapism would culminate in a golden age for the animated cartoon.[21]

THE CHALLENGE OF THE MOVIES
TO THEATRICAL TRADITIONS

Although by the 1920s the movies and the growing popularity of radio were making inroads into attendance at both the theater and vaudeville, the latter suffered the greater loss of patrons. As an omen of vaudeville's precarious status, 1923 was the peak year of the Palace Theater's two-a-day shows. Ziegfeld's *Follies,* because of its appeal to a more select audience, had not yet felt the threat these mass entertainment venues posed. But popular *Follies* and vaudeville performers were beginning to look to the movies and radio as lucrative outlets for their talent. Concerning the predictable demise of what he termed the "theater of the people," vaudeville historian Douglas Gilbert theorized that vaudeville started to fail when it "dressed up" to compete with lavish productions like the *Follies.*[22] To him, vaudeville's crowd-pleasing way of delivering "low comedy" was a major reason why it had appealed to the mediated vision for nearly fifty years. During its gradual demise, then, it had remained for burlesque to develop an off-color kind of "low" comedy that appealed mainly to male audiences. And even though it forged a moral divisiveness between the conservative and liberal views of the mediated vision, the ongoing appeal of burlesque was due to its natural license to present programming that vaudeville could not and that family-oriented movies dared not.

From the time of the penny arcade's risqué peep show and the *Police Gazette*'s daring pictorial spreads to the appearance of Ziegfeld's *Follies* and later Broadway revues, a socially marginal acceptance of the near nude display of the female body had come about. In promoting and selling female sexuality as theatrical spectacle, then, burlesque of the 1920s was humorously referred to as the poor man's *Follies,* even though it was patronized by high and low alike. In the late teen years the enterprising Minsky brothers began to define program standards for modern burlesque in New York's National Winter Garden Theater. One of them described their show as the kind of theater "whose basic ingredients were girls, gags, and music. The girls showed as much of themselves as the law and what passed for local option allowed. The gags were broad and topical and were often takeoffs on the Broadway shows uptown."[23] Of course, the satirical intent of the takeoff was indigenous to the word "burlesque" in its etymological sense, but in its modern format male clowns presided over the predictable gags and comedy skits that audiences had come to relish. In this role, they were masters of the double entendre, a punchline whose ambiguity allowed them to get away with about any kind of joke with sexual or scatalogical implications.

But it was the girls the customers came to see, and to create a more intimate relationship between audience and performer the Minskys' theater featured a runway that extended out into the audience. Here, amidst raucous male whistles and entreaties, the girls went into their routines: the bump and grind accompanied by the impromptu music of a small band and, of course, the striptease, which by this time had become a standard feature of the burlesque show. Thus for its patrons burlesque was yet another visual form of fantasized escape. The fact that it was frowned upon by the moralists made it that much more alluring.

Although the 1920s had become a more liberal time regarding sexual matters, the traditional public posture toward censoring that which did not meet its approval was still formidable, as the highly publicized police raid on the Minskys' theater in 1925 demonstrated. Despite the good things that such highbrow literary types as Edmund Wilson, H. L. Mencken, and Brooks Atkinson had to say about the lowbrow entertainment the Minskys served up, law enforcement officials were not as sympathetic about the undulating breasts of one of the brothers' specially endowed performers. The "raid" precipitated a seven-week trial of comic proportions that the tabloids capitalized on, only to result in dismissal of the charge of indecent exposure. But the puritanical fear of theatrical sex as a threat to long-standing bourgeois values would persist throughout the century, splitting the general public into two camps of reactionary and moderate attitudes toward sexual matters.

The most outspoken stage personality who decried society's hypocritical attitude toward sex was making a livelihood out of it as both a playwright and an actress. Mae West probably would have been perfectly suited for the socially transgressive role of a burlesque performer. But in departing vaudeville in the 1920s for the Broadway revue, she found the proper milieu to prepare for her later career. Way ahead of her time in her criticism of society's attitudes toward the traditional gender roles of men and women as well as its condemnation of homosexuality, West found a voice for her personal opinions about these controversial areas in a series of plays she wrote. As expected, the moralists condemned them for their frankness and sensational elements. Her first play, structured around a central character who learns to use her sex appeal to counter the dominant role men play in society's affairs, was blatantly titled *Sex* (1926). Though it was eventually shut down on obscenity charges, Mae West had created the character that would become her stage and movie persona for the rest of her career. Accordingly, in the title role of the stage production *Diamond Lil* (1928), she played a coarse-talking, alluringly dressed madam type who uses her sexuality to control the men in her life. Thus, by satirizing puritanical elements inherent in the American social system, Mae West conditioned the mediated vision to a more accommodative attitude toward sexuality as a normal human function.

By this time, the *Follies* was being openly emulated by the Broadway revues of George White's *Scandals* and Earl Carroll's *Vanities*. Ziegfeld's way of getting back at his competition was to criticize its brand of theatrical nudity as vulgar and lacking in good taste. But the real thing that separated

Ziegfeld from his competitors was his personal zeal for creating the best in set design and fashionable costumery as well as signing up the most talented entertainers around. Accordingly, the years 1914–29 represent a golden age for the productions of Florenz Ziegfeld. Building on the popularity of his annual *Follies* revue, he succeeded in about every project he turned his hand to.

Nevertheless, as something of an omen of the kind of competition he would encounter from the movies, Ziegfeld's wife Billie Burke initiated a longtime movie career in 1915. And over the years he would lose such promising beauties to Hollywood as Marion Davies, Billie Dove, Louise Brooks, and Paulette Goddard, as well as headline entertainers like W. C. Fields and Will Rogers. By 1921 radio was also becoming a factor in attracting talent that Ziegfeld had discovered and nurtured. But Broadway's leading showman still had an important role to play, especially in the development of the musical genre, as discussed later in this section.

Until the late 1920s, Broadway still fancied the European operetta, and even with America at war in 1917, Sigmund Romberg's *Maytime* was a smash hit in spite of the composer's Germanic name. The production's romanticized setting and captivating melodies lent it the right kind of escapist mood at this critical time. As heirs of Victor Herbert, both Romberg and Rudolph Friml created tuneful operettas that dominated the music scene up through the mid 1920s. Friml turned out two big hits in *Rose Marie* (1924) and *The Vagabond King* (1925), but Romberg had rivaled him with *Blossom Time* and *The New Moon* (both 1921), and later, *The Student Prince* (1924) and *The Desert Song* (1926). All these productions were blessed with a plethora of songs that would become perennial favorites in the mediated culture. But musical theater was on the verge of giving way to a revolutionary way of interpreting it.

Respecting the future of the Broadway musical, the figures who played the greatest roles were Jerome Kern and Oscar Hammerstein II, not so much for their considerable talents as composer and lyricist respectively as for their vision of what the stage musical could accomplish in a dramatic sense. In 1926, following the popular reception of Edna Ferber's novel *Show Boat*, Kern and Hammerstein acquired the rights to transform it into a musical. At the time, Florenz Ziegfeld had many irons in the fire, among them the construction of his own theater. In addition to planning his annual *Follies* production, he was also looking to stage other big musicals after the 1923 success of Eddie Cantor in *Kid Boots*. He decided first on *Rio Rita* and then *Show Boat*, for which he contracted Kern and Hammerstein to do the music, lyrics, and book. *Rio Rita*, which opened in 1927, followed by *Show Boat* later in the year, were both staged in the newly opened Ziegfeld Theater. As a model of theatrical splendor, it was a fit setting for both productions, boasting a seating capacity of over sixteen hundred and on its ceiling an imposing mural designed by Joseph Urban.

While *Rio Rita* received high praise from the critics, it was *Show Boat* that won the greater laurels, mainly because no one had ever seen anything like it. Emphasizing character and plot, Hammerstein and Kern had merged book and score into what was essentially a musical play. In marked contrast to the day's conventional format in which song and dance numbers were isolated from any semblance of a plot, *Show Boat's* musical component related naturally to its narrative development, revealing its characters as real people. The upshot of this production's positive reception was that it changed the course of American musical theater, as Hammerstein, who would go on to even greater achievements in the genre, and Kern, who composed some of the most beautiful songs in American music, proved that the musical was adaptable to treating life's darker side. Thus *Show Boat's* attention to subject matter heretofore unfamiliar to the traditional musical—racism, miscegenation, and alcoholism—informed the mediated vision that even the musical could transcend its conventional romanticized aura and portray reality as compelling entertainment.

Not one to rest on his laurels, Ziegfeld presented his final regularly scheduled *Follies* in 1927 (he would produce one more in 1931), then promptly turned to the production of three more musicals in 1928. Although four more *Follies* would be staged periodically after his death in 1932, the Ziegfeld era faded with the 1920s. But the cultural heritage of this master showman is embodied in the visual impact he had on the mediated culture. As Richard and Paulette Ziegfeld comment in *The Ziegfeld Touch:* "Ziegfeld's genius lay in his grasp of what appealed to the American public. He had an uncanny ability to combine the exotic with the familiar, 'high' culture aesthetics with 'low' culture entertainment."[24] In fact, to Florenz Ziegfeld the art of entertainment had no cultural divide.

During these years a new wave of songwriters and lyricists, who produced a veritable cornucopia of favorite show tunes, were helping change the course of American popular music. Among the most talented was George Gershwin, who inspired listeners to appreciate compositions with classical overtones as well as the more modern sounds that were incorporated in his longer works. In 1924, when he performed his *Rhapsody in Blue* in concert with Paul Whiteman's orchestra in New York's Aeolian Hall, a new kind of American music was heard for the first time. By introducing jazz and blues themes into the traditional piano concerto format, Gershwin created an intensely visual style that conjured up the sights and sounds of the modern urban scene. Recognizing that jazz, as a successor to ragtime, is an art of both visual and aural dynamics, Gershwin utilized this characteristic quality in much of his music to entice and compel the listener to become an active participant in its expression. In ranging from the romantic ballads he composed with his lyricist brother Ira to compositions of a more classical bent, then, Gershwin's versatility seemingly knew no bounds. He had called *Rhapsody in Blue* his

"musical kaleidoscope of America—of our vast melting pot, of our undupli-
cated national pep, of our metropolitan madness," and in the spirit of that
work he continued to insert indigenously inspired themes and motifs into his
serious output.[25] The first movement of the *Concerto in F* (1925), for example, employed the exciting rhythm of the era's signature dance—the
Charleston. *An American in Paris,* first performed in 1928 on his return from
Europe, captured the sights and sounds of the French capitol from a tourist's
point of view. By the end of the twenties, George Gershwin had made his mark
both nationally and internationally. Yet much of his best work was still to
come.

Irving Berlin, the most prolific of all the Tin Pan Alley songwriters, was
still churning out the kind of hit tunes he had been producing since the teen
years, working either independently or for the revues. By 1921 he was composing songs for his own show, *Irving Berlin's Music Box Revue,* from which
emanated some of his most beloved melodies: "Say It with Music," "What'll
I Do," and "All Alone," to name a few. In fact, in his entire career as a songwriter Berlin hardly ever suffered a waning of melodic creativity.

As his own composer and lyricist, Berlin seemed to hold the advantage
over songwriters who worked as a team, and as a result the songs kept coming in a torrent throughout the twenties. Al Jolson made "Blue Skies" (1926)
an even bigger hit by singing it in *The Jazz Singer,* foreshadowing the long
relationship Berlin would have with the movies. In 1929, the full score he
had composed for the 1925 production of *The Cocoanuts* was integrated into
the Paramount film version, featuring its original stars—the Marx Brothers.
Even in this early point of his long career, Irving Berlin had established himself as the most representative songwriter of the mediated culture.

A sampling of the hundreds of songs generated by Tin Pan Alley composers during the 1920s, from, for example, "Ain't We Got Fun" (1921) to
"When You're Smiling" (1928), reveals the times as optimistic and high-spir-
ited, very much in keeping with the general mood of the nation. And an appreciative audience reciprocated, playing these songs on the piano (for those
less gifted the fad of the ukulele provided an outlet), dancing to them, listening to them on the radio and the Victrola, and, by 1929, seeing them performed in the sound movie. Indeed, those who came under the sway of popular music at this time were enticed into envisioning themselves as
performers in their own personalized escapist dramas.

The Resurgence of African American Music

Following World War I and the continuing popularity of jazz-styled music,
black performers were still spreading their music in their inimitable way.
Many of them had attracted loyal followings through a national black vaude-

ville circuit that precipitated a revival of the all-black Broadway musical in the early 1920s. *Shuffle Along*, highlighted by the songs of Noble Sissle and ragtime pianist Eubie Blake, was one of the more popular shows of 1921. Similarly, the high point of *Runnin' Wild* (1923) was James P. Johnson's "Charleston," the song that inspired the trademark dance of the Jazz Age. The black musical revival culminated in Lew Leslie's *Blackbird* revues of the late 1920s, of which the most successful was *Blackbirds of 1928*. Ironically, its score that included the hit song, "I Can't Give You Anything but Love," was composed by the white team of Dorothy Fields and Jimmy McHugh.[26] *Hot Chocolates* closed out the decade featuring the piano stylings of Fats Waller, among which was "Ain't Misbehavin'," a song he would always be identified with. Not a few entertainers in these productions would go on to greater fame, among them Josephine Baker as an expatriate performer in the more racially tolerant milieu of Paris, bandleader Cab Calloway, tap dancer Bill "Bojangles" Robinson, and singer Ethel Waters.

These shows' most significant contribution to the popular song was to help free it from the formulaic conventions that Tin Pan Alley composers had adhered to since the 1890s. They also helped make music composed and performed by black artists culturally respectable to white audiences. However, a more significant factor in the acceptance of black music was the "whitening" process engineered by songwriters like Fields and McHugh and the most prominent bandleader of the 1920s, Paul Whiteman, whose jazzed-up arrangements looked ahead to the dance-band music of the Swing era.

New Directions in the Legitimate Theater

By 1915, as the popularity of the movies kept spreading across the country, the provincial theater of the town hall and river showboat began to fade. The traveling tent show that catered to the less sophisticated tastes of rural folk lasted into the twenties, but when the nearest town opened up a movie house, it had to bow to the more appealing lure of the silver screen. To supplant the demise of professional drama in their communities, many towns and cities organized amateur groups, which not only responded to a cultural need, but also served as a training ground for many a future actor of note. Naturally, New York, the cultural center of theater, had great appeal to the would-be dramatic star and playwright who cultivated their talent in a group like the Provincetown Players, which, in fact, had relocated in New York's Greenwich Village around 1917.

Although some theater groups were staging the works of daring, revolutionary European playwrights, whose expressionistic technique, attention to psychological problems, and a frank depiction of human relationships had a pervasive influence, the Provincetown Players strived to produce original works that related to American life and themes. Spearheaded by the prolific output of a daring new playwright named Eugene O'Neill, their efforts would inspire a renaissance in American drama.

In a career that extended from 1916 to the 1940s, O'Neill turned out an abundance of short plays and longer works, most of them thematic revelations of his obsessive search for life's meaning. In 1920 his first Broadway productions appeared—*Beyond the Horizon* and *The Emperor Jones*—whose bold combination of naturalistic and expressionistic techniques would recur throughout the O'Neill canon. With a dramatic vision uniquely his own but highly controversial as well as critically acclaimed, O'Neill attempted to transcend the constraints of the conventional stage in unconventional ways, from the naturalism of *Anna Christie* (1921) and an increasing emphasis on Freudian themes to the epitome of his bold experimentation, *Strange Interlude* (1928). In this overly long production the performers resort to asides to reveal their private thoughts and, by extension, their psychological states of mind. The critical reception of such a technique that made the inner lives of a play's characters visible saw it as only one of O'Neill's brilliant innovations. In recharging American theater with a new dramatic vision, then, O'Neill gained worldwide recognition for his work.[27] While he decried film as a medium of dramatic expression, it was the movies that offered the public the most accessible way to view O'Neill's plays, as after *Anna Christie* was filmed in 1923, it and a number of his other plays would be filmed in the sound era. But as cinema the plays tended to lose much of their dramatic impact.

Though a number of dramatists who contributed to the awakening of the American theater utilized experimental techniques in their works, most preferred to work in realistic modes, in particular those who gained the attention of the filmmakers. Maxwell Anderson, who had collaborated with Laurence Stallings on the antiwar play, *What Price Glory?* (1924), saw it filmed in both the silent and sound eras. Sidney Howard's *They Knew What They Wanted* (1924) and Robert Sherwood's *The Road to Rome* (1927) displayed their creators' flair for compelling drama, leading to their departure from Broadway to become Hollywood scriptwriters in the sound era. Another playwright whose output the movies took to was Elmer Rice, who began the twenties with his satirical allegory of modern life, *The Adding Machine* (1923), and closed the decade with *Street Scene* (1929), his tragic indictment of the social conditions affecting the plight of the urban poor. In anticipating the drama of the Depression years, this play was yet another that sensitized the mediated vision to the realization that the promise of the American Dream was largely a myth. As O'Neill's plays dwelled on the big, unanswerable questions about the human condition, the plays of social criticism would present more questions than answers about contemporary life.

Other kinds of drama of the time offered vicarious escape through the less serious problems they attended to. A socially marginal kind of comedy popular during the years 1915–22 revealed the theater's growing attraction to racy subject matter and sexual innuendos, as posited by the risqué plots and suggestive titles of *Up in Mabel's Room* (1919) and *Getting Gertie's Garter* (1921).[28] The diverse ethnic backgrounds of the lead characters in Ann Nichols's *Abie's Irish Rose* (1927) made it popular enough to become Broadway's longest-running play at 2,327 performances and a testimonial to the kind of humor that had the broadest appeal to the mediated vision at this time.

Influenced in the main by modernist art techniques, the time's poster publicizing a Broadway play helped transform the New York subway station into a kind of art gallery for busy commuters. Though the theater poster was a graphic reminder of Broadway's resurgence as an entertainment force in American culture (with 280 productions the 1927–28 season was its biggest), an upstart electronic medium was beginning to make itself known (and heard) by the mid 1920s—one that assured its audience that it didn't even have to leave home to be entertained.

ADJUSTING TO RADIO AS A VISUAL MEDIUM

By the 1920s the telephone had long been accepted as an essential household implement of interpersonal communication. But another medium of communication was promoting itself as an integral part of the home, primarily for family-shared entertainment purposes. During the first two decades of the century, radio, or what its pioneer Guglielmo Marconi had termed "wireless" communication, underwent extensive experimentation as a means for conveying emergency and informational messages. At the time, a commercial or entertainment purpose seemed out of the question, as most theorists wondered how radio could pay for itself in such a role. Initially a hobby for amateurs, by 1917 thousands of these so-called "hams" were utilizing crystal sets to transmit and receive radio talk. A sign of things to come had occurred the previous year when young David Sarnoff submitted a proposal to his superiors at the American Marconi Company for the production of "radio music boxes" for the reception of broadcast music. The idea seemed so absurd at the time it was promptly rejected. But in 1919, the formation of the Radio Corporation of America (RCA) from the Marconi assets presented the ambitious Sarnoff a ripe opportunity to promote his visionary concept. And by 1922, having risen to the position of general manager of the Corporation at the age of thirty, he began manufacturing his radiola consoles for the mass market.

In 1920, when Pittsburgh's KDKA, the first reputable commercial station, came on the air under the auspices of the Westinghouse Company, the potential for radio as both an informational and entertainment source began to be realized. In fact, on 2 November 1920, KDKA inaugurated an electronic media tradition when it beamed the Harding-Cox Presidential election returns on its first regularly scheduled broadcast. Even though early programming included a wide variety of educational material, market reports, local news, and even church services, it was soon apparent that live music programs would be radio's strong suit. As early as 1921, when Vincent Lopez's band presented the first such broadcast, radio proved itself as a conducive medium for transmitting music, either for listening or dancing purposes. It also conditioned listeners to the realization that here was an entertainment medium that created celebrity personalities on the spot, as Lopez paved the way for such musical headliners as Paul Whiteman, Fred Waring, Guy Lombardo, and Rudy Vallee, the most popular romantic crooner of the 1920s.

After the forces of corporate America discovered that radio and consumer advertising could function hand in hand, the commercial sponsorship of regularly scheduled programs started to appear as early as 1922 when the American Tobacco Company established a broadcast model with its *Lucky Strike Radio Show*. Such sponsored broadcasts ranged from the antics of a two-man comedy team in 1923 called the Happiness Boys, who promoted a candy product, to the *Voice of Firestone* orchestra, starting out on a long run in 1928 under the auspices of the tire company. From a similar perspective, classical music authority Dr. Walter Damrosch headed up a musical appreciation program in 1928 that adapted the elitist interpretation of such music to popular taste. Thus early radio programming cut across a wide spectrum of listener interests, whether commercially sponsored or not.

To expand radio's geographical range, the American Telephone and Telegraph Company and RCA had linked up their independent stations in 1922 to form the nucleus for the first radio network. And in 1926, RCA announced the formation of the National Broadcasting Company (NBC), which, along with the establishment of the Columbia Broadcasting System (CBS) in 1927, helped establish New York as the cultural center of the mass media industry. Although some had thought corporate advertising was too intrusive for acceptance into the home, the radio network system, in allowing for network broadcast to a national audience, soon made its listeners both star conscious, as the movies had done, and consumer-product sensitive through the marriage of advertising and the personalities of mediated culture. Eddie Cantor's radio appearance in 1926 and Al Jolson's in 1928 were indicative of radio's efforts to ensure a solid relationship with its commercial sponsors by showcasing well-known stars of vaudeville, theater, and the recording industry.

To disseminate newsworthy events of national and international import, radio was a natural, of course. President Warren G. Harding had discovered the medium's worth as a political tool, while his less volatile successor Calvin

Coolidge was elected to office at the right time for his inaugural address to be the first ever broadcast. By 1928 radio was covering the national party conventions, a move that would prove highly influential over the years in conditioning the mediated vision to the serious implications as well as entertaining side of party politics. As a celebrated exemplar of a new profession, Ted Husing reported just about anything from politics to sports, as did Graham McNamee, whose nationwide hookup in 1927 described Charles Lindbergh's impressive Washington reception following his heroic flight to Paris.

McNamee was also the premier sportscaster of his day, whose vivid description of headline events in the twenties clearly demonstrated that radio and sports were made for each other. The year 1921 had presaged this relationship when New York's WJZ engineered the first broadcast of the World Series between the New York Yankees and the Brooklyn Dodgers to area listeners. But it was network radio that fostered national interest in sports through its power to transform the listening experience into an event of nationwide immediacy. Cases in point were the coast-to-coast airing of the 1927 Rose Bowl football game between Alabama and Stanford and NBC's broadcast of Jack Dempsey's championship fight with Gene Tunney, emanating from Chicago over sixty-nine stations. Thus, the mediated vision's growing perception of sport as a form of escapist entertainment was greatly enhanced by radio's capability to "visualize" the national import of an event for rapt listeners.

By the late 1920s, then, David Sarnoff's "radio music box" had attained such a centralized place in the American household that manufacturers were advertising the console set as an essential piece of living room furniture. But as another sign of how huge the radio industry had become in less than a decade, lawmakers were alerted to the need for regulated control of the congested airways. When President Coolidge advocated responsible legislation to restrain radio's uncontrolled expansion, the result was the Federal Radio Act of 1927, ironically passed the same year of another breakthrough attesting to the medium's pervasiveness—the automobile radio. The newspapers, which had been observing the growing power of radio with a critically wary eye, naturally welcomed any legislation that would regulate a medium whose capabilities for reporting the news appeared to pose a threat to their very existence.

But as the trend toward interdependence among the mass media soon revealed, the newspapers' fears proved unfounded. The thing that made radio unique was its ability to transform what was heard into a visual kind of sensory experience that stimulated the imagination. Whether attending to the broadcast of a sporting or news event, dance band, or concert, the listener was mentally compelled not only to visualize what he or she heard but often to recall the personal circumstances in which a broadcast was heard.[29]

RADIO'S SYMBIOTIC RELATIONSHIP
WITH OTHER MEDIA FORMS

Although the radio boom of the 1920s contributed to a decrease in the sale of phonographs, pianos, and sheet music, radio's promotion of the day's popular music revealed a growing interdependence between itself, the recording industry, musical theater, and, with the advent of the sound era, the movies. This symbiotic relationship expressed itself primarily through the era's fascination with dance music and the attendant popularity of the dance band, particularly as jazz influenced the kind of music many bands played. As the improvisational heir of ragtime, jazz seemed to reflect the rebellious mood of the postwar era, especially that created by college-age youth. And many considered it a contributor to the decline in morals, making it a highly controversial issue. Nevertheless, the new dance styles inspired by black jazz artists found receptive outlets in public dance halls, hotel ballrooms, and speakeasies, as well as through radio's late-night broadcasts of dance-band music.

In the twenties dancing had become a more self-indulgent activity as the social milieu turned hedonically escapist, generating a flurry of spontaneous, exhibitionist-type stylings—among them the Shimmy, the Black Bottom, and the era's most popular, the Charleston. For the rebellious flapper dancing was the kind of self-expression that offered a natural outlet for her newfound freedom. She hardly suffered for places to try it out, as all over the country public dance halls and hotel ballrooms became centers for such revelry. While music with a syncopated beat may have inspired the most frequent requests for dance numbers, society bands were expected to perform the exotic rhythms of Latin imports like the tango and the rumba. Although the "hot" jazz beat predominated, Tin Pan Alley was still turning out standards like "Charmaine" (1926) and "Stardust" (1929), proving that the traditional ballad was still alive, which to the older, more conservative sector was the only kind of music fit to dance to or listen to.

By producing a cross between this kind of music and that influenced by jazz, Paul Whiteman's orchestra played the most representative dance music of the 1920s. Whiteman, of course, was destined for bigger things than playing the ballroom of a reputable hotel. In 1921 his orchestra debuted at the Palace Theater, followed a year later with an appearance in George White's *Scandals,* and, in 1923, Ziegfeld's *Follies.* In the Aeolian Hall concert, mentioned earlier, Whiteman's main purpose in organizing the program was to introduce the audience to his concept of "symphonic jazz," yet another attempt to bridge the gap between elitist taste and popular culture. As the so-called "King of Jazz," though, Whiteman must have realized the ironic connotation of his surname, for he was not a jazz musician in the true black tradition. He would have been more deserving of the title "King of Show-manship" because of his success in all the areas of his day's entertainment modes: vaudeville, musical theater, radio, recording, and later the movies.

Numerous white musicians helped create a favorable climate for jazz by revealing the influence of black music on their playing style as, for example, cornetist Bix Beiderbecke did. The recording success of Sophie Tucker's black-styled singing and the wide reception of the all-white Original Dix-ieland Jazz Band pointed up the growing marketability among white fans of what was still termed "race" music. Tucker, in fact, took two songs by the black team of Henry Creamer and Turner Layton—"After You've Gone" and "Way Down Yonder in New Orleans"—and turned them into big hit record-ings. In fact, many would consider "After You've Gone," which first appeared in 1918, the first truly modern popular song because of the way its lyrics fo-cused on personalized emotions rather than abiding by the conventional bal-lad technique of relating a mini-story.

Dependent on a rhythmic beat more so than melody, black music in both its jazz and blues forms demanded improvisation by a performer, the qual-ity that made it a uniquely visual kind of musical expression. The early recording careers of Bessie Smith and Louis Armstrong offer prime evidence of the role that improvisation played in attracting large followings of both black and white fans through radio and recordings.[30] After Smith contracted with Columbia in 1923, she established her image as "Empress of the Blues" by recording classic songs that perpetuated the blues conventions of Ma Rainey. Armstrong, through his natural way of improvising on the trum-pet and uninhibited scat singing, pioneered the role of the jazz soloist with a dynamic style that transcended the Dixieland tradition of integrated in-strumental performance.

By the 1920s, then, the spontaneous jazz style of New Orleans had mean-dered from its roots by way of Chicago's Prohibition speakeasies to the night-clubs and recording studios of New York. By then, too, studios like Victor, Co-lumbia, and Okeh were ignoring their musical prejudices in favor of the profit motive, especially after Okeh's windfall with Mamie Smith's "Crazy Blues" in 1920, the first blues recording by a black woman. Black performers knew that to compose or perform a real blues-styled number, one had to have either ex-perienced or identified with the source of its emotional feeling. In this sense the blues provided the appropriate orientation for women vocalists like the legendary Ma Rainey and her rural-roots style and the later big-city mode of Bessie Smith. Both expressed the down-and-out feeling that comes from life's bitter disappointments, either in romance or urban alienation.

So while white songwriters ritualized the blues format from their own dis-tanced perspectives, black composer W. C. Handy was realizing the com-mercial rewards of this kind of music from his naturally indigenous posture, creating the compositions that the mediated culture would relate to as classic blues, in particular "The St. Louis Blues" (1914). This number, which continued to find renewed life in a string of recordings over the years, typified the cultural legacy of black music that became entrenched in the mainstream of American popular music. Whether from the black or white perspective of the mediated vision, the blues provided a way to help transcend life's problems by facing them head on through music's salving power.

Thus, by the late 1920s, New York, with its influx of talented black musicians, had become the jazz center of the nation, not just through radio and recording outlets but socially in such dance venues as Broadway's Roseland Ballroom and a Harlem nightspot called the Cotton Club. Regardless of how it expressed itself, the thing that made black music so appealing to listeners was its capacity to free the self from its mundane moorings. In assessing the recording industry's sociocultural contribution to modern life, André Millard concluded: "The single most important cultural accomplishment of recorded sound in the 20th century was to make the music of black Americans the popular music of the world."[31] Indeed, its mediated sounds would have as great a democratizing influence on modern life as any other cultural force.

By the late twenties another category of popular music was starting to make itself heard, if at first only on a regional basis. Country, or what many disparagingly called hillbilly music, had its roots in the folk music of the Southern mountains, which was revitalized by such groups as Virginia's Carter family. When a yodeling/singing railroad man named Jimmie Rodgers recorded some of his songs, the country style began to develop a bigger following. But its widest exposure came through the numerous radio stations that sprang up during the South during the 1920s. Their programming was patterned after Nashville's WSM, the station that introduced the *Grand Ole Opry* radio show in 1925. Through its ongoing popularization in radio and recordings, country music offered the mediated vision yet another kind of escapist mode, which like the blues, attempted to transcend the problems of life by singing about them.

The fact that popular music was now being categorized by *Billboard,* the magazine of show business, pointed up the diverse range of audiences that existed for it within the scope of the mediated vision. This practice soon began equating performers with signature songs as a way to promote and sell recordings and sheet music as well as establish a cult of fans to market these songs to.

After the phonograph transitioned from the acoustic into the electronic era, Victor introduced its Orthophonic player in 1925, allowing for increased volume and clearer reproduction. Now all the recording companies were attempting to emulate the sound of radio through the electrically recorded disc. Ironically, though, by learning how to coexist, each medium in this highly competitive enterprise actually profited from the other's achievements. Emblematic of this outcome was the marketing of combination radio-phonograph components by the end of the decade as well as the merger of Victor and RCA in 1929.

With the advent of the talking picture, the union of sound and image provided another opportunity for the mediated culture to benefit from interdependent relationships. In 1927, for example, Brunswick records issued Al Jolson's big hits from *The Jazz Singer* to highly profitable sales. Two years later recording companies were marketing the songs of MGM's first musical, *Broadway Melody.* These undertakings clearly demonstrated how the movies would open up new economic vistas for the electronic media and a whole new dimension of escapist entertainment for the mediated vision in the process.

The Newspaper's Evolving Role in the Mediated Culture

Dominant forces in reflecting and maintaining a mediated posture during these years were the newspaper and mass-circulated magazine. As literacy continued to spread, journalism geared itself to concentrate on the interests and concerns of the mediated culture, both to inform and to entertain. The New York newspapers of the 1920s were prime exemplars of this trend. Of seventeen papers publishing by 1923, those with the largest circulations in order were the *World,* the *Times,* and the *American.* In 1919 an upstart tabloid called the *Illustrated Daily News* had begun publishing and, in time, would offer all the established New York dailies some stiff competition. But to compete with the perceived threat of radio, renewed emphasis was placed on tabloid-like accounts of crime and scandal, especially when they involved celebrity types. Recurrent features were added or expanded, both to keep and attract readers. With the New York papers as models, then, newspaper editors across the country realized that readers wanted diversion as much as information. And through the syndication system many of these papers were able to offer big-city features along with front-page news circulated by the wire services of the Associated and United Presses. In 1928 wirephoto services also came into being, adding a new visually immediate dimension to reporting breaking news. Now, for just a few cents a copy, and not much more for a weekly subscription, the newspaper customer had an abundance of news and entertainment features at his or her fingertips.

Thus, in reporting the sociocultural implications as well as the escapist appeal of the popular attractions and zany distractions the times fell heir to, the newspaper was a highly receptive medium. The social behavior of the decade was colored by the "noble experiment" of Prohibition, which became law in January 1920, ironically turning law-abiding citizens into "criminals" through their involvement in ingenious schemes to procure alcohol. Its illegal status made social drinking even more enticing, with the big-city speak-

easy a ready source to indulge one's habit. As a result, the profits from boot-
leg liquor and other illegal activities were sufficient to make a multimillionaire out of a celebrated Chicago mobster named Al Capone.

Because of its focus on the time's social eccentricities and the mediated
vision's propensity for fantasizing life through such reportage, the sensationalism of tabloid journalism was an apt social mirror of the twenties. As though
to affirm this metaphorical concept, William Randolph Hearst added tabloid
journalism to his empire in 1924 when he introduced a paper called the *New
York Mirror*. But during its life this paper would never surpass the circulation of publisher Joseph Patterson's, whose name was now shortened to the
Daily News. Now, too, pictorial content dominated its text in such a way that
viewers were drawn into the drama of the situation or event depicted. The
rapid pace of the times, Patterson contended, demanded the ascendancy of
the visual image over print.

The *Daily News*'s formula for tabloid journalism cast a widespread net,
from coverage of Gertrude Ederle's momentous feat of swimming the English
Channel in 1924 and Babe Ruth's setting baseball's homerun record in 1927
to reporting the most violent crimes and outrageous celebrity scandals. All
such stories were accompanied, of course, by an abundance of explicit photographs. Whether the mediated vision realized it or not, tabloid journalism
was conditioning it to a new kind of visual escapism that capitalized on an
inherent power to transform reality itself, no matter how graphic, into a kind
of fantasy experience.

While the *Mirror* attempted to attract customers by publishing as many
photos and crime stories as the *News,* if not more, another tabloid suddenly
emerged in 1924 that intended to outdo them both, mainly by sensationaliz-
ing sex. In fact, Bernarr Macfadden's *Evening Graphic* was a tabloid version
of his romance and physical culture magazines' main focus. As big on crime,
too, as the other tabloids, the *Graphic* outdistanced them both with its sleazy
stories of sex scandals, deviant behavior, and the seamy side of celebrity
lifestyle. To lend them even more impact, Macfadden often resorted to what
was called the composograph, which merged different photographs to reveal
well-known individuals in compromising or highly theatrical situations. As
a purposeful distortion of reality, the composograph created a fantasized
viewing experience that would become a tabloid tradition.

Among the most popular features of the *Graphic* was Walter Winchell's
Broadway gossip column, written in a candid manner that assured readers
they were getting the inside scoop on the latest goings-on in the show business world. Winchell was well trained for his job, having started out delving
into the affairs of Broadway entertainment figures in 1919 with a column for
Billboard. Such was his power and influence that the *Daily News* attempted
to hire him, but he stayed on with the *Graphic* until the *Mirror* secured his
services in 1930. Winchell's reporting style became a model for the probing,

no-holds-barred approach that seemed to thrive on dissecting the errant ways of celebrity personalities.[32]

The tabloids also exploited the times by keeping abreast of the mediated culture's attraction to manic fads—from Emile Coué's personalized plan for self-improvement and the fascination with zany marathon activities to the fashion and design craze inspired by the 1922 discovery of King Tutankhamen's tomb in Egypt. However, one such "fad" destined to outlive the era was the crossword puzzle. In 1924, when two young publishers, Richard Simon and Max Schuster, began marketing a book of such puzzles with a No. 2 pencil attached, their ploy was such a success that the foundation for both a daily newspaper feature and a publishing empire was established.

Although numerous stories of the time's scientific breakthroughs and technological discoveries were generally played straight, tabloid journalism was always tempted to sensationalize the facts to respond to the mediated vision's faith in such marvelous achievements as omens of a wondrous future. In this light, the advent of the first liquid-fueled rocket flight in 1926 was of special import since it heralded space travel and the kind of fantastic world a new comic strip began dramatizing in 1929—*Buck Rogers in the 25th Century.*

During this era, the newspaper comic strip continued to proliferate and grow in popularity, as most urban papers carried daily and Sunday color sections. By the 1920s, Joseph Patterson and Robert McCormick's Chicago Tribune-New York Daily News Syndicate and Hearst's King Features were circulating the most popular comics of the era to newspapers all over the nation, and their success encouraged other fledgling syndicates to enter the comic strip distribution business. As a proven means to help sell a paper, the comics were now an integral part of its makeup, which undoubtedly accounted for the deluge of strips that appeared during these years. Something for everybody seemed to be the editorial reasoning for the wide range of new strips, though many quickly fell by the wayside while others went on to long-running popularity.[33]

The most appealing strips were those that presented humorous insights into the everyday incidents of family life, particularly those depicting the boyish pranks and shenanigans of an innocent time that the mediated vision saw rapidly disappearing. Of the veritable flood of strips based on such antics, one stood out over all—Percy Crosby's *Skippy.* Even the title character's attire was unique for an eight year old, dressed as he was in checked hat, ill-fitting jacket, short pants, and a polka dot bow tie adorning his high collar, all defiantly set off by floppy socks. But it was Skippy Skinner's personal commentary on the world around him that caught the fancy of his many adult fans. First appearing in the old *Life* as a panel feature, *Skippy* began a syndicated comic strip life in 1925 that would last for twenty years, inspiring a multitude of merchandise spin-offs as well as movie and radio versions. Enlivened by an animated drawing style that seemed to offset its droll humor, the strip covertly functioned as its creator's voice, whose tone could be either philosophical or politically critical. To the mediated vision, however, *Skippy* was reminiscent of what Jules Feiffer has described as a nostalgic "yearning to reclaim a nonexistent past: a society more homey, more congenial, free of cutthroat values and offensive change."[34]

Another popular offshoot of the family genre saw the independent young working girl's self-assertive manner complemented by the latest fashions, much to the delight of female fans. As a sign of the times, the business office setting of these strips that afforded the opportunity to focus on the interaction between the sexes made for intriguing fare to their readers. But whether in the workplace or the social scene, the image of the working girl in *Winnie Winkle the Breadwinner* and *Tillie the Toiler* was that of one definitely in the know on how to dress, socialize, and if so motivated, lure a man into marriage.

The institution of marriage was still fair game for satire, as George McManus's improving draftsmanship continued to reveal in *Bringing Up Father*. However, in *Moon Mullins*, Frank Willard created the antithesis of family life by bringing a group of low-life characters together in a boardinghouse setting. What they lacked in togetherness, though, con-man Moon and his assortment of loser-type cronies made up for in an ongoing series of hilarious escapades. The elements of continuity in this strip also informed the day-to-day story line of two highly popular family strips.

In 1917, Sidney Smith introduced *The Gumps*, whose dailies functioned as a soap opera rendering of a middle-class family's bouts with life's ups and downs. Although Smith's drawing style was decidedly inferior to that of most of his peers, his work demonstrated that suspense was the essential quality in maintaining reader interest. After *Gasoline Alley*, a 1918 panel feature about a group of auto tinkerers, evolved into a daily strip, Frank King's expanded cast of players—adults and children alike—were allowed to age over the years, in contrast to most conventional comic strip characters who remained frozen in an ageless world. In particularizing the American experience through the day-to-day lives of its small-town personalities, *Gasoline Alley* grew popular enough still to be running at the close of the century.

Presaging the adventure strip was a variety of other titles in this era. Billy DeBeck's *Barney Google*, which began in 1919 as a cross between a domestic- and a sports-oriented feature, later focused on the picaresque misadventures of the short, bug-eyed Barney, who was out to make his fortune, initially through horseracing. DeBeck's reliance on the language of the street as well as his coining of slang expressions in the manner of Tad Dorgan helped make the title character of *Barney Google* popular enough to inspire a hit song in 1923.

Although *Wash Tubbs* began as a humorous feature in 1924, it was creator Roy Crane's penchant for action-packed continuity that saw his unlikely protagonist soon venturing into exotic locales around the world, thus making this work a candidate as the first pure adventure strip. As another character short in stature but long on falling into one mishap after another, Washington Tubbs II found many of his problems resulting from his weakness for women, and when it came to picturing beautiful femme fatales, Crane was a master. In 1929 the Sunday page's adventure element was enhanced when he introduced the roguish Captain Easy, whose strong physical presence promised a fast-paced, exciting scenario at the expense of pushing Wash Tubbs into the background. As the early strips' artwork evolved into the more mature style of the late twenties, readers were witness to Crane's unique manner of depicting adventure—a cinematic approach to visualizing the atmosphere of remote, romantic locales that was the stuff of dreams made real.

A character who challenged the flapper/working-girl stereotype was the heroine of Frank Godwin's beautifully illustrated *Connie*. Starting out in 1927 as a Sunday-page feature, it evolved by 1929 into the first adventure strip with a female protagonist. As a beautiful liberated woman in the high-fashion style of the time, Connie Kurridge not only drove a car as fast as any man, she could pilot an airplane. She also had a propensity for stumbling into one perilous situation after another, a sign of things to come in the heroic adventure strips of the 1930s.

Anticipating the mediated culture's growing interest in science fiction, *Buck Rogers in the 25th Century* first appeared as a syndicated strip in 1929. In its highly imaginative picture of life five hundred years into the future, it was such a smash hit that its title character soon became an icon of American mediated culture. Although the future was depicted as a perilous time when wars and criminal activity have become an interplanetary operation, it was also seen as a time of marvelous technological advances when rocket ship space travel, ray guns, and antigravity belts that allowed the wearer to fly have become realities. In functioning as a dream world unto itself, *Buck Rogers* intimated to the mediated vision that the escapist concepts of fantasy and reality were interchangeable.

The appearance of *Tarzan* on the very same day in 1929 as *Buck Rogers* convinced readers that the newspaper adventure strip had truly arrived. In marked contrast to the artwork of *Buck Rogers,* though, that of commercial illustrator Hal Foster, who first drew the *Tarzan* daily, was far superior. His later assignment on the Sunday page presented him an even better opportunity to showcase his magnificent technical skills in original stories sanctioned by Edgar Rice Burroughs. Through its idealization of the noble savage theme, Foster's *Tarzan* became the model for the comics' jungle genre, visualizing Burroughs's philosophical theme of the natural man's environment being despoiled by power-mad despots of lost civilizations and the modern encroachment of self-aggrandizing poachers from the urbanized world. Although the jungle setting that Foster depicted was highly fantasized, the perils and problems that Tarzan confronted in it were as real and treacherous as the alien forces of outer space that threatened Buck Rogers. And while the latter's fantasized experiences in space conjured up the mediated vision's dream of a future made more manageable by technological progress, Tarzan's jungle world suggested the inherent yearning for a lost pastoral world where the self could be more fully realized.

On a more mundane level, the panel cartoon, in the hands of such socially observant cartoonists as H. T. Webster, Clare Briggs, and J. R. Williams, grew even more popular in the twenties. At a time when the editorial cartoon, as practiced by the *Chicago Tribune*'s John T. McCutcheon, targeted both the decade's exuberance and excesses, the comic panelists were more concerned with portraying the humor emanating from the petty trials and tribulations of everyday life. In 1924, Webster created *The Timid Soul,* a title that was popular enough to become a Sunday page and add a word to the language—"Milquetoast," after the name of its overly apologetic, weak-willed title character. Clare Briggs was a master of the alternating theme panel, which he had been drawing since the teen years. His ability to recapture nostalgic moments from the past of a simpler America endeared his work to the mediated vision. However, in *Out Our Way,* J. R. Williams inaugurated a panel series that resonated with what could be termed nostalgic realism. His work targeted the whole gamut of the American scene, from the everyday incidents of family life and on-the-job shenanigans to the rough and tumble of ranch life—all played out under thematic headings.

While the panelists were at the peak of their popularity during this era, another comics innovator was enjoying his greatest period of creativity. Rube Goldberg, who had been a newspaper cartoonist since 1904, tried his hand at every comics genre of his day—from the panel format to the continuity strip and, later, the editorial cartoon. Even after starting a Sunday page in 1915 about the zany problems of a dumb innocent named Boob McNutt that would last nearly twenty years, Goldberg continued to experiment with a wide variety of projects. But no cartoonist ever topped the impact of a panel series he drew intermittently and from which he derived his greatest fame. In the absurdly impractical "inventions" ascribed to one Professor Lucifer G. Butts, Goldberg devised overly complicated designs of specialized contraptions to carry out the simplest process or action like sharpening a pencil or hitching a car ride. His satire of the machine age's growing technocratic dominance in the mediated culture made "Rube Goldberg" a descriptive synonym for any unnecessarily complex plan or procedure. But in the 1930s the comic vision of Goldberg and his peers would find increasing competition from the proliferating adventure strip that functioned as an escapist antidote to the hard times of the Depression.

The Diverse Roles of the Magazine
in the Mediated Culture

While the mainstream magazine informed by analyzing important news events of the day in retrospect as well as discussing the impact of political, technological, and cultural developments, it also entertained through pieces on the popularity of certain media personalities and new social patterns inspired by the mediated culture.[35]

In response to the dynamic spirit of the times, newspaper publishers Joseph Patterson and Robert McCormick introduced a new mass-circulated magazine in 1924 whose name *Liberty* carried the slogan "A Weekly Periodical for Everyone," meaning primarily the American middle class. As a general interest, easy to read magazine, *Liberty* was outranked in popularity only by the *Saturday Evening Post*. Yet, by publishing quality authors for a mass audience, it distinguished itself as yet another sign of the ongoing democratization of highbrow culture.

Both to inform and entertain, *Liberty* featured articles about such famous figures as Henry Ford, Jack Dempsey, and Rudolph Valentino, as well as pieces authored by luminaries like Mary Pickford ("Shall I Bob My Hair?") and Florenz Ziegfeld ("What Makes a Woman Beautiful"). It also carried recurrent features like puzzles, panel cartoons, and, of course, that longtime magazine fixture—fiction illustrated by reputable artists. One of its most popular innovations was the one-page or "short short" story with its reading time indicated for busy readers, as it was for other stories and articles. With so many attractions, *Liberty* would find itself in for a long ride.

Bolstered by a bountiful flow of advertising revenue, the *Saturday Evening Post* continued to hold its position as the top-ranked general interest family journal. While its rank was secured by publishing the fiction of such authors as Mary Roberts Rinehart, F. Scott Fitzgerald, and P. G. Wodehouse, the *Post* also beguiled its readers with stories about successful real-life figures, particularly the American businessman. In the eyes of editor George Horace Lorimer, the leaders in business and industry were the heroes of an ever expanding corporate world, to which his editorials and the articles and fiction he chose to publish attested. Heedless of the economic debacle that reckless stock market investing and trading would precipitate by the end of the twenties, Lorimer continued to view his magazine as not only a source of information and entertainment but also an ongoing advertisement for the mediated vision's faith in the American Dream.

Based on a similar approach to the worth of the American value system, a new publication appeared in 1922 that, in spite of its inauspicious startup on a minimal investment, would evolve into the most successful magazine in publishing history respecting total circulation. *Reader's Digest*, in its beginnings, was a most nondescript publication to catch the attention of a magazine customer. There were no cover and internal illustrations; instead, only a listing of articles on the cover, which were condensations of pieces that had appeared in leading magazines. Most incredulous of all, the *Digest* was expected to subsist through subscriptions and newsstand sales, without revenue from display advertising. But the inspiration for its inception was derived from a perceived need to offer a way to cope with the information overload that the rapid pace of modern life was imposing on the individual's daily time frame. By reading its "Articles of Lasting Interest," as the inscription under the masthead proclaimed, one could stay duly informed (and entertained) through the monthly *Digest*'s provision of an article a day.

Reader's Digest was conceived by midwesterner DeWitt Wallace, who with his wife Lila parlayed their sense of what middle-class Americans wanted to read about into an enterprise that succeeded in a way they never could have dreamed at the outset. True to their idealistic goals, Wallace saw his magazine existing as a kind of public service, helping people lead fuller lives by reading mainly about the positive side of life. Nevertheless, in the years ahead the *Digest* would function increasingly as a barometer of the mediated vision's changing social views in an increasingly complex society.

Another new magazine that got off the ground the following year responded to a growing need to analyze the significance of current events and sociocultural developments in the fast-moving modern world. But publisher Henry Luce's *Time* saw its mission as more than informational by reporting its version of the news as a form of entertainment with each issue featuring a cover story about a newsworthy personality. Though it replicated the *Literary Digest*'s manner of departmentalizing reportage under topical headings, *Time* reporters wrote in a peculiar prose style that utilized tag names, compound words, and inverted sentences. This practice played a key role in *Time*'s method of humanizing the news. The very first issue in 1923 reported a "Beer Hall Revolt" in Munich in which an Austrian upstart named Adolph Hitler proclaimed his political ambitions. In the ten years it took for him to assume the leadership of the German people, *Time*, "The Weekly Newsmagazine," would establish itself as much a reflector of world affairs as the daily newspaper.

Though their covers reflected the modernist graphics stylings of the 1920s and their content, changing perspectives on women's social role, *Good Housekeeping,* the *Ladies' Home Journal,* and the *Woman's Home Companion* maintained their longtime missions of keeping the homemaker apprised of her role in managing the household as well as entertained through fiction inspired by her romantic interests. While they also carried articles on fashion styles and beauty hints, these topics were more the province of publications like *Harper's Bazaar* and *Vogue,* now highlighting the latest Paris fashions with photographs, especially the popular informal look of designer Coco Chanel.

In addressing males' practical, do-it-yourself interests, publications ranged from the automotive advice of *Motor* magazine to the project plans of

Home Craft and the latest scientific developments and prophecies of *Popular Science* and *Modern Mechanix*. Categorized as hobby magazines, these latter two magazines' covers, with their dynamic illustrations of marvelous inventions, seemed inspired by the mediated vision's ongoing fascination with a wondrous future resulting from the fruits of technological advances.[36]

Special interest magazines addressed to both men and women covered a wide spectrum of topics. While Bernarr Macfadden's *Physical Culture* preached the gospel of diet, exercise, and healthy sex as cures for bodily ailments, editor Harold Ross's witty, urbane *New Yorker*, which started out on its long run in 1925, addressed social behavior, cultural developments, and political digressions in the satirically humorous light of such writers as Robert Benchley, Dorothy Parker, S. J. Perelman, and James Thurber. Enhancing this magazine's image over the years was a panel cartoon tradition whose one-line caption caught the flavor of the times more tellingly than that of *Judge* or *Life*. Through a unique blend of graphics style and trenchant humor, *New Yorker* cartoons consistently offered hilarious insights into the follies of the human condition, even helping democratize the magazine's sophisticated aura over the years.

New publications also appeared for youths that revealed interests differing in social context from those reflected in the long-running *St. Nicholas*. Now, even the staid *Youth's Companion* had merged with *The American Boy* to compete with *The Open Road for Boys*, which dealt mainly with exciting adventure stories, camping, and sports topics. Well established by the twenties, *Boys' Life*, with its emphasis on scouting, had little trouble attracting subscribers. In fact, all these magazines, in their attention to a youthful version of the mediated vision, bolstered their readers' faith in the American way through stories and articles that extolled personal achievement in the changing times of the modern world. As such, they came across as updated versions of the Horatio Alger myth in which the idealized athlete now played a key role in the formula for success in life.

Of course, the most solicitous way in which a magazine addressed a potential customer was through its cover art and design. Now even the most popular magazines were experimenting with modernist approaches to cover design and interior layout. In the vanguard of this trend was the talented typographer Will Bradley, who as art director of *Collier's* and later the Hearst magazines, developed an interior layout style that merged text and photograph, a key factor in the democratization of the magazine's modernist look. But a magazine's main attraction to the reader was still its cover's pictorial content.

A standard feature of *Liberty*, after the manner of the *Post* and *Collier's*, its biggest competitors, was the thematic cover painting that gave the magazine its trademark look. Among the most popular of the many illustrators who contributed to this tradition was Leslie Thrasher. Though he was not as technically gifted as Norman Rockwell, he possessed a similar talent for merging both the actual and the ideal in the familiar situations he projected about American life—the domestic scene, youthful romance, sports, and especially children at play.

The sentimental, nostalgically inspired narrative art of Norman Rockwell, which came into its own during these years, would appear in over three hundred *Post* covers from 1916 to the 1960s. As the most representative artist of the mediated vision, he generally ignored the frenzied pace of urban life to portray the leisurely lifestyle that characterized the small-town/rural scene. Rockwell's blunt confession that he painted life as he would like it to be is the key to understanding his artistic intent in numerous covers that either fantasized the present or rendered the past in a warm, nostalgic light, thus delighting *Post* readers in the escapist passage such covers provided.

More attuned to contemporary realities was the cover art of J. C. Leyendecker, which helped inspire patriotism during the war years in either a humorous or serious vein. *Post* readers were particularly attracted to his tableau-like covers that commemorated a holiday and his long-running New Year's baby series that signaled the beginning of another year. But Leyendecker, like Rockwell, was also a master at conveying sentimental moods. Jan Cohn has assessed the overall escapist tenor of the *Post* covers at this time as a nostalgic search "for an irrecoverable American past, the past of boyhood or a fast-disappearing rural America." Thus she concludes: "it is Rockwell and Leyendecker who most clearly figure in their work this subtle escape from the present."[37]

Although Leyendecker would produce an abundance of covers for both *Collier's* and the *Post* during his career (his total for the latter was surpassed only by Rockwell), he was also well known for his advertising work. If the Gibson Girl idealized the young woman of turn-of-the-century America, Leyendecker's Arrow Collar Man, who showed up in his detailed promotional art for the prominent shirt company, was the fantasized conception of American manhood from the late teens into the 1920s.

More elegantly rendered than Rockwell and Leyendecker's work was the cover and advertising output of Maxfield Parrish, who brought the painter's disciplined eye to his unique illustration style. Indeed, from the fantasized, poster-like covers he did for *Collier's* early in the century to the antic characterizations of his *Life* covers in the 1920s, Parrish's artistic vision was unlike that of any of his contemporaries, especially in the brilliance of its colorfully glazed look that characterized even his advertising work for a number of well-known commercial products.[38]

The magazine artist whose art best captured the youthful spirit of the 1920s was John Held Jr. In the myriad covers and illustrations he created for *Life, Vanity Fair,* and *College Humor,* Held projected an epicurean lifestyle in his satirical drawings of partying, boozing, and petting collegiate types.

The illustrative art of John Held Jr., which conveyed the youthful spirit of the 20s, appeared in a wide variety of media forms, including this ad for the movie *So This Is College* (MGM, 1929). Author's collection.

Because of the trendy fashions he bestowed on them and his syndicated comic strip about the flapper lifestyle, Held's art was in great demand to promote consumer products. Visually his work contributed more to the myth of the Jazz Age's social side than any other source other than the movies. Though his style was a distinct departure from other notable magazine illustrators, the one thing they all had in common was an intensely personal vision that was a key factor in the commercial success of the American magazine during this era and the 1930s.[39]

If the main purpose of cover art is to promote a magazine, then the sensational covers of the pulp publications stood out as the most daringly ostentatious in the overcrowded showcase of the urban newsstand. Now more aware of the larger world due to the pervasive media forms of the movies and radio as well as the newspaper and the general interest magazine, readers had cultivated a more receptive attitude toward unique social behavior and diverse subcultural interests. Accordingly, the 1920s saw a plethora of specialized pulps begin to infiltrate the newsstands. There their garish, action packed covers defied modernist literary tastes to persist as an open invitation to the romanticized world they so boldly promoted.[40]

Assuring the continuing popularity of the fantasy/adventure pulp was the growing demand for more tales about Edgar Rice Burroughs's jungle hero Tarzan, evidenced in the 1920s by eight Tarzan novels serialized in the pulps. Also during this time the prolific Burroughs continued publishing his Martian series as well as originating the Pellucidar tales about life at the center of the earth. Displaying a versatility unsurpassed by any of his contemporaries, Burroughs even tried his hand at writing Westerns. But he would be primarily identified with the character of Tarzan, the natural man of aristocratic origins.

While the unparalleled success of Burroughs spawned a host of imitators in the jungle story genre, the two most popular pulp genres during this time were the Western and the detective story. The house of Street & Smith, by introducing *Detective Story* in 1915 and *Western Story* in 1919, instigated new lineages through the link with past dime novel icons Nick Carter and Buffalo Bill. Soon to be as popular an interpreter of the Frontier myth as Zane Grey, Frederick Faust sold his first work of fiction to *Western Story* in 1920 and never looked back. Writing under a multitude of pen names before he settled on Max Brand, Faust saw his career parallel the origin of dozens of Western pulps that became a market for his prolific output. As the pulp Western grew in popularity, many writers heeded the call. But only those with a strong sense of heroic characterization and visual feel for the Western scene would inform both the mediated vision and the movie people of the kind of ingredients that made for a good Western story.

While Max Brand and his ilk elaborated on the Frontier myth and its version of Western justice, detective fiction was beginning to reveal a close kinship with this manner of meting out justice. By the 1920s the urban milieu's growing susceptibility to organized crime was providing the backdrop for the appearance of a vigilante-type character who could function as a self-appointed agent of the law, in essence, a new kind of detective—the private eye conditioned by an increasingly lawless urban environment to react in his own special way to set things right. Ironically, such a character, in his private mission to right a wrong beyond the jurisdiction of legal authority, would be looked upon as something of an outlaw himself. But therein lay his appeal. Prior to the 1920s, what was referred to as detective-mystery fiction was written mainly as literary puzzles in the British tradition of the Sherlock Holmes stories in which the reader is challenged to solve a mystery prior to a story's denouement. This was the kind of fiction then appearing in *Detective Story* magazine. But it would soon be countered in a new pulp called *Black Mask* by a tough-talking, doggedly persistent detective who viewed crime not as an avocation but a business.

Ironically, *Black Mask* was founded in 1920 by H. L. Mencken and George Jean Nathan, who saw it as a way to generate funds to support their new magazine of social satire, *The Smart Set.* While its early stories were similar to those in the formulaic British tradition, in 1922 a fledgling writer named Carroll John Daly sold *Black Mask* a story about a tough-guy adventurer who, by the following year, evolved into a private detective called Race Williams. As a prototype of the hard-boiled detective, he narrated his own rough-and-tumble dealings with the criminal element in a first-person voice that resonated with the language of the street. Though Daly's writing was not the most polished of literary styles, readers liked the blunt dialogue of his wisecracking detective, especially when he became involved in sexual intrigue and violent action. In effect, then, Race Williams was the cowboy vigilante come to the city where the mounting problems of criminal activity justified a self-serving antiheroic type whose modus operandi transcended the constraints under which the police operated.

What Carroll John Daly had begun Dashiell Hammett improved upon to the extent that his body of fiction came to be admired as classics of the detective genre. Of the *Black Mask* school, in particular, Hammett was the consummate stylist, especially in the way he utilized vernacular English to define individual character. Not only did the Hammett vision have a profound influence on other writers, its attention to the integral function of spoken language in fiction sensitized readers to the way characters in a story should actually talk.

In contrast to Daly, Hammett's writing was more focused on the motivation behind a criminal act than it was on the act itself. From the first protagonist he created in 1923, the generally law-abiding Continental Op (so called because he was an operative for a national detective agency) to Sam Spade, the epitome of the self-resourceful tough-guy detective in *Black Mask*'s 1929 serialization of *The Maltese Falcon,* Hammett's developing emphasis on the effects of criminal involvement on character charged the action of his plots. As a result, his fiction comes across as a series of vivid scenes in which the problem at hand controls the characters' interaction. This dramatic technique accounts for the intensely visual quality of Hammett's writing, which enabled it to translate so readily into film. Even though detective-mystery fiction focused mainly on the dark, transgressive side of American life, it would continue to be one of the mediated culture's most compelling modes of escapism.

While fiction inspired by a Poe-like horrific experience had appeared in the pulps before the appearance of *Weird Tales* in 1923, it was this publication that, in spite of its ongoing financial problems, became the most recognized pulp medium for horror in a supernatural vein. For over thirty years it would introduce fascinated readers to a veritable who's who of writers in the horror/fantasy tradition, from Clark Ashton Smith and Robert E. Howard to Robert Bloch and and Ray Bradbury. But in the twenties the *Weird Tales* writer who made a name for himself as the most imaginative in the genre since Edgar Allan Poe was H. P. Lovecraft. His tales told of a dark, sinister world in which demonic forces that had once inhabited the earth were conspiring to regain their dominance. The bleak atmosphere of Lovecraft's stories, made even more forceful through his unique power to describe his protagonists' terrifying ordeals, accounted in large part for their compelling appeal. Both the output of Lovecraft and others who wrote for *Weird Tales* in the 1920s presaged the appearance of a number of horror/fantasy pulps in the coming Depression years when escapism would become a way of life.

Inspired by Lindbergh's transatlantic flight, pulp stories about the daring experience of flying, whether in World War I combat or for pure adventure, uncovered an appreciative audience who saw the airplane as a symbol of individual freedom. But there were those who saw beyond the achievement of flight to other frontiers. According to futurist Hugo Gernsback, the concept of "scientifiction," as a blend of scientific fact and prophecy, offered a new way to present highly imaginative visions that merged a fantasized cosmos with the known world. In follow-up to the theories of H. G. Wells and his own ideas advanced in his magazines dealing with radio and invention, Gernsback started publishing a pulp in 1926 that would provide the inspiration for a new field of creative endeavor soon called science fiction. Though *Amazing Stories*'s editorial policy was to publish only fiction that was scientifically plausible, it informed readers that the wonders of the future would be unlimited in scope. To enhance such an outlook, special attention was given to the magazine's cover art and interior illustrations. As the cover art of *Weird Tales* portrayed the fantasy world of the supernatural, so that of *Amazing Stories* set the style for the kind of artwork that seemed to authenticate science fiction's highly fantasized but visionary tales—especially the kind of fiction that began showing up in 1928. In the same issue that featured the genesis of the Buck Rogers character appeared the first installment of E. E. Smith's *The Skylark of Space*. In this novel of space travel that took on galactic dimensions, the conventions for many a science fiction tale to follow were established, thus, transforming a seemingly incredible future into credible reality.[41]

MARKETING POPULAR FICTION TO A GROWING DIVERSE AUDIENCE

In this early day of the mass-marketed trade book, much of the popular fiction serialized in both the slick and pulp magazines was reappearing in the hardback format. The trend was clearly evident in the popularity of the detective-mystery genre. Beginning in 1925 with *The House without a Key*, a total of six Charlie Chan novels was serialized in the *Saturday Evening Post*, all destined to appear as hardback publications. Their popularity derived from Earl Derr Biggers's characterization of the Chinese-American Chan as a shrewd individual whose intuitive understanding of human nature was pivotal in solving the crimes that came under his purview. His philosophically humorous insights also revealed him as among the most humanized of the literary detectives, thus breaking the stereotype of the sinister Oriental. As a rare minority figure presented in a commanding light, Chan's character was appealing enough for other media forms' portrayal, alerting publishers to another sure way to promote the sales of their books.

That even the British-styled detective still had a following was evidenced in the class-conscious character of Philo Vance. Starting in 1926 with *The Benson Murder Case*, arts critic Willard Huntington Wright, under the pen name of S. S. Van Dine, involved his snobbish, intellectual sleuth in a series of murder mysteries of best-seller caliber. But when readers' tastes transitioned to the hard-boiled private eye, Philo Vance's patrician manner fared better in fourteen films made from 1929 to the 1940s.

The reading public also continued to find an escapist outlet in the well-established genre of the Western. Zane Grey in particular affirmed his reputation as the master of Western fiction by staying on the best-seller lists with novels like *The U.P. Trail* (1918) and *The Mysterious Rider* (1921). As James D. Hart has commented on the formula for Grey's success: "In the minds of millions he shaped a myth of the western range involving a stereotyped struggle between ruthless villains and noble heroes unyieldingly faithful to a frontier code of justice in the protection of friends and homespun heroines."[42] Accordingly, Grey's vision would continue to inspire endless variations in the Western's plots and movie scenarios.

If adult readers found much of their escapist fiction in hardback novels, young readers, especially boys, also enjoyed their own outlet in the proliferating format of series books. While interest in invention and technology assured the ongoing popularity of the Tom Swift character, dozens of new series also featured stories inspired by other interests of the time: aviation, sports, frontier life, and the Boy Scouts. The late twenties' fascination with science fiction spawned the Great Marvel Series dealing with explorations into outer space, under the sea, and even into the earth but none of these books was any more popular than those featuring the Hardy Boys, originated in 1927 as the juvenile answer to the popularity of detective-mystery fiction. Under their author's house name of Franklin W. Dixon, these books, in which their youthful heroes are drawn into challenging mysteries to solve, would enjoy long life as updated reprints over the rest of the century. Similarly, young girl readers would find a detective heroine to identify with in the Nancy Drew books that started out on their long run in 1930.[43]

By the 1920s, then, book publishing had become a highly competitive business, and to counter the distractions of the movies and radio, as well as the mass-circulated magazine, book jackets, many adorned with the latest Art Moderne stylings, assumed the function of a miniposter to promote a book's worth. Taking their cue from the other visually-oriented cultural forms, publishers capitalized on the sensibility of an increasingly image-conscious society, directing their marketing strategy to the growing, more democratized readership of the mediated culture.[44]

THE ONGOING DEMOCRATIZATION OF THE MAINSTREAM LITERARY SCENE

During a time when reading popular fiction had become a national habit, a number of attempts to broaden the literary horizons of the mediated culture were under way. Chief among these efforts was publisher Bennett Cerf's founding of Random House, which in 1925 took on the mission of publishing both literary and philosophical classics in its Modern Library series. The next year saw the establishment of the Book of the Month Club, whose main intent was to promote what Janice Radway has categorized as "middlebrow" reading matter for a largely professional/managerial class and those who aspired to this status.[45] Shunning the complexities of literary modernism and the distance such writing established between reader and text, the Club's judges chose both fiction and nonfiction books of more popular bent—works that strived to make sense of an increasingly complicated world. Although there were those who criticized the Club for its marketing of books as cultural commodities to enhance one's social image, the Club's success and that of its imitators proved that the time was apparently right to publish books that responded to the variables of middle-class desire.

In fiction, Harold Bell Wright's moralizing, Gene Stratton Porter's sentiment, and Booth Tarkington's intimate depiction of midwestern life still found
large audiences in the 1920s. But the modernist vision that fomented fiction
of an esoteric and controversial nature, as did James Joyce's banned novel
Ulysses (1922), held very little appeal to the reading public, except for the
notoriety it generated. Nonetheless, the mediated vision now realized that
even serious fiction written in an accessible, realistic style had taken on a
more liberal posture toward controversial subject matter. The new realism,
for example, saw Sherwood Anderson's *Winesburg, Ohio* (1919) exploring the
inner lives of repressed small-town people with Freudian hang-ups. For Sinclair Lewis the whole spectrum of American life was the target of his satire.
In a prolific outpouring of best-selling novels, he attacked the narrow-
minded ways of small-town life in *Main Street* (1920), chamber of commerce
tactics in *Babbitt* (1922), the medical profession in *Arrowsmith* (1925), and
evangelical religion in *Elmer Gantry* (1927). But it was *Main Street* that had
the strongest impact on one of the mediated vision's most idyllic conceptions,
for after Lewis reviled the American small town for its enshrinement of medi-
ocrity, it lost much of its idealized charm in the urbanized eyes of the mediated vision.

With college attendance after World War I higher than it had ever been,
youth was provided a more open way to display its rebellious tendencies, both
socially and sexually.[46] If John Held Jr.'s idiosyncratic drawings portrayed a
comically satirical side to collegiate social behavior, F. Scott Fitzgerald's *This
Side of Paradise* (1920) described it more graphically than ever before
through its social focus on the college girl now free to smoke, drink, and express her sexuality. A spate of college life novels ensued, all seeking to outperform their model in sensationalism.[47] By the time Fitzgerald published
The Great Gatsby in 1925, his reputation was secure enough for him to be acclaimed the literary spokesman for the Jazz Age and its excesses. Both the
high critical reception of his novels and the popular appeal of the short stories he wrote for the *Saturday Evening Post* made him the golden boy of the
literary set and a favorite of the mediated culture. In fact, his fiction's vivid
imagery that limned the social high life of the 1920s would linger on in the
nation's collective memory.[48]

In contrast to Willa Cather's well-crafted fiction centering on strong pioneer women characters, as in *My Antonía* (1918), and Edith Wharton's on
New York socialites of the Gilded Age in *The Age of Innocence* (1920), some
daring women novelists were beginning to deal with the taboo topic of illicit
sex and its consequences. The new realism in women's fiction, which derived
from a variety of personal problems women identified with, was only the beginning of a proliferation of reality-based topics and themes once considered
too daring and controversial for fiction.

Among the most shocking novels of the 1920s was Theodore Dreiser's *An American Tragedy* (1925), in which he established a model for many a best seller to come by basing his story on a real-life happening—the alleged premeditated murder of a factory girl by a coworker who has impregnated her. Seeing the girl as a barrier to his status-seeking romance with the factory owner's socialite daughter, the novel's central character plots to rid himself of her. Dreiser, in his earlier novels focusing on the powerful businessman, had revealed his fascination with the drive for material success in American life. In *An American Tragedy,* he attempted to show how this compulsion can lead to tragic consequences. At a time when tabloid journalism was obsessed with reporting the morbid, sensational side of murders of passion, Dreiser's blockbuster novel commanded a powerful hold on its readers, confronting them with the hard reality that lurked just below the surface of the American Dream's fantasized promise.

Although America's original reluctance to enter the Great War was eventually resolved by viewing it as the war to end all wars, the initially naive idealism of those who survived it had been shattered by the harsh realities of their frontline experiences. Thus the war itself was the catalyst for a postwar mood of disillusionment and cynicism among certain writers. In John Dos Passos's *Three Soldiers* (1921), the war's shattering effects from three different viewpoints sensitized readers to the dehumanizing damage of modern warfare on the human psyche. After this first novel, Dos Passos applied his panoramic vision to criticizing the capitalist system in *Manhattan Transfer* (1925), a prelude to his major 1930s trilogy *U.S.A.* But *Three Soldiers* was the first of a number of other war novels in the tradition of Stephen Crane that undermined the mediated vision's pulp magazine fantasies about war as a great, heroic adventure.

The American writer who drew on the realities of war to espouse an intensely personal kind of stoicism in both his life and his writings was Ernest Hemingway. Critically acclaimed worldwide by the 1930s as one of the era's greatest writers, he was also a favorite of the mediated vision, due mainly to the real-life macho image he fostered as a sportsman. Although the Hemingway persona manifested in his fictional characters derived in part from his own youthful sporting experiences, the wounding he suffered in the war was also a significant factor. As another American expatriate attracted to the creative freedom and liberated lifestyle of Paris in the 1920s, Hemingway began there to produce the well-crafted fiction in which he forged his own philosophy of existence. It would be dramatized in *The Sun Also Rises* (1926) by its characters' pursuit of the sensual life and in *A Farewell to Arms* (1929) in its rejection of the idealized abstractions of duty, glory, and honor that the horrors of war had rendered meaningless. To Hemingway, the stoical, adversarial posture personified in his highly individualized protagonists represent a defiantly forceful way to confront the uncertainties of life and realize personal identity in an otherwise nihilistic existence. Thus his sporting-type heroes' sense of self-resolution in the face of any kind of physical challenge had wide appeal to the mediated vision. Then, too, Hemingway's deceptively simple style appealed to most readers, making his writing easy to digest, even if they missed out on its philosophical import. His organic emphasis on the precise, exact word's function would have a great influence on other writers who saw in it a way to capture the intensity of the immediate moment. To Hemingway, the disciplined control of the word in creating his visually styled fiction was tantamount to expressing the personal philosophy of life that made him an icon of media culture.

Closing out this era were two major writers whose literary vision derived from their special insights into the traditions of the Southern past that conflicted with the cultural changes that had impacted on the modern South. While the complex style of William Faulkner's *The Sound and the Fury* (1929) kept it from becoming anything like a popular work, this novel drew on familiar terrain—the tragic impact of the South's lost cause on the old landed aristocracy and disenfranchised dirt farmer, white and black alike. To formulate a universal message out of this situation, Faulkner transformed his Mississippi Delta area's peculiar problems of race and lost family honor into a microcosm of the human concerns of the world at large. Although Faulkner's psychological exploration of a character's inner self through his stream of consciousness method may have repelled many readers, it would have a stylistic influence on writers who saw in it a viable way to reveal the inner thoughts of their characters—even those who wrote in a manner that appealed to the mediated vision's sense of fiction as escapist entertainment.

Both the realistic and poetic revelation of the self found full expression in the autobiographical fiction of Thomas Wolfe, beginning with *Look Homeward, Angel* (1929). In this novel, and later in *Of Time and the River* (1935), Wolfe, as Eugene Gant, tells the painful story of his attempt to escape the sociocultural ties of his conservative Southern roots and find fame as a writer, centering all the while on himself as emblematic of the American experience, hopefully to fathom its meaning for himself and, by extension, his readers. To achieve this lofty goal, Wolfe structured his fiction around Eugene's memories of the past, his struggles in the present, and his hopes for the future—all of which were filtered through the sensory experiences of Wolfe himself. Thus he bravely attempted to impose meaning and order on the fragmented experiences of American life by synthesizing the whole of his own personal experiences in the novel form. Because of his idealistic quest to ascertain the meaning of the American experience and the promise underlying its contradictions, Wolfe's writings would stand as a beacon of hope during the dark times of the 1930s.

THE NEW POETRY AND THE
POPULARITY OF NONFICTION

Like Ernest Hemingway, some poets of this era sought to express themselves by employing both the precise word and the language of the people, as in the poetry of Amy Lowell and the Imagists. At a time, too, when media imagery was starting to pervade society, this visually oriented poetry manifested itself through a variety of collections, as in Vachel Lindsay's *The Congo and Other Poems* (1914), which was infused with a lively folk spirit; Robert Frost's *North of Boston* (1914) and its poems' compelling conversational manner; and especially Carl Sandburg's *Chicago Poems* (1916). Purposely avoiding the obscure, Sandburg drew on visual metaphors of the urban scene to emphasize the worth of the American way and its people. As a poet also attracted to the land (his *Cornhuskers* in 1918 celebrated the prairie), Carl Sandburg persisted as *the* poet of the mediated vision during this era. This role was enhanced by his work in resurrecting the American folk song through an anthology titled *The American Songbag* (1927) and the publication in 1926 of the first volume of his monumental biography of Abraham Lincoln.

In response to a spreading literacy, such nonfiction as the Lincoln biography was finding an increasingly popular reception, prompting the Modern Library series to keep adding titles to its list. The most revealing autobiography of the time, *The Education of Henry Adams* (1918), saw its patrician author lamenting the passing of a conservative older culture due to the industrialization and urbanization of society. The ongoing democratization of education was also generating a popular interest in history and even the esoteric field of philosophy, making best sellers of Hendrik Van Loon's *The Story of Mankind* (1922) and Will Durant's *The Story of Philosophy* (1926). As "stories," these works appeared more accessible to the mediated vision and its awakening to the significance of the real historical past as opposed to its fictional revelation. The ongoing interest in self-improvement inspired a publishing area that became a field unto itself with books that ranged from Emily Post's *Etiquette* (1922), in answer to the social climbing bent of the middle class, and Emile Coué's *Self-Mastery through Conscious Auto-Suggestion* (1923), which started a national fad among readers who were told to keep reminding themselves, "Every day in every way I am getting better and better."

Two of the era's most celebrated figures also responded to the mediated vision's perennial quest to get ahead in life with best-selling autobiographical books that stressed the traditional American values of hard work, self-reliance, and determination. In *My Life and Work* (1922) Henry Ford recounted how his personal work ethic enabled him to produce the affordable automobile that changed the lifestyle of the average American family. The success of Charles Lindbergh's lonely flight across the Atlantic in his tiny plane, as described in *We* (1927), symbolized his faith in pioneer-like motivational qualities, helping him prove to a skeptical world that long-distance air travel had a promising future. As moral fables about the worth of the American way, then, books about successful people would continue to have great appeal to the mediated vision.

Evolving Opportunities for Leisure Activities and the Growing Popularity of Sports

In response to a spreading liberal attitude toward the use of leisure time, new venues were being introduced and promoted while old ones were being transformed. By 1919 the Chautauqua movement, for example, had expanded into a summer circuit of towns and communities across the country that attracted some fifteen million participants. As a congenial way to satisfy the mediated vision's perennial goal of improving the self, enrollees were treated to noted lecturers' stimulating topics, musicians' inspiring concerts, and a colorful array of cultural specialists, some of whom radiated the appeal of a vaudeville entertainer. Thus the Chautauqua demonstrated that leisure time could be productive as both an entertaining and elevating experience.

As a national holiday like the Fourth of July presented the nation the opportunity to stage spectacular fireworks displays, it also inspired the staging of idealized pageants that celebrated memorable events of an area's past while offering its citizens recreational release. Highly popular during the Progressive years, such pageantry evolved into nationalistic, patriotic endeavors during the war era, often presented to help promote war bond sales. Following the cessation of hostilities, interest in historical pageants was renewed on a more regionalized basis. What Percy MacKaye, son of dramatist Steele MacKaye, was to the creation of historical pageantry, Frederick Koch, drama professor at the University of North Carolina in the 1920s, was to the development of regional folk drama that Paul Green, one of his students, would play a key role in writing and producing. In addition to its entertainment value, historical pageantry instilled a sense of collective memory that revived insights into the fading ideals of the past, hopefully to serve as inspiration for the future.[49]

Modeled after their Coney Island prototype, some two thousand amusement parks were located near the nation's larger cities by war's end. In the 1920s, though, the automobile, which park management expected to provide more immediate accessibility, was affording potential visitors the latitude to head out for other competing attractions. Despite the diverse opportunities for self-expressive entertainment that had made the amusement park the fantasized embodiment of the American spirit, it was now entering its most trying time in striving to compete with other escapist venues for a piece of the leisure time pie.

The circus, striving to maintain a long tradition of appealing to the masses, was also feeling competition from other amusement attractions. In 1918, the Ringlings combined with Barnum and Bailey as "The Greatest Show on Earth," and by 1929 it was monopolizing the circus industry, having driven many of the smaller circuses out of business. Nevertheless, the circus still maintained its image as vaudeville on a grandiose scale, featuring its usual exotic animals and assorted trapeze/aerial performers, lion tamers, high divers, acrobats, clowns—not to mention the sideshow's gallery of freaks, a tradition that had branched off from P. T. Barnum's dime museum to other amusement venues. Whether real or fraudulent, they were always visually fascinating to viewers. A much ballyhooed circus attraction was the appearance of a famous personality like cowboy movie star Tom Mix. In 1929 he brought Buffalo Bill's Wild West Show full circle in an updated version of the Western myth that reflected its ongoing crowd appeal. What really helped the circus survive, then, was its ability to respond to the mediated vision's escapist desires within the ever changing social scene, and in so doing, maintain its sense of creating ritualistic order out of grandiose spectacle.

With automobile ownership a middle-class reality in the 1920s, the roads filled up with vacationing families on their way to the seashore, the mountains, and the national parks. There were plenty of places to see, too, motivating local tourist boards to attract travelers to whatever their colorful brochures promoted. In 1927 the state of Virginia set a precedent for others to emulate by staking out highway markers identifying historic sites for motorists to visit. Thus, making a pilgrimage to any one of these shrines of American history was like returning to a time when things seemed more stable and purposeful, which in itself was incentive enough for motorists to take to the highway and exchange present concerns for the nostalgia of the past or the simpler life of the hinterlands.

The democratization of travel even saw some middle-class families engaging in what once only the wealthy could afford—a tour of Europe, where they showed up in places like London, Paris, and Rome with their cameras at the ready. But most chose to explore the expanses of their own country, as travel by automobile was now possible all the way to California. Some compromising souls were compelled to take home life with them by pulling a house trailer behind their cars. Though the automobile may have modernized camping by making it a less hardy experience, the lure of "roughing it" in the great outdoors was still very much alive in the 1920s.

Out of the popularity of the Western movie sprang the commercialization of cowboy culture, inspiring some of the more adventurous wealthy types to look and live like a cowboy on a "dude" ranch. Here, they affected the stylized dress and mannerisms that were integral to the riding and roping skills of the rodeo show. Recognized by 1914 as a rising entertainment venue, rodeo evolved from its indigenous roots to become popular enough by the 1920s to play New York's Madison Square Garden before thousands of eastern "dudes."[50]

Children, naturally motivated by what they saw in the numerous Tom Mix movies released during the twenties, had their play-acting stimulated by the toy guns and cowboy regalia available from stores and mail-order catalogs. While board games continued to reflect the major interests of the times, the most popular items from a boy's viewpoint were the toy soldiers and weaponry inspired by the war and the time's technological advances. Thus, miniature automobiles, trucks, buses, boats, and airplanes (especially in the wake of Lindbergh's momentous flight) appeared in multiple forms of stationary and wind-up models. The most singularly popular item modeled after its real-world counterpart was the new electric train, particularly that manufactured by the Lionel Company. Recognizing its merchandising appeal to adult males as well as boys, department stores put the electric train on display in their show windows at Christmastime, often in the anachronistic setting of a Nativity scene.

For children reaching adolescence, a new type of play had now come to the fore as a group participant activity—team games involving ball play and its requisite accessories. In follow-up to the growing popularity of organized team sports in the schools and colleges, sporting goods companies that catered to the needs of baseball, football, and basketball teams enjoyed an economic boom during the 1920s' so-called Golden Age of Sport. Although individualized games like tennis and golf were still dominated and controlled by the country club set, a large and prosperous middle class was beginning to make inroads into these traditionally elitist activities.

A major reason for the spreading popularity of sports as both participant and spectator activities was the expanded reportage accorded them by the media. In appealing to the mediated vision, writers emphasized the understanding that achievement in sports addressed values fundamental to being an American. As though to substantiate this viewpoint, the athlete who excelled in a particular sport was adulated as a public icon by the mass media. Paradoxically, by succeeding at playing a game rather than engaging in an honored profession, the athlete was looked upon as an heroic type who had made something of himself through dedication to physical achievement. As a measuring stick, sports statistics, such as the batting average or pitching record of a baseball player, were assimilated and touted by fans. Accordingly, the cult worship of media-made athletic heroes of the twenties contributed to a visual mythology of American sport that became part and parcel of a mediated national identity.[51] Only a few writers saw sport and the kind of person it defined in a negative light. And in spite of Ring Lardner's fictional portraits of flawed baseball players and John Tunis's indictment of organized sports in a 1927 article titled "The Great American Sports Myth," sportswriters like Grantland Rice helped reinforce the notion that the lessons taught by participation in sports were integral to the American way.[52]

Now publishing a section unto itself, the sports department of big-city dailies embellished its layouts with halftone action photographs of notable sporting events. Columnists editorialized about the fortunes and misfortunes of sports figures and teams as did that old standby, the sports cartoonist. Both *Collier's* and the *Saturday Evening Post* devoted a significant amount of space to stories about sports personalities of the day, while the movies enhanced their popularity through incorporating notable sporting events into the newsreel format and by signing famous athletes to film roles. And radio, which invented the profession of sportscasting, made a leisure activity out of listening to sports, either on a local or national basis, thus showing how sports and a mass medium complemented each other.

By the twenties, college football, with its strong alumni support, had become something of a grandiose public spectacle. If a notable team had a successful season, then it might be invited to play in the Rose Bowl on New Year's Day, an event that became increasingly popular in the 1920s. This prototype of all the bowl games was sponsored by the annual Tournament of Roses festival at Pasadena, California, which decided to host an annual football game beginning in 1916. Taking its name from the festival and the shape of the stadium in which the game would be played, its festivities consisted of a big parade and an elaborate halftime program in which the principal players were bands and cheerleaders engaging in intricately planned formations. To the mediated vision, such a spectacle proved that college football and pageantry were made for each other.

Mechanized sport in the form of automobile racing continued its surge in interest as major races during 1915–29 saw average racing speeds approach 150 miles per hour. Later, these years would be considered the Golden Age of car racing when drivers like Barney Oldfield and Eddie Rickenbacker blazed a glory trail for the high-powered engines to come. Rickenbacker, who had been an ace fighter pilot in the war, also helped organize a new aerial sport in which fellow pilots reunited to participate in airplane racing. It ultimately evolved into the daredevil exploits of stunt flying or aerobatics, an exciting spectator attraction that would remain popular for the rest of the century.

On a darker side, baseball fans were shocked when a scandal was uncovered in 1919, pointing out that not even organized athletics were immune to the deviant side of human nature. When eight members of the Chicago White Sox baseball team were accused of involvement in a gambling scheme to throw the World Series, the game of professional baseball appeared doomed.[53] After the players who had plotted to pull off the scheme were banned from the game, branded thereafter as the "Black Sox," baseball appointed a czar to oversee its operation and hopefully maintain the honorable image the system demanded.

But problems common to the real world were even infiltrating so-called amateur athletics, and by 1929 the release of the Carnegie Commission report on the state of intercollegiate athletics revealed that the game of football had become so commercialized that a number of institutions appeared to be losing sight of their primary educational mission. While the growing emphasis on professionalization and winning at any cost had begun to cloud over the long-time idealized perception of sport, the mediated vision, ironically enough, would continue to look on sport as an escapist refuge from real-world issues.

Although sport was still considered a predominantly male preserve for both participant and spectator, it was socially fashionable for women to attend sporting events like college football games. But as participants, women athletes, such as Gertrude Ederle in endurance swimming and Helen Wills in tennis, were accepted because they performed in socially approved sports for women. Those who excelled in the more masculine activities like track and field were seen as betrayers of the feminine ideal. During this era, too, an honored place for the black athlete was practically nonexistent. Although Fritz Pollard, a football player at Brown University, was honored as the first black All-American in 1916, white sports fans at this time could never have foreseen the breadth and depth of impact that the black athlete would have on not only American but international sport in future years.[54]

By the 1920s the international theater of the Olympic Games had become more culturally meaningful to the mediated vision, mainly due to sports journalism's emphasis on their nationalistic significance. More informed, too, about the special events that comprised the Olympics, sport fans were eager to follow American athletes' chances against worldwide competition. Although they dominated the summer Olympics of the 1920s, U.S. athletes realized they had a lot of catching up to do in competing against the Europeans in the winter Games, which were established in 1928. Though prejudices still persisted over the participation of women athletes in certain events, in 1928 some were allowed to compete for the first time in track and field events. Overshadowing the lack of minority participants was a growing tendency for competing countries to use the Olympics as a showcase for nationalistic politics, a portent of future developments.

THE SOCIOCULTURAL IMPACT OF THE 1920s ON THE MEDIATED CULTURE

The degeneration of the Victorian moral code and the mood of postwar disillusionment fomented a youthful lifestyle in the 1920s that was as improvisational as the jazz music that dominated the era. Its credo of living for the moment represented the mediated vision's first real disconnect with its communal views on the worth of the past and the promise of the future. Now, for the first time in the nation's social history the attitudes of youth were superseding those of the old order, planting the seeds for an adversarial dichotomy that would challenge middle-class values for the rest of the century.

It was the so-called New Woman who was the most revolutionary force in toppling social tradition as her parents had known and understood it. Even though by 1920 she had won the right to vote, the flapper type generally ignored the political process to affirm her new social image. In rebelling against the restrictions imposed on their corseted mothers, young women, enshrined by the visual power of the movies and magazine advertisements as objects of sexual desire, were using a variety of cosmetics to complement their bobbed hair, flesh-colored stockings, and knee-length dresses. The evolution in women's fashions that had begun around 1914 had culminated in this new image of the American woman, the latest version of Carrie Meeber.[55]

During the late teen years, wearing swim attire at the beach that displayed more flesh than guardians of the peoples' morals were willing to permit saw women frequently cited and even arrested for "indecent exposure," though their swimwear was quite modest by later standards. In the twenties the spread of beach resorts along the coastal areas made the daring, formfitting one-piece suit more socially acceptable, especially after the success of Atlantic City's first Miss America beauty pageant in 1921, when all eight participants wore one-piece suits. By the decade's end, the virginal, golden-haired image of the movies' Mary Pickford had given way to the sexually provocative image of Clara Bow, and, in the eyes of the mediated vision, the revolution in women's fashions had played an instrumental role in this transition.

Women were also growing more independent and self-expressive in a number of ways other than through fashion. Some were even driving automobiles, a practice many men considered not only absurd but foolhardy. As the more aggressive women were daring to smoke, the social institution of the cocktail party in the era of Prohibition allowed them free rein to imbibe alcohol with men. Also an aura of sexual openness in mixed company revealed women as more tolerant of strong language and even the telling of off-color jokes and scandalous stories. With women's rights advocate Margaret Sanger dispensing birth control information since 1914, sexual relationships could now be indulged in with less fear of an unwanted pregnancy. Yet not a few wondered about the kind of deleterious influence the New Woman's social freedom might have on public propriety.

Many blamed the loosening of morals on the modernist temper, particularly its emphasis on the New Psychology and its revelations, while others praised this pioneering behavioral science's innovations that set standards for measuring the intelligence of school children and testing the individual abilities of workers. Still others were moved to praise the therapeutic technique of the psychiatrist as a highly effective way to diagnose mental problems and illnesses. Thus, to liberals the psychoanalytic theories of Sigmund Freud stood as yet another triumphant modern breakthrough. In probing the subconscious self to deal with the problems of the repressed libido, Freud introduced the social order and the realm of literature and the arts to a new awareness of the inner self's role in relating to or escaping from everyday reality. In fact, Freud's exploration of the inner world of the individual uncovered a rationale for interpreting dreams and myths as keys to revealing the complex mysteries of the self. In this process, he singled out the diagnosis of sexual problems as providing a significant clue to understanding the vagaries of human behavior. As a result, his findings became a major force in the sexual liberation of the twentieth century, in particular for women.

Though Freudian theory was attacked as another way of rationalizing selfish motives and fantasizing the realities of life, its influence became widespread during the first half of the century, extending from the areas of medicine and education to business's reliance on the persuasive power of advertising to influence the masses' buying habits. In their attention to the problems of human sexuality and deviant behavior, Freud's theories also had a significant impact on both the modernist vision in literature and the arts, introducing the mediated vision to the dark inner world of the self as it was revealed in the socially aberrant behavior of numerous characters in fiction, drama, and the movies.

In the 1920s, the Bohemian lifestyle of Greenwich Village became a big attraction to outsiders intrigued by the social rebels who had forsaken conventional behavior to live by a code of their own.[56] Accordingly, a number of landmark gathering places sprang up that catered to the curiosity of those who either wanted to observe or become a part of the Village scene. Not only was it a haven for freethinkers, intellectuals, and creative geniuses, but also for self-styled pretenders whose main purpose was to engage in an endless round of revelry that defied the standards of morality. In their own way, then, they contributed to a counterculture milieu that would continue to attract opponents of the Establishment and crusading idealists throughout the century. Paradoxically, the social manners of each rebellious wave would be absorbed into the very thing it sought to rebel against—middle-class culture.

An African American parallel to the Village's creative energy was embodied in the movement known as the Harlem Renaissance of the 1920s. Its primary purpose, as leading representatives like Langston Hughes, Carl Van Vechten, and Zora Neale Hurston contended, was to show that black-generated art and literature had a great deal to offer mainstream American culture. But to the general public, exposed as it was to movie sterotypes and the mass-mediated images of Edgar Rice Burroughs's fantasized Africa, the output of black artists and writers was slower to be recognized than the more audible and visible sector of black culture that was producing jazz music.

Such spontaneously creative environments as those of Harlem and Greenwich Village were also natural breeding grounds for radical pundits who openly attacked what they thought was not only wrong but sorely lacking in American culture. In 1919 the Russian revolution had precipitated a Red scare that resulted in a national fear of the country being infiltrated by Communism. Agitating this situation, leftist magazines of socialist bent, in particular *Revolt* and *The New Masses,* were declaring that only a people's uprising could right the wrongs that capitalism had inflicted upon them. From a more intellectual point of view was the iconoclastic commentary of editor Harold Stearns and his fellow critics in the anthology *Civilization in the United States* (1922). Pointing up the cultural deficiencies of a country that had sold its soul to Big Business, this volume of thirty essays launched one caustic attack after another on the capitalistic system as a major contributor to the cultural barrenness and conformist social behavior of American society.

As a reputable gadfly in such cultural debates, H. L. Mencken started up a journal in 1924 called *The American Mercury* in which he and other acerbic commentators had their say about the reasons for the low status of American culture. Mencken was especially fond of citing the Puritan ethic and narrow-minded provincialism as significant factors. A former newspaper man sensitized to the peculiarities of mass taste, Mencken was a paradoxical composite of social critic and learned scholar, as he revealed in championing Theodore Dreiser's controversial fiction and in his highly respected multivolume study, *The American Language.* Ironically, critics like Mencken and Stearns's essayists were too close to their times to realize that the 1920s, in retrospect, would be judged as one of America's richest eras in creating a native literature. A parallel to this situation lay in the belated recognition accorded the nation's artists.

American painting of the 1920s directed its attention to both the vitality and oppressiveness of the urban scene, almost as though artists were carrying on a love-hate relationship with it. Attendant to this trend, and one that still affected the way the mediated vision viewed art, was the ongoing conflict between portraying subject matter in either a conventionally realistic or modernist abstract manner. While the early abstract work of John Marin, who had exhibited in the 1913 Armory show, was charged with the organic dynamism of New York's skyscraper construction period, Edward Hopper's realism reflected the alienation and isolation of urban life. He captured this mood even in the communally oriented amusement forms of the urban scene, as, for example, in his painting of preoccupied, anonymous faces in a movie theater audience. The realistic styles of both Hopper and Charles Burchfield seemed to echo the same kind of literary vision that the fiction of Sherwood Anderson and Sinclair Lewis expressed about the cultural bleakness of modern American life. Both artists, in their projection of visual metaphors that resonated with the darker side of the American experience, presented viewers a poignant rendering of a decadent present that ironically conjured up memories of a lost, irrecoverable past.[57]

In general, American artists of this era, who worked in watercolors or oils, wavered between the abstract styles of Marin and Charles Demuth and the subtle realism of Hopper and Burchfield. But modernist artists like Marin, in his intensely energized abstractions of New York's machine-made landmarks, Demuth, who subtly satirized the machine age in his industrial landscapes, and Charles Sheeler, who caught the spirit of technology's formidable presence in his photographic scenes of modern machinery, all saw technology for what it was—a powerful symbol of America's explosive expansion toward a technocratic future. Although the modernist movement in the arts had little impact on the mediated vision during this era, it would burst full blown on the American scene in the 1930s through Art Moderne's widespread influence on machine and architectural design.

Due to the general prosperity of the twenties, most criticism leveled at the time's cultural failings went largely ignored by the general public. Indeed, the economic windfall generated by big business and industry and their relationship with consumer advertising was a sign to many that material success had begotten a new kind of religion. To justify this outlook, unique compromises were made between the world of the material and that of the spiritual, as Bruce Barton speculated in *The Man Nobody Knows* (1925), his best-selling book about how Jesus and his disciples would succeed as modern businessmen. During this time, though, the Christian fundamentalist movement had been gathering strength, even at the expense of an occasional scandal. But to fundamentalism the real problem to contend with was the scientific theory of evolution, which contradicted believers' literal interpretation of the biblical version of creation.

The conflict came to a head in 1925 when a small-town Tennessee school teacher was brought to trial, charged in violation of a state statute prohibiting the teaching of evolution. Over a period of three weeks the east Tennessee town of Dayton took on the air of a mediated circus in which townspeople, outsiders, and media figures vied for attention. With renowned trial lawyer Clarence Darrow defending, in essence, the individual right to accept the theory of evolution as valid, and populist politician William Jennings Bryan supporting the fundamentalist stand to condemn the theory outright, the center ring of the circus was set. Although the defendant, a high school biology teacher, was eventually found guilty of having broken the law and fined one hundred dollars, the symbolic clash between Darrow the agnostic and Bryan the fundamentalist would become known as the trial of liberal thought versus conservative narrow-mindedness. Through the fiery denouncements of media evangelists' reaction to the ongoing spread of liberal thought, this irreconcilable conflict would continue to erupt on occasion throughout the century.[58]

The so-called Monkey Trial served to showcase the rural South as a benighted region where ignorance, lack of progress, and racism reigned. But the region that H. L. Mencken dubbed the "Sahara of the Bozarts" was still a place that prided itself in the cultural traditions of its past, an inheritance from antebellum times that advocated agrarianism as the major source of economic sustenance while promoting an inherent mistrust of the Northern industrial system. Nevertheless, as both whites and blacks left the land of cotton and tobacco in larger numbers each year to pursue the industrial North's promise of the mediated vision's hope for a better life, the South would lie economically dormant until the war years of the 1940s.

But one area of the South enjoyed a bountiful economic boom in the 1920s, if only for a short while. The propitious combination of Northern prosperity, new Southern highways, and aggressive promotion generated the wheel-and-deal atmosphere of the Florida real estate boom of 1924–26. Millionaire automotive speculator Carl Fisher was the chief architect in conceiving and building what would become the dream city of the mediated vision. Carved out of a tangled, seemingly impenetrable mangrove forest, the nucleus for Miami Beach soon found itself the focal point of enticing real estate offers, especially after the construction of new roads and a railroad improved accessibility to the area. In a carnival-like milieu of get rich schemes, the promotion of the area's year-round tropical climate and exotic image as an escapist haven from winter's chill helped sales proliferate. Although Fisher kept pouring his profits back into improvements for his dream city, the unchecked system of option and binder deals soon burst the profiteering bubble. Nevertheless, from this time on, Florida became fixed in the eyes of the mediated vision as a glorified haven of escape.

Real estate booms were fairly common in the 1920s, as it was a time when the desire to own one's dream home in a cultivated residential neighborhood was on the way to becoming a reality. Along with the availability of the automobile, suburban America would ultimately grow out of real estate agencies promoting the advantages of the suburban community and its ready access to a nearby city. But long before the flight to the suburbs would turn the inner cities into devastated ghettos, downtown areas also realized building booms, as the construction of planned civic centers and skyscraper office buildings helped transform the appearance and skyline of the American city, all of which were aspiring versions of New York or Chicago. In merging art and the machine to produce a new aesthetic of construction, the Bauhaus movement, which German architect Walter Gropius inaugurated in 1919, was another modernist force that would impact on the future of architecture and the notion of functional design. However, the dominant architectural styles of the 1920s were still influenced by past tradition, and the most impressive structure to combine the best of the past with a future look was the Chicago Tribune Tower's neo-Gothic design.[59]

Unfortunately, though, events transpired that did not bode well for the future. For one, the collapse of the Florida land bonanza in the late 20s was a portent of what was to come on a national scale. Like those who had speculated in Florida real estate and made fortunes before things came apart, thousands of investors were lured into trying their luck on the booming stock market. But by October 1929, the Great Bull Market had generated more shares than there were traders or buyers, and with the disappearance of billions of dollars in market value, collapse was assured. What followed was an economic depression of such magnitude it would last through the 1930s until the advent of World War II. Moreover, it would prove to be a severe time of testing for both the American way of life and the mediated vision's faith in the promise of the American Dream. Indeed, it would be a time when many would find more solace in the escapist outlets of the mediated culture than in any other source.

4

1930–1945—Testing the Dream in the Great Depression and World War II

> Not only did the movies amuse and entertain the nation
> through its most severe economic and social disorder,
> holding it together by their capacity to create unifying
> myths and dreams, but movie culture in the 1930s became
> a dominant culture for many Americans, providing new
> values and social ideals to replace shattered old
> traditions.
>
> —Robert Sklar, *Movie-Made America:*
> *A Cultural History of American Movies*

By 1932, WITH AMERICAN INDUSTRY CUT TO LESS THAN HALF OF ITS 1929 volume and something like twelve million unemployed, the Horatio Alger formula for success in life was being put to its severest test. Even so, most of the nation's down-and-out population, in coping with the Great Depression, resisted the tendency toward a fatalistic posture by identifying more intimately and frequently with the modes of escapism that the mediated culture had created for it. The upshot was a unique kind of homogenized experience that offered a sense of personal solace and refuge from the grim realities of the times.

But the escapist mood responded to by the movies, magazine fiction, comic strips, and radio was hardly an answer to the bleak reality of day-to-day living, and with so many out of work the mediated vision saw the economic problems of the national scene as a nightmarish perversion of the American Dream. Such a pervasively austere outlook presented an open invitation to Leftist thinkers and political radicals to champion Marxism as a way to supplant the victimizing nature of capitalism. And not a few disenchanted citizens responded to their cry to revolutionize the system.

To counter former President Herbert Hoover's contention that the country's economic problems were temporary and would resolve themselves in time, his successor, Franklin D. Roosevelt, established an action-oriented

posture from the very start of his administration in 1933. Although the re-
formist policies of his revolutionary New Deal program appeared as so much
fantasy to his political opponents, Roosevelt's take charge posture impressed
those tired of governmental machinations and promises that had failed to de-
liver. From his initial fireside chat over the radio and in many others to follow, Roosevelt exuded a positive, sincere manner that made him popular
enough for listeners to overlook his political excesses. Most, in fact, perceived him not as the self-aggrandizing politician type they were accustomed
to but as a selfless savior of his people.

Because so many banks had failed in the Crash, a major goal was to reaffirm the stability of the banking system and the people's faith in it, not an
easy task to carry out in view of those unfortunate citizens whose savings accounts had been wiped out. Striving to foster a more positive outlook, the
ubiquitous Blue Eagle logo of the National Recovery Act (NRA) served as a
symbolic reminder, to paraphrase the words of Roosevelt's campaign song,
that happy days were here again. But not for those who took a negative stand
toward the socialistic trend of Roosevelt's acronymically named reform plans
for putting the country back to work, such as the Public Works Administration (PWA), the Works Progress Administration (WPA), and the Civilian Conservation Corps (CCC). Though these programs would be phased out by the
war years, the most controversial would last the century—the Social Security Act of 1935, denounced by his political enemies as socialistic madness
that would lead the country down the road to a communist state.

But a pervasive faith in Roosevelt as an authoritative representative of
the people and the "American Way of Life"—a commonly used phrase by
this time—was clearly evidenced in his re-elections to office in 1936 and
1940. His strong leadership during the war years even assured him a fourth
term in 1944, which would end with his death in 1945 near the end of the
war. Despite the polio attack in 1921 that had cost him the use of his legs,
Roosevelt maintained his popular image in the eyes of the mediated vision
through the reassuring manner of his radio addresses and open press con-
ferences as well as wife Eleanor's public visibility in her role as First Lady.
Together they projected an air of supreme confidence that helped carry the
American people through the dark days of the Depression and the crises of
World War II. As journalist Joseph Alsop assessed the legacy of the Roosevelt presidency: "Hope was . . . Franklin Roosevelt's greatest gift to his
fellow Americans. He gave us hope by his deeds, when he came to office in
a time that seemed utterly devoid of hope. But even more, he gave us hope
because all could see that he himself felt not the slightest doubt about the
future at any time in his years as President."[1] Clearly, the dominant figure
of this era was Franklin Delano Roosevelt, whose mass-mediated image au-
gured for better times.

THE FUTURISTIC MODE OF THE
MEDIATED VISION IN THE 1930S

A psychological barrier against the dominant problems of the Depression years was the mediated vision's inherent ability to look ahead as well as back to make the harrowing present more tolerable. Envisioning the promise of the future was greatly enhanced by the era's technological achievements. The year 1935, for example, was a watershed time when marvelous breakthroughs were announced in the areas of communications, automation, and what would become the electronics industry. Even though most of the new consumer products that appeared were unaffordable to many, seductive magazine advertising inspired readers to look ahead to the time when such coveted items as a Coldspot refrigerator and a modern-designed automobile would be theirs.

Mirroring the influence of aerodynamic design while shunning ornamentation, the 1934 Chrysler Airflow came closer than any model to depicting the car of the future. Significantly, modernist designers Raymond Loewy and Norman Bel Geddes's conceptualization of the streamlined look as the criterion of form and function suggested a futuristic milieu that extended to other areas of creative endeavor. Seemingly ignoring the economic problems of the present, such a vision connoted an idyllic future when all would be right with the world. That this outlook pervaded the times was attested to by the number of world's fairs that continued to celebrate the technological progress and cultural achievements of the modern era.

During 1933–34, the city of Chicago hosted another great fair to promote its centennial as a "Century of Progress." Purposely avoiding the realities of the Depression by epitomizing the spirit of modernity in its theme and overall building design, it drew over twenty million visitors. Promulgating its perception of the future as a golden age were such popular exhibits as designer George Keck's prefab-styled House of Tomorrow with its flat surfaced exterior and free-flowing interior, and the Wings of the Century exhibit, a history of transportation that culminated in the achievement of aviation as an apt symbol of America's faith in the progress of technology and the future opportunities afforded by it.[2]

Anticipating Walt Disney's revolutionary amusement park concept in the 1950s, the Chicago Midway showcased attractions like "The World a Million Years Ago," which featured mechanically operated prehistoric animals, and the "Enchanted Island," a fantasy land that appealed to both adults and children. An update of the 1893 Exposition's popular Ferris Wheel was the "Sky Ride" that transported passengers high above the fair's expanse. But to socially daring adults the most exciting concession was the "Streets of Paris," where they could revel in a nightclub atmosphere and view the notorious fan dance of Sally Rand. Her arrest for exhibiting too much of herself naturally helped popularize the act, and she returned in 1934 to present her even more risqué bubble dance. From its cultural venues to Sally Rand's shocking update of the 1893 fair's bellydance, the overall impact of the "Century of Progress Exposition was at once an escape from the trials of the Depression, an adult education center, a successful business venture, and a contributor to the development of modernist architecture."[3]

But the most heralded fair of the era was another optimistic monument to the future—the New York World's Fair of 1939–40. With its thematic emphasis on "Building the World of Tomorrow," the Fair's only ostensible link to the past was to commemorate the 150th anniversary of George Washington's inauguration as the country's first President. Like its San Francisco counterpart, the New York Fair was another in the tradition of the great expositions that proclaimed progress amid a fantasized milieu of spectacle and illusion. In its bold promotion of modernity through the streamlined look of its buildings and progress through the corporate efforts of industry and technology, the Fair staged one of its biggest attractions in General Motors's "Futurama" exhibit. Envisioning what the American landscape might look like in the 1960s, designer Norman Bel Geddes avoided any sign of urban problems to depict a society in which the automobile reigned, automatically transporting its passengers any place they desired on superhighways spread across the land.

The Fair's omnipresent trademark emblem—the combination seven hundred-foot tall Trylon and adjoining Perisphere—was more than just a symbolic tribute to high aspirations. The hollow Perisphere housed one of the Fair's most prophetic exhibits—a six-minute show in which visitors could view from a moving balcony a metropolis of the future called "Democracity." Purposely designed to cater to the mediated vision's perspective on the way things should be in an ideal world, this exhibit, like the others, tactfully ignored any signs of domestic or international issues.

Indeed, at the New York Fair the mundane present became the idealized future, for its structurally unified, modernist image came across as something of a "Futurama" in itself. By showcasing many of the wonders that technology had wrought, particularly television, the New York Fair functioned as a barometer of a still spreading, though sluggish, consumer economy and its promise of a brighter future. In drawing some thirty-three million visitors, it also persisted as a defiant beacon of hope in the face of the ominous threat of another world war.

In contrast to the fairs that celebrated progress and faith in the future were the monuments to the past that attracted multitudes of visitors. While John D. Rockefeller's money had financed the restoration of Colonial Williamsburg, the stubborn persistence of sculptor Gutzon Borglum resulted in the finished heads of George Washington, Thomas Jefferson, Abraham Lincoln, and Theodore Roosevelt carved out of the side of South Dakota's Mount

Rushmore. At the monument's dedication in 1941, President Roosevelt hailed it as a "shrine of democracy," a visual testimonial, like Williamsburg, to remind visitors of past achievements that made the American way of life possible.

The modernist architectural stylings that the Chicago and New York fairs promoted also characterized the most visible symbols of urban progress during the 1930s—the mushrooming skyscrapers of the larger cities like New York and Chicago. And in spite of the lack of investment money during the lean Depression years, American architecture realized one of its richest periods of creativity. Reacting to the spare, rectilinear look derived from Germany's Bauhaus school, New York's burgeoning skyline took on an ornamental Art Deco appearance with the completion of the Chrysler Building in 1930 and the world's tallest structure the following year—the 102–story Empire State Building. As proud symbols of American capitalism, these edifices also stood in paradoxical defiance of their economic system's most critical testing time.

In addition, the RCA Building, completed in 1932, thrust upward from the Rockefeller Center as a fitting monument to the nation's wealthiest family dynasty. Looking ahead to the urban mall, the Center's open plaza concept inaugurated the use of downtown public space to mix entertainment with consumerism, as the nearby Radio City Music Hall also opened in 1932. Billed as "The Showplace of the Nation," it boasted 5,900 seats for movie and stage productions that featured the precision dancing of the high-kicking Rockettes.

From a regional perspective, other unique architectural styles were also expressing themselves during this time. The explosive growth of Los Angeles and its environs, which included the Hollywood movie capitol, resulted in a type of commercial and residential structure known as California style, whose mix of Spanish and Oriental cultures reflected the American desire for a special identity of place. Thus novelist Nathanael West rightfully labeled this "mishmash of exotic styles" as the epitome of "escapist daydreams," conjuring up the dreamworld imagery of the movies.[4] Most representative of this era's preference for modernist design, though, was the Art Deco look that glamorized the commercial buildings, apartment houses, and theaters of Miami Beach.

MEDIATED LIFESTYLES AND POPULAR TASTE IN THE 1930s

Despite its generally less than well-off economic status, the family remained at the center of home life in the thirties, and instrumental in holding it together was a kind of communal culture redolent of the past. Accordingly, Gary Dean Best has noted that the time's "emphasis on home entertainment—whether radio, reading, games, puzzles, gardening, or others—and family 'togetherness' resembled the 1890s, and such fads of the 1930s as bicycle riding caused the bike paths and streets of towns and cities to resemble those of 40 years earlier."[5] Thus the simplest game that helped fill time or distracted the mind from more serious matters could capture the imagination. Families not only played cards, checkers, and dominos but also engaged in joint efforts to finish patience-trying jigsaw puzzles or compete in the marathon-length board game of *Monopoly* that Parker Brothers began marketing in 1935. In this popular game that had players transacting business deals with play money, the opportunity to acquire immense wealth was a welcome fantasy trip in the heart of the Depression. A more earthy diversion for the socially minded was the conviviality of the neighborhood tavern, which was enjoying new life after the repeal of Prohibition.[6] Generally, though, most people avoided the pitfalls of alcohol for the mediated pastimes of listening to the radio or the phonograph and going to the movies.

In contrast to the 1920s, hard times dictated generally conservative styles of dress for both men and women. For formal dress, males wore a double-breasted suit with the essential tie and fedora hat as the movie actors did. Women's fashions reacted to the androgynous look of the flapper by dropping hemlines and adapting the waistline to the natural flow of the feminine form. However, the economic duress of the times had a democratizing impact as the popularity of women's ready-to-wear fashions revealed. Featured in magazine ads and the Sears catalog, women's cultural models for the latest styles were Hollywood stars like Joan Crawford, Ginger Rogers, and Loretta Young, shown attired in the newest hats, dresses, and shoes. Beauty parlors, in responding to their customers' desire to emulate the hair style of a favorite star, capitalized on the permanent wave craze. Cosmetics were now seeing their most widespread use, as the products of Max Factor were into their greatest period of glamorizing the faces of movie stars. Thus, the distaff perspective of the mediated vision, in looking to a glamorous appearance as not only a fantasy experience but the key to romantic happiness, saw it as best achieved in adopting Hollywood standards of fashion and beauty.[7]

The most obvious influence of the modernist look on 1930s fashions was in bathing suit design. With the invention of a rubber-based fiber called Lastex, swimwear companies began producing what they called "swimsuits"—streamlined, form-fitting outfits that emphasized the natural curves of the body, particularly the female's. To promote their public acceptance, companies looked to such popular movie stars as Joan Blondell and Loretta Young to model them. Also George Petty's idealized artwork for Jantzen swimwear advertisements, which depicted physically well-endowed men and women wearing the latest modernized styles, was a big factor. By the 1940s, the ongoing democratization of swimming as a healthy, enjoyable experience had legitimized the seminude display of the body as socially acceptable.

Still, this more tolerant attitude aroused a degree of concern about the kind of social effects the new swimsuit styles would have on youth for whom they were mainly designed. The situation of encountering the opposite sex in such attire, which by the 1940s had become the most revealing in the nation's social history, was seen by the moralists as an open invitation to sexual experimentation. Sex, of course, was a subject that upright people did not openly talk about, though the economic consequences of supporting a large family had to be a factor in the practice of contraception to which the time's low birth rate attested, despite any moral edict against it. At such a critical time, when religious faith was thought highly essential to one's morals and morale, competition from radio, movies, and other diversions was contributing to a mediated lifestyle seemingly moving too fast for the Church to keep pace. As a result of the compromise between the material and the spiritual, the mediated vision was now looking increasingly to the escapist venues of mass culture to circumvent the pressing problems of the here and now.

With so many breadwinners jobless and the employment of youth at its lowest point (posing the choice of joining the CCC or taking to the road to find work), as well as two-thirds of the population earning less than fifteen hundred dollars a year, consumer spending was dedicated to the essential needs of food, clothes, and housing. The leading luxury item was cigarettes, with the cheap roll-your-own tobacco brands among the most popular, though in rural areas chewing tobacco and snuff still held sway. Indeed, the soothing power of nicotine had become even more of a widespread habit following the late 1920s' advertising campaign to make smoking socially acceptable for women. Because of the abundant items priced at five to ten cents, the 1930s has been fittingly labeled the "Nickel and Dime Decade."[8] Never again would the mediated vision see such cheap prices, a fact that in itself would contribute to the later nostalgic feel for a time that ironically is at once appallingly grim and curiously appealing.

THE PATRIOTIC MOOD OF THE MEDIATED CULTURE
DURING THE WAR YEARS

As late as 1939, when international conditions worsened after Hitler's invasion of Poland, America's involvement in another war seemed remote, especially when 70 percent of the people indicated they wanted no part of it. Although they kept indulging their favorite escapist habits of going to the movies and listening to the radio, their serenity had been undermined since the mid-1930s by the news heard over the air and seen in the weekly newsreels. By the early forties, radio was regularly broadcasting the latest war news, while newsreels projected graphic scenes of Germany's air raids on London and its submarine warfare's impact on Atlantic shipping. After such dire reportage, most felt gratefully relieved when a favorite program came on the air or a movie short featuring a popular comic flashed on the screen. To audiences these were escapist refuges from not only the problems of the immediate scene but the world at large.

It took the emotional shock of Japan's sneak attack on the naval base at Pearl Harbor in 1941 for the American people to realize that involvement in the war had been inevitable. As it had been in World War I, too, they discovered that before future dreams could be realized, the exigencies of the present had to be attended to. Thus, the rapid mobilization of a dormant military force into a mighty fighting machine, supported by an unparalleled show of industrial power, was representative of a collective desire to get the war over with as soon as possible. Key players in this goal, of course, were the military recruit and the defense worker.

An underlying motivation to the men who endured the drudgery and horrors of combat was the recurrent dream of returning to an even better world than the one they had left. To a large extent, the women awaiting their return were integral to realizing that idealized world. In the meantime, their sexual promise was symbolized in the erotically inspiring pinups of Betty Grable, Rita Hayworth, and the Varga Girl, as well as the romantic ballads troops heard over the Armed Forces Radio Service or sung live by the entertainers who comprised the war zone troupes of Bob Hope and Carole Landis.

In the long run, then, it was the concerted effort of the military forces and home front support that helped bring the war to an end by 1945. From 1942 to 1944, the city, that longtime lure to the mediated vision, was once again flooded with job seekers, mainly where work was readily available at defense plants, military bases, and shipyards. With eligible males gone to war, women took their places on the job and established the independent image of Rosie the Riveter as the latest version of Carrie Meeber. An ever-growing number of blacks, mostly from the South, also showed up in urban areas, where they found themselves enduring another form of segregation that compelled them to live in the ethnic neighborhoods of the large cities. The massive influx of newcomers resulted in severe housing shortages, and even though well-paying jobs generated more money to indulge in consumer buying, the strict rationing of essential items curtailed liberal spending. But most citizens were patriotic enough to comply with rationing edicts, realizing that such sacrifices could help bring about an early end to the war.[9]

As a visual medium of pointed advice and information, the stylized poster popped up everywhere, warning how loose talk could aid the Axis powers, urging the purchase of war bonds, and encouraging increased production at defense plants. While movie stars headed up bond rallies, either in film trailers or in live appearances, many of the most famous, such as Katharine Hepburn, Bette Davis, and Jane Wyman, entertained servicemen at places like

New York's Stagedoor Canteen and the Hollywood Canteen. At a time when the serviceman was the focal point of attention, even popular male stars like Henry Fonda, James Stewart, and Clark Gable volunteered for induction, as did well-known athletes, of which the most famous was heavyweight boxing champion Joe Louis, who willingly served in the time's segregated army. Women were recruited to do their bit, too, most visibly in the WACS (Army) and the WAVES (Navy). To the mediated vision, the call to duty was no respector of sex, race, or profession when it came to answering the nation's call to serve.

Indeed, old-time patriotism had returned in full force, reaffirming the posture that America and its allies represented the good that would win out over evil in the long run. Thus the mediated culture was geared to remind citizens of this end, not just in the movies but in the songs of Kate Smith, Bing Crosby, and the Andrews Sisters, whose music was heard throughout the land on the radio and the jukebox as well as through sheet music purchased for the rejuvenated parlor piano.

During this time, then, when the clash between good and evil forces was clear cut, patriotic-inspired toys abounded. The Shirley Temple doll that little girls of the 1930s cherished had now evolved into a variety of plastic dolls which were no less adored in their WAC or nurse's garb. While boys had been building model airplanes since the 1930s, they now welcomed the larger challenge of constructing models of both the allies' and enemies' planes from kits of precut balsa wood to stage their own mock aerial battles. Those less inclined to engage in such activity found satisfaction in playing war-theme board games or reading comic books that inspired the new hobby of collecting them, many of which featured a dynamic superhero like Captain America taking on Hitler and his spies.

Older youths now found themselves with more money than ever before by benefiting from the part-time job demand. Anticipating the social behavior of the postwar years, high school students began taking on a more independent and self-expressive air, buying recordings of the latest hit songs and dancing to them by a jukebox at their local soda shop hangout. As far as dress was concerned, they experimented with a code of casual informality that subscribed to their own conformist standards. But in reflecting the ongoing trend toward fashion as a personally expressive mode, such dress was an omen of revolutionary variations to come.

As far as the progress of the war was concerned, the years 1943–45 were an optimistic time, since the Axis powers were now forced into a defensive stand. The newsreel and magazine pictures of the D-Day landings at Normandy in June 1944 became etched in the memory of the mediated vision, in addition to a succession of memorable images along the advance toward Berlin, in particular, the liberation of Paris, the aerial bombardment of German cities, and the suicide of Adolph Hitler. Even the untimely death of Franklin Roosevelt and the appointment of the relatively unknown Vice President Harry Truman to succeed him could not deter the nation's resolve now, for the end of the war was in sight. However, when the ominous sight of a mushroom-shaped cloud clinched the close of hostilities with Japan, it also signaled the beginning of the Atomic Age and a new set of concerns for the future. Even though some fifty million people had died in the war, including those at Hiroshima and Nagasaki, the question looming now was what kind of monstrous threat to mankind did this new weapon of destruction pose. To the mediated vision, the promise of the postwar years suddenly seemed a lot less bright.

ESCAPING THE DEPRESSION AND CONFRONTING THE WAR YEARS VIA RADIO

That radio was a pervasive cultural force during 1930–45 was attested to by the diffusion of radio sets showing up in American homes. By 1931, two out of five households boasted radio ownership, a statistic that would keep rising. By this time, too, there was a decided shift to realizing the medium's capability for pure entertainment. And in reaching out to both urban residents and rural folk alike, radio, once it had the economic security of commercial sponsorship, became highly instrumental in nationalizing the mediated culture as well as fragmenting it by addressing special interests.[10]

Initially, complaints were voiced that the commercialism of advertising was too obtrusive, that it constituted an invasion of privacy in the home. Nevertheless, listeners soon accustomed themselves to their role as targeted consumers once they realized the rationale for advertising's support in providing them with free entertainment. By the 1930s, then, the corporate forces behind America's spreading habit of tuning in to its favorite programs had formulated the basic elements of network programming. And as a sign of its faith in radio's future, the National Broadcasting Company (NBC) moved into its prestigious Radio City headquarters at Rockefeller Center in 1933. The very next year it collaborated with the Columbia and Mutual Broadcasting Systems (CBS and MBS) to link up their 180 stations in a national broadcast of the World Series baseball championship, sponsored by the Ford Motor Company, who paid the then munificent sum of $100,000 for the broadcast rights.

By the mid-1930s the role of the corporate sponsor was well established, with many programs even named for the products that sponsored them, such as the *Kraft Music Hall* (cheese), the *Chase and Sanborn Hour* (coffee), and the *Lux Radio Theatre* (soap). As a result, the mediated vision was conditioned to equate a program's product with its featured star as, for example,

Jell-O was with Jack Benny, Kraft cheese with Bing Crosby, Pepsodent tooth-paste with Bob Hope, and, from a younger perspective, the breakfast cereal Ralston with cowboy star Tom Mix.

American Tobacco Company president George W. Hill capitalized on the power of radio advertising in a number of ways during this era, among them a campaign plugging Lucky Strike cigarettes as a diet aid. During the war years this brand also promoted its image by jumping on the patriotic band-wagon with the announcement that henceforth the color of its pack would be white because the green dye it had been using was essential to the war effort. Hence, the recurrent message, "Lucky Strike green has gone to war!" As re-flected in its mounting sales, this proved an effective kind of advertising, an-other sign that the age of mass media electronic advertising had become a persuasive force in American society. Through catchy product slogans, mu-sical jingles, and celebrity testimonials whose familiar voices lent them a kind of visual presence to the listening audience, corporate sponsors were able to manipulate the consumer desires of a materialistic society.

From the C. E. Hooper agency's rating system to that of A. C. Nielson, ra-dio also began experimenting during the 30s with ways to measure audience interest in its programming and function as a more reliable broker for the messages of consumerism. There was a real diversity of interests to measure, too, as programming ranged from music, news, and daytime serials to the likes of former vaudeville entertainers, current stage personalities, and even movie stars in "live" evening broadcasts for just the cost of electricity to run a radio. Although some programs would endure into the postwar years, most would die out long before, casualties of the mediated vision's evolving out-look as it was being subjected to societal change.

The most appealing genre, during a time when laughter had an essential therapeutic function, was the comedy-variety show. Some of the earlist fea-tured former vaudeville performers like Ed Wynn (*Texaco Fire Chief* pro-gram) and Eddie Cantor *(Chase and Sanborn Hour)*. Starting out on their own program in 1933, the former vaudeville team of George Burns and Gracie Allen would become one of the most popular husband-wife comedy teams in the history of media culture. Reprising their vaudeville routine, which fo-cused on straight man George's bemused reaction to Gracie's zany logic, they capitalized on a brand of verbal humor that would also engage movie and tel-evision audiences over the years.

Fred Allen, who first appeared on radio in 1932, displayed a penchant for acerbic wit of a topical nature that reached its peak in the 1940s. In doing most of the writing for his show, he was not averse to satirizing the system that had made him what he was, bringing down the wrath of his sponsors on occasion. But Allen's satirical kind of humor was a sign of things to come in a more liberal time. One of the comic highlights of his show was the crossover "feud" he carried on with Jack Benny, who returned the favor in his own show.

Among the top-ranked shows for years, Benny's program built its humor around the interaction of character and incident, with much of it based on the Benny character's personal frustrations and idiosyncrasies, particularly his miserly ways, and his cast's reactions to them. Of the cast, Eddie Anderson, as Benny's black valet, "Rochester," played a unique role in breaking the time's racial stereotype by often upstaging his boss.

Another of the era's most popular comedy shows starred a wooden dummy named Charlie McCarthy, whose dueling dialogue with his ventriloquist master Edgar Bergen and the show's celebrity guests contributed to the show's comic highlights, among them the irreverent repartee between Charlie and W. C. Fields and Mae West. No matter the situation, though, Bergen usually allowed his brash dummy to get the better of his human associates and spark a fresh, occasionally suggestive kind of humor for its times.

As the movie/radio fan magazines revealed, an interdependent relationship between radio and the movies developed during this time, allowing many radio stars to find further fame in the movies. In 1932, Paramount's *The Big Broadcast* became the first big film to feature radio stars like Bing Crosby, Kate Smith, and the Mills Brothers. The trend peaked with *The Big Broadcast of 1938,* which spotlighted the radio identity of Bob Hope along with movie comedy star W. C. Fields. The power of radio as a star-maker was clearly evidenced in the push it gave to the entertainment careers of Crosby and Hope, both better known in the 1930s as radio performers than movie stars. Their ongoing comical radio feud led to their teaming up in *The Road to Singapore* (1940), the first of Paramount's long-running "Road" series.

To many, the most popular radio format of the era was the situation comedy series with its set cast of characters that listeners came to know and love. Undoubtedly, the most appealing program in the genre was the ground-breaking *Amos 'n' Andy* show, which had started out on a Chicago station in 1926. After its lead performers signed with NBC in 1929, it began to attract national attention as listeners tuned in to its weekday early evening time slot to catch the latest hilarious episode of two naive black men trying to make a go of it in the big city. Although the comic dialect that white actors Freeman Gosden and Charles Correll affected in the old blackface minstrel style resonated with racial overtones, the show's widespread appeal transcended most criticism at the time. Listeners, no matter their ethnic background or social class, seemed to identify with the title characters' problems in plots that reinforced the mediated vision's attraction to the theme of natural innocence tested by urban chicanery.[11]

As small-town life was a naturally appealing radio milieu to the mediated vision, one of the most listened-to programs that celebrated it was *Fibber McGee and Molly,* which started airing in 1935. The serenity of the title characters' household at seventy-nine Wistful Vista was always undermined by the weekly visitations of an assortment of neighbors whose zany personali-

Radio and the movies' symbiotic relationship resulted in films that featured the stars of both media forms, as in Paramount's *The Big Broadcast of 1938*. But radio stars Bob Hope and Bing Crosby went on to greater fame in films. Author's collection.

ties and Fibber McGee's reaction to them accounted for much of the program's humor. Clearly, the only sensible person in this show's lineup of eccentric characters was Fibber's wife Molly, who revealed herself as not only in control of her household but her wits as well. Each week listeners tuned in, anticipating the comic repercussions of Molly's role as well as Fibber's ritual of opening the hall closet to retrieve an item, only to forget that it had been packed to overflowing for years. The ensuing deluge, which always drew the program's biggest laugh, was a classic example of radio sound effects' integral role in visual stimulation.[12]

That radio had now become a medium catering to audiences and age groups with special interests was exemplified by the daytime serials tailored for women and the after-school adventure series for children. Because the former were sponsored in the main by detergent companies, they assumed the label of "soap operas," and with a natural audience of housewives looking to alleviate the dullness of their household routines, the soaps quickly became a mass listening habit, proliferating into daily fifteen-minute formats. Emotionally enhanced by organ-played themes, melodramatic plots were structured around the basic women's concerns of romance and family life, and among the more popular programs whose titles suggested their subject matter were *The Romance of Helen Trent, When a Girl Marries,* and *Portia Faces Life.* With their emphasis on how their characters deal with the problems of day-to-day living, either through bold determination or stoic endurance, these programs' heroines, in their struggle for a better day, actually served as role models for many listeners.[13]

As early as 1930, writer-director Nila Mack produced a Saturday morning radio program for children known as *Let's Pretend.* Dramatizing classic fairy tales, this series enjoyed a popularity that lasted until the 1950s when television programming for children began to dominate. But in the late afternoons of the 1930s and early 40s, it was the daily fifteen-minute serials that lured school kids home to hear the latest episodes of their favorite heroes, many of which were based on popular comic strip characters such as Buck Rogers and Dick Tracy. Also commanding attention were original characters like Jack Armstrong, the "All-American Boy," sponsored by Wheaties, one of the many breakfast cereals that pioneered the sponsorship of juvenile radio programming. A Western original featured the mysterious masked figure of the Lone Ranger, who, after starting out in 1933, found renewed life from 1941 to 1955 promoting Cheerios cereal. Though these action-packed stories were marked by plenty of violence, most parents overlooked it, viewing them as a way to keep their children home and away from any kind of trouble. So youths kept listening and responding to premium invitations to send in box tops of a sponsoring cereal like Ralston Wheat Chex for an autographed picture of Tom Mix or seals from Ovaltine food-drink for Captain Midnight's decoder badge.

The essential ingredient that made radio drama appealing to both child and adult was the effective use of realistic sound effects, inducing listeners to visualize what they heard. In aspiring to a visual medium, radio ironically countered the movies' visually direct manner that left little to the imagination. Prime examples of this dramatic intent were the eerie sound effects for such popular thriller series as *The Shadow* and *Inner Sanctum* and those that enhanced the aura of reality-based crime drama like *Gang Busters.*

In 1938, a radio production that ominously demonstrated radio's power to stimulate the visual imagination was Orson Welles's dramatization of H. G. Wells's science fiction novel *The War of the Worlds* on the *Mercury Theater.* In fact, listeners who tuned in late mistook the program for actual news coverage of Martians invading Earth. With news broadcasts sensitizing the American public to the immediacy and threat of involvement in another war, it was only natural that Welles's fictional radio drama seemed too real to jittery listeners at the time, causing widespread panic. While many of them thought the world as they knew it had come to an end, in a figurative sense it was actually about to, for the war that was descending upon the nation would irrevocably transform the communal focus of the mediated vision that had pervaded the culture for some fifty years.

By the early 1940s, foreign correspondents such as Howard K. Smith, Eric Sevareid, and Edward R. Murrow were inventing broadcast journalism by directly reporting the advances of the German war machine, while their home front counterparts H. V. Kaltenborn, Gabriel Heatter, and Lowell Thomas were analyzing the upshot of the disturbing reports from overseas.[14] Also, the radio version of *The March of Time*'s dramatic approach to news commentary added a new dimension to the documentary format. Yet, despite all the war talk's pervasive air of uncertainty, radio news reports helped forge a nation-wide sense of community, functioning in effect as a psychological buffer against the negative impact of such talk.

But radio's capability to initiate on-the-spot reportage and provide expert commentary on the controversial sides of current issues and concerns fomented a heated rivalry between it and newspaper journalism. In such live programs as *America's Town Meeting of the Air* and *American Forum of the Air,* radio appeared to be superseding the newspaper as far as updated commentary on current events was concerned. During election years, too, listeners were given the opportunity to hear the actual voices of candidates to evaluate their leadership capabilities. In the area of breaking news, reporters responded with either on-site or quick followup coverage of such momentous events as the trial of the culprit in the kidnap/murder of the Lindbergh baby in 1935, the assassination of political demagogue Huey Long that same year, and the fiery crash of the zeppelin *Hindenberg* in 1937. On a lighter side, significant sporting venues such as championship boxing matches, baseball games, horse racing, and big-game football matchups were accorded colorful, even occasionally concocted, descriptions by announcers Ted Husing, Don Dunphy, Clem McCarthy, and Bill Stern. Radio also afforded Walter Winchell the opportunity to develop his tabloid style of journalism and fashion a long-time career out of the mediated vision's fascination with celebrity and Hollywood gossip. By the 1940s, then, radio had become the newspaper in its aural form but one with a more direct impact by drawing the listener into the mental process of "seeing" what was programmed.

But with radio now largely an entertainment medium, the airwaves were awash with such venues as talent and quiz shows. While the talent show kindled listeners' interest in a contestant's quest for fame and fortune, the quiz show offered a contestant the promise to win money and a listener the chance to foster a vicarious sense of self-pride in answering questions that contestants failed to. Thus, *Take It Or Leave It* became so popular that its "Sixty-four Dollar Question" contributed a new phrase to the American language. In making the most of radio as a fertile proving ground for television programming, both the talent and quiz show formats would remain favorites of the mediated vision. In his sociocultural study of radio's heyday, J. Fred MacDonald states that these kinds of shows with their emphasis on self-reliance to succeed "were fully compatible with American social values. . . . At a time when unemployment, economic sluggishness, and governmental experimentation diminished popular faith in the American system, these radio programs reaffirmed social premises."[15]

A major cultural accomplishment of radio during this era was the large number of programs that contributed to the development of a mediated culture tempered by elitist standards and a narrowing of the divide between the elite and the popular cultures. In the classroom, children listened to *The American School of the Air*, learning of important events from history through their dramatization, and the glories of classical music through its rendition. For adults, in addition to being challenged to think for themselves by the various radio forums of the time, there were adaptations of classic drama and fiction by such authors as Shakespeare, Henrik Ibsen, and Leo Tolstoy, as well as the productions of talented scriptwriters Norman Corwin and Arch Oboler. In addition, CBS's "theater of the mind," the *Columbia Workshop*, which aired for the first time in 1936, dramatized the works of reputable contemporary authors, demonstrating how the radio medium could function in an artistic as well as escapist dimension.

However, music, which had been a big part of radio's offerings from the beginning, still attracted more listeners than any other programming. And in accommodating the special interests of its audience, radio helped foster an appreciation for listening to classical as well as popular music. Accordingly, Milton Cross, the knowledgeable voice of the Saturday afternoon Metropolitan Opera broadcasts during these years, introduced the art of operatic drama to high and low alike. Of the latter group he once declared that they were, in the main, "plain, average, American 'folks,' who have never attended an operatic performance . . . but who have made acquaintance with it and come to love it entirely through radio."[16] In 1937 NBC's *Symphony of the Air* was organized, and under the masterful direction of Arturo Toscanini, the symphonies of Beethoven as well as the works of many other composers were aired to the general public. By offering its listeners a choice between classical and popular music, radio now functioned as a viable democratizing agent of the mediated culture. But there was another newer, more audacious kind of music that radio was attending to at this time, a musical style that would become a classic itself of American culture—the Big Band sound of Swing music.

THE SYMBIOSIS OF BROADCAST MUSIC AND THE RECORDING INDUSTRY

Hurt by both radio and the Depression, the recording industry suffered a decline it would not recover from until the end of the 1930s. As a natural outlet for listening to music, radio had surpassed the phonograph as the more practical, certainly cheaper, source for musical entertainment. But various technical innovations helped rescue recorded music and create a resurgence of interest in it. While the automatic record changer/turntable provided a more efficient way to play records, the amplification of electronic sound enhanced their reproduction. It also made the jukebox a popular source of public entertainment. With the repeal of Prohibition it began to show up in bars, diners, and hotel lounges so that by 1941 the colorfully embellished Wurlitzer model was a standard fixture. Supplying it with the latest hits also helped pull recording companies out of the economic doldrums, as customers who invested their nickels for plays had a range of choices from Tin Pan Alley songs to the less reputable race and hillbilly music popular in taverns and roadhouses. But the most momentous impetus to reviving the recording industry came from the radio appearances of the Big Bands whose distinct sound would have a significant influence on the mediated culture of this era.

Music historian Donald Clarke has commented that "the history of modern popular music may be seen as the repeated rescuing of a moribund scene by the music of African Americans."[17] And in the thirties radio played a key role in this process by promoting the visionary jazz of Duke Ellington's modernist compositions and Louis Armstrong's inimitable improvisational ability as a trumpet soloist, to name only two black talents who anticipated the development of Big Band music. But it was the white bands who, in absorbing the influences of black-styled jazz, were in a more socially advantageous position to introduce any new breakthrough to the larger society.

Accordingly, Benny Goodman's band, which had achieved something of a national reputation via a radio program called *Let's Dance,* inauspiciously kicked off the Swing era in 1935. Booked at the Palomar Ballroom in Los Angeles at the end of an unsuccessful tour, Goodman made a daring decision when he had his band perform some Fletcher Henderson arrangements before a subdued audience of young dancers. Surprisingly, they responded in such positive fashion that the future of dance band music was revolutionized on the spot. By incorporating black arranger Henderson's emphasis on the interplay between the brass and reed sections to produce a rhythmic dance beat, Goodman, along with his trademark clarinet playing, established Swing's unique sound that adapted African American style to white tastes. Indeed, white musicians discovered that specialized arrangements in the black music tradition could turn even the most formulaic Tin Pan Alley tune into a fresh listening or dancing experience. Thus, the cross fertilization of black and white music to produce Swing charged ballroom dancing with a kind of visual energy it had never known before. Ranging from the sweet sound of Guy Lombardo's band that older listeners preferred to the youth-directed hot stylings of Goodman and many others of his ilk, each band went its own way in producing the Big Band sound. Though Swing had its detractors, the near hypnotic appeal of both the Big Band's improvisational style and the romantic/inspirational moods of its vocal music offered its devotees escapist release not only through dancing but listening.[18]

The new physicality of expression also showed up in the dynamic solo styles of both black and white band performers. Improvisational jazz, in fact, generated a number of small-group bands, such as those of Goodman, Fats Waller, Lionel Hampton, and Artie Shaw, enabling individual performers to display their talent. That racial barriers were slowly breaking down was evident in the participation of black performers in previously all-white ensembles. Goodman had even featured a young black female vocalist named Billie Holiday in some early recordings. To lend a more personalized dimension to their instrumental focus, the Big Bands began to spotlight vocal stylists like Ella Fitzgerald and Frank Sinatra, as well as close-harmonizing groups like the Pied Pipers and the Modernaires.

With numerous bands keeping hotel ballroom dates on late-night radio, the airwaves became a listening and dancing boon to the country's youth as well as young-at-heart older people looking to renew the happy-go-lucky mood of the 1920s. Whether predominantly white or black, Swing music's popularity was spread by name bands like those of the Dorsey brothers (Jimmy and Tommy), Harry James, Artie Shaw, Woody Herman, and Count Basie, who were among the many playing various venues. Despite their critics, who saw in their stylings a lowering of musical taste, many listeners were first introduced to classical music by the bands who adapted the public domain work of famous composers to modernized treatments, as in the themes from Tschaikovsky's Second Piano Concerto and the Fifth Symphony. In 1938, Benny Goodman championed the cause of his music when he performed in concert at the venerable Carnegie Hall.

As would be expected during this time, the Arthur Murray dance studios were kept busy teaching the intricacies of the new dance steps whose visual kind of expression ranged from the Big Apple to the exotic styles of Latin America. Also coming on the scene were the impromptu acrobatic gyrations of jitterbugging that certain Swing numbers compelled those impulsive or "high" enough to perform. By this time, New York's Roseland and Savoy ballrooms had become popular centers for showcasing the jitterbug craze as well as the radical fashion of the "zoot suit" some daring males wore to complement this dance style's manic aura.

For the era's song hits, vocalists and their bands were indebted to the established songwriters and composers who were still around in the early forties. But younger ones were making names for themselves, too, in particular Johnny Mercer, Frank Loesser, and Jule Styne, who with lyricist Sammy Cahn turned out some of the vintage songs of the war years. Such songs were made to order for soloists like Bob Eberly and Helen O'Connell, whose voices resulted in an ideal blending of instrumental and vocal expression in the Jimmy Dorsey band. But another such vocalist with Tommy Dorsey would go on to greater heights in the entertainment field.

Like his predecessor Bing Crosby, Frank Sinatra demonstrated a special ability to meet the challenge of the microphone and make a song uniquely his own. Indeed, he displayed a natural, yet sophisticated singing style that merged the romantic ballad artlessly with the Big Band sound. Though Sinatra had been making radio appearances on *Your Hit Parade*, a weekly ratings show of the nation's top songs, the hysterical reaction of a schoolgirl audience to his first concert at New York's Paramount Theater in 1944 helped make him a media icon, marking the first time a popular singer had generated such an on-site emotional reaction. It was an omen of things soon to come in the youth sector of the mediated culture.

If Sinatra's singing and the Swing stylings of the Dorsey brothers brought popular music to a new level of sophistication in the eyes of the mediated vision, the counter play of the Glenn Miller band's brass and reed sections, beginning in 1939, gave the war years their most distinctive musical sound. In both its aural and visual appeal to listeners and dancers, Miller's signature sound would become integral to the nostalgic recall of that time, conjuring up memories of an era when music was a key factor in maintaining the nation's morale, from the hot, jazzy energy of "Chattanooga Choo-Choo"—the first million-dollar recording, made in 1941—to the rhythmic cadences of "In the Mood" and the sweet, slow-dance style of "Moonlight Serenade."

By 1945, the impact of jazz on the Big Band sound had influenced American popular music to the extent that it was leading the mediated culture toward other musical frontiers, particularly that referred to as Progressive jazz. Throughout the 1930s Duke Ellington had been composing experimental pieces that equated musical sounds with emotional states or moods, as his prototypal "Mood Indigo" expressed in 1930. It was a kind of visualized sound that related musical themes to color, just as the titles of many of Ellington's later compositions suggested. The sophisticated artistry of his music, in its elitist approach to elevating a mass-oriented form, came to be regarded in such high esteem that in 1943 his band presented a concert in Carnegie Hall.

By this time, though, such talented individual performers as pianist Thelonious Monk, trumpeter Dizzy Gillespie, and saxophonist Charlie Parker were reacting to the regimentation of the Swing band through a highly improvisational style of musical performance that came to be known as Bebop, or Bop. From the toe-tapping jazz renditions of the 1920s, through the Swing music era of the 1930s and 40s, to the beginnings of Progressive jazz, the mediated vision had witnessed jazz-inspired music evolve toward a greater focus on the individual performer's expressive interpretations within a group. It was a foreshadowing of the self-promotional performances of the 1950s' rock bands.

Although Swing music dominated the era, other musical sounds were making themselves heard, too. As the war years demanded closer political ties with the nation's neighbors to the south, an upshot of this relationship was the cultural infiltration of their exotic dance rhythms, such as the samba, a variation of the earlier rumba style. Beyond the escapist milieu of ballroom dancing lay the darker world of social and labor unrest that had sprung up in the 1930s. To bring attention to the plight of the poor and the dispossessed, as well as to inspire hope, balladeer Woody Guthrie's singing and guitar playing dwelled on both protest and plaintive personal experience in the folk ballad tradition. Paralleling this kind of expression was the country music of the Southern mountain region, which continued to gain widespread popularity in the 1930s after radio reached out to areas beyond the rural. Both the *National Barn Dance,* broadcasting over Chicago's WLS, and the *Grand Ole Opry,* over Nashville's WSM, utilized their powerful night signals to spread the sounds of country music. Fittingly, the South's sense of apartness, despite its poverty, illiteracy, racism, and religious fundamentalism, provided the inspirational background for its music's natural manner of expressing the lonely sound of rural isolation. While the fiddle and guitar were the instruments of choice for old-time country music performers, the banjo and mandolin forged an indigenous style of playing soon to be promoted as Kentucky "bluegrass." Although it would grow more sophisticated over the years, country music, from the honky-tonk songs of Hank Williams and Ernest Tubb to the mellow voice of Eddy Arnold, never lost sight of its basic roots in the rural culture of the American South.[19]

In contrast to the country singer as a disenchanted loner who endures problems in romance, marriage, and life in general by emoting about them, western-styled music, popularized in the main by the movies' "Singing Cowboy" roles of Gene Autry and Roy Rogers, formulated a more positive outlook inspired by romance and the West's natural scene. The hybrid music of country/western also invited experimentation, as the close-knit vocal harmony of the Sons of the Pioneers and Swing's influence on the flamboyant manner of Bob Wills's Texas Playboys revealed.

The breakthroughs in communications technology, which played such an integral role in the development of radio and recorded music and the ensuing popularity of their performers, were major factors in the democratization of American culture and its influence on the mediated vision. But another, even more marvelous electronic triumph was waiting in the wings. Although static-free Frequency Modulation (FM) radio was demonstrating its potential in the 1930s, its implementation was reserved for a later day, as RCA was showing a greater interest in television. In fact, had it not been for the intervention of World War II, television would have become the much earlier reality that the New York World's Fair had promised.

MOVIES: THE GREAT ESCAPE IN THE DEPRESSION AND THE WAR YEARS

During the Depression, the most popular medium of entertainment regularly seeking to procure what little money Americans had was the movies. After a decline in attendance in the early 1930s, the film industry began to enjoy a steady upturn in business that continued on through the war years. Undoubtedly, the improved quality of sound movies produced from 1934 on, along with their mass media promotion, was hard for the public to resist investing in a few hours of escapist entertainment. Ironically, many films released in the early thirties were not nearly as inspirational as one would expect for such desperate times. In an era when the murderous, bank-robbing sprees of John Dillinger and the team of Bonnie Parker and Clyde Barrow received extensive media coverage, Hollywood found an abundance of source material from which to create films that responded to the public's fascination with the criminal mind. Accordingly, a veritable parade of such movies as *Little Caesar, The Public Enemy,* and *Scarface* lured fans into theaters, mainly for the sensational content their advertising promised. The criminal's lifestyle also provided many moviegoers a way to fantasize their frustrated dreams of material success through the inverted ambition of the gangsters portrayed by Edward G. Robinson and James Cagney.

Reactions to the Production Code of 1930

To establish a moral philosophy that the moviemakers would presumably adhere to, the Hays Office promulgated the Production Code of 1930, whose guidelines operated on the general principle that "No picture shall be produced which will lower the moral standards of those who see it."[20] Because of the resultant conflict between dramatizing life as it is and as the Code wanted it to be, production problems soon developed. Although an advertising code was also enacted at the time to regulate the language and pictorial content of posters and other promotional material, most movie advertising continued to be blatantly sensational, as it sought to justify the studios' intent of promoting entertainment rather than morality. In the Code's zealous quest to rid the screen of undesirable elements, other forces were recruited to support it—in particular the appointment in 1934 of a tough, uncompromising enforcer in Joseph Breen and the watchdog role of national religious organizations such as the Catholic Church's Legion of Decency. And because the crime film subverted the success ethic that the culture idealized, the censors reinforced their mission of condemning the rewards of deviant behavior. So like their real-life counterparts, movie protagonists of criminal bent often met with a violent end, either by a hail of police gunfire or a prison execution. Though censors justified such endings as well-deserved and necessary comeuppances, an unfounded fear of theirs was that the movies' graphic portrayal of violence would be conducive to violent behavior in real life. As genres other than the gangster film also came across more realistically through the enhancement of sound, the problem of violence in the movies escalated to an alarming extent. Naturally, dialogue became a major factor in enhancing realism as censors now had to monitor any offensive indiscretions of speech that a script assigned an actor.[21]

As the leader in the production of crime and social problem films, the Warner Brothers studio was also a leading offender of the Code. Drawing much of its source material from the reportage of current newspapers and nonfiction exposés, Warners produced films like *I Was a Fugitive from a Chain Gang* (1932), an indictment of prison conditions in the South based on a true-life experience. By not only depicting the American justice system from a negative perspective but showing the criminal in an heroic light, this film created problems for the censors by suggesting that the criminal behavior of its central figure was attributable to a corrupt system.[22]

When J. Edgar Hoover of the Federal Bureau of Investigation (FBI) introduced his scientifically trained government policemen known popularly as G-Men, the Warners studio found a way out of its problems with crime films, while the mediated culture acquired another heroic figure to mythologize.

Even though intensely violent situations of rampant gunplay still persisted in a film like *G-Men* (1935), the fact that the G-Men came out on top in the end helped placate the censors.

When presented in the appropriate context, then, violence epitomized the heroic virtue of manliness in righting a wrong. Sex, on the other hand, presented an altogether different problem to justify. And with the coming of the Production Code, the censors were more sensitive than ever to the role of woman as sex symbol. In 1933, Warners's production of *Baby Face* confronted a moral issue similar to that Theodore Dreiser had encountered in 1900 with *Sister Carrie:* how to morally justify a woman's rise in the world at the expense of the men around her. This situation was openly exploited in the roles of Hollywood's first female sex symbols of the sound era—Jean Harlow and Mae West. After displaying her star quality in Howard Hughes's production of *Hell's Angels* (1930), Harlow began to capitalize on her sexuality in *Red-Headed Woman* and *Red Dust* (both 1932). While Jean Harlow was a product of the Hollywood promotional system up to her untimely death in 1937, Mae West, in flaunting her sexual image throughout her film career, was more the result of her own personal methods. In *She Done Him Wrong* (1933), the film version of her Broadway production *Diamond Lil,* West demonstrated in her special way how a woman's sexual role is a kind of game in which she ultimately holds the upper hand. The dialogue she wrote for this and other films like *I'm No Angel* (1933) and *Belle of the Nineties* (1934) was filled with sexual innuendos that were enhanced by her provocative mannerisms. In countering the conventional social role of woman in both film and real life, Mae West was a brazen symbol of moral turpitude to the censors, obviously delighting in challenging the rules of the Code. Nevertheless, because of the roles she and Jean Harlow portrayed in the 1930s, the mediated vision began to take a more tolerant view toward women as moral transgressors in the movies.

Even though the Production Code barred the "justification of adultery" and suggestions of "sex perversions," among other forms and signs of deviant social behavior, the moviemakers found loopholes to exploit.[23] Ultimately, some scriptwriters and directors even resorted to literary symbolism and allusion that left a plot's moral concerns or problems up to the audience's imagination. But by the late 30s, real-life issues were becoming too pervasive to be avoided, foreshadowing the time when all the edicts of the Code would be violated.

Also portending this trend were the independent theaters, which by not belonging to the studio chains, were free to exhibit exploitation ("Adults Only") films lacking the Code's sanction. Even though urban movie houses on the so-called "grindhouse" circuit were subject to being closed down, they skirted most problems by promoting cheaply made "educational" films like

She Done Him Wrong (Paramount, 1933) centered on the flamboyant sex appeal of Mae West to attract moviegoers. Author's collection.

Independently made "Adults Only" exploitation films like *The Burning Question*, or *Reefer Madness* (1938), may have avoided the censors' mandates, but they hardly ever lived up to their wild promotional tactics. Author's collection.

The Birth of a Baby (1938), forerunner of the 1940s' sex hygiene sensation *Mom and Dad.* Although any illicit topic was considered fair game as subject matter, titillating titles like *Girls of the Street* (1935) and *Reefer Madness* (1938) promised much but delivered little as naive patrons were often taken in by these films' sensationalized publicity. The real thing was reserved for the underground pornographic or "stag" movies that offered the explicit sexual activity their ambiguous titles suggested.[24]

The mainstream movies' growing liberal approach to fantasized sex was manifested in the publicity accorded Jane Russell's role in Howard Hughes's overrated Western *The Outlaw.* Originally scheduled for earlier release, it was held up for three years by Hughes's stubborn battle with Joe Breen concerning the overt display of Russell's cleavage. When it finally appeared in 1943, *The Outlaw*'s attendant notoriety naturally attracted curious audiences everywhere it was shown.

Now, with the Code's mission weakening, the movie studios were looking to justify sexual situations and questionable language that mainstream fiction and the theater had gotten by with for years. In 1939 Clark Gable had actually uttered "damn" at the end of *Gone with the Wind,* and the first half of the forties saw grippingly realistic films like *Double Indemnity* (1944) and *Mildred Pierce* (1945) appear. In subverting the innocent world the Code had strived to preserve, they offered the mediated vision a compelling kind of entertainment by focusing on the aberrant behavior and personal problems of their main characters.

Ironically, the horror genre, despite its inherent equation of sex and violence, fared fairly well with the censors. The Universal studio's monster cycle, featuring the Mummy, Dracula, and Frankenstein characters, spawned fantasized sequels throughout the 1930s and into the 40s in which the curse of a revived Egyptian mummy, vampirism, and the Frankenstein monster's rampages implied that sex was elemental to their violent plots. In the first sound remake of *Dr. Jekyll and Mr. Hyde* (1932), sex took on a more degenerate air in Frederic March's portrayal of a respected doctor as a sexual predator, a role reprised by Spencer Tracy in 1941. However, some scenes in *King Kong* (1933) dealing with the giant ape's sexual play with a captive Fay Wray were later excised. When the classic Universal films fragmented into vapid sequels that parodied the earlier versions, RKO responded with what seemed to be a new approach to horror. Ironically, it was as old as the dramatic experience itself in intimating that what happens off stage can be more terrifying in a psychological sense than what occurs on. Thus, in *Cat People* (1942) and other films of the early forties director Jacques Tourneur centered on the basic fears of the unknown to evoke an ominous mood of horror that kept his films in the good graces of the censors as well as audiences.

COMIC AND SERIOUS REACTIONS TO THE TIMES

If the movies that centered around sex, violence, and horror emanated from the perception of a social order that needed righting, the films of the Marx Brothers were based on an antic kind of humor that suggested the only way to put up with an absurd, chaotic world was to laugh at it. And in transitioning their zany vaudeville escapades from the Broadway stage to the movie screen, hardly anything dear to the social order escaped the merciless wit of the Marxes. After the popular reception of their first two films, *The Cocoanuts* (1929) and *Animal Crackers* (1930), which were direct transcriptions of the musical comedy versions, Paramount provided original scripts for the iconoclastic characters of Groucho, Chico, Harpo, and, to a lesser degree, Zeppo. The result was the classic film comedies—*Monkey Business* (1931), *Horse Feathers* (1932), and *Duck Soup* (1933)—in which they targeted such diverse topics as the lifestyle of the upper class, the collegiate educational system, and the spread of Fascism. In 1935 the Brothers took their brand of comic lunacy to Metro-Goldwyn-Mayer for what many consider their best film, *A Night at the Opera*, highlighted by its madcap stateroom scene. Though their final four films appeared in the 1940s, the heyday of the Marx Brothers was the 1930s, when their unique way of undercutting conventional social behavior helped moviegoers escape the time's anxieties through laughter.

While the Marxes teamed up to poke fun at sacred cows and human foibles, the irascible, misanthropic posture of W. C. Fields represented a one-man foray against such an honored social idol as family life, as well as mores in general. After beginning his film career in the silent era, the advent of sound afforded Fields the opportunity to merge voice and manner in his peculiar way of intoning the vitriolic comments and asides that became his trademark. In his most characteristic films—*You Can't Cheat an Honest Man* (1939), *The Bank Dick* (1940), and *Never Give a Sucker an Even Break* (1941)—he either won over or turned off audiences through his encounters with an indifferent society's onslaughts on his personal sense of dignity. Regardless, the Fields persona, in its inimitable way, enabled many moviegoers to laugh at a man who, in enduring his daily frustrations and putdowns, always remained his own man.

A more sophisticated comedy style had begun to appear in the 1930s that took a uniquely different approach to interpreting societal behavior.[25] Directors Ernst Lubitsch's *Design for Living* (1933) and Frank Capra's *It Happened One Night*, 1934's Academy Award winner as best picture, established the screwball comedy models for the sound era. In structuring its comic vision around the romantic problems of the well-to-do, whether single, married, or about to be, this genre's involved plot was an intriguing viewing experience for economically stressed moviegoers who undoubtedly derived considerable satisfaction laughing at the improbable yet human escapades of beleaguered rich people in such films as *My Man Godfrey* (1936) and *The Philadelphia Story* (1940). Then, too, it was in the wild social behavior of the screwball comedy's characters that moviegoers saw the visual embodiment of their own escapist dreams.

However, Frank Capra went on to fashion a filmic vision seemingly designed to inform moviegoers of real issues common to the Depression years that screwball comedy necessarily avoided. In such films as *Mr. Deeds Goes to Town* (1936), *Mr. Smith Goes to Washington* (1939), and *Meet John Doe* (1941) he projected serious messages about the American experience in highly entertaining ways. In fact, these films were sufficiently liked to be praised by both critics and audiences. Essentially, they tell the same story about the need to recover the lost verities of the past or the worth of communal solidarity to counter the exploitation of the little man by those in power. By this time, too, the Depression had demythologized the urban myth of the city as a place of promise and self-fulfillment, creating an acute awareness of the wide gulf between the haves and the have-nots. Through idealized protagonists whose personal conflicts reflect problems arising from this division, these films functioned as modern-day morality plays. In their basic message, then, Capra sought to bring the antithetical elements of small-town/rural and big city interests together in a new understanding of how the American system should work. Although his populist heroes, forcefully portrayed by Gary Cooper and James Stewart, were intended to personify this message, some critics attacked it as much too sentimental and overly idealized. But a rejuvenation of ideals was precisely Capra's intent, hopefully to remind audiences of the need to reaffirm what he perceived as the nation's fading sense of traditional values.

THE HEYDAY OF THE MUSICAL AND OTHER DEVELOPMENTS

Because the sociopolitical realities of 1930–45 were too formidable to be avoided in the movies, the advent of sound saw the all-singing, all-dancing musical become the most escapist genre of the era. In fact, these years were Hollywood's most prolific in creating the fantasized viewing experience that only the visual/aural combination of image and music could generate. Since a script with a solid plot was usually secondary to a musical's score, numerous teams of reputable composers and lyricists were lured to Hollywood to meet the demand for new songs. They, as well as the marquee names of Berlin, Gershwin, Kern, Porter, and Rodgers, produced many of the movie musical's most enduring songs, attesting to their inventiveness in coming up with endless variations on the formulaic theme of young romance.

Although the first years of the Depression saw a falling off in the production of musicals, due mainly to cost factors, the spectacular films directed by Busby Berkeley for Warners in 1933 inaugurated a resurgence of interest. Not only were *42nd Street, Gold Diggers of 1933,* and *Footlight Parade* notable for stronger story lines, they were eye-dazzling showcases for Berkeley's cinematic/choreographic skills. While the basic inspiration for his unique vision stemmed from the showmanship and sexuality of Ziegfeldian theater, the thematic influence of Depression-era problems is apparent in many of his production numbers. Even the kaleidoscopic patterns formed by phalanxes of scantily attired pretty girls seemed to remind audiences of the collective unity necessary to cope with the dark days of the Depression. More likely, the ultimate intent of Berkeley's astonishing pieces of choreographic fantasy was to make people happily forget their problems, if only for a short while.

The RKO studio, by introducing the exotic team-dancing style of Fred Astaire and Ginger Rogers in lavish scenarios like the "Carioca" number of *Flying Down to Rio* (1933), unleashed a box office bonanza in the films these two made together over the decade. *The Gay Divorcee* (1934) was highlighted by their marathon interpretation of "The Continental," while *Top Hat* (1935) featured Irving Berlin's music for them to dance to, and *Swing Time* (1936), that of Jerome Kern.

If RKO capitalized on the fabulous dancing of Astaire and Rogers to help keep it solvent, the Fox studio came up with a windfall investment in the talented little Shirley Temple, who proved so popular at the box office that Fox took over the ailing Twentieth Century studio in 1935 to become one of the film production giants.[26] Until she grew up in the early 1940s, it was indeed a difficult task for any child star (and many adults) to outperform the singing, dancing, and acting appeal of Shirley Temple. Whatever role she played, whether a waif abandoned by her penniless father in *Little Miss Marker* (1934) or an orphan in *Curly Top* (1935), Temple remained the bright-eyed personification of optimism and hope, inspiring moviegoers to face up to their problems in a manner only she could project. Her popularity was evidenced by her rating as the number one star of the Hollywood Top Ten from 1934 to 1939, when she was finally surpassed by Mickey Rooney.[27]

Mickey Rooney and Judy Garland enjoyed a unique popularity of their own in such MGM musicals as *Babes in Arms* (1939), *Strike Up the Band* (1940), and *Babes on Broadway* (1941). With show business as their plots' central focus, the team of Rooney and Garland generated an infectious brand of optimism that moviegoers relished during this troubled era. In 1939 Judy took time out from the show business musical to star in one of the all-time film musicals, *The Wizard of Oz.* In it she introduced "Over the Rainbow," the song she would always be identified with, one, too, that expressed the mediated vision's longing for better times more emotionally than any other song of this era.

During the Depression years the movie musicals' escapist mode was a natural attraction, particularly those featuring the exciting dance team of Fred Astaire and Ginger Rogers in films like *Top Hat* (RKO, 1935). Author's collection.

THEY WEREN'T AS TOUGH
...as they thought they were!

Gamblers, sharp-shooters, blondined dolls...calloused and mercenary! Their icy hearts were melted by a little tot whose daddy hocked her for $20!

DAMON RUNYON

Takes you along the Great White Way to introduce the oddest set of characters since his 'Apple Annie' of "LADY FOR A DAY"

"Little MISS MARKER"

A Paramount Picture with

ADOLPHE MENJOU
as 'Sorrowful Jones' ready to bet on anything except love..

DOROTHY DELL
as 'Bangles Carson' singing love songs she doesn't believe ...

CHARLES BICKFORD
as 'Big Steve' whose heart is as hard as the pavements ...

SHIRLEY TEMPLE
as 'Little Miss Marker' making Broadway mugs believe in fairies...

a B. P. Schulberg Production

Films like *Little Miss Marker* (Paramount, 1934) focused on lovable Shirley Temple's optimistic outlook no matter how adverse her situation, a winning combination in the Depression years. Author's collection.

By the late thirties, the major studios began to respond to the mediated vision's musical inclinations in a variety of ways. Enjoying renewed popularity was the operetta in the films Nelson Eddy and Jeanette McDonald made for MGM. With the coming of the war years, nostalgic subjects began to dominate. MGM had anticipated interest in the entertainment luminaries of the past with its Academy Award for best picture of 1936—*The Great Ziegfeld.* Twentieth-Century Fox came on with the success stories of composer Stephen Foster in *Swanee River* (1940), Tin Pan Alley tunesmith Paul Dresser in *My Gal Sal* (1942), and a famous figure of the vaudeville era in *Lillian Russell* (1940).[28] MGM produced a real classic in the eyes of the mediated vision with *Meet Me in St. Louis* (1944), a nostalgic return to the seemingly more secure times of turn of the century America. But Warners mixed both nostalgia and patriotism in *Yankee Doodle Dandy* (1942), the life of Broadway musical icon George M. Cohan, in which James Cagney earned an Academy Award as the dynamic theatrical personality. At a time when American morale needed a big boost, Cagney's spirited acting and dancing along with the revival of Cohan's World War I songs were a great stimulus to carrying out this mission.

While the Fox musicals featured Big Band names, another reason for their box office success was Betty Grable, whose American-girl looks made her one of the top stars of the 1940s in such films as *Down Argentine Way* (1940) and *Springtime in the Rockies* (1942). In *Pin-Up Girl* (1944), she assured her popularity as the serviceman's favorite girl in a bathing suit in the publicity shot of her smiling back over her shoulder, one of the most memorable photos of the World War II era.

During this time, the movies even started featuring performers with a classical music background. The appearance of Kirsten Flagstad singing Wagnerian opera in Paramount's *The Big Broadcast of 1938* was an early sign of the movies' expanding role in introducing high culture to moviegoers. But MGM did more to popularize classical music than any other studio, especially in the performances of pianist José Iturbi and operatic singer Lauritiz Melchior, both of whom appeared in a number of its musicals in the 1940s. Of all the studios, it was MGM's magical blend of music, stars, and Technicolor that kept its musicals high on the list of moviegoers' must-see films.

With the conventional movie musical starting to lose its escapist appeal by the mid forties, some regard *State Fair* (1945) as "the old-time musical's last hurrah."[29] A remake of the 1933 film, this version was enlivened by the music of Richard Rodgers and Oscar Hammerstein, a team just beginning to make a name for itself in the Broadway musical. But the realities of the war years had begun to anticipate a less innocent time for the movies, a time that would see Hollywood take on a more realistic perspective toward its subject matter.

During these years, thematic background music was now being utilized as a way to merge plot development and atmosphere without intruding on an audience's sense of reality. Two pioneers of this aural/visual effect were Max

Steiner and Alfred Newman, who both demonstrated the worth of original soundtrack compositions to highlight a film's emotional moments. Steiner achieved this end in films as disparate in mood as *King Kong* (1933) and *Gone with the Wind* (1939), whose score won him an Academy Award. Newman, who began scoring films in the early thirties, developed a style that enhanced the realism of many of Hollywood's classic films—*Dead End* (1937), *Gunga Din* (1939), *The Grapes of Wrath* (1940), and *How Green Was My Valley* (1941). Without the contribution of these and other composers whose styles seemed especially right for certain kinds of movies, the emotional experience in viewing them would have been sorely lacking.[30]

Directors, too, were more attuned to the expansive sense of creativity that sound afforded them in the scripts they shot from. Both Billy Wilder and Preston Sturges, who started out as scriptwriters, parlayed their writing and later directing skills into such box office hits in the 1940s as *Double Indemnity* (1944) and *Sullivan's Travels* (1941). Overall, though, the making of a movie remained a collaborative effort between writer, director, and producer. The latter, of course, had the final say so in the approval of a shooting script, which, in turn, was dependent on budgetary constraints and the dictates of a studio's factory-like production schedule.[31]

The perfection of color in the filmmaking process was another important factor that added to the escapist appeal of the big productions of the late 1930s. Although the movies had experimented with color enhancement from their beginnings, it was not until 1935 and the release of the film version of W. M. Thackeray's novel *Vanity Fair* as *Becky Sharp* (after the name of its central character) that the potential of the Technicolor process was realized, though most studios considered it too expensive. It was MGM that effectively demonstrated the mesmerized impact Technicolor could have on audiences in two classic 1939 films. Elaborating on L. Frank Baum's popular children's story, *The Wizard of Oz* projected a fantasized aura that appealed to both children and adults, due mainly to its outstanding visual effects. An ingenious stroke was filming the bleak reality of Dorothy's Kansas home setting in sepia tone in order to contrast it with the colorful fantasy world of Oz. During a time when many best-selling novels were being transcribed to the screen, *Gone with the Wind,* Margaret Mitchell's story about the South of the Civil War years and their aftermath, made a highly successful transition to film through the selective dramatization of the novel's big scenes. Magnificently enhanced by the Technicolor process, many of them would long remain in the collective memory of the mediated vision. By the 1940s, then, Hollywood studios that could afford it began to release an increasing number of films in Technicolor, figuring that box office returns would justify the expense.

By this time, too, the movies had achieved their status as the nation's favorite form of paid entertainment. To meet the demand of some fifty million moviegoers who were attending thousands of theaters throughout the land at least once a week, studios were turning out some four hundred films annually. At most second-run houses, where ticket prices ranged from ten to twenty-five cents, audiences took in a program usually comprising both A and B features, a newsreel, short subject, and cartoon. The installation of vending machines and refreshment counters helped make their stay even more enjoyable, especially children escaping parental domination at a Saturday matinee that included cartoons and an exciting serial. For adults, air cooling systems in the summer and the chance to win money and prizes during bingo and bank/dish nights made going to the movies a much anticipated event. As the movies themselves were the main attraction, most moviegoers felt they had gotten their money's worth if a film had a happy, inspirational ending that met the mediated vision's standards for a satisfying escapist experience. Even though social problem films were inclined toward painting a negative picture of life, Hollywood studios of this time always seemed to find a way to end a serious story on a positive note, even if it was critical of the American way. But it was a criterion that was about to change, the signs of which were already appearing.

At a time when women's real-life roles were undergoing dramatic change, the movies depicted them as either dominantly forceful or long-suffering types, most exemplary in certain roles of Bette Davis and Joan Crawford. Davis typified the new young star whose name would be linked with a problematic kind of role, as in her Academy Award-winning performance in *Jezebel* (1938). Joan Crawford's offbeat mother role in *Mildred Pierce* (1945), for which she also won an Academy Award, earned her as large a following among women moviegoers as Bette Davis. Evidently, to these stars' fans it hardly mattered if their films ended on an ambivalent note. Their movies, after the manner of the radio soap opera, offered the distaff sector of the mediated vision a way to escape the problems of their own lives through vicarious identification with those dramatized on the screen.

By this time, then, the movies had cultivated a generation of female stars who projected an emancipated demeanor, also exemplified in the versatile roles played by Barbara Stanwyck and Katharine Hepburn. Expanding on the love goddess image of the 1920s were such leading ladies as Rita Hayworth, Linda Darnell, and Veronica Lake. But foreign-born actresses seemed more acceptable in sex-oriented roles that the censors might frown on—the kind Greta Garbo played in *Anna Christie* (1930) and *Grand Hotel* (1932); Marlene Dietrich, in the exotic locales of *Morocco* (1930) and *Shanghai Express* (1932) and the earthier backgrounds of *Destry Rides Again* (1939) and *The Spoilers* (1942); and Hedy Lamarr in *Algiers* (1938) and *White Cargo* (1942). To the mediated vision the female star of alien origins brought a sophisticated aura and/or sexual intrigue to their roles.

In the process of responding to women's sensibilities (and men's sexual fantasies), the movies were also responsive to the social role of women as consumers. As a result, the good life mirrored in films kept them up to date and informed of the latest developments in fashion, cosmetics, and even home furnishings. Other than magazine advertising, it was the movies that influenced the mediated vision's impressions as to what the ideal woman (and man) should look like. The close-ups of the stars' faces, particularly those of Marlene Dietrich, Hedy Lamarr, and Joan Crawford, in their intensely illuminated appearances, demonstrated to an entire generation of women how makeup could be utilized for the most glamorous effects. As the new center of fashion and its accessories, Hollywood was, in essence, selling as well as promoting the kind of glamorous image that most women desired to cultivate. Assisting them toward this end were such figures behind the scenes as Edith Head, the Academy Award-winning costume designer, and, of course, cosmetics genius Max Factor, whose makeup adornment of the stars was now being mass-marketed to women in department and drug stores as well as beauty shops.

Judging from the kind of social impact the Hollywood film was having on women fans, an important part of its escapist mission now, it seemed, was to show how they could make themselves over into their own image of the movie star. As an aid to this end, the fan magazine, which continued to function as a pipeline for the studios' promotion departments, achieved its greatest popularity during this era. Among the most popular articles were those of a positive slant, but not a few catered to a growing trend toward the sensational exposé.[32]

With the reality behind the illusion becoming a more intriguing subject, the relatively new profession of the Hollywood gossip columnist found its most influential figure of this time in former movie scriptwriter Louella Parsons. Whereas the studios had some control over the fan magazines in their reportage, Parsons had the prerogative to say almost anything she wanted concerning those involved in the Hollywood scene, especially those who fell from her favor. Much of Parsons's power to make or break a Hollywood personality was reflected in the syndicated column she wrote for the Hearst newspapers at a time when the communications magnate also had a hand in the moviemaking business. Similarly, her competitor Hedda Hopper, a former minor movie actress who also wrote a syndicated column about the stars' social activities and indiscretions, developed a powerful reputation beginning in the late 1930s.[33]

While most women stars were glorified in reports of their beguiling lifestyles, the image of many male stars helped counter the time's waning masculine identity due to the Depression's employment dearth and the war years' military draft. Humphrey Bogart rose above his criminal roles to become his own man in *The Maltese Falcon* (1941) and *Casablanca* (1942). Alan Ladd established his tough-guy image in *This Gun for Hire* and the film version of Dashiell Hammett's *The Glass Key* (both 1942). Certain other actors exerted a film presence that gave them a special identity in the eyes of moviegoers: Clark Gable's sex appeal, Cary Grant's comedic flair, Spencer Tracy's acting versatility in numerous roles, Errol Flynn's suave acts of derring-do, Henry Fonda's portrayal of American populist types, and Gary Cooper's quiet-spoken but strong-willed cowboy roles.

Though the sound era saw directors experimenting with the new technology to make Westerns outdoors, it wasn't until the late thirties that the real potential of this genre was realized. In 1939, John Ford expanded on his 1924 production of *The Iron Horse* to make the most realistic Western to date. Although *Stagecoach*'s dramatic emphasis was on characterization, Ford also focused on the West's panoramic vistas to temper the viewer's sense of its majestic expansiveness, a trademark of his future films. It was a visual quality attuned to the mediated vision's traditional perception of the West as a place of eternal challenge and, as such, an ideal site to test character.

In 1936, the epic-minded Cecil B. DeMille had anticipated Ford's vision in *The Plainsman,* which focused on the real-life but legendary characters of Wild Bill Hickok, Buffalo Bill Cody, and Calamity Jane. Then, in 1939, DeMille turned to a more ambitious project in *Union Pacific,* his version of the railroad's great achievement in creating a national linkup in the 1860s. As the world situation grew more uncertain in the late 1930s, the Western's historical base became more meaningful to moviegoers by reminding them of the great challenges that had to be surmounted to establish the American nation.

But this was also a time when the Western genre inspired productions that would be termed offbeat for the variant interpretations of its conventions. *Destry Rides Again* (1939), for example, came across as a parody of the whole Western scene, highlighted by its riotous saloon brawl. *The Westerner* (1940) brought the person of Judge Roy Bean and his brand of frontier justice to life in the superb acting of Walter Brennan. The overall effect was a deglamorized image of the mediated vision's traditional view of the West. In this vein, the most unique Western of the era was that based on Walter Van Tilburg's novel, *The Ox-Bow Incident* (1943). During this heart of the war years when inspirational films were in great demand, producer Darryl Zanuck dared to present audiences with a social protest message against lynch-mob justice in the guise of a Western. Indeed, in looking ahead to the reality-based films of the postwar years, this production was very much ahead of its time.

THE DAY OF THE B MOVIE, SERIAL, AND SHORT SUBJECT

With respect to addressing serious issues, the B Western was never too involved, of course. It was naturally more intent on pleasing the tastes of its largely youthful, impressionable audience in a fast-paced format that normally lasted no longer than an hour. Adhering to formulaic plots in which the

Director Cecil B. DeMille may have exaggerated historical fact in *The Plainsman* (Paramount, 1936), but it was another example of his special flair for producing the epic film. Author's collection.

cowboy hero always overcame his adversaries after a great deal of gunplay and fisticuffs, the B Western was primarily designed to generate exciting, violent action. But since it all took place in a fantasized setting, the threat of such goings-on having a harmful effect on young moviegoers was hardly ever questioned. With sound now a big factor in enhancing the action, the silent-era cowboy stars like Ken Maynard, Tim McCoy, and Buck Jones established the heroic image for many Saturday matinee cowboys, whose colorful dress style also lent them a strong visual presence.[34]

Though studios such as Paramount, Columbia, and Republic produced B movies in a variety of genres, the Western was among their most popular. Paramount's Hopalong Cassidy series, for example, was among the most prolific, with over sixty-five films produced from 1935 on into the 40s. In William Boyd's forceful but genial conception of the lead character, moviegoers saw the reassuring presence of an old friend, which, of course, was the reason why any film series, Western or otherwise, succeeded. Republic, the most productive studio of the genre, hit on a box office windfall when it began featuring its "singing cowboy" heroes Gene Autry and Roy Rogers in the thirties. Autry, whose positive reception soon accorded him star status, not only took on cattle rustlers and the usual assortment of stock evildoers but also took time out to sing songs, to the extent that Autry's films bordered on the musical genre. This mode coupled with a modern look in setting and dress belied the conventional trappings of the Western, informing viewers that in this format the past and the present were merged into a fantasy world of pure escapism, the likes of which would pass with this era.

The explosive action of the B Western also found expression in the Saturday matinee serial that brought young fans back week after week to their neighborhood theater to find out how their favorite horseback hero survived his latest perilous predicament. But for all its nonstop violent action, the serial never had a real problem with censorship. The closest it ever came to sexual innuendo was in Universal's three Flash Gordon serials. The first, *Flash Gordon* (1936), saw a sexily clad Dale Arden (Flash's girl played by Jean Rogers) ardently pursued by the despotic Ming the Merciless, whose daughter showed no less affection for Flash, played by Buster Crabbe, who was perfectly cast as a look-alike for the comic strip hero. But physical violence rather than physical attraction between the sexes was what sold a serial to its predominantly adolescent audience.

Another selling point of the serials was the studios' recognition of young moviegoers' fascination with comic strip and comic book heroes. In addition to Flash Gordon, among the many popular newspaper comics' characters brought to life in the serials were Buck Rogers, Red Ryder, Dick Tracy, and the Phantom. The comic book's lineup of superheroes who came into prominence in the late thirties was another rich source, providing one of the better serials in Republic's *Adventures of Captain Marvel* (1941). While the war

Among the most popular of the cowboy heroes was William Boyd in the role of Hopalong Cassidy, shown here in an ad for *Heart of Arizona* (Paramount, 1938). Author's collection.

years saw costumed characters like Spy Smasher, Batman, and Captain America taking on the nation's enemies, masked radio characters such as the Green Hornet and Captain Midnight also came to the serials to do their part. This trend toward the visual conceptualization of the media culture's fantasized heroes was only the start of a phenomenon that would become a box office bonanza in the latter years of the century when technical advances resulted in more realistic interpretations.

In the late 1930s, even the major studios found themselves competing in the B movie market, particularly for the series film audience that had come into its own by now. Like the serial heroes, much of the series characters' popularity was attributable to the fact that they were already established in other media forms like fiction, radio, and the comics, attesting to the growing interdependence of the forms of mediated culture. With the coming of sound, the murder mystery's essential ingredient of dialogue naturally enhanced plot development, placing the detective hero at the proper center of the action and contributing to the demand for a film cycle. The Charlie Chan series is a case in point, as during 1929–45 a total of forty-five movies appeared, most made by Fox until Monogram took over in 1944. Coloring his methodology with choice aphorisms that were more a fixture of the films than the novels, the Chan character was the most affably appealing movie detective in the pantheon of the mediated vision. His genial presence, in fact, helped counter the reigning prejudicial attitudes toward the sinister Oriental type, most deviously characterized in Sax Rohmer's fictional villain Fu Manchu and the pulps' Wu Fang.

In general, the time's most popular series detectives were modeled after the suave, articulate, logically thinking British image of Sherlock Holmes, reflected in the actors chosen to play this role. Of these, Basil Rathbone proved the most effective, playing Holmes in fourteen films (1939–46). His American variations were legion, from the Ellery Queen character in nine films to the fourteen featuring Philo Vance. Other than their immense popularity with moviegoers, the one thing the movie series detectives had in common was their origins in popular fiction.

The escapist mode of fantasy adventure found its most popular expression in the series based on Edgar Rice Burroughs's fabulous jungle hero Tarzan. While former athletes Buster Crabbe, Herman Brix, Glenn Morris, and Johnny Weissmuller took on the role in the 1930s, it was the latter who presented moviegoers with the most favorably received image by virtue of the six movies he made for MGM from 1932 to 1942. The basis for the popular reception of this series lay in the humanizing of its lead characters, transforming the remote, exotic setting of the films into the familiar rituals of family life by casting Weissmuller as a surrogate husband in *Tarzan and His Mate* (1934) and as a "father" in *Tarzan Finds a Son* (1939). With its appealing balance of the fantasized fiction/comics versions and the more down to earth approach of the movies, MGM's Tarzan series was a major box office attraction during these years.

Family life was also at the heart of a popular series that originated in the comics—Chic Young's *Blondie,* on which Columbia based twenty-nine titles from 1938 to 1950, all with Penny Singleton in the title role and Arthur Lake as husband Dagwood. As in the widely syndicated comic strip, the series was structured around the humorous episodes of a middle-class household. Looking ahead to the situation comedy of the television age, this series, like most, presented characters that audiences never seemed to tire of.

However, it was a 1937 MGM film called *A Family Affair* whose idyllic perception of small-town family life was so appealing to the moviegoers that it resulted in a long-lasting series featuring its lead characters. While the ingredients of the original film were derived from a 1928 Broadway play, the Andy Hardy series parlayed them into audience-pleasing plot situations in fifteen more films that lasted well into the 1940s. The Hardy family and their antiseptic home town of Carvel were an inspirational tonic at a time when the country's problems were initially compounded of economic woes and then the horrors of war. In fact, the popularity of the series was such that Mickey Rooney, as the key figure on whom all the series' plots focused, continued playing Andy Hardy long after he had obviously outgrown the role.

The popular series with the most obvious "aging" problems featured the principals from the original Dead End Kids films. When *Dead End,* Sidney Kingsley's 1935 play about urban crime's effects on juvenile delinquency, was made into a movie in 1937, the acting of its youthful leads won such acclaim that Warners cast them in a series of social problem films. In turning slum youths with criminal tendencies into appealing characters, the fantasizing power of the movies was clearly evident. But the series soon splintered into vapid imitations of its former self, as it became, in turn, the Little Tough Guys, the East Side Kids, and, by 1946, the Bowery Boys, who appeared in a seemingly endless run of ludicrous comedies into the late 1950s.

Jackie Cooper's audience-winning roles in *The Champ* (1931) and *Treasure Island* (1934) overshadowed the fact that he had started out in the highly popular *Our Gang* shorts, better known to later television viewers as *The Little Rascals.* Among the most successful movie series ever, *Our Gang,* with its lineup of appealing child actors, came under the production auspices of Hal Roach at MGM. There, a prolific total of 132 shorts were turned out between 1929 and 1944 that, in their attempt to recapture the lost innocence of childhood, appealed to adults as well as children.

In the 1930s and 40s the promotional phrase "Also Selected Short Subjects" in a movie ad was a big inducement to moviegoers, especially if it cited a comedy short starring a favorite comic or team like Stan Laurel and Oliver Hardy. In successfully transitioning to the sound era, they made forty shorts from 1929 to 1935. Of these, *The Music Box* (1932), which won an Academy

Award, was an example of their propensity to involve themselves in hilarious situations that bordered on the catastrophic. Their feature films of similar bent continued to appear into the 1940s until age and changing comedy tastes caught up with them. Judging from the 190 films the Three Stooges made from 1934 to 1959, theirs have to be deemed the most popular comedy shorts ever. Relying on the crudest form of slapstick humor and punctuating their antics with a kind of animated-cartoon violence, the Stooges maintained a following into the television era.[35]

In a movie-short comedy category unto themselves were the *Pete Smith Specialties* and the Robert Benchley and *Joe McDoakes* series. Their appeal derived mainly from the mock-serious documentary style that foreshadowed a trend toward reality-based humor. While a *Pete Smith* short could be educational, it utilized sight gags and timely sound effects to get a point across as producer Smith intoned his signature narrative style. The series was popular enough to approach a twenty-year run from 1936 to 1955. Humorist Robert Benchley was a one-man show in which his identification with the average person's frustrations derived from the mundane affairs of everyday life, as featured in the episodes of 1935–42. Similarly, the *Joe McDoakes* shorts were structured around a fall-guy type in a series of sixty-three situation comedy shorts of topical interest from 1942 to the 1950s, when television programming contributed to the demise of the movie-short genre. But the Benchley and *McDoakes* shorts offer significant insights into the social behavior of an era when the mediated vision was first being subjected to humor tempered by the realities of the time.

Although the escapist mode was most prevalent during this era, reality infiltrated the movies in a variety of ways. MGM's *Crime Does Not Pay* shorts (1935–47) dramatized the consequences of such mounting problems as drunk driving and juvenile delinquency. From travelogues to the bizarre findings of Robert L. Ripley's globetrotting in *Believe It or Not!*, the cinematic version of his popular illustrated newspaper feature, moviegoers found access to the larger world at their local theater.

By the mid 30s, then, when global issues of more alarming dimensions were undermining the mediated vision's escapist outlook, the climate was right for the resurgence of the documentary film, and some classic examples appeared that induced the mediated vision to become more sensitive to serious social issues and concerns underlying the dominant escapist mood of the times. Independent productions such as Pare Lorenz's *The Plow That Broke the Plains* (1936) and *The River* (1937) dealt respectively with the agricultural problems resulting from the midwestern dust storms and the pressing need for soil conservation and flood control.

A significant breakthrough in the revival of the documentary-type film came in 1935 when the Time-Life Corporation began producing filmed versions of radio's *March of Time* series. By this time, movie audiences were conditioned to a program starting off with a Paramount or Fox Movietone news-reel highlighting the latest happenings of national and, now more frequently, international import. Although the coverage of such events appeared later than that of the radio and newspaper, the newsreel offered an on-site, intensely visual kind of reportage that only film was capable of. Its style would temper an entire generation to a more immediately visual sense of what was going on in the world. *The March of Time,* in its exploration of the underlying factors behind the news to create both an insightful perspective and theatrical effect, foreshadowed the entertaining style of the television documentary, which by the 1950s would supersede the very form that had influenced it.

The Serious and Comic Versions of Hollywood's War

In 1939, Hollywood began propagating its own messages about the threat of war with *Confessions of a Nazi Spy* in which crusading FBI agent Edward G. Robinson exposed the presence of German spies and espionage agents in the U.S. In 1941, just months prior to the nation's entry into the war, a justifiable rationale for fighting for a cause was personified in converted pacifist and World War I hero Alvin York in *Sergeant York,* as Gary Cooper in the title role turned in an Academy Award-winning performance. Entry into the war saw a veritable torrent of inspirational films about the military's role and civilians' reactions on the home front. Battle-action films like *Wake Island* (1942) and *Bataan* (1943) focused on the uncertain times of the war's early years by portraying the courageous fighting of outmanned troops. By the time of *Thirty Seconds over Tokyo* (1945), the bombing devastation of Japan signaled the end of the war. Throughout, the war films' themes remained steadfast in inspiring unswerving patriotism and continued faith in the democratic system as powerful forces that would ultimately help win the war.

On the home front the role of patriotic fervor was dramatized in such films as *Joe Smith, American* (1942), about a defense plant worker's bravery in uncovering a spy ring; *The War against Mrs. Hadley* (1942), in which a society matron's self-centered lifestyle becomes an object lesson for everyone to do his or her part in the war effort; and *Since You Went Away* (1944), a sentimental tribute to the American family's attempt to maintain a stoical attitude while loved ones are serving in the war. To Hollywood, patriotism expressed through communal spirit was clearly a key factor in helping win the war.[36]

The realities of the war were mitigated by film comedy, particularly that featuring the hilarious escapades and burlesque routines of Bud Abbott and Lou Costello. Apparently right for the times, Abbott and Costello's comedic reactions to military life in their 1941 films—*Buck Privates, In the Navy,* and

Keep 'em Flying—made them the top box office attraction of 1942. In thirteen more movies released up to 1945, they exhibited a brand of humor that was as much verbal as slapstick in which Costello's wacky logic countered Abbott's deceptive tactics—a situation that audiences delighted in.

The satirical characterization of the enemy also helped perk up home front morale. In follow-up to Charlie Chaplin's daring lampoon of Adolph Hitler's megalomaniacal tactics in *The Great Dictator* (1940), the Axis military was frequently depicted in films (as well as propaganda posters) as gross caricatures, bestial in appearance and inhumane in their ways. In particular, the Japanese military leaders and their spies were revealed as scheming, brutal adversaries who should be dealt with accordingly. Whether factually based or not, these films succeeded in their intent of painting stereotyped portraits of a treacherous enemy for the mediated vision's perception and ultimate judgment.

A well-received film that caught the duress of wartime life, due mainly to its actors' honest portrayals of their characters, was *Casablanca* (1942). In fact, all its dramatic ingredients merged to create a memorable viewing experience: the exotic locale teeming with exiles looking to escape the exigencies of the war, others their pasts; the central conflict generated by the ominous presence of the Nazis; a fast-moving plot structured around the complementary roles of Humphrey Bogart and Ingrid Bergman; and even the musical interludes that give the story an emotional balance. At a time when the uncertain world situation demanded a stoic-like posture to endure impersonal forces encroaching on individual worth, the story seemed just right.

SIGNS OF A COMING NEW REALISM IN FILM

The reality-based aura of the war films was reflected in other genres as well, especially that depicting criminal activity. Like *Casablanca,* these films depended on atmosphere as an important dramatic component. As such, they looked ahead to the later cinematic style dubbed *film noir,* a French term that implies the filming technique of low-keyed lighting to complement inner-directed characterizations whose revelation of paranoia, guilt, or greed figure prominently in the plot. In this light, director John Huston's 1941 remake of Dashiell Hammett's *The Maltese Falcon* (the best of the three made) came across as an intriguing character study, actually a morality play disguised as a detective story.

It was a mood beginning to infiltrate even more familiar territory. Alfred Hitchcock, who had arrived in the U.S. in 1939 to lend his directorial touch to the gothic air of *Rebecca,* turned out an updated suspense thriller in *Shadow of a Doubt* (1943), which intimated that evil can lie even below the surface of the mediated vision's idyllic small town. To project such a seem-

Hollywood's growing attention to real world problems in the 1940s was evident in a chilling film like *Double Indemnity* (Paramount, 1944). Author's collection.

ingly innocent milieu, Hitchcock utilized the setting of a pleasant, real-life California town. This film's riveting suspense induced the mediated vision into a new kind of escapism, compelling the viewer to relate to an on-screen character's problems, no matter how fearsomely real they seemed to be.

One serious psychological problem that Hollywood had mostly avoided, except to depict it in a humorous way, was alcoholism. Fearing a negative reaction to a film version of *The Lost Weekend*, Charles Jackson's graphic novel about the consequences of alcohol addiction, Paramount initially hesitated to make it. But the time was apparently right for this film as it garnered four Academy Awards for best screen script, Billy Wilder's direction, Ray Milland's acting as an alcoholic writer, and best picture of 1945. It also offered further evidence of the growing fascination moviegoers were cultivating toward characters with serious flaws, sensing that the problems they saw depicted on the screen may very well be their own. Thus the movies' longtime fantasized mood was beginning to evolve into a whole new way of perceiving reality as a form of escapist entertainment

Because of its literary-like exploration of the consequences of psychological stress on the inner self through a variety of technical innovations, *Citizen Kane* (1941) was hailed by many as the greatest film ever made. Like its influential precursor, *The Birth of a Nation*, this film pioneered a new visual grammar to depict dramatic experience, setting a high standard for film as a narrative medium. As both director and lead actor, Orson Welles relates the story of newspaper magnate Charles Foster Kane (whose real-life counterpart was William Randolph Hearst) through the flashback perspectives of six key individuals who knew Kane prior to his death. As significant events from Kane's life unfold, clues reveal what made him the kind of man he was. To express the importance of setting or milieu in defining character, Welles photographed many of his scenes in deep focus to delineate singular personalities; others he took from unique angles in long shot to create a mood of dissension or divisiveness. By equating character with atmosphere, Welles created an expressionistic kind of realism that involved viewers in a powerful study of what can happen when chasing the American Dream goes awry. Noted film critic Bosley Crowther contended that in *Citizen Kane* Welles "had made a picture of overpowering scope . . . a motion picture that really moves."[37] Most everyone else, except moviegoers, agreed, for the film was not a box office success, probably because most movie fans at the time were more receptive to escapist fare. Nevertheless, *Citizen Kane*'s technical innovations would inspire later films of great visual appeal to an increasingly sophisticated mediated vision.

THE AFRICAN AMERICAN CINEMATIC EXPERIENCE

During this time another cinema, separate from the Hollywood production system, was churning out movies for black audiences. Although they featured "all-colored" casts, the crime, horror, and romance melodramas, musicals, and Westerns of producers/directors Oscar Micheaux and Spencer Williams were largely derivative of Hollywood genre traditions.[38] Attendant to the B

Western craze in the 1930s, Williams even performed in movies like *Harlem on the Prairie* (1938), which featured a black counterpart to singing cowboy Gene Autry in Herb Jeffrey, a popular radio and recording performer of the time.

Since the mediated vision's escapist inclinations cut across sociocultural differences to merge in a common vision, these films clearly demonstrated that black movie audiences' interests were hardly any different from those of white moviegoers. But while the mediated vision itself was color-blind, the posture of the dominant culture was decidedly not. In fact, the story of African Americans in the movies clearly reflects white society's racist attitudes toward the black roles in mainstream films from the beginnings. In the 1920s, these roles were still being performed by whites in blackface, while in the 30s the jungle movie added to black stereotyping through a distorted perception of the African continent and its natives. With the coming of sound, signs of a breakthrough in mainstream film roles appeared with the casting of Paul Robeson in the film version of Eugene O'Neill's *The Emperor Jones* (1933), Louise Beavers in *Imitation of Life* (1934), Bill Robinson's tap dance routines with Shirley Temple in several of her films, and Hattie McDaniel's Oscar-winning performance in *Gone with the Wind* (1939). But Hollywood chose mainly to showcase blacks as headline entertainers in all-black-cast musicals like *Cabin in the Sky* and *Stormy Weather* (both 1943), while the popular series films assigned blacks like Willie Best and Mantan Moreland to obsequious roles for comic relief. Not until the social upheaval of the 1960s would Hollywood begin to depict what it was really like to be black in America.

ANIMATION'S RESPONSE TO THE FEATURE FILM CHALLENGE

The coming of both sound and color were godsends to the animated cartoon in its mission of charging a fantasized world with life. Sound, in particular, had been the needed component to complement a character's actions. Now, not only dialogue but the onomatopoeia of the comic strip could be aurally replicated through well-timed sound effects and the interpolation of music. Though numerous comic strip characters were brought to the screen in the 1930s, they met with little success until the Fleischer studio introduced Popeye the Sailor in 1933. With his unique voice and brusque mannerisms, Popeye soon overtook the studio's sexy bimbo image of Betty Boop in popularity. The character's continuing appeal derived mainly from the audience's anticipation of his spinach eating ritual and the ensuing climactic, explosive battle with the villains he encountered. The formula never seemed to grow old, as the animated version of the Popeye character would last on into the 1950s. In 1941 the Fleischer studio came up with another big hit in the comic book hero Superman in a series that would be acclaimed among the best animated shorts ever made, mainly for their realistic action sequences.

However, at this time it was the Disney studio that was winning more plaudits, which were mainly the result of its creation of a more reality-based fantasy world where good must undergo a period of testing before overcoming the forces of evil. Such a viewpoint was clearly evident in "The Three Little Pigs" (1933), whose timely theme inspired moviegoers to counter the bad times of the Depression. Disney cartoons were now so anticipated by movie fans that exhibitors took to promoting them along with their feature-film programs. This was particularly true of those starring Mickey Mouse, whose character grew popular enough to become a cultural icon, inspiring dolls, toys, books, games, a newspaper comic strip, and even a best-selling wristwatch. But Mickey's personality was so consistently cheerful that the irascible Donald Duck was apparently created in 1934 to offset his character. Surprisingly, his movie popularity soon surpassed that of his famous predecessor to compete with the output of MGM and Warners.[39]

The burgeoning success of the Disney studio precipitated an undertaking that many at the time considered foolhardy, if not impossible—the creation of a feature-length cartoon. The result in 1937 was the highly acclaimed *Snow White and the Seven Dwarfs*, which spawned a golden age of the animated feature film in the 1940s, when Disney produced such box office successes as *Pinocchio* (1940), *Dumbo* (1941), and *Bambi* (1942). But the experimental *Fantasia* (1940), even though it would become a cult classic, was not too well received when it was first released. In attempting to demonstrate how the art of animation and the new system of Fantasound could capture and project the essence of musical expression through exemplary works of some of the greatest classical composers, the Disney animators produced a brilliant tour de force. Unfortunately, they failed to realize that most moviegoers' level of musical taste at this time had not prepared them for such a sophisticated visual experience.[40]

Only the Fleischer studio boldly dared to emulate Disney in the production of feature cartoons. But though *Gulliver's Travels* (1939) and *Mr. Bug Goes to Town* (1941) contain some fine moments, they were not up to the overall standards of the Disney productions. Fleischer's forte was the cartoon short, as the Popeye and Superman series attested to. With movie houses clamoring for more cartoons to enliven their programs, other studios answered the call, including those of MGM and Universal. But it was Warners, with its talented staff of Tex Avery, Bob Clampett, Friz Freleng, and Chuck Jones, that created the most diverse lineup of popular animated characters. Indeed, it was difficult for any studio to top the likes of those appearing in the *Looney Tunes and Merrie Melodies* series, from Daffy Duck to the wisecracking Bugs Bunny, one of the most popularly received animated characters ever. By the end of this era, then, the creators of the animated cartoon had introduced the mediated vision to a colorful, fantasized world where anything was possible, limited only by the creative power of the animators and their understanding of the mediated vision's escapist desires.[41]

The Legacy of Moviegoing, 1930–1945

These fifteen years represent a time when the Hollywood film became a powerful sociocultural force indoctrinating moviegoers into a new vision of the individual's place in society. Having cultivated a greater appreciation for the art of the motion picture by the 1940s, moviegoers were sensitized to the movies' power to respond to their basic desires and dreams, conditioning them to certain expectations of life itself—in particular, how good life should be as opposed to how it really is. Thus, through the magical combination of image and sound, the movies generally depicted life as the mediated vision wanted it to be. And for those coming of age during these years, the movies were a strong formative influence, not just through their display of glamorous lifestyles to emulate but in conditioning social attitudes, particularly toward the opposite sex. Though the moralists were quick to criticize the movies for their undermining of conventional codes of social mores, youths were equally quick to pick up on the very things they condemned—rebellious lifestyles, vulgar speech, and unseemly fads. To go to the movies, then, was to stay young, evidenced by this social outing having become too entrenched for fans to be undone by any kind of moralistic denouncements. Enhancing this habit, too, was the omnipresent promotional imagery of Hollywood seductively beckoning to one's escapist dreams.

But the movies also helped create a cultural appreciation for drama as well as classic and best-selling fiction that found interpretation on the screen. Many moviegoers who were not initially attracted to the printed page were frequently motivated by a favorite movie to check out its literary source. In effect, then, they were being conditioned to a higher level of literary perception while hardly ever realizing it. While film biographies of famous figures of the past helped educate moviegoers to the nation's cultural and political traditions, documentary films alerted them to important issues and concerns of the time.

From the graphic realism of the gangster films of the 1930s to the developing *film noir* mood of the 1940s, and the technical advances and imaginative dimensions that enabled the animated cartoon to fashion a make-believe reality all its own, the movies responded naturally to the mediated vision's desire to exchange the realities of the immediate scene for the escapist solace of an illusionary world.

THEATER AS ESCAPE AND CONFRONTATION
AND OTHER THEATRICAL DIRECTIONS

If the Depression hurt the American theater more than it did any other entertainment form, its effects were hardly noticed by the creative sector, as this
era was one of the richest and most diverse for the production of musical comedy and drama. In contrast to the 1920s, the spirit of theater in the 1930s
was more attuned to the grim realities of contemporary events. Even the escapist mode of musical comedy drew on satire to lash out at such unlikely
topics as the folly of war, political corruption, and the clash between democratic and totalitarian forces. As Thousands Cheer (1933) mirrored this mood
but mostly in a humorous light, staging its scenes in the format of a newspaper inspired by the day's headlines. Scored by Irving Berlin, the show enjoyed a run of over four hundred performances by inducing audiences to
laugh at the time's foibles and problems. Similarly, Of Thee I Sing (1931),
with a score by George and Ira Gershwin, had a long run spoofing the presidential election ritual and its attendant political shenanigans. Ironically, it
became the first musical comedy to win a Pulitzer Prize, beating out Eugene
O'Neill's Mourning Becomes Electra for the honor.

For composer George and his lyricist brother Ira, the 1930s was a prolific
time of creativity, as it was for Jerome Kern, Cole Porter, and the team of
Richard Rodgers and Lorenz Hart, all of whose songs would become perennial favorites of the mediated culture. From 1930 on into the forties over two
hundred productions appeared featuring the songs of these and other songwriters in the formats of musical comedies, revues, operettas, and George
Gershwin's landmark opera Porgy and Bess (1935). In merging jazz idioms
and the operatic form to dramatize Southern blacks' lifestyle, it would be
deemed his masterpiece.

Like the inspiration for this work, the primary sources of many of the times'
musical productions were plays and novels, pointing up the ongoing interdependence among creative forms for source material. Certainly, Hollywood was
indebted to the musical comedy, as twenty-six of them were made into popular films during the years 1931–44. The songs of these shows found additional
mass appeal not only through the movies but sheet music, recordings, and, of
course, radio. By the 1940s, then, the cultural image of the Broadway musical comedy had become more mass-mediated than it ever had.[42]

Subsequently, the enduring songs of talented composers like Jerome Kern,
Cole Porter, who was as adept at creating lyrics as he was melodies, and the
team of Rodgers and Hart's six shows, from Jumbo (1935) to The Boys from
Syracuse (1938), were highly influential in advancing the art of the musical
comedy. After their final collaboration on Pal Joey in 1940, Rodgers teamed
with Oscar Hammerstein to create some of the greatest hits in musical theater history and, in doing so, expand on the musical theater tradition initi-

ated by *Show Boat.* In 1943, the heart of the war years, they turned out *Oklahoma!*, a classic example of total theater in which music, dance, and story merged in a visually engrossing theatrical experience. For five years this show generated such wide audience appeal it ran for over two thousand performances, foreshadowing the even more popular *South Pacific.* The continued success of Rodgers and Hammerstein's partnership brought this era to a close in 1945 with *Carousel,* yet another big hit. In the successful careers of these two creative geniuses, the future of the Broadway musical looked as bright as that of the nation's situation at the end of the war that same year.

The folkloric elements of dance that were such an integral and effective part of *Oklahoma!* derived from the pioneering efforts of choreographer Martha Graham. Rebelling against the ritualized form of traditional ballet, she developed an intensely energized kind of theatrical dance in the 1930s that expressed a democratic feel for American values through her dancers' plain dress and dynamic movement. Its visually expressive manner was epitomized in the dance sequences of Aaron Copland's *Appalachian Spring* (1944) as well as those suggested by the thematic music of his ballet compositions inspired by the Western myth—*Billy the Kid* and *Rodeo.* Graham's dance style and Copland's populist music, with its kindred feel for regional distinctions, was an ideal marriage through which to indoctrinate the mediated vision into the artistic intent of an art form that had been largely incomprehensible to it. Another who would be instrumental in popularizing the twin roles of theatrical music and dance was just beginning to make a name for himself in the 1940s—a dynamic young composer/conductor named Leonard Bernstein. His Gershwin-like feel for urban life found expression in 1944 in *On the Town,* a musical comedy that attempted to capture the sights and sounds of New York City in music and dance.

Having had the legitimate stage as a viable training ground, actors like Spencer Tracy and Melvyn Douglas began to head for Hollywood for its lucrative film contracts, followed by such future stars as Humphrey Bogart, Bette Davis, Henry Fonda, Katharine Hepburn, and James Stewart. With the advent of sound, movies demanded performers who could speak with the authority of their assigned roles, and many of those who had acted before live audiences on the Broadway stage were naturally qualified to meet the demand.

Of course, numerous stage plays of the time were made into movies, with not a few starring the featured performers of the original stage productions. A notable example of the crossover trend was Vicki Baum's novel *Grand Hotel,* which arrived on Broadway as a play in 1930 and became a highly publicized, star-studded film in 1932. Although no dramatic production with significant audience appeal was overlooked by Hollywood, the long-running stage version of *Tobacco Road,* Erskine Caldwell's earthy novel about impoverished Georgia sharecroppers, was not made into a movie until 1941. The eight-year delay, of course, was due to the problematic task of coming up with a script that met Production Code standards. While both fiction and drama were traditionally allowed a more liberal interpretation of the transgressions of social behavior, the movies, whose audience ranged across all ages, were still expected to maintain strict standards for what could or could not be shown on the screen. In striving to keep up with the mediated vision's changing perspectives on social behavior in difficult times, Hollywood, as noted earlier, was in the ironic position of having to sanitize the realism of its major dramatic sources to make film, the most visually realistic of creative forms, less realistic.

Preparing the way for a more liberal approach to a play's film interpretation was the drama of topical protest, which provided a highly visible mode through which to promote the sociopolitical issues and concerns of the 1930s. The era's sensitivity to labor problems was evident in the critical posture of Clifford Odets's *Waiting for Lefty* and *Awake and Sing* (both 1935). Robert Sherwood, who satirized the ploys of warmongering nations in *Idiot's Delight* (1936), won a Pulitzer Prize for his efforts. Earlier, in *The Petrified Forest* (1935), he dramatized the symbolic clash of traditional values and self-centered individualism in the tragic confrontation of a poet and a gangster. But the lure of Hollywood was not lost on either Odets or Sherwood, as both compromised their commitment to the legitimate stage by taking on the more profitable assignment of writing scripts for the movies, a vocation other authors would also pursue.

Despite competition from film and other entertainment forms, mainstream drama continued to stage memorable works. Eugene O'Neill, at the peak of his creative powers, carried on the experimental tradition of the 1920s in *Mourning Becomes Electra* (1931), a lengthy, psychological exploration of its lead characters' inner selves. Two years later his most uncharacteristic work appeared, *Ah, Wilderness!*, which in its nostalgic revival of small-town life at the turn of the century held a natural charm for the mediated vision. Similarly, Thornton Wilder's *Our Town* (1938), structured around the lives of two American families at the beginning of the twentieth century, had an emotional appeal that would make it a classic of the American theater. With hardly any semblance of a set, this play clearly demonstrated how the interrelationship of characterization and thematic development functioned as the key dramatic components in winning over an audience. No less attractive to the mediated vision was Clarence Day's *Life with Father* (1939), a lighthearted view of the role that strong family ties played in the urban setting of turn of the century New York. In fact, this play proved so popular that it became the era's longest-running Broadway production with well over three thousand performances.

Although sophisticated comedy with a contemporary setting like Philip Barry's *The Philadelphia Story* (1939) was popular, the ongoing trend toward realism portended of things to come. *Native Son*, Richard Wright's controversial novel about racism, was dramatized as a play in 1941; and Tennessee Williams's *The Glass Menagerie* (1945) was the first hit of the playwright whose plays about individuals with deep psychological flaws would soon become highly anticipated Broadway events.

As in the musical, inspiration for dramatic exposition was found in many diverse sources. Maxwell Anderson's *Winterset* (1935) derived its plot from the controversial Sacco-Vanzetti trial of the 1920s, whose principals were seen by many as martyrs to the American justice system. In 1934 Sidney Howard based a play on *Dodsworth*, Sinclair Lewis's best-selling satirical novel about the American newly rich. Drama also took on some unique formats. In 1936 Orson Welles, as revolutionary in theater as he was in radio, produced a highly experimental version of *Macbeth* that drew on the voodoo sector of Haiti for its setting. The following year, under the auspices of the Mercury Theatre, Welles and John Houseman collaborated on a modern-dress production of *Julius Caesar*. In addition to the ongoing experimentation in set design by New York's Theatre Guild, the Group Theatre, founded by Harold Clurman and Lee Strasberg, made significant contributions to the development of realistic acting techniques. Pioneered by Stanislavsky of the Moscow Art Theatre, the "Method" acting system would soon find its way to Hollywood and generate a cinematic revolution.

But the most unique experiment in the history of American theater was the Federal Theatre Project (FTP), which during 1935–39 offered notable theatrical productions to the general public. Ranging from mediocre to outstanding, many of its plays were in tune with the times by projecting sociopolitical messages. However, supporters of the FTP saw it as a significant step toward democratizing the elitist status of the American theater. Hallie Flanagan, the FTP's dynamic director, contended that to appeal to the people as the movies had done, the "stage too must experiment—with ideas, with psychological relationships of men and women, with speech and rhythm forms, with dance and movement, with color and light."[43] She, in turn, advocated a return to the roots of American culture for source material, as Paul Green did in *The Lost Colony*, his annual outdoor drama that opened in 1937 as an example of the "people's theater."

At a time when the amusement park and the circus were in direct competition, the circus as the original "people's theater" was now promoting more sensational acts to lure people to the Big Top. Among them were the Flying Concellos, a husband and wife trapeze team who performed the first triple somersault in 1933, and the nail-biting highwire routines of the Wallenda Family. In 1931, renowned animal tamer Clyde Beatty, who had his own circus, was performing in a cage with a dozen lions and tigers, while by 1938 the Ringlings' jungle connection capitalized on an even more sensational ploy with the appearance of a gorilla billed in the tradition of P. T. Barnum's Jumbo as "Gargantua the Great—the World's Most Terrifying Living Creature!" But the disastrous fire that engulfed the Ringlings' Big Top in 1944 at Hartford, Connecticut, was an omen of the future, inducing circuses to put on their shows in the safer confines of an indoor arena. To the mediated vision, though, the three-ring circus was always its own fantasy advertisement, a place where adults could escape everyday life and, along with their children, become young again.

Burlesque, still socially marginal as theater, continued to capitalize on the lure of sex as fantasy, and therein lay the reason for its success, especially during the more open time of the war years when performers were sent around the country on a wheel circuit to wherever such entertainment was allowed. This system was especially popular along the east coast where in a Navy town like Norfolk lonely sailors lined up at the Gaiety Theater on Main Street to catch the latest road production. Thus, burlesque remained profitable because, as Morton Minsky and Milt Machlin put it: "Comics were what people loved once they were in the theater, but it was sex on the marquee that pulled them in."[44]

In this vintage era of striptease artists like Ann Corio, Margie Hart, Rose la Rose, and Georgia Sothern, a star stripper was a big attraction. But in contrast to the headline performer who had a specialty that lent her a degree of notoriety, the highly literate Gypsy Rose Lee gave burlesque a special kind of class it never had before. And even Ann Corio parlayed her sexuality into starring roles in a series of B movies in the early forties. But with crusading zealots like New York Mayor Fiorello LaGuardia waging a personal war against it, the days of organized burlesque were numbered. Nevertheless, like Florenz Ziegfeld's *Follies,* burlesque played a significant part in cultivating the controversial image of woman as a glorified sex object. As social historian Robert C. Allen has commented: "burlesque's principal legacy as a cultural form was its establishment of patterns of gender representation that forever changed the role of woman on the American stage and later influenced her image on the screen."[45] His observation would also obtain to the visual role of woman in consumer advertising in which she was now expressing a more sexually expressive or, to some, transgressive image.

ADVERTISING AND ITS PROMISE OF THE GOOD LIFE

Although the movies were playing a key role in projecting images of the good life in a mediated culture, it was consumer advertising that promised form and substance to the mediated vision's goal of realizing the American Dream—if not immediately, then, it was hoped, in the near future. By the 1930s the rhetoric and pictorial content of mass advertising, which now utilized abundant photography, had established a seductive posture that sought to counter the harsh realities of the time. In fact, this kind of advertising inferred that even though one's present possessions might not be as adequate or as fashionable as desired, ultimately one could have it all—from home ownership to the necessary material things that signaled class status. Nevertheless, in 1932 a backlash to this kind of deception had appeared in the form of a muckraking book titled *100,000,000 Guinea Pigs.* In essence, it accused the advertising industry of promulgating false promises to cajole a gullible public into coveting and purchasing items many could not afford.[46] In effect, though, the kind of cajolery appearing in the full-color display ads of the *Saturday Evening Post,* which could make even a soft drink appear essential to the cultivation of a desirable lifestyle, was merely the latest update of the mediated vision's escapist dreams of a better day.

In the 1930s, when radio and print advertising confirmed that women were the ultimate consumers, they were showing up more frequently as principal players in magazine ads, particularly those structured around dramatized scenes either illustrated or photographed. A more liberal moral climate found women themselves directly targeted by the cigarette companies in ads that not only depicted social gatherings in which women were smoking but women celebrities endorsing a particular brand. Through visual techniques that mixed the psychological with the hard sell, advertising promoted consumer products as either a therapeutic need or a status symbol. When a national poll revealed that newspaper comics were highly popular with adults, advertising agencies resorted to minidramas in comic strip form to promote products that addressed the American obsession for health therapy and self-improvement. Some ads even relied on popular comic strip characters to get their messages across, as the Cream of Wheat cereal company did with Li'l Abner. Underlying this era's advertising imagery, then, was the personally directed message that one's success and health in life depended a great deal on the products such imagery extolled.

To enhance this message and command immediate attention, advertising graphics began placing more emphasis on eye-catching modernist designs, a move that also extended to packaging. Following the spread of the self-service grocery stores in the 1930s where multiple brands openly competed with each other for selection, this brand identification process helped transform the customer into more of a self-reliant shopper. During these trying times, too, relief from inner anxieties became a reliable sales pitch for such longtime items as soft drinks, candy bars, and chewing gum. Thus, their trademark logos, as symbols of American commerce, persisted as familiar friends to the mediated vision, their appealing images reminiscent of better times.

Advertising in the 1930s was especially big on travel as a glamorous way to escape, at least for those who could afford it. Though the popularity of the streamlined, diesel-powered luxury train peaked in the late thirties, railroad brochures were still pushing their scenic routes to national parks and seasonal resorts. But to its converts, the airplane, promoted as the fastest way to get

around, represented the future of travel. By 1939, Pan American was complementing its Far East connection with ads for flights to France. To compete
with the domestic airlines of American and Eastern and promote flying as a
service-oriented way to travel, United had hired the first stewardesses in
1930. And as the other airlines soon followed suit, the airplane was on its way
to surpassing the luxury train as the celebrities' way to travel. While Art Deco-
styled posters promoted steamship lines offering periodic sailings to Europe
as well as the Caribbean, its exotic advertising would cease with the ominous
appearance of German submarines in Atlantic waters in the early 1940s.

Even though wartime travel was curtailed by gas rationing restrictions, the
American sense of personal mobility had been conditioned by the automobile since the 1920s by offering motorists the independent means to set their
own pace. But as the beckoning highway system continued to expand across
the nation, they were witness to the development of an intrusive roadside advertising mission that attempted to address all on-the-road needs. Thus, in
taking to the highway during this time, one discovered that no matter how
scenic the drive, roadside entreaties of commercial import frequently inter-
rupted it.

As the competition for business was quite intense among the myriad roadside diners, cafés, and fast-food drive-in stands that sprang up practically
overnight, the most creative highway advertising was that for food. Accordingly, not a few of these venues concocted a flamboyant style of architecture
that drew attention to their food-service function, a kind of folk art imagery
that, as John Margolies and Emily Gwathmey have commented, was "often
overlaid with highly regionalized flavors [that] symbolized the new-found and
vitally exciting ambience of life on the open road."[47] In democratizing the
eating habits of mobile Americans, roadside diners looked ahead to the fast-
food chains that would dominate both the highway and urban scene in the
second half of the twentieth century. Before then, though, the peculiarly
American institution of the diner, which became a sociocultural icon by the
1940s, attracted the familiar road types who appeared in the settings of fiction, drama, and the movies.[48]

In the thirties, family sight-seeing tours could be readily planned from the
detailed information offered in the state travel guides produced by the Federal Writers Project. They, in fact, uncovered an America rarely ever known
or seen by a motorist.[49] But for most families on vacation, the garish, comical advertising for roadside tourist attractions helped them decide what to
see. The state of Florida, for example, was showing a more egalitarian posture toward tourists by endorsing an infinite variety of ways to attract them.
Accordingly, highway vistas grew thick with fantasized signage, statuary, and
symbolic structures that publicized alligator farms, oddity museums, exotic
bird jungles, and shell shops—all competing for the attention of curious
highway adventurers and their demanding offspring.

As far as lodging was concerned, motorists usually drove until they spied a sign for tourist cabins or an auto/motor court offering the welcome opportunity for an overnight respite from driving fatigue. Eventually, the "motel," a contracted term for motor hotel, would become a major focus of the road culture created by the automobile revolution. Ironically, the trails where pioneers had trod on their way west to fulfill the dream of a better life were now dotted with highway stopovers for modern-day pilgrims, who, from the viewpoint of the mediated vision, were still looking for that better day, whether down the road in the form of a good job, business deal, new home, or merely the temporary pleasures of a vacation destination. Despite its myriad commercial distractions the romance of the road had now become a nationwide "ritual" that, in a philosophical sense, "help[ed] explain where Americans have been and where they think they might be going."[50]

Promoting the War Effort and Home Front Diversions

During the war years when motorists lined up at a local gas station for their prescribed quota of fuel, they could only hope that the necessary sacrifice they were making would ensure better days ahead. For this very reason, personal sacrifices were expected of everyone on the home front as well as the big corporations like the automobile manufacturers, who stopped making cars in 1942 to produce trucks, tanks, and ammunition/weaponry for the military. They, as well as other industries that converted to wartime production, devoted their advertising to the war effort by utilizing it to boost home front morale and provide public service information. For example, the Goodyear rubber company issued magazine ads on tire conservation, while the Oldsmobile division of General Motors publicized its proud role in producing "Fire-Power" for airplanes.

During the 1930s the Federal Poster Project had provided unemployed artists a livelihood by using their talent to promote public service messages. By the war years such proclamations gave way to posters that kept the public informed of their responsibilities in supporting the war effort. While the stylized art that depicted the enemy was done in a blatantly racist manner, showing the foe as repulsively grotesque in appearance, the American fighting man was heroically idealized to inspire a sense of patriotism or to generate feelings of guilt for not contributing more to the war effort by buying bonds, car-pooling, and abiding by the rationing regulations. Even miniscule matchbook advertising, at the peak of its circulation during this time, warned knowledgeable smokers of the dangers of loose talk. ("A slip of the lip might sink a ship.") Due to the public's mass bombardment by propagandistic advertising, from billboards to matchbook covers, the mediated vision was readily indoctrinated into a justified rationale for shoring up the war effort.[51]

By this time, a city's major commercial area, which still clustered around one major thoroughfare, had survived the 1930s to reassert itself through flamboyant neon advertising that promoted the attractions of a recovering economy. In this presuburban era, newspaper advertising also reminded its readers that downtown, or areas close to it, was the focal point of social life. Small town or big city, "Main Street" remained an escapist mecca to the mediated vision, abounding with food venues (ranging from the drive-up diner to the deluxe restaurant), department and drug stores, movie theaters, and businesses that catered to special consumer interests. For the high school set, growing fairly sizable by now, soda fountain shops flourished as popular hangouts. But for those with cars there was the gregarious appeal of the drive-in restaurant, serviced by a cadre of carhop waitresses who hustled orders out to vehicles awaiting in the parking lot.[52] Still an enticement to many was the movie theater marquee that was at the peak of its magnetic powers in announcing the latest attractions. The model for it, of course, was the great movie palace of New York, which, to promote first-run films, transformed neon and electronic lighting into pyrotechnic tableaux that often excelled the other promotional efforts of the Times Square area.

Just as the Hollywood musical was publicizing the glamorous side of café society, so the real-life nightclub, with its name dance bands and nightly revues, imitated art by attracting celebrated personalities, from New York's El Morocco and Stork Club to those that graced the Hollywood scene—Ciro's, the Coconut Grove, and the Brown Derby. With movie culture at its height, these places became prominently recognized as the favorite eateries and watering holes of famous film stars. In such a fantasized milieu the newspaper, magazine, and radio gossip reporters found a ready-made source of "hot" material that not only helped publicize the high life but also contributed to the mediated vision's ongoing fascination with the off-screen affairs of a movie star or public personality.[53] To the mediated vision, then, these venues were natural advertisements for the good life that beckoned in the postwar years.

THE MAGAZINE'S DEPICTION OF BOTH THE REAL AND FANTASIZED WORLDS

To approach a newsstand in the 1930s and 40s was to be overwhelmed by the proliferation and diversity of magazine titles that vied for attention on the racks, ranging in taste from the elitist opinion journals to the fantastic pulps. Little wonder, then, that such a competitive array strived to attract potential customers through covers that sensitized them to a mass-mediated "perception as to what art—or at the very least what popular art—should be."[54] A major reason the general interest magazines like the *Saturday Evening Post,* *Collier's,* and *Liberty* maintained their popularity during these years was their covers' portrayal of the sentimental rituals of home life, young love, and the innocence of childhood that represented an America the mediated vision still wanted to believe in, despite the problems of the time.

Although magazine fiction was still bountifully illustrated, the visual impact of its nonfiction pieces was more realistically enhanced by the photograph, pointing up the growing influence of photojournalism. Indeed, in the 1930s many magazines were attending to the real-world province of photographers Roy Stryker, Walker Evans, and Dorothea Lange, who were motivated to record the dominant reality of the time as social deprivation. Roaming the offbeat byways of the country, particularly the rural South, they captured the Depression's impact on the bleak, downtrodden lives of the common people—mainly the dirt farmers whose children seemed destined to perpetuate the same way of life. In both its unblinking honesty in demythologizing the rural scene and the primary intent of sensitizing rather than inspiring, the photography of social realism saw its function as more didactic than artistic.

Nevertheless, the theatrical nature of the photograph made it highly conducive to an entertaining interpretation of life's high as well as low moments, from the depiction of great achievements to tragic natural disasters and nefarious criminal acts, as well as the scandalous affairs of celebrated personalities. In the 1930s, then, magazine photography was beginning to reveal that the camera was no respecter of social standing when it came to observing people in their offbeat, even intimate moments. One of the first to recognize and capitalize on photography's visual power to project the intriguing drama of the human condition was Henry R. Luce.

The popular success of Luce's *Time,* which had been using photographs in its reports since the 1920s, inspired the appearance of two more photo-oriented weeklies in 1933—*Newsweek* and *U.S. News and World Report.* Fortuitously, the 1930s was a decade whose abundant newsworthy events were tailor-made for photojournalism. Tempered by the administration of Franklin Roosevelt and the repeal of Prohibition, media events and their repercussions flowed in an endless stream. *Time* and its competitors readily responded with stories on the Dionne quintuplets, the tragic plane crash death of humorist Will Rogers, the disappearance of aviatrix Amelia Earhart's plane somewhere in the Pacific, J. Edgar Hoover's war against the gangster element, the rise of dictator Adolph Hitler, the trial and execution of the man charged with the kidnapping and murder of the Lindbergh baby, Edward VIII's abdication of the British throne to marry a commoner, and the meteoric rise of black boxing champion Joe Louis. These and many more topics took on added visual impact through a wirephoto service that transmitted photographs electronically.

But *Time*, in its unique journalistic style that made readers feel they were being entertained while they were informed, remained the model for such print reportage. As the pioneer of the modern magazine format, Luce next gambled on a magazine devoted to the world of high finance in the uncertain economic times of 1930, appointing highly talented art director T. M. Cleland to see that *Fortune* was the paragon of modernist design. The first issue promulgated its visually-oriented credo of presenting "a clear and readable text profusely illustrated with pictures, mostly photographic, in a form ample and agreeable to the eye."[55] While conceptual art in the modernist style adorned this magazine's cover, its interior layout of photographs and graphics looked ahead to *Life*, which became the first photo-dominated magazine in 1936.

Undoubtedly, the 1935 film version of radio's *March of Time* series and its visual approach to documentary journalism played a big part in Luce's formulation of a picture news magazine like *Life*. Certainly, his magazine was more aptly named than the defunct humor journal which had relinquished the rights to its name. So with "life" itself as its major subject, Luce's new magazine set out to articulate a visual language that not only showed famous people involved in activities that ranged from the mundane to the heroic (and frequently the absurd), but ordinary people engaged in the affairs of everyday life. While *Time* and its competitors maintained a posture of reporting the news through the dominance of print, *Life* relished its method of telling a complete story in pictures with a minimum of words. Even its photographic cover that referred to an interior feature posited a degree of narrative power.

In a society that was now placing more emphasis on images than words, *Life* was an immediate hit. In fact, the mediated vision found this weekly an exciting visual repository for both its love of the familiar and fascination with the new and different. Nevertheless, certain pieces, like those that dealt with the birth of a baby and the underground culture of American blacks, stirred up a degree of public controversy, as revealed by letters to the editor and the banning of the "birth" issue in some areas of the country. In the main, though, this new visual medium was sensitizing the mediated vision, in Luce's words, to "see life; to see the world; to eyewitness great events . . . to see and take pleasure in seeing; to see and be amazed; to see and be instructed."[56] It was a mission that foreshadowed the dynamic breakthroughs in visual communications in the second half of what Luce in 1941 dubbed the American Century.

If, as the saying goes, imitation is the sincerest form of flattery, then *Life* succeeded on an unprecedented scale. In 1937 *Look*, the magazine that became its biggest competitor, began publishing, while other clones showed up by the score, most with visually evocative names like *Pic, See, Peek,* and *Foto*. As a rule these publications catered to the more prurient inclinations of the mediated vision. But *Life*, in its move humanized visual approach to reporting both the ordinary and the significant, was clearly the leader.

Although the editors of many American magazines had denounced involvement in a potential war, the coming of World War II soon revealed news magazines as reliable ongoing sources of information about it, attracting eager readers who only a short while ago were strict isolationists. Since to Henry Luce words were for editorializing, he had commented in the late 1930s on the dangers of imminent war and the nation's unpreparedness for it. Now he found a receptive audience not only for *Life*'s on-the-spot photo stories of the battlefront, but for features that covered the home front's reaction to the war.

Among the most popular pieces were those about the nation's rapid coming together at such a critical time, dealing with the mobilization of a vast military machine, the transition to mass production for the military, the patriotic dedication of movie stars conducting bond drives, and the sacrifice of doing without desirable consumer items due to rationing. For such reportage, Luce recruited perceptive photographers like Alfred Eisenstaedt, whose camera work resulted in memorable visual images that captured both the emotional moods and communal spirit of the time.

Life also helped distract readers from the war by publishing photo essays on achievements in science and the arts, and even topics usually reserved for the women's journals, such as the newest fashion trends. Popular, too, were articles on the latest fads, as well as those on the world of entertainment, especially the movies whose sexy stars *Life* frequently spotlighted. In fact, *Life*'s approach to displaying female sexuality was among its most anticipated features. Here was yet another media source that helped acclimate the mediated vision to a cultural acceptance of such subject matter, mainly because it appeared in a socially approved publication as opposed to the more sensationalized material carried in the era's "girlie" magazines.

First and foremost, though, *Life*'s wartime role was committed to focusing on the experiences of the American fighting man. Whether through the photograph or the art of painting/illustration, *Life* commanded all its resources to record the triumphs as well as the day-to-day drudgery and horrific ordeals of combat. Thus, the artists, correspondents, and photographers who showed up everywhere the military fought brought the war's immediate scene into the purview of the mediated vision. Robert Capa, for example, was seemingly fear-less in the face of imminent danger, producing some of the war's classic photo-graphs. In this category, the most famous was Joe Rosenthal's shot of five marines triumphantly raising the U.S. flag atop Iwo Jima's Mt. Suribachi. It was a symbolic image reverberating with the inherent American values of determination and goal achievement, foreshadowing the war's end and the future's bright promise. But *Time*'s subjective commentary on the future implications of the atomic bomb, whose use ended the war in 1945, was not so optimistic in noting that humankind now had possession of "the fires and force of the sun itself. . . . Was man equal to the challenge? In an instant, without warning, the present had become the unthinkable future. Was there hope in the future, and if so, where did it lie?"[57] This ominous observation with its apocalyptic overtones portended a coming postmodern era when the mediated vision's idealistic view of the future's promise would never be the same.

With the country's entry into the war in 1941, the *Saturday Evening Post* abandoned its conservative stance for an intensely supportive patriotic role reflected in its editorials and cover art. The retirement of longtime editor George Lorimer in 1937 saw some change as inevitable, of course. While Wesley Stout, his successor, sought to maintain the traditional rapport the magazine had with its readership, his biggest innovation in the *Post*'s appearance was to intersperse occasional photographic covers with its traditionally painted ones, a move undoubtedly influenced by the success of *Life*. While numerous new artists produced cover art that met Stout's standards, it was the output of J. C. Leyendecker and Norman Rockwell that still dominated the late thirties, projecting their familiar visual magic that had enthralled the mediated vision over the years.

When, in early 1943, Leyendecker painted his last inimitably-crafted cover for the *Post,* the way was now open for Rockwell to become its signature cover artist. In addition to his special talent for producing idyllic as well as comical anecdotal scenes, Rockwell created two legendary figures of the war years: Rosie the Riveter, in a 1943 cover that posited her as the symbol of women's contribution to the war effort, and, beginning in 1941, a series of covers about Willie Gillis, who was depicted as the average enlisted man. Rockwell's Willie was a more appealing image than that of cartoonist Bill Mauldin's dog-faced infantrymen Willie and Joe in the military newspaper *Stars and Stripes.* Clearly, Rockwell's version of the war was colored by the mediated vision's idealistic home-front viewpoint. This outlook served him well from a commercial standpoint, too, as these years were among the most productive for his work in consumer advertising, in addition to his memorable posters of President Franklin Roosevelt's "Four Freedoms," that reaffirmed the mediated vision's faith in the American way.

Even though the *Post* lost its circulation lead to *Life* in 1942, its subject matter, along with its cover art, continued to appeal despite radically changing times. The *Post* had always been a repository of high quality, entertaining fiction, but when Ben Hibbs assumed the editorship in 1942, he began promoting nonfiction features over that of fiction. However, in deference to publishing biographical pieces about successful industrialists and business entrepreneurs as champions of free enterprise, more attention was paid to popular figures of the entertainment and sports sectors, obviously in response to the mediated vision's growing interest in icons of consumption rather than production. During this time, too, *Collier's*, the *Post*'s longtime competitor, modified its exposé approach to place more emphasis on entertainment features, as though it realized the war's critical times of privation and sacrifice demanded subject matter that offered escapism. Thus, its covers competed with those of the *Post*, in the main, assuring its readers that the familiar rituals of the American lifestyle were still alive and well. With even its name a boost to morale, *Liberty* was the other general interest magazine that thrived during the war years. Even though it carried feature stories about contemporary concerns and issues, its mostly lighthearted narrative covers reflected both this magazine's feel for its readers' escapist needs and its idealistic outlook. Bernarr Macfadden had voiced his publication's optimistic outlook when he dared to prophesy in a 1939 editorial that there would be no war for a year, perhaps five. It was certainly the kind of positive message readers wanted to believe.[58]

Macfadden's editorializing revealed another side to the general interest magazines—their role as instruments of psychological and propagandistic intent, functioning in effect as national newspapers whose editorial views helped influence public opinion. Indeed, the *Saturday Evening Post* operated as a national forum which evaluated wartime policies, programs, and current as well as future issues of concern, thus alerting the mediated vision to the reality behind the appearance of things and events. As early as 1940, in fact, the *Post* was exploring the future ramifications of atomic energy for modern living. But the general interest publication that addressed the current concerns and future hopes of the mediated vision more appealingly than any other was the *Reader's Digest*.

Though still devoid of pictorial content and advertising, the *Digest* in the 1930s was well on its way to becoming the most widely circulated magazine in the world. During the war years its circulation jumped from under four million to over nine, an astonishing growth rate that can be attributed to founder DeWitt Wallace's inherent feel for correlating the *Digest's* contents to changing times. Over the years, in fact, its inspirational, informational, and self-help selections had sought to ameliorate the concerns and problems fomented by an increasingly complex world, with the implied purpose of helping make it into a better place for living. Intellectuals branded such a posture as incredibly naive and overly idealistic, but as the *Digest's* popularity continued to reveal, readers obviously relished the good news of its therapeutic pieces. While it had started out reprinting appropriate articles from contemporary publications in condensed form, the *Digest* began publishing original articles in the 1930s, and by the 40s, as its success continued unabated, was including more original pieces than reprints. Peter Canning has assessed the amazing success of the *Digest* during this era as resulting from its manner of "clearly reflecting something deep in the national psyche."[59] That "something," of course, was the mediated vision's persistent desire for a better life than that present circumstances offered.

Other magazines responded to the quest for self-improvement and specialized information in a variety of guises during this time. The hobby magazines were still informing their readers how to "Build It Yourself"—from a motor boat to a mobile trailer. Others, like *Popular Science* and *Popular Mechanics,* with their futuristic cover art, extolled this era as one of marvelous invention. One of the latter's covers brought the miracle of flight closer home by forecasting "An Airplane in Every Garage." In the bleak 1930s, readers were naturally susceptible to such a positive outlook on the future's promise.

Seemingly above all this were the magazines directed at a more sophisticated, well-to-do audience, though in the Depression years *Vanity Fair* found it increasingly difficult to relate its light-hearted views to the times, and by 1936 it was gone. *The New Yorker* may have strived to march to a different drummer, but its unique cover tradition, inspired by the urban scene, was enticing enough to lure the casual reader into its bland black and white interior pages, to discover the funniest panel cartoons of any magazine that satirized the social aberrations of the times—ranging from the bold strokes of Peter Arno's urbane vision to George Price's absurd sense of reality.

Among the most popular sources of humor during this era, the panel cartoon was also featured in general interest publications like the *Post* and *Collier's.* While magazines devoted to social satire, such as *College Humor, Ballyhoo,* and *Judge,* crowded the newsstand racks, in the 40s the pocket digests of low-brow cartoon humor depicting sexually suggestive situations found a responsive audience in military personnel, selling by the thousands at post exchanges around the country. Whether directed at the lowliest army recruit or the most educated *New Yorker* subscriber, the panel cartoon kept its audience laughing during a time when there was not much to laugh about.

Esquire, whose cartoons reflected a more urbane raciness, began publishing in 1933 as a major medium for men's fashions. It also featured fiction and nonfiction by distinguished authors such as Ernest Hemingway, John Steinbeck, and Gilbert Seldes. From their cosmopolitan perspective, *Esquire*'s editors also took the initiative to update their readers with evolving conceptions of female sexuality. Among the time's most fantasized versions was artist George Petty's idealized feminine image that became so popular by 1939 it was featured in the magazine's first fold-out section. Although Petty departed after a contract dispute, the Petty Girl tradition was expanded on by Albert Vargas's Varga Girl, beginning in 1940. In the style of the portraits he did of *Follies* showgirls in the 1920s and movie starlets in the 30s, Vargas created a seminude type whose glossily voluptuous appearance became a classic of its kind. The Varga Girl, in fact, set a standard for fantasized feminine beauty during the war years, as servicemen plastered their quarters with her pinups, and flyers highlighted aircraft nose art with her morale-boosting, sexually alluring image.

In the context of a class-conscious magazine like *Esquire,* the glorification of sex as it was embodied in an idealized female form was generally acceptable since it met the standards most readers of this publication thought of as "art." Another kind of magazine designed for a more working-class male audience fell far short of such criteria and consequently drew the wrath of the moral custodians. This was the prurient "girlie" magazine that featured photographs of women in high heels and silk stockings but little else. In the 1930s, *Film Fun's* erotic covers of young women posing in lingerie or swim suits, provocatively painted by Peter Driben or Enoch Bolles, signaled its interior's enticingly lurid contents. Publisher Robert Harrison extended this tradition in the forties by originating a stable of picture magazines with come-on titles directed at men's sexual fantasies. In a sense, the newsstand's now open display of girlie magazines was yet another sign that the mediated vision, from the complementary perspectives of the male as voyeur and the female as performer, was becoming attuned to a rapidly changing social climate reflected by daring new visual trends in the print media.

A similar development in this era appeared in the rise of the magazine that featured the exposé-type story, as, for example, the aptly named *Exposed!* As an updated version of the *National Police Gazette,* its illustrated covers of women in direful situations promised "Inside Stories the Papers Dare Not Print." Likewise, the pulp-like covers of *Sensation* in the early forties touted its coverage of the underground activities of white slavery and drug orgies as "Stories No Other Magazine Dares to Print." From the 1950s on, this kind of publication would splinter into a variety of magazines as well as tabloids.[60]

Poles apart from the publications depicting women as sex objects, of course, were the traditional women's periodicals. Due to women's ongoing sense of social independence, resulting in large part from their role in the work force during the war years, these magazines began assessing the positive and negative consequences of this new status, particularly in articles that looked ahead to the postwar years. To alert women to issues and concerns beyond the routine of homemaking, for example, the *Ladies' Home Journal* carried a series in the 1940s titled "How America Lives." It prophetically implied that the challenging world beyond the kitchen was one in which women would soon play an active role.

Nevertheless, whatever challenges lay ahead could not detract from women's natural interest in contemporary fashion. The venerable fashion journals *Harper's Bazaar* (now spelled with two As) and *Vogue* were still around, but their mission was supplemented by a number of competitors, including a new publication in 1939 called, fittingly enough, *Glamour.* By the 1940s, college women were relying on *Mademoiselle* to keep them posted on the latest styles, while in 1944 teenagers discovered *Seventeen,* the magazine that helped establish a new social image for the adolescent girl. She would generate a significant impact on the informal dress and changes in youthful lifestyle of the postwar years.

Though the traditional woman's magazine had begun to evolve into a kind of national forum for informing its readers of their rightful place in a changing world, many women whose personal lives were directly affected by the realities of the time found escape in the popular romance story magazine. The spin-offs from Bernarr Macfadden's *True Story, True Confessions,* and *True Experiences* (all ostensibly pledged to the dictum that "Truth is Stranger than Fiction") addressed their readers through compelling first person narratives with posed photographs of the stories' dramatic moments to enhance their realism. Actually, many well-to-do women who would never admit it read them, relishing subject matter that dealt with the consequences of quickie marriages, unwanted pregnancies, marriages on the wane, and divorce. Whether fabricated or not, these stories ironically revealed many of the social problems of the time. Thus, the war years, when women were more sexually aggressive due to the scarcity of available men, saw these magazines take a more realistic approach to sex. The concerns of the present may have been quite real to most women of the time, but the romance magazines paradoxically offered escape through the vicarious experience of reading about the real problems of others, the upshot of so many disrupted lives during this time.[61]

By the 1940s, magazines designed for a growing black urban audience were also expressing the fantasies and dreams emanating from blacks' gradual absorption into the mainstream culture. In success stories and features, as well as advertising derivative of the predominant white lifestyle, the leading African American magazines modeled themselves after those of the publishing establishment. *Negro Digest* and *Ebony,* for example, were outright imitations of *Reader's Digest* and *Life* respectively. Publisher John H. Johnson also cashed in on the exploitative magazine by producing photo-oriented digests with color-conscious titles like *Jet, Tan,* and *Hue,* as well as a romance tale magazine called *Tan Confessions.* Even as socially separate entities, these publications' subject matter reflected the mediated vision's natural affinity to cross the racial divide, foreshadowing a time when black lifestyle and culture would have a dominant influence on the mainstream experience of American life.

In 1941, social historian Frederick Lewis Allen observed that the practice of reading magazines was not only educational and entertaining in effect; it allowed readers "to escape from provincial limitations, to acquire a sense of taste and style and at least outward distinction, to widen the horizon, to become . . . in some degree citizens of the world."[62] The visually-oriented slick magazine, then, with its photographic essays and nonfiction features, played a key role in conditioning the mediated vision to the fact that the realities of the present could not be easily ignored. This situation was undoubtedly the reason why the fantasized fare of the pulp publications attracted such an avid following during this time.

In the 1930s the pulp magazine, in expanding on its tradition of responding to even the most bizarre escapist tastes, produced its most graphically explicit covers to promote its content. This was especially true of the titillating sex, fantasized horror, and futuristic science fiction genres. By now the standard romance tales of Street & Smith's pioneering *Love Story* had evolved into a deluge of pulps with suggestive titles like *Spicy Stories, Stolen Sweets,* and *Saucy Stories.* Offering the male eye tantalizing images of seminude females in seductive poses, their colorfully painted covers by such skilled artists as H. J. Ward and Enoch Bolles promised much, but due to censorship restrictions usually fell short of what many readers expected. Perhaps the permissiveness that mainstream fiction began to employ in describing sexual matters was their undoing, as by the 1940s the spicy pulps were gone. If they bequeathed any kind of literary influence, it was probably Robert Leslie Bellem's stories in *Spicy Detective,* whose blunt-talking private eye Dan Turner, in mixing business with sex, looked ahead to Mickey Spillane's Mike Hammer character in the 1950s.

Competing with *Weird Tales,* the long-established fantasy/horror pulp, was the "weird menace" genre. Typically, the covers of pulps like *Horror Stories* and *Terror Tales* mixed sex and mayhem by depicting scantily clad, sensuous women in bondage situations, helplessly enduring or awaiting the insidious torture methods of a demonic captor and his crazed henchmen. If the real world of the Depression was generating a seemingly endless run of economic horrors, then these publications strived to circumvent them through a gory kind of violence that made readers' problems seem trivial compared to those endured by the stories' lead characters. But their covers' gruesomely-worded titles, which informed prospective readers what to anticipate in these magazines' interior pages, naturally invited censure from the moralists, portending a similar fate for the horror comics of the 1950s.

Fittingly, the futuristic emphasis of the 1930s made this a highly favorable time for the reception of the science fiction (SF) pulp. Editor Hugo Gernsback's pioneering efforts in *Amazing Stories* had inspired a new wave of SF writers, among whom was John W. Campbell. Appointed editor of *Astounding Stories* (later *Analog*) in 1931, he promptly capitalized on this position to set forth a new vision of SF's literary purpose. If Gernsback had trumpeted the official arrival of SF as a legitimate literary genre, it was Campbell's timely emphasis on the sociological and psychological effects of science and technology on human experience that gave it a more mature vision. To visualize this posture, inspired artists like Leo Morey, H. W. Wesso, and Howard V. Brown expanded on the tradition begun by Frank R. Paul to create enthralling pulp cover illustrations of relevant visionary import.

Campbell's editorial stance flowered in the work of such talented writers in the genre as Isaac Asimov and Robert Heinlein, who went on from the pulps to attract a wide audience for SF in the slick magazines, as well as in best-selling novels, some of which would later appear as films. To many, Asimov, Heinlein, and Campbell were the founders of modern SF. While Gernsback had editorialized that SF's role was to inform the mediated vision of science's potential for making the world a better place, Campbell and his disciples sensitized readers to the perils involved in technology's quest to transform the future.[63]

As a bridge between science fiction and fantasy adventure, the prolific output of Edgar Rice Burroughs continued to appear in both magazine and book publications. The man's imagination was seemingly boundless, as he also created numerous pulp stories dealing with a variety of themes and subject matter. Realizing the sales potential of the Burroughs name, editors took to highlighting it on a cover along with the title of a story and what purported to be an exciting scene from it.

The jungle may have spawned its most popular hero in Tarzan, but the urban milieu was also generating a bountiful share of fantasized types. Among the most popular were the Shadow and Doc Savage, who, in taking on a legion of master criminals, enjoyed lengthy careers in their own magazines. The Shadow, in fact, appeared in the pulps from 1931 to 1949 in an astounding total of 325 novels. Created by Walter B. Gibson, writing under the Street & Smith house name of Maxwell Grant, this mysterious character became popular enough to be featured in other media forms, in particular a long-lasting radio series in which his sinister laugh struck terror in the hearts of his enemies (not to mention youthful radio listeners). According to Chris Steinbrunner, the Shadow's appeal lay in his ambivalent characterization, as he "was both the force of good and lurker in the darkness. In the unstable and turbulent times in which he flourished . . . it was somehow right for him to operate completely outside traditional institutions and methods of justice."[64] As the people's avenger, the Shadow provided cathartic release by overcoming his villainous adversaries who epitomized the wrongs of a highly troubled era. At a time when pulp villains abounded, some even served as omens of an imminent real-world war as, for example, the series centered around the sinister Asian, Wu Fang, and the tyrannical invading forces encountered by a secret service agent known simply as Operator 5.

But no pulp hero ever confronted a more insidious cast of monstrous villains than did Doc Savage, the superheroic character whose superb physical strength matched his scientific genius. With his five assistants, each of whom possessed a specialized talent or ability, "The Man of Bronze" became involved in adventures that took him and his team from his New York base to alien and exotic locations around the globe. The fertile imagination of Lester Dent, writing for Street and Smith as Kenneth Robeson, propelled *Doc Savage Magazine* to a total of 181 issues from 1933 to 1949. In them, the titular hero was featured in stories that ranged from science fiction adventure to supernatural fantasy. But all of them revealed Doc Savage as an updated composite of Frank Reade Jr., Nick Carter, and Frank Merriwell in his attempt to revive American ideals during a time when they desperately needed recharging.[65]

By spawning numerous pulp imitations, the legendary characters of the Shadow and Doc Savage offer significant clues to fathoming the mediated vision's escapist urges at this time. Nevertheless, the most popular pulp genres continued to be the Western and the detective-mystery. Though many writers who had helped establish the Western story in the 1920s were still publishing, the form had become so popular that editors were hard pressed to meet the demand. Consequently, hack writers by the score were grinding out formulaic tales designed to appeal to the longing for escapist adventure in the wide-open spaces of a mythical West. But it was detective fiction's urban-centered setting, with its private eye counterpart to the Western hero, that offered a more realistic and compelling kind of escapism. By this time, too, the genre achieved its greatest popularity publishing in the more reputable hardback format.

MAINSTREAM LITERARY TRENDS: FROM HARDBACKS TO PAPERBACKS

A listing of the most popular novels published from 1930 to 1945 reveals detective-mystery fiction high among the best sellers. As escapist fare, the subject of violent crime evidently had wide appeal to the mediated vision as long as it was someone else's problem. Thus, the American detective hero, in his ability to cope with this problem whenever and wherever it occurs, would persist as a favorite literary type throughout the twentieth century. By enduring the uncertainties of his profession in a take-charge, self-reliant manner, the fictional detective took on an heroic dimension in the 1930s that was uniquely his own.

One of the most popular and durable detectives in this mold was Ellery Queen, who first appeared in *The Roman Hat Mystery* in 1929. Created by the team of Frederic Dannay and Manfred Lee, writing under the pseudonym of their detective hero so as to portray him as the author of his books, Ellery Queen helped transform the conventional image of the intellectual detective into a more humanized character with a practical bent over the course of forty novels and crossovers into other media forms. In contrast to the British social class tradition of detective-mystery fiction, the democratization of American culture helps explain why the American genre evolved as it did and why the characterization of Ellery Queen, which initially functioned as a variation of the British detective, became less cerebral in manner.

But if Ellery Queen came across to the mediated vision as a more convincing model of the American detective's modus operandi, Dashiell Hammett's fiction posited the way in which he was expected to talk. In the 1930 hardback publication of the original pulp version of *The Maltese Falcon,* the laconic speech of Sam Spade received its widest exposure. To readers this fresh kind of dialogue not only helped define both character and plot development, it also contributed to a visual kind of writing style that forged an organic relationship with its subject matter. In their realistic portrayal through an indigenous urban patois, Hammett's characters become involved in complex plots that seem to be always in motion, which is why *The Maltese Falcon* and his other works were so visually right for the movies.

Although many other writers emulated the Hammett style by creating detectives in the Sam Spade mold, none was more skilled at this kind of characterization than Raymond Chandler. An avowed disciple of Hammett, he, in some ways, improved on his master's skills through the depiction of a wisecracking but dedicated private eye named Philip Marlowe, beginning in 1939 with *The Big Sleep*. In delineating his socially marginal portrait of a loner-type detective motivated by personal goals, Chandler produced novels that were also naturals for the movies, as six of his works featuring Marlowe were filmed. In spite of their ambivalent lifestyles, the detective heroes of Chandler and Hammett hold to their traditional mission to set things right by functioning as the moral center of their fragmented world. The variations in personality of all the American detectives who followed the self-realized figures of Ellery Queen, Sam Spade, Philip Marlowe, and even the eccentric Nero Wolfe, display this honorable but often frustrating quest to make things right in a world gone woefully awry.

The American detective fiction style even influenced writers who were not strictly in the private eye tradition. In his best-known novels, James M. Cain displayed masterful control of a spare, visual kind of prose that focused on the psychological effects on those who commit criminal acts for personal gain. For this reason *The Postman Always Rings Twice* (1934) and *Double Indemnity* (1941) were readily translated into films that were both critically and popularly acclaimed. Similarly, former pulp writer and attorney Erle Stanley Gardner, developed a riveting style suited to courtroom drama. Beginning with *The Case of the Velvet Claws* (1933), he introduced in trial lawyer Perry Mason, one of the most memorable characters in the history of popular fiction. In evolving into an American cultural icon, he ironically transcended the usual negative image of the real-life lawyer by appearing on radio as well as a later long-running television series. In over eighty novels centering around the melodramatic theater of the courtroom, Gardner depicted his self-confident attorney as a new kind of heroic figure, the ironically idealized conception of a demeaned authority figure who stood up for the right during an era when a sense of what was right seemed to have lost its true meaning.[66]

The reason Western fiction also rode high on the best-seller lists was due mainly to established authors who kept responding to readers' fascination with the West as a viable escapist source. Even after his death in 1939, Zane Grey maintained a big following, and the prolific output of Max Brand (Frederick

Faust) reflected its ongoing popularity. His version of the mythical West centered on visually-oriented, fast-paced plots, as exemplified in *Destry Rides Again* (1930), a prototype for the "adult" movie Western. Monuments to the visual qualities of the Max Brand stories, as well as their appeal to the mediated vision, are the three film versions of this novel in which such representative stars of their times as Tom Mix, James Stewart, and Audie Murphy played the title role in 1932, 1939, and 1955, respectively. Brand's strong visual sense for relating character to scene also made him a natural as a movie scriptwriter, a penchant that by the late 1930s found him in Hollywood.

That the American frontier provided ongoing inspiration for the historical novelist was demonstrated in best sellers like Edna Ferber's *Cimarron* (1930) and Kenneth Roberts's *Northwest Passage* (1937). Both their epic qualities and the escapist experience that the perennially popular historical novel afforded made this genre prime property for Hollywood. Naturally, the film versions of these and other popular works were highly anticipated media events.

During these trying times, novels with inspirational themes were natural candidates for the best-seller lists and ultimately the movies. There were, for example, Pearl Buck's *The Good Earth* (1931), whose Chinese agrarian setting was unique in extolling the work ethic at a time when America's faltering economy had undermined its worth; *Lost Horizon* (1933), James Hilton's vision of an idyllic paradise that instilled hope for a better future; Lloyd C. Douglas's religious-centered works, from *Magnificent Obsession* (1932) to *The Robe* (1942); Marjorie Kinnan Rawlings's *The Yearling* (1938), the sensitive story of a backwoods Florida boy's love for an orphaned deer; Betty Smith's *A Tree Grows in Brooklyn* (1943), which focused on a young girl's awakening to life's challenges; and an optimistic approach to the personal exigencies of the war in William Saroyan's *The Human Comedy* (1943). Ironically, it didn't seem to matter if the less literary-minded failed to read these books, for they were assured of seeing them in their highly publicized film versions. But the novel that received the most media attention as both a pre-publicized and released film was Margaret Mitchell's *Gone with the Wind* (1936). In it, she produced a balanced blend of character, historical incident, and action along with the nostalgic aura fomented by the South's "lost cause" and its aftermath. The 1939 film's admirable attempt to capture these elements and recreate a past truly "gone with the wind" still stands as one of Hollywood's greatest triumphs in translating a best seller to the screen.

If popular fiction was the most adaptable choice for movie production during this time, the movies, conversely, had a direct visual influence on the writing styles of many novelists, among them some of the most reputable. John Dos Passos, looking back on the reception of his panoramic trilogy *USA* that dealt with the turbulent problems of the American scene during the first third of the twentieth century, observed in 1937: "In the last fifty years a change has come over the visual habits of Americans as a group. . . . From being a word minded people we are becoming an eye minded people."[67] In fact, Dos Passos's own "eye minded" writing technique in *USA* had mirrored this visual transition, most auspiciously in his "Camera's Eye" and "Newsreel" sequences as well as Reginald Marsh's lively illustrations that broke up the fiction and nonfiction sections. From pulp fiction to the most critically acclaimed novels, writers were increasingly influenced by a mediated culture in which visual imagery dominated.

In this day of the camera's eye, then, the Marxist-inspired proletarian fiction of the 1930s that focused on the economic plight of the downtrodden complemented the photography of social realism. Reflecting the literary mainstream's mood, sociological overtones infiltrated the subject matter of such diverse novelists as Erskine Caldwell, James T. Farrell, Richard Wright, and John Steinbeck. Whether it was Caldwell's graphic depiction of the impoverished conditions of poor white Georgia farmers or Farrell's of the ghetto-bound Irish of Chicago's South Side, the naturalistic approach to their writing reinforced the social message their works implied. Filtered through the bleak vision of Farrell, the Dreiserian tradition of the city as a formidable social force was given its most devastating portrait as a result of the failure of capitalism and the ensuing subversion of individual will in the Depression years. To Richard Wright, though, the more ominous social force that pervaded both the urban and rural scenes was racism, and his first novel, *Native Son* (1940), was strongly autobiographical in its vivid portrayal of a young black man's fight against the injustices of a racist society. Ironically, during the same year that Wright's controversial novel appeared, Ernest Hemingway published his widely acclaimed *For Whom the Bell Tolls.* Its underlying message transcended the Spanish Civil War setting to proclaim the universal need for brotherhood among peoples.

Through an ever developing media culture the reading public was becoming more informed about the sociocultural significance of fiction that had formerly obtained to a more elitist audience. Although the issues and concerns that major novels focused on were more acclimated to the real world as compared to the intent of escapist fiction, their promotional copy usually took a sensationalized approach to their content, promising a momentous reading event. As a daring trailblazer of the kind of fiction that exploited sex, Erskine Caldwell made his mark with the widely banned *God's Little Acre* (1933). But the obscenity charge brought against its publisher was eventually dismissed, the sign of a more liberal interpretation of what now determined the difference between literary intent and pornography. By the postwar years, Caldwell's seemingly scatological approach to his subject matter would become even more commonplace in realistic fiction.

Among the most controversial major novels of this era was John Steinbeck's *The Grapes of Wrath* (1939). Focusing on the plight of a down-and-out

Midwest family during the Dust Bowl time of the Depression, Steinbeck employed a documentary style, but one that often rose above the novel's candid revelations to achieve a poetic manner in its observations about the dark side of the American experience in the 1930s. In a larger sense, Steinbeck's visually intense style sought to interpret the Joads' search for a better life as a macrocosmic experience that related to all the world's dispossessed and the insensitive forces that had brought them to such an end.

The new realism in fiction played an instrumental role in assuring the success of the up-and-coming paperback publishing industry, which would ultimately supplant the pulp magazine as a popular reading source and provide best-selling hardback novels new life. Founded in 1939, the Pocket Books line was originally designed for people on the go, which, along with its modest price of twenty-five cents, was the major reason the pocket-sized book was a hit from the start. By publishing subject matter that ranged from the classics to the popular, the earliest of these publications helped broaden the cultural perspective of the mediated vision. Later, paperback nonfiction would introduce the reading public to numerous classics of philosophy, the political and social sciences, and literary/arts criticism.

After publisher Robert de Graff had successfully sampled the market with a trial balloon in 1938—Pearl Buck's best-selling novel *The Good Earth*—it was apparent that reissuing hardback books in cheap, paperback reprint format had additional marketing potential. In follow-up to the impressive sales of nine other titles, de Graff secured the reprint rights to works of the most popular authors he could find, and from that point on the paperback publishing business was off and running.

A well-received nonfiction entry in the original ten books was Dorothy Brande's *Wake Up and Live!*, which offered a formula for success in life. Such a work clearly demonstrated that a solid paperback market also existed for self-help guides that addressed the American people's inherent desire for personal improvement. To answer the demand, de Graff made one of the publishing industry's most profitable coups in 1940 with the publication of Dale Carnegie's *How to Win Friends and Influence People*, a hardback best seller since 1936. Promoting Carnegie's simplistic plan for success in business and life as learning how to get along with one's associates, the book would continue in paperback format for years to come as one of the most popular self-help publications ever.

Replicating a distribution method that magazines had employed over the years, paperbacks were soon catching the eye of potential customers unaccustomed to seeing books on display at the corner newsstand and in drugstores. Like its hardback counterpart whose jacket functioned as a poster designed to promote its contents, the paperback capitalized to an even greater extent on the selling power of an appropriately illustrated cover. In direct competition with a magazine's familiar appearance aligned on a nearby rack, the paperback cover reflected the stylized approach of artists who realized that to market the paperback's packaging of fiction and nonfiction to a mass audience, they had to reconcile art with business.

Initially, the modernist design pioneered by the hardback jackets of the 1930s and early forties showed up on the covers of the paperback reprints of classic fiction and nonfiction works. But during the war years covers would become more pictorially graphic and sensational, especially those promoting fiction with socially subversive content. In a sense, the paperback cover supplanted the lurid cover artwork of the fading pulp magazine, and some publications even assumed its disreputable literary status. The artwork for popular fiction, in particular, by leaning toward a titillating and suggestive cover style would cajole even conservative readers into a more tolerant posture toward literature dealing with questionable subject matter and sensational themes.[68]

Soon, the spreading popularity of the paperback saw publishers like Avon Books, Popular Library, and Dell Books coming on the scene in the early 1940s. By 1945, Bantam Books had arrived, armed with the publishing rights to the works of such notable authors as Ernest Hemingway, F. Scott Fitzgerald, and John Steinbeck. Along with a British-based company called Penguin Books that had invaded the U.S. market in 1940, Bantam sought to maintain respectability for the paperback format. But while many of Penguin's covers were nondescript in highlighting only a work's title and author, Bantam's revealed the growing competition in the field by relying on exploitative cover scenes to promote its fiction.

In responding to reading tastes that ranged from instructive nonfiction to fiction that exploited reality-based subject matter, the downside of the paperback's democratization of Americans' reading habits lay in its growing reliance on sensationalism. Despite the cultural custodians' condemnation of such writing, it now appeared that the paperback book had a bright future in providing the mediated vision both an educational tool and an entertaining portable companion for travel and leisure-time activities. But during these years another kind of entertaining visual fiction was making a significant impact on the mediated vision.

THE COMICS TAKE TO ADVENTURE
AND OTHER CHALLENGES

To compete with the scores of popular magazines that crowded newsstands, newspaper editors took a cue from the magazines themselves by expanding their entertainment/amusement features to include more of everything, in particular serialized fiction, syndicated columnists, advice to the lovelorn, puzzles, stories about entertainment figures, and, of course the syndicated

now you can SEE the thrill-a-minute excitement of AMERICA'S GREATEST DETECTIVE STORY WRITER

in smashing, vivid, action PICTURES!

SECRET AGENT X-9

daily detective strip by today's most popular, fastest-selling author of detective novels..

DASHIELL HAMMETT

Only Dashiell Hammett could have created the swift, breathless suspense and excitement of this great new daily strip. Here is all of the stark, stirring drama, grim humor and baffling mystery that made Hammett's detective novels the favorites of all America—plus the added thrill of SEEING the story in PICTURES that bring you the action with vivid, gripping realism. There has never been a sleuth like Secret Agent X-9. He fights gun-fire with gun-fire — matches racketeers' cunning with his finely trained wits—faces any danger or runs any risk to bring the underworld into the hands of the law! Be sure to watch for Secret Agent X-9.

drawing by the sensational new illustrator **ALEXANDER RAYMOND**

begins Monday, Feb. 12, in

The Scranton Times.

Promotional ads for syndicated comics like this one reveal that by the 1930s the comic strip had assumed an important sales role for newspapers. Author's collection.

comic strip. Now an essential adjunct to a newspaper's makeup, the comics peaked in the 1930s–40s in the amount of space allotted them, particularly in the Sunday section's full or half-page, multicolored features. As an eye-enchanting format that would never again appear on a scale of such magnitude, the comics were the visual literature of both children and adults during this era. Though many old favorites were still around, a new trend was touched off by the adventure strip, the comics' latest response to the mediated vision's yen for an exotic kind of visualized escapism.

When Harold Foster left *Tarzan* in 1937 to inaugurate *Prince Valiant in the Days of King Arthur,* Burne Hogarth, an artist of equally superlative talent began drawing Edgar Rice Burroughs's perennially popular hero. He, in fact, charged the Tarzan character's physical appearance with a baroque kind of dynamic energy that pervaded all the action scenes, supplanting the movies' humanized characterization with a more mythically appealing image. Foster, in going on to his majestic illustrative style on *Prince Valiant,* also assured himself a revered place in the history of newspaper comics. His heavily researched and meticulously drawn Sunday pages of life in medieval times, with their incomparable blend of realism and fantasy, soon commanded the respect and admiration of artists and comics fans alike. Both Foster's interpretation of an historical past colored by myth and Hogarth's depiction of a fantasized jungle world afforded the mediated vision passage to wondrous places it heretofore could only dream about.

Following the popular reception of *Buck Rogers,* other strips inspired by science fiction made their appearances, some better drawn than their prototype. A prime example that set the highest standards for the genre was Alex Raymond's *Flash Gordon,* which came to the Sunday comics page in 1934. In depicting how life might exist on other worlds, Raymond, like Foster and Hogarth, brought the controlled pen of the illustrator to the comics page, thus lending a compelling air of authenticity to his work. He also demonstrated his versatility by working in the jungle tale genre of *Jungle Jim* and that of the detective story in *Secret Agent X-9,* which he initially did in collaboration with writer Dashiell Hammett.[69]

The serialized genre of the 1930s that had the greatest influence inspiring variations was that of the police detective of which Chester Gould's *Dick Tracy* was the most imitated. As a hit from its first appearance in 1931, this strip's artwork soon evolved into an expressionistic style that was highly effective in depicting the ominous atmosphere of its criminal world. With violence an integral ingredient of this milieu, Gould transformed the urban scene into a starkly rendered stage that made *Dick Tracy* a kind of morality play in which the forces of good and evil were clearly delineated. As though to underscore this end, many of Gould's gallery of grotesque villains possessed names that in signifying their physical characteristics also suggested the nefarious deeds they were capable of.

Among the more popular strips after *Dick Tracy* was Alfred Andriola's version of *Charlie Chan*, which started up in 1938. By this time the appealing Asian American sleuth was a familiar figure to the mediated vision as a result of his crossover from fiction into the movies, as noted. But a major reason for the popularity of Andriola's comic strip was a drawing style that lent it a highly realistic aura, undoubtedly an upshot of his work as assistant to Milton Caniff who had developed an illustrative mode for *Terry and the Pirates*.

The influence of Milton Caniff's style on comic strip art would be widespread and enduring. In 1934 he had begun drawing *Terry* in the conventional comic strip manner, but Caniff's professional relationship with artist Noel Sickles introduced him to a brush-type, impressionistic approach that transformed *Terry* into one of the most technically admired strips in the history of comics. Attending to the high-charged action sequences of Sickles's aviation strip *Scorchy Smith*, Caniff forged a new cinematic way of rendering movement and the interaction of his characters. Many later artists would capitalize on this breakthrough, but the real winner was the mediated vision in the way this style enabled it to relate to comic strip escapism as though it were film on paper.

As aviation had inspired numerous strips since the late 1920s, the war presented their artists a ripe opportunity to focus on the strategic role of air power as well as dramatize the patriotic zeal of their central characters. The strong characterization and narrative power of *Terry and the Pirates*, for example, enhanced the morale-boosting adventures of a grownup Terry Lee as a combat pilot. Some artists created new strips for the occasion, in particular Roy Crane, who forsook *Captain Easy* in 1943 for *Buz Sawyer*, which featured the exploits of a carrier-based Navy pilot. While many newspaper cartoonists were promoting war bond sales through their popular characters, others had them taking part in the war itself.[70]

Beginning in 1942 the military life cartoons of Army enlisted men Bill Mauldin, George Baker, and Dave Breger were supplemented in the day's military publications by a unique feature called *Male Call*. Drawn in the polished style of civilian Milton Caniff, it featured a beautiful, sexily attired young woman known simply as Miss Lace. Relying on double entendre and tongue-in-cheek humor, Caniff depicted her character as the center of attention to off-duty servicemen, most of whom were vying for her affections. Besides its suggestive humor, the visual pleasure for the military man derived from Caniff's erotic rendering of Miss Lace, a task he was well suited for, having created such alluring characters as the Dragon Lady, Normandie, and Burma in *Terry and the Pirates*. According to Caniff, though, Miss Lace was created as "a wish fulfillment for the readers. She was always there, always available, and yet *not* available. The whole thing hung on the point of view of the American G.I. . . . What he's really thinking about is the girl back home."[71] Functioning as an ideal, then, Miss Lace's mediated morale-building role inspired servicemen to anticipate the good life awaiting them after the war.

The comics first realized their visual power to bring people together in the Depression years when editors emphasized both the daily gag and continuity strips as escapist fare. Though many strips had established a longtime communal following, new ones also found fans during these years, a trend especially true of the humorous family strips. Dominated by women, in particular a wife or single girl, the genre found a highly appealing interpretation in Chic Young's *Blondie,* which debuted in 1930. In terms of worldwide circulation, this strip in both its daily and Sunday format would become one of the most popular and enduring of all time, simply because it made the most of the family's basic concerns of eating, sleeping, raising children, caring for pets, and earning a livelihood. But the strip's humor derived mainly from the misadventures of Blondie Bumstead's bumbling husband Dagwood, whether at home, at work, feuding with his boss or neighbors, or dealing with neighborhood children.[72]

One of the most avidly followed continuity strips of this era featured the female lead of Harold Gray's *Little Orphan Annie,* then at the peak of its popularity. Essentially, Gray utilized Annie's adventures to dramatize his conservative opinions about the problems of American society he saw emanating from a spreading liberalism in the 1930s. Despite Gray's periodic habit of voicing his thoughts through Annie's soliloquies, a great deal was happening in this strip as its story line moved resolutely toward a climactic moment when Annie's foes (and Gray's as well) got their comeuppance. Thus, Annie, through her self-reliant nature, always managed to overcome any difficulty, then reflect on the state of things, only to encounter other problems of equal or more ponderous import down the road. Although Annie's guardian, the self-made billionaire Daddy Warbucks, epitomized the role big business had played in building the nation, his part in the strip became highly controversial during the Depression years, testing Gray's rationale for championing a wealthy man at a time when many people were doing without. But overall it was Gray's storytelling ability that kept readers following his comic strip epic and attending to its basic message urging a return to the core values that an increasingly liberal society had undermined.

Among the most popular strips showing how comedy and continuity could work together was *Thimble Theater Starring Popeye.* In 1929, after creator Elzie Segar brought Popeye the Sailor on stage as a minor character, positive fan reaction soon saw him moved into the lead role. Voicing a combination of nautical terms and his own unique mispronunciations, Popeye endeared himself to comics fans by overcoming his uncouth manner through an innate wisdom in dealing with an assortment of eccentric associates. Of these, the standouts were the conniving J. Wellington Wimpy and the gawky, spinsterish Olive Oyl, with whom Popeye carried on a longtime romance. But the highlight of *Thimble Theater* was Segar's special way of narrating episodes of high adventure in which Popeye encountered a colorful lineup of grotesque villains. As one of the first superheroes, whose strength was attributed to a fondness for spinach, Popeye always succeeded in subduing his most powerful adversaries. By the 1940s his character had become legendary as both a merchandising image (not to mention the promotion of spinach as a health food) and the star of the Fleischer studio's animated cartoon series, as noted.

Another humorous continuity strip structured around a physically strong but incredibly naive character quickly attracted a devoted following. Al Capp's *Li'l Abner*, which first appeared in 1934 as a takeoff on the ignorant ways of rural mountain folk, soon had its title character involved in a series of madcap episodes that, in mirroring the turbulent times of the 1930s, laid the foundation for Capp's later attacks on the follies and foibles of American society from the 1940s to the 1970s. The naiveté (or stupidity) of Abner Yokum, as well as a degree of physical strength he seemed unaware of, merged in a character who was both fall guy and foil in the picaresque escapades he became embroiled in. But fans loved his characterization, and the strip soon grew so popular that cults sprang up, particularly after the advent of the first Sadie Hawkins Day in 1937, when the women of Abner's hometown of Dogpatch were allowed to enter a race to catch eligible bachelors as a prize for matrimony. College males made it their own special event, adapting Capp's lampoon of the dominance of women in American life to their own advantage. Such a send-up was only the beginning for Capp as he unleashed his liberal views in an ongoing series of bizarre episodes that work to complicate Abner's life in particular and satirize modern life in general.[73]

That fantasy in the tradition of *Little Nemo* was still alive was demonstrated in a little-known strip that first appeared in 1942. Crockett Johnson's *Barnaby*, in which a little boy and his comically conceived fairy godfather are privy to a world that adults cannot perceive, caught the fancy of those who found it in the few papers that carried it during its ten-year run. Though *Barnaby* maintained the fantasy milieu of *Krazy Kat*, which ended in 1944, the realities of the real world were now offering newspaper cartoonists a richer territory to explore.

As in the magazine, the humor of the newspaper's panel cartoon was inspired by peoples' inability to live up to the realities imposed on them by such societal institutions as courtship, family, work, and law enforcement. And in the 1930s–40s, panel series satirizing the foibles of human nature were abundant. Others covered familiar topics ranging from sports to politics. Robert L. Ripley, a former sports cartoonist, parlayed his experience in the field into a highly successful panel called *Believe It or Not!* Initially focusing on sports oddities, he soon took a wider perspective on unusual topics and bizarre subject matter around the globe in a popular syndicated series. After the manner of P. T. Barnum, Ripley capitalized on the mediated vision's fascination with the strange and mystifying to create a unique fantasy venue out of reality, as he also did in his movie short version, noted earlier.

With war clouds on the horizon in the late 30s, the output of the editorial cartoonists reflected a division between an isolationist posture and one that advocated girding for war. However, when war became a reality, their perspectives were energized by a collective patriotic fervor directed at an enemy whose actions they perceived as contrary to the laws of the civilized world. As much an influence in sensitizing the mediated vision to the war's exigencies as the most heated editorials were Pulitzer Prize winners C. D. Batchelor of the *New York Daily News* and Vaughn Shoemaker of the *New York Herald Tribune*. Thus, the newspaper editorial cartoon remained a strong visual force in informing the mediated vision of the time's realities that could no longer be ignored.[74]

During this era the art of the newspaper comics had become such a highly familiar type of visual expression that corporations were requesting ad agencies to promote their products in the comic strip format. Among the artists who responded to this demand in the 1930s were Milton Caniff and Noel Sickles, who supplemented their incomes creating ministrips promoting various products, one in particular that dramatized the physical problems attendant to "coffee nerves" and their remedy by drinking a coffee substitute called Postum. By the 40s, then, comic strip characters had become so widely recognizable that they, like movie stars, were seen as highly effective agents of salesmanship in the consumer process.[75]

Proof that the comic strip had become a strong social force during these years was revealed in the ongoing criticism of its vulgar appeal by the keepers of public morals. While sexual relationships were never overtly delineated in the comic strip, they were certainly implied, as in Moon Mullins's womanizing, Jiggs's leering at the fashionably dressed young women who appeared in *Bringing Up Father,* and the erotically alluring females who showed up in *Terry and the Pirates*. Explicit sexual activity was reserved for the crudely drawn underground comic strip booklets that flourished in the 1930s. The leading performers in these eight-page minimelodramas, whose rampant sexual escapades enacted suppressed male fantasies, were popular comics characters, movie stars, or mediated public figures. Ironically labeled "Tijuana Bibles," their unwitting function as sex education manuals introduced many a pubescent male to the mysteries of the sex act.[76]

Whether the visual power of newspaper comics made them a natural vehicle for influencing the morals of their audience has never really been determined. But they were forerunners of the controversial comic book whose subject matter revealed an obsessive emphasis on crime and violence. By the late 1930s the comic book that featured costumed superheroes had become a publishing phenomenon, mainly through its attraction to the nation's youth. In 1939, Jerry Siegel and Joe Shuster's *Superman*, which had started out the previous year, was also appearing in 230 newspapers. Anticipating the appeal that the comic book might have for an adult audience, Will Eisner introduced the Spirit, a refreshingly different kind of masked hero who headed up a sixteen-page comic book supplement in a number of major newspapers beginning in 1940. At a time when the mediated vision's escapist inclinations placed a high premium on heroic adventure, fantasized characters who took on the forces of crime as well as those of the Axis responded to the demand in full force during the superhero craze of 1939–45.

The Comic Book Superhero:
The Alter Ego as Escapist Identity

The familiar format of the comic book that the public came to recognize was modeled after the promotional giveaways featuring popular newspaper comics characters that department stores produced for children, beginning in 1933. One of these evolved into *Famous Funnies,* the first monthly comic book to appear on the newsstand as a sixty-four-page, all-color publication selling for ten cents. Sensing big profits to be made in this fledgling business, competitors sprang up overnight, most publishing syndicated comics reprints of characters like Dick Tracy, Flash Gordon, and Tarzan. Then, with the appearance of *Detective Comics* in 1937, the modern comic book had arrived, for it included a lineup of all original private eye and police characters, obviously inspired by their pulp fiction counterparts. *Detective Comics* would not only become the longest-running comic book, it provided an identity for a major comic book enterprise—DC Comics.[77]

In 1938 the character of Superman made his appearance in the first issue of DC's *Action Comics,* an event that would revolutionize the comic book industry and turn it into one of the most profitable in the publishing field. Consequently, the hundreds of superheroic character variations that followed can be attributed to the successful reception of this one character, who seemed a composite of the pervasive escapist desires of the time. Ultimately, Superman would become one of the most universally recognized figures of the mediated culture. He, in fact, has been called "*the* great American hero" who achieved "truly mythic stature, interweaving a pattern of beliefs, literary conventions and cultural traditions of the American people more powerfully and more accessibly than any other cultural symbol of the 20th century."[78] Over the years, the popularity of Superman found additional mediated expression in radio, movies, and television, as well as in the form of games and toys, and even as endorsements of food and beverage products.

In 1939, another protean character arrived in *Detective Comics.* In contrast to the seeming invincibility of Superman, whose powers derived from an alien source, Bob Kane's Batman was a mortal being, who, like pulp hero Doc Savage, relied on his own scientific knowledge, ingenuity, and physical skills to subdue depraved villains like the Joker, the Penguin, and Two-Face, character types who naturally abounded in the superhero comic books. With the appearance of Robin the Boy Wonder in 1940, *Batman* also introduced the tradition of the young sidekick, thus enhancing sales potential through young readers' identification with a role model.

The characters of Superman and Batman were prototypes of the two basic kinds of comic book heroes—one endowed with superhuman powers and the other dependent on his own human capabilities. While the former character, who gained his powers in a variety of ways, predominated, both types had one thing in common—the way they dressed when countering their foes. From its inception, the superhero character was attired in a skintight costume, usually complemented by a mask or hood and cape. Despite such a pretentious appearance, young fans recognized in it a symbol of what a favorite hero stood for. It also represented a way to realize their own alter-ego fantasies of escape from an indifferent world in which a sense of personal identity was not easy to come by.

As a catastrophic world war called forth the energies of not only the nation but also the comic book heroes to combat totalitarian forces bent on world conquest, the publication of comic books approached floodtide in the early 1940s. To meet publishers' production demands, assembly-line shop systems were set up, whose output ranged from the mediocre work of hacks to the expert draftsmanship of skilled artists like Will Eisner and Lou Fine. Indeed, the comic books' action packed covers featuring the seductive styles of such artists as Fine and Alex Schomburg helped mesmerize American youths' attraction to the superhero during this era.

With some 150 titles appearing monthly on newsstands by 1940, even long-established pulp magazine publishers scrambled to reap the benefits of the comic book explosion. That year, Fawcett came up with the biggest original hit in *Whiz Comics'* Captain Marvel. Soon outselling even Superman, Captain Marvel's adventures had a humorous aura about them that came across as a lampoon of the superhero concept. The gimmick of young Billy Batson uttering the magic word "Shazam" to be transformed into the mighty image of Captain Marvel not only contributed to endless plot possibilities, but also offered a fascinating diversion for young readers in its mystical connotation, suggesting a self-realized way to escape the repressions of school and family that was only a spoken word away.

A major factor in the popularity of comic books was the war itself, whose real-life villains of Hitler, Mussolini, and Hirohito were depicted as pure evil incarnated, fully deserving of their comeuppances from a colorful array of superheroes. Most of the patriotic heroes were modeled after Timely's Captain America, who first appeared on the cover of his own magazine taking it out on Hitler some nine months before the country was drawn into the war. The

This copy of *Captain America: The Classic Years*
is one of a very limited number containing this
special bookplate signed by Joe Simon.

Image by Joe Simon © 1998 Marvel Characters, Inc.   June, 1998   Bud Plant Comic Art

During the war years, the comic book superhero Captain America, created by Joe
Simon and Jack Kirby, spawned many patriotic imitations. This signed bookplate
replica of a 1941 *Captain America* cover accompanied a reprint book of the character's early years. © 1998 Marvel Comics. Author's collection.

team of Joe Simon and Jack Kirby, the creators of Captain America, was among the most prolific in the comic book industry, as their output for both Timely and DC demonstrated. Kirby's dynamic artwork ideally complemented Simon's fast-paced stories by providing them a cinematic focus. In fact, Kirby has commented on how his drawing style was influenced by his fascination with movies: "I saw myself as a camera . . . I developed a kind of three-dimensional style so you can see a player from all angles. . . . I put a lot of movement into my characters."[79] In effect, Kirby's cinematic vision characterized the look of everything he produced for an audience that in itself was highly sensitized to the movie-viewing experience.

Although most of the artwork in comic books was mediocre at best, artists on the order of Kirby, Will Eisner, and Jack Cole brought a high degree of competence and experimentation to this fledgling form of creative expression. Cole was as ingenious in his creativity as Kirby and Eisner, turning out a long line of original characters, both comic and heroic. Plastic Man, his most famous creation, typified Cole's energized explosive drawing style and his highly original approach to visualizing a story. As a superhero who has the power to assume any physical shape, Plastic Man, from his first appearance in 1941, provided the ideal expressive mode for his creator's comically absurd, unrestrained imagination. While Cole would die at forty-four (tragically by his own hand), Will Eisner went on to a long, distinguished career, contributing a great many innovative techniques to the art of the comic book.[80] The work he did on *The Spirit,* his magnum opus, would stand as an impressive achievement in displaying what comic book art is capable of. Influenced by the movies and the American short story tradition, Eisner merged the visual techniques of the former with the compressed, ironic mode of the latter to relate a weekly story in the space of no more than seven pages. Setting a mood right from a story's start was an Eisner trademark, even to the point of incorporating the title page's stylized letters into a thematic layout. As in most comic book stories, a surfeit of violence characterized *The Spirit's* crime fighting exploits, but in directing his stories toward an adult audience, Eisner was not averse to sex playing a key part, as intimated in the Spirit's encounters with various femme fatales throughout the series. However, it was all tempered by an underlying comical tone that made for a kind of tongue-in-cheek spoof of the comic book crime fighter with a secret alias.

It was the comic book's tendency to fantasize real life with an undue amount of violence that most concerned parents, teachers, and social critics at the time. In 1941, to enhance the cultural image of the comic book, the Parents Magazine Institute began publishing titles like *True Comics* and *Real Heroes,* which, in portraying the experiences of people of historical and contemporary significance, were not really "comic" books in the word's fantasized sense. To test the reception of classic fiction in comic book format, the Gilberton Company brought out Alexander Dumas's *The Three Musketeers* in

1941. As the first title of 169 that would appear in the *Classic Comics* (later *Classics Illustrated*) series over a twenty-eight-year span, the venture proved to be a big success as well as a boon to students who covertly relied on them for the book reports English teachers demanded. However, fiction, whether classic or popular, was also, in effect, a form of fantasized experience, and although reality may have been more thrilling than fiction, as the real-life comics contended, visualized fantasy as escapist experience was still the major ingredient that continued to sell comic books.

However, when one so-called comic book depicting the subversive lifestyles of real-life criminals made its debut in 1942, it became not only the most widely read in this format but the most controversial. *Crime Does Not Pay* was the brainchild of publisher Lev Gleason, who hired one of the most versatile talents in the comic book industry to edit it. Equally at home in the roles of editor, writer, and artist, Charles Biro had created some of the most appealingly popular heroes in comic books as well as some of the best-plotted stories relating their adventures But he saw this new assignment as taking the comic book in a whole new direction, and to enhance the realism of the biographies of notable criminals like John Dillinger and Lucky Luciano, he called them "illustories." Although a large adult following read them, it was their supposed harmful effects on young readers that raised considerable concern in the minds of the cultural custodians who still considered the audience for comic books to be children. Because this publication and its many imitations visualized criminal activity in graphic detail, they charged that young readers were being directly exposed to the most violent crime sprees of the twentieth century. It mattered not that the criminals were depicted as coming to a deserved end; critics were more upset over what appeared to be the dramatization of violence for violence's sake. In beginning a trend that would culminate in the uproar over the horror comics of the 1950s, the crime genre also marked another step toward conditioning the mediated vision to a general understanding of media-made violence as another form of fantasized entertainment.

The manner in which women were being presented, not only in crime-oriented comics but in some other comic books, also raised the problem of suggestive sex and its effects on young, impressionable male minds. Like their pulp magazine counterparts, the Fiction House and Fox lines of comic books seemed to revel in displaying flimsily dressed, buxom young women on their covers and in their stories. While the bondage scenes of these comic books presented many adolescent boys their first up-close look at female anatomy, it was the appearance of the superheroine who best caught the social temper of changing times. And the most emblematic of them, whose self-assertive ways presaged the feminist movement of the 1970s, was Wonder Woman. Created by psychologist William Moulton Marston to counter the dominance of the superhero and supposedly respond to the young girl audience of the time, Wonder Woman was depicted as utilizing her Amazonian powers to champion women's rights.[81] However, to show her role as more than that of a feminist, she was attired in a skimpy, red-, white-, and blue-colored costume that promoted her persona as a kind of female Captain America aligned against the enemies of democracy, as were a number of other costumed female characters and variations of the superhero genre.[82]

Even though the superhero craze would die out by war's end, the year 1946 would see some forty million comic books being published every month. Their universal appeal attested to their role as social barometers of American youth culture—where it was at the time and where it might be headed. With its roots entrenched in the ideals of the American past, the comic book and its escapist tales of triumph over immediate problems were inspired by the mediated vision's idealistic dream of making the world into a better place. Moreover, Les Daniels, a comic book historian, has reacted to this form's status as an underrated cultural influence, noting that comic books "have become part of the modern consciousness, and their influence has spread into the arts from painting to literature to cinema. . . . They offer excitement, adventure and spectacle. They appeal to the dreamer in all of us."[83]

THE ESCAPIST DIMENSIONS OF SPECTATOR AND PARTICIPANT SPORTS

Recognizing the American people's growing preoccupation with organized sports as another visually appealing mode of escape, the mass media directed even more attention to them during this era. Expanded newspaper coverage of high school athletic programs, particularly football, helped build a supportive audience for them as fans began to realize that prep schools were the training grounds for the collegiate heroes of tomorrow. At a time when problematic events pervaded the news media, reports of achievements in both amateur and professional sports were a big boost to the morale of the American people. Also the hoopla attendant to championship boxing bouts, baseball's World Series, and important college football games contributed a great deal to the mediated vision's perception of sport as a theatrical event of high dramatic import.

Although the war years put the development of television on hold for the duration, radio's broadcast monopoly of sports continued in full swing. With attendance at college football games reaching an all-time high in the 1930s, the realization that radio brought football schools widespread publicity as well as money from the commercial investment of sponsors was another sign of things to come in sport's evolving relationship with the electronic media. While sportscasters capitalized on the realization that football had become a more wide-open game through their intensely dramatic descriptions, its role as public spectacle had also been enhanced by the inauguration in the 1930s of such postseason games as the Orange Bowl in Miami, the Sugar Bowl in New Orleans, and the Cotton Bowl in Dallas. By this time, football's linkage to past traditions and school alumni's perennial hope for a national championship had affirmed the mediated vision's ongoing fantasized relationship with it.[84]

While the northern-based game of professional football was shunned by most college players in the 1930s, those recruited by the developing National Football League were talented enough to lend credibility to an image long overshadowed by the college game and baseball. But in the 1940s a timely innovation called the T-formation helped transform football's offensive style of play into a more visually exciting game. Since that time the offensive strategy of both the collegiate and professional games has proliferated into evolving variations of this prototypal formation. Indeed, its qualities of speed and quickness, in addition to frequent passing, field goal attempts, and the specialization of positions saw football become a corporate-styled game that, in adopting the collegiate game's defining competitive characteristic of pride in the place that a team represents, would evolve into *the* game of the mediated vision by the 1960s. However, in the 1930s baseball was still ascendant as the "National Pastime." To die-hard fans, baseball and mediated culture were one and the same, as the game's legendary player statistics and records offered both an historical and nostalgic referent to the game's past.

In the meantime, college basketball's style of play, which was still languishing as slow, deliberate, and low scoring, was on the brink of revolution, particularly after Stanford's Hank Luisetti introduced a flamboyant style that made the game more exciting to watch. Shunning the standard two-handed set shot advocated by conservative coaches, Luisetti perfected a one-handed jump shot at which he became so proficient he scored the unheard-of total of fifty points in a 1937 game. Recognizing that a faster-paced brand of basketball could make for entertaining spectacle, promoter Ned Irish started booking double-header college games in Madison Square Garden. Ironically, blacks, who would ultimately dominate college and professional basketball, were initially barred from it as well as other pro team sports. That the general racist posture toward blacks at the time perceived them more as entertainers than athletes undoubtedly explained the public's ready acceptance of the Harlem Globetrotters and their clownish antics on the court. The emergence of the black athlete in America awaited the profound social changes of the postwar world. Ironically, in the television era sports would take on even more of an entertainment function.

An anomaly of the time, though, was Joe Louis, the young impoverished black boxer who rose through the ranks to become the world heavyweight champion in 1937. To black people he was their fighter, a symbol of hope in an oppressive white man's world, and when he fought they gathered around their radios to cheer their "Champion" on to another inspiring victory. But one fight, as a media event of great political significance, made Louis an American hero of both whites and blacks, the 1937 rematch with the boxer who had previously defeated him—Nazi Germany's Max Schmeling. By knocking him out in less than two minutes of the first round, Louis was lauded by the press as more a champion of the American way than a symbol of any minority cause, much for the same reason sprinter Jesse Owens was praised for winning four gold medals in the 1936 Berlin Olympics.

By now the Olympic Games had evolved into a form of international theater, a grandiose media-made stage for participating countries to showcase their political systems through the success of their athletes. Indeed, Adolph Hitler had designed the 1936 Nazi Olympics to reveal to the world the sociocultural revolution of the new Germany, looking also to focus on athletic achievement as visible evidence of his nation's racial supremacy.[85] But Owens's victories over Hitler's "Aryan-pure" athletes clearly demonstrated the fallacy of the racial superiority myth, signifying to many the triumph of American democracy over Nazi totalitarianism. The irony of both Louis's and Owens's success was further compounded by their unwillingness to use their prestige as champion athletes to speak out against the racial injustices of their own country.

Not only was sport in this era predominantly racist, it was blatantly sexist. When Mildred "Babe" Didrikson, a great athlete in her own right, won two track and field medals in the 1932 Olympics, many perceived her success as something of an aberration because of her exceptional ability to excel in traditionally male-dominated sports. Some even saw her accomplishments as detrimental to the ideal of American womanhood. By contrast, the Norwegian ice skater Sonja Henie was a popular favorite in winning a gold medal in a "gender-appropriate" sport in the 1932 Winter Olympics. In fact, Henie's star quality earned her a Hollywood contract that cast her feminine good looks in conventional romantic roles. At a time when the closest a "real" female was expected to participate in athletics was as a cheerleader, the 1932 Olympics offered the woman athlete her first real chance to prove her worth. But until the century's latter years, the status of American sport as a male sanctuary would remain a formidable barrier for women to overcome.

Although the individualized sports of golf and tennis maintained their class-oriented ways during these years, municipal golf courses and the tennis courts of public recreational parks presented middle-class enthusiasts more opportunities to play these demanding games. A key factor in the democratization of participant sports was the varied opportunities for self-realization they now offered. Competing in mixed-gender bowling leagues became a communal ritual for many couples, while the game of softball developed into a national mania, with both men and women fielding teams in company, community, and church leagues. While cycling maintained mass

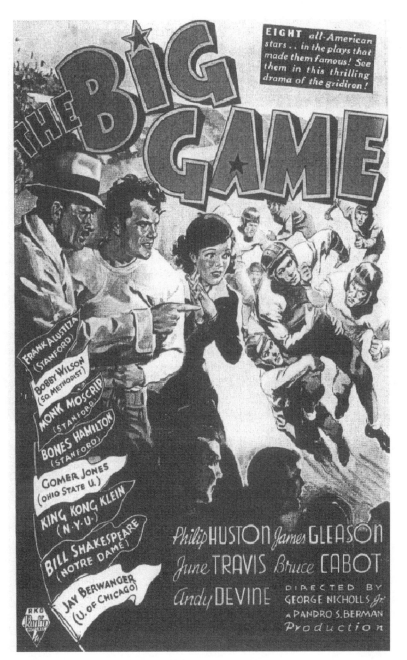

This ad for *The Big Game* (RKO, 1936) dramatized Hollywood's penchant during this era for signing real-life sports stars whose roles responded to the American fascination with the athlete as sociocultural hero. Author's collection.

appeal at a time when cars were not so readily available, indoor roller skating in commercial rinks inspired media interest in the spectator sport of Roller Derby, an offshoot of the six-day bicycle races that reflected the thirties' craze for endurance activities. Of these the most bizarre was marathon ballroom dancing, which awarded the last remaining couple a cash prize.

A sense of self-fulfillment was the reward for the serious participant in sporting activities, while other dedicated fans found vicarious escapism in merely watching a favorite team or athlete perform. Because the media were now promoting the spectator sports of college football and professional baseball as a form of show business, the adulation of athletic heroes that had begun in the 1920s continued on into the 1940s. Naturally, Hollywood played a big role in this ongoing process through the production of numerous sports-centered movies, which, in substantiating the positive side of sports experience, expanded on its mythical implications.[86] Thus, the signing of real-life athletes to help promote these formulaic films saw them functioning as icons rather than actors. To the mediated vision at this time, then, champion athletes were more than fantasized entertainers; they were actualized symbols of the success ethic that the American way extolled. Such an heroic role not only helped establish a strong sense of community by positing the athlete at its center; it was also instrumental in defining what it meant to be an American.

Although sport had played a key sociocultural role in mythologizing the American experience, it, like other social institutions in the coming postmodern era, would be subjected to the problematic trends of a fragmented mediated culture and function increasingly as a microcosm of society's ills. Accordingly, such topics as the demise of the athlete's heroic ideal, the overemphasis on winning, and fan misbehavior invite further sociocultural analysis in an ensuing book on the ever-evolving media-made culture and its visual impact on American life in the second half of the twentieth century.

Epilogue: Detecting the Signs
of a Coming Postmodern Era

> By conferring the benefits of affluence on every member of the
> population, America created the notion of a popular culture. It
> toppled the barriers between art and ordinary life, and put into
> practice a revolution which all the [post]modernists had hoped for.
> —Peter Conrad, *Modern Times, Modern Places*

From the opportunistic times of Carrie Meeber's symbolic Chicago pilgrimage to the end of World War II and the generally optimistic expectations of the future, the visual focus of media-made culture was mainly communal in intent. From the 1890s to the 1940s its purveyors had responded to the nation's escapist dreams and desires with a wide variety of mediated attractions that cut across the class, gender, age, and ethnic components of the society to unite Americans in the egalitarian outlook of the mediated vision. Paradoxically, though, the communal perspective harbored the seeds of its own disintegration that, during the century's second half and the evolving democratization of American culture, would result in an ethos fragmented into multiple subcultures of mediated special interests.

The earliest signs of this development had appeared in the variety of late nineteenth-century escapist venues and diversions designed to counter the alienation of the urban scene and transcend the ordinariness of everyday life. The Chicago Exposition of 1893, as a repository of both elitist interests displayed in the White City and those of mass appeal in the Midway Plaisance, was a model for future amusement parks and other great fairs in this vein. In bringing together the polar interests of both these entities in one place, then, the Chicago fair was a touchstone media event that epitomized the inception of a mediated milieu in which one could be both edified and entertained.

In the ensuing years, momentous technological breakthroughs made it possible for musical recordings, movies, and radio to introduce new ways to cut across the cultural divide. As the most visually and escapist oriented of these entertainment forms, the movies were also the most culturally influential in narrowing the gap between the popular and elitist sectors in the first half of the twentieth century, especially after critics accorded film the status of an art form. In the 1920s, radio, in its broadcast of entertainment and information programming, first introduced listeners to an immediate shared sense of belonging to a community of like interests. But from its beginning, the medium also proved highly sensitive to the special interests of its listeners as, for example, in its response to audiences for both popular and classical music, a portent of later "format" programming for special tastes. Technological advances were not lost on the musical performance scene either, as electronic developments in the innovative Swing era prefigured the self-promoted type of recording performer who would respond mainly to the youth sector. Similarly, the improvisational style of musical expression that was a natural outgrowth of the African American social experience and its contributions to popular music presaged the myriad styles of rock music and those of other musical genres that would spring up in the century's second half.

In seeking to entertain as well as inform, the newspaper, through the escapist appeal of tabloid-type journalism and daily diversions like the comic strip, played a strong democratizing role by offering fare that attracted a wide range of readers across the social spectrum. The pictorial magazine, with its coverage of topics and themes of communal as well as special interests, and the fantasized pulps, whose attention to unique subject matter seemingly knew no bounds, also looked ahead to the diverse subcultural sectors that the electronic media would respond to. To survive, then, the print media were compelled to find diverse audiences, as from the 1950s on, they, as well as the movies, would see their major competition emanating from the visually immediate role of television. Thus, sensational journalism that had spotlighted the lifestyles and social indiscretions of celebrities, especially those made famous by their careers as entertainers, would generate even more sensationalized reportage in the century's second half. By then, the mediated vision would see celebrity culture as a kind of fantasized reality that had invaded all spheres of American society. Also, as sport continued to gravitate toward spectacle and entertainment, creating its own celebrated performers in the process, play, as opposed to work, would clinch an ascendant place in the social scene. With more leisure time available, the upshot would be an ongoing investment of it in individualized leisure activities as well as in the proliferating spectator sports fostered by the media, especially television.

Consumer advertising, in its targeting of both mass and special interest sectors, revealed the inherent power of celebrated and commonplace images to convey its messages, anticipating a postwar era dominated by televised imagery that entertained as it attempted to promote a product. Still among the most mediated products that equated directly with the good life was the automobile, and its advertising continued to focus on self-esteem as a major factor in stimulating the American people's ongoing quest for the ultimate in personal mobility.

In the century's early years, the social experimentations of the Bohemian lifestyle in New York's Greenwich Village signaled the role that youth would play in the fragmentation of society from the 1920s to century's end. Following World War I and the mood of cynicism and youthful rebellion that characterized the era, the New Woman, as the latest version of Carrie Meeber, established a social image that would grow increasingly self-assertive in the years ahead. Women's revolutionary fashion styles, reflected in the magazine ads and the movies of the time, were among the most telling signs of social change. Certainly the movies played a major role in not only depicting women's "coming out" but influencing their social image from the 1920s through the 1940s. Although censorship strived to restrict film's focus on sex and violence, a number of daring movies foreshadowed what was to come in the more self-indulgent and socially liberal times of the century's second half. Indeed, the mediated vision, conditioned by the modern era's cinematic affinities, would become even more voyeuristic as society evinced a growing escapist propensity to identify with visually-mediated reality as escapist experience.

The ongoing democratization of the literary scene, evidenced by the best-selling novel in either the hardback or the new paperback format, saw both their mainstream and popular authors expounding on a varied cross-section of topics and themes of either inspirational or, increasingly, controversial bent—the result of a growing liberal posture toward formerly taboo subject matter, especially sex. By century's end, novelists would be freely expressing themselves with hardly any fear of censorship. As though in reaction to the media's graphic emphasis on life's problematic issues and concerns, a nostalgic mood would pervade the last years of the century, cajoling the mediated vision to look back ironically to the media icons of the century's first half as emblematic of better times.

From a sociocultural perspective, though, it was the visual arts that offered some of the more revealing insights into where American culture was headed in the coming postmodern era. If sports had functioned as a strong communal force to bring people together, the visual arts still played a culturally divisive role during this era. By 1945, the American people, in looking ahead to the promising new way of life that the postwar world portended, envisioned a world not without some semblance of doubt and foreboding, emanating mainly from a fear of what the accessibility to atomic power might hold in store. It was a mood more psychological than that fomented by the Depression's economically uncertain times or the war years' sense of social isolation. By the mid-1940s, then, the arts movement known as Abstract Expressionism had begun to reflect the new uncertainties. Its nonrepresentational perspective appeared to emanate from a willful retreat from depicting the real (or what many artists deemed "unreal") world to fomenting a personal vision that was more internalized than outward-directed, as in the works of Willem de Kooning and Jackson Pollock.

Earlier, regionalist artists Thomas Hart Benton and John Steuart Curry had looked to the heritage of the nation's past to express a more concrete vision of its collective memory. In their attention to populist traditions, they drew on their respective styles of romantic realism to portray a rural America that aspired to nostalgic myth. Whether ennobling or satirical, as in the paintings of Grant Wood, the difference between these artists' regional subject matter and that of the urban-tempered painters like Edward Hopper and Charles Sheeler, lay in the ongoing cultural conflict between the worth of an agrarian past and the polarizing aura of the city and the industrial scene that had been undermining the mediated vision's idealized sense of a pastoral past for over fifty years.

In 1935, the Federal Arts Project put a veritable army of unemployed artists to work, assigning many to paint panoramic murals of the American scene in public buildings. Mostly avoiding the modernist tendency toward abstract expressionism, they created a kind of visionary realism that, in the mode of Benton and Curry, idealized the American past as well as a hopeful future by appealing to both the nostalgic and aspirational inclinations of the mediated vision, though some were motivated by a proletarian sense of social consciousness that tended toward the controversial.

Nevertheless, the mediated vision perceived this kind of art as "real" in contrast to the expressionists' output, which persisted as something of a sham in its disregard of the formal conventions of art. More acceptable was the earthy realism of Reginald Marsh's impressions of urban life's ongoing vitality during the bleak years of the Depression. Inspired by the prevalence of the city's popular culture and its artifacts, Marsh's art suggests a postmodernist vision that, in reflecting the vibrant spirit of the urban milieu, countered the expressionists' disdain for the mediated culture's consumer obsessions. Ironically, Stuart Davis, one of the leading expressionists, often incorporated the American scene's material reality and elements of media culture in his work, a technique that seemingly looked ahead to the Pop Art movement of the 1960s. But the highly private manner of the expressionists reinforced the avant-garde notion that a work of art, as its own excuse for being, was intended to be accepted more in terms of its technique than its content.

Yet, Abstract Expressionism, similar to the way in which Art Deco sensitized the public to the visual culture of the 1930s, would become a cultural force during the postwar years when its intangible imagery would seemingly connote the personal anxieties common to the era. Setting the stage for this development and abstract art's growing public presence was the appearance of the new art museums. The Museum of Modern Art had opened its doors in 1929, and the Whitney Museum of American Art, in 1930. Later came the

National Gallery of Art (1941) and the Guggenheim (1959), Frank Lloyd Wright's monument to architectural expressionism. These museums' exhibits would subtly indoctrinate the mediated vision into the expressionist perception suggesting the seemingly disjointed state of contemporary life through an eccentric arrangement of colors in painting and purposively distorted shapes in sculpture.

Instrumental in this process were the European artists who migrated to the U.S. in the 1930s to produce their craft in a freer political atmosphere. Their presence not only helped bring the nation into the cultural mainstream of modern art, it also saw New York City become its center by the end of the 1940s. A leading figure in this development was the American artist Jackson Pollock. Rebelling against the provincialism of much American art, Pollock began experimenting with a radical, anarchistic manner of painting that by the end of the 1940s made him into an heroic figure of the avant-garde, though his work remained a bona fide mystery to the mediated vision, which at the time was more attracted to the folk art of Grandma Moses.[1] But Pollock's antipictorial manner of "drip-painting" with its emphasis on the creative act itself—an automatic or accidental technique dubbed "action painting"—pointed the way for other artists searching for a freer, more self-expressive approach to the creative process.

Even though Pollock refuted the melodramatic realism of Thomas Hart Benton, under whom he had studied at New York's Art Student's League in the early 1930s, the theatrical manner of his mentor's murals lived on in the spontaneous "action" paintings. In fact, it was art in the manner of Pollock's that, in denying the worth of media-made culture, would precipitate a reactionary movement called Pop Art. It, in turn, would help define the coming postmodern era, when the communal aura of Carrie Meeber's day and the ensuing years of the century's first half would be transformed into disconnected sectors of the mediated culture. If Jackson Pollock saw the creation of art as a theatrical performance of the inner self, he bequeathed a similar posture to the Pop artists. Their seemingly self-promotional approach to replicating the iconic images of media-made culture would reflect the ongoing escapist mood of a burgeoning postwar consumer society.

By the 1960s, then, avant-garde approaches to the creative process—exploring the inner self in fiction, free association in poetry, atonal sounds in music, and abstract expression in art—would find the shock of technique that initially baffled the mediated vision giving way to the shock of content, a dominant characteristic of the postmodern era and a major theme of this chronicle's concluding volume.

Notes

PROLOGUE. THE RISE OF MEDIA-MADE CULTURE IN AMERICA

1. Theodore Dreiser, *Sister Carrie* (1900; reprint, New York: New American Library, 1961), 7–8. Relevant to my book's focus on the mediated vision is Dreiser's attention to consumer desire and the American motivation for material success amid present discontent, dominant forces in the makeup of his novels' main characterizations.

2. L. Frank Baum, *The Wonderful Wizard of Oz* (New York: Airmont Classic edition, 1965), 32.

3. The American literary archetype of the mediated vision's conflict between present reality and a romanticized past or the future's promise is Washington Irving's early nineteenth-century fable about the legendary Rip Van Winkle. Awakening from his twenty-year "nap," Rip finds himself in an unfathomable future that is now the present, while the present he once knew has vanished into the past. Thus the psychological confusion implicit in the Rip Van Winkle syndrome is also immanent in the mediated vision's sociocultural conflict.

4. Dreiser, *Sister Carrie*, 19–20.

5. Roland Marchand, *Advertising the American Dream: Making Way for Modernity* (Berkeley: University of California Press, 1985), 235.

6. Daniel J. Boorstin, *The Image: A Guide to Pseudo-Events in America* (New York: Atheneum, 1980), 252.

CHAPTER 1. THE 1890s—SETTING THE STAGE FOR A MEDIA-MADE CULTURE

1. For a personal reaction to the fair's transformation at night, see author W. D. Howells's comments in Neil Harris, ed., *The Land of Contrasts: 1880–1901* (New York: Braziller, 1970), 347.

2. The visitor was French poet, novelist, and critic Paul Bourget. See ibid., 23.

3. William Dean Howells, *A Hazard of New Fortunes* (1890; reprint, New York: New American Library, 1965), 66. The visually oriented descriptions of Howells's fiction are often related in a theatrical manner.

4. The time's special feel for the night as fantasy is pointed out in Lewis A. Erenberg, *Steppin' Out: New York Nightlife and the Transformation of American Culture, 1890–1930* (Chicago: University of Chicago Press, 1984).

5. Quoted in Preface to ibid., xiv. As a stage for this "great drama," New York offered abundant space, as by 1898 the merger of the boroughs of Manhattan, Brooklyn, Queens, Staten Island, and the Bronx made it the second largest city in the world after London.

6. Howells, *A Hazard of New Fortunes*, 12.

7. Burlesque as a sociocultural inversion of the Victorian ideal of femininity is discussed at length in Robert C. Allen, *Horrible Prettiness: Burlesque and American Culture* (Chapel Hill: University of North Carolina Press, 1991).

8. Reid Badger, *The Great American Fair: The World's Columbian Exposition and American Culture* (Chicago: Nelson-Hall, 1979), 118.

9. Robert W. Rydell, *All the World's a Fair: Visions of Empire at American International Expositions, 1876–1976* (Chicago: University of Chicago Press, 1984), 2.

10. The appearance of the picture postcard during this time was another popular offshoot of photography that allowed visitors to the fairs to "show and tell" the folks back home what they were missing. This practice would soon become an inveterate social custom of tourists and vacationers. See Sander Davidson, "Wish You Were Here," *American Heritage* (October 1962): 97–112.

11. See Howells, *A Hazard of New Fortunes*, 56.

12. Mark Twain, Vol. 1 of *Autobiography* (New York: Harper & Brothers, 1924), 110.

13. Dreiser, *Sister Carrie*, 20. But in the spectrum of the mediated vision, the city's potential to provide opportunities to achieve personal goals, despite its obstacles, is what keeps a character like Carrie Meeber motivated.

14. Willa Cather, preface to *The Country of the Pointed Firs and Other Stories*, by Sara Orne Jewett (Garden City, N.Y.: Doubleday Anchor, 1956). Similarly, Cather's fiction elegized the strong social values inherent in the Nebraska prairie society of her girlhood.

15. See "When Romance Was in Flower," in *The Nineties*, ed. Oliver Jensen (New York: American Heritage Publishing Co., 1967), 83.

16. Ron Goulart, *The Dime Detectives* (New York: Mysterious Press, 1988), 2.

17. According to Michael Denning the dime novel's popularity as an escapist medium was due to its code of manliness that responded to working-class values. See his *Mechanic Accents: Dime Novels and Working-Class Culture in America* (London: Verso, 1987).

18. Marcus Klein, *Easterns, Westerns, and Private Eyes: American Matters, 1870–1900* (Madison: University of Wisconsin Press, 1994), 23.

19. Books on the rise of consumerism and advertising's role in it are legion, but integral to the ideas advanced in this chapter are Daniel J. Boorstin, *The Americans: The Democratic Experience* (New York: Vintage Books, 1974), and Charles Goodrum and Helen Dalrymple, *Advertising in America: The First Two Hundred Years* (New York: Abrams, 1990).

20. David Nasaw, *Going Out: The Rise and Fall of Public Amusements* (New York: Basic Books, 1993), 60. See also Robert C. Toll, "Show Biz in Blackface: The Evolution of the Minstrel Show as a Theatrical Form," in *American Popular Entertainment*, ed. Myron Matlaw (Westport, Conn.: Greenwood Press, 1979), 19–32.

21. For an overview of late nineteenth-century developments in American theater, see Joseph Csida and June Bundy, *American Entertainment: A Unique History of Popular Show Business* (New York: Watson-Guptil, 1978). More germane to my book's focus is Robert C. Toll, *On with the Show: The First Hundred Years of American Show Business* (New York: Oxford University Press, 1976).

22. Gerald Carson, "The Piano in the Parlor," *American Heritage* (December 1965), 56.

23. Quoted in Russell Sanjek, *American Popular Music and Its Business*, vol. 2 (New York: Oxford University Press, 1988), 250. In addition to the monumental work of Sanjek, the early years of popular music as a growing media force have been discussed in numerous books. Among the most stimulating is Donald Clarke, *The Rise and Fall of Popular Music* (New York: St. Martin's Griffin, 1995).

24. Andre Millard, *America on Record: A History of Recorded Sound* (New York: Cambridge University Press, 1995), 12.

25. Sousa's flair for showmanship was particularly suited to the social exuberance of the 1890s. See Neil Harris, "John Philip Sousa and the Culture of Reassurance" in *Cultural Ex-*

cursions: Marketing Appetite and Cultural Tastes in Modern America (Chicago: University of Chicago Press, 1990), 198–232.

26. Gene Smith, "A Little Visit to the Lower Depths via the *Police Gazette*," *American Heritage* (October 1972), 69.

27. In New York Anthony Comstock's all-out crusade to eradicate all forms of vice drove them underground where they thrived in light of David Loth's observation: "The spirit of the age held that an evil not seen or heard or flaunted did not exist." See David Loth, *The Erotic in Literature* (New York: Julian Messner, 1961), 142–46.

28. Richard Kluger, *The Paper: The Life and Death of the* New York Herald Tribune (New York: Alfred A. Knopf, 1986), 148.

29. Robert C. Harvey, *The Art of the Funnies: An Aesthetic History* (Jackson: University Press of Mississippi, 1994), 9.

30. But according to comic strip historian Bill Blackbeard the term originated from a promotional cross-country bicycle marathon that Hearst's papers sensationalized as news. See Blackbeard, *R. F. Outcault's* The Yellow Kid (Northampton: Kitchen Sink Press, 1995), 56–61.

31. Dreiser, *Sister Carrie*, 406–7. For a cultural analysis of the contemporary impact of the print media's pictorial content on the mediated vision, see Neil Harris, "Pictorial Perils: The Rise of American Illustration," in *Cultural Excursions*, 337–48.

32. Frank Luther Mott, "Is There a Best Seller Formula?" in *Mass Culture: The Popular Arts in America*, ed. Bernard Rosenberg and David Manning White (Glencoe, Ill.: Free Press, 1957), 113–18.

33. Amy Janello and Brennon Jones, *The American Magazine* (New York: Abrams, 1991), 34.

34. Norton Wood, ed., foreword to *The Spectacle of Sport* (Englewood Cliffs, N.J.: Prentice-Hall, 1957). This book is a compilation of articles from *Sports Illustrated* that reveals how photography complements sport as spectacle.

35. Quoted in Earl Pomeroy, *In Search of the Golden West: The Tourist in Western America* (Lincoln: University of Nebraska Press, 1990), 65

36. John F. Kasson, *Amusing the Million: Coney Island at the Turn of the Century* (New York: Hill and Wang, 1978), 72. This observation also suggests that a puritanical fear of idleness still influenced attitudes toward the proper use of leisure time, as Cindy S. Aron contends in *Working at Play: A History of Vacations in the United States* (New York: Oxford University Press, 1999), 5–10.

37. Dreiser, *Sister Carrie*, 464.

CHAPTER 2. 1900–1913—INTRODUCING THE MEDIATED VISION TO NEW WAYS OF SEEING

1. Lena Lencek and Gideon Bosker, *Making Waves: Swimsuits and the Undressing of America* (San Francisco: Chronicle Books, 1989), 34.

2. Quoted in Douglas Tallack, *Twentieth-Century America: The Intellectual and Cultural Context* (New York: Longman, 1991), 257.

3. Among youth itself, the origin of the Boy Scout movement in 1907 inspired a vested interest in nature study, conservation, crafts, and camping. The Girl Scouts, which started up in 1912, responded to similar interests as well as the need to inculcate a sense of self-reliance in young girls through the challenges of outdoor ventures.

4. Roderick Nash, ed., *The Call of the Wild: 1900–1916* (New York: Braziller, 1970), 266.

5. William Dean Howells, *A Hazard of New Fortunes* (1890; reprint, New York: New American Library, 1965), 35.

6. Quoted in Theodore P. Greene, *America's Heroes: The Changing Models of Success in American Magazines* (New York: Oxford University Press, 1970), 175.

7. For an account of the trial and its upshot, see Warren Forma, *They Were Ragtime* (New York: Grosset & Dunlap, 1976), 142–47.

8. David Pascal, "The Art of the Comic Strip," *Graphis* 28, no. 159 (1972), 6.

9. In 1906 the prestigious *Atlantic Monthly* branded the comics a "national menace," calling them coarse, vulgar, and violent. See Ralph Bergergren, "The Humor of the Colored Supplement," *Atlantic Monthly* (August 1906): 270–73.

10. For a bountifully illustrated appreciation of McCay's art, see Richard Marschall, *America's Great Comic-Strip Artists* (New York: Abbeville Press, 1989), 75–95.

11. John Canemaker, McCay's biographer, wrote that *Nemo* is "unlike any comic strip before or since . . . an exhilarating weekly adventure, a cartoon epic of sustained drama, both visually beautiful and compelling." See *Winsor McCay: His Life and Art* (New York: Abbeville Press, 1987), 82.

12. Also in this vein was the brief comic strip output in 1906 of modernist painter Lyonel Feiniger, whose *Wee Willie Winkie's World* and *The Kind-der-Kids* were done in an expressionistic manner. For a profuse sampling of Herriman's output, see *Krazy Kat: The Art of George Herriman*, ed. Patrick McDonnell, Karen O'Connell, and Georgia Riley de Havenon, (New York: Abrams, 1986). Also included is Gilbert Seldes's evaluation of Herriman's art from his book *The Seven Lively Arts* (1924). Note, too, movie director Frank Capra's high opinion of Herriman's work, 76–77.

13. For numerous examples from the golden age of sports cartooning and later, see Murray Olderman, "The Sporting Life," *Hogan's Alley: The Magazine of the Cartoon Arts*, no. 6 (1999): 122–36.

14. Thus, O'Neill was yet another artist whose works reflected an inherent desire to unite the high and the low, both the popular and the serious in art. See Shelley Armitage, *Kewpies and Beyond: The World of Rose O'Neill* (Jackson: University Press of Mississippi, 1994), 145–77.

15. Judith O'Sullivan, *The Great American Comic Strip: One Hundred Years of Cartoon Art* (Boston: Bulfinch Press, 1990), 10.

16. By 1908 one of the uncredited performers in *The Great Train Robbery*, G. M. "Andy" Anderson, was producing and acting in dozens of formulaic two-reel Westerns. Indeed, as "Broncho Billy" he created the prototypal image of the action-oriented cowboy that Tom Mix and many others would expand on.

17. Neal Gabler has shown how the movies created a "new sensibility of infinite possibilities" personified in the movie star, whose real-life image implied that life could be like the movies. See *Life the Movie: How Entertainment Conquered Reality* (New York: Knopf, 1998).

18. An in-depth study of the animated cartoon in the silent era is Donald Crafton, *Before Mickey: The Animated Film 1898–1928* (Cambridge: MIT Press, 1982).

19. Quoted in Anthony Slide, *Early American Cinema*, rev. ed. (Metuchen, N.J.: Scarecrow Press, 1994), 182.

20. Although a multitude of sources were consulted as the basis for this section's thoughts on the silent film, the sociocultural bent in Robert Sklar, *Movie-Made America: A Cultural History of American Movies*, rev. ed. (New York: Vintage Books, 1994) is more aligned with this book's sociocultural focus.

21. This expansive era of American advertising has been a ripe area for recent study from which this book profited, for example, the trademark as "a reflection of our cultural history" in Hal Morgan, *Symbols of America* (New York: Penguin Books, 1986); magazine advertising in Amy Janello and Brennon Jones, *The American Magazine* (New York: Abrams, 1991); and the history of the billboard in James Fraser, *The American Billboard 100 Years* (New York: Abrams, 1991).

22. See Ralph K. Andrist, "Paladin of Purity," *American Heritage* (October 1973), 5. See also James R. Petersen, *The Century of Sex:* Playboy's *History of the Sexual Revolution, 1900–1999* (New York: Grove Press, 1999), 10–18.

23. Florenz Ziegfeld, "What Makes a Woman Beautiful," Liberty: *Then and Now* (summer 1974), 47. A provocative study of the Ziegfeld showgirl as a "powerful icon of race, sexuality, class, and consumerist desires" is Linda Mizejewski, *Ziegfeld Girl: Image and Icon in Culture and Cinema* (Durham, N.C.: Duke University Press, 1999).

24. To moralists, major contributors to a young woman's downfall were the dance hall, cabaret, and ballroom, where she might easily fall prey to the devious schemes and desires of amoral men. See chapter 9 of David Nasaw's *Going Out: The Rise and Fall of Public Amusements* (New York: Basic Books, 1993).

25. A nostalgic and informative trip back to the forgotten products of this era is offered in Arnold Schwartzman, *Phono-Graphics: The Visual Paraphernalia of the Talking Machine* (San Francisco: Chronicle Books, 1993).

26. The sociocultural role of sheet music in this era and beyond is both discussed and profusely illustrated in Lynn Wenzel and Carol J. Binkowski, *I Hear America Singing: A Nostalgic Tour of Popular Sheet Music* (New York: Crown, 1989).

27. The popularity of this novel assured its success as a play in 1910 and in three film versions—of which the most popular were those starring Mary Pickford in 1917 and Shirley Temple in 1938. Other popular novels of the time in a similar vein were Lucy M. Montgomery's *Anne of Green Gables* (1908) and Eleanor H. Porter's *Pollyanna* (1913).

28. In addition to Zane Grey's literary bequest to the mediated culture of over sixty Western novels, his visual legacy comprised over one hundred movies as well as 145 television shows inspired by his interpretation of the old West.

29. Lee Server, *Danger Is My Business: An Illustrated History of the Fabulous Pulp Magazines, 1896–1953* (San Francisco: Chronicle Books, 1993), 22.

30. Gore Vidal, "Tarzan Revisited," *Esquire* 80 (October 1973): 281. Richard A. Lupoff has noted how the Tarzan character also inspired a multitude of spin-off characters and themes by other authors over the years. See his *Edgar Rice Burroughs: Master of Adventure* (New York: Ace Books, 1968), 257–77.

31. Quoted in Allen Eyles, *The World of Oz* (Tucson: HP Books, 1985), 40.

32. Walter Blair et al., eds., vol. 2 of *The Literature of the United States* (New York: Scott, Foresman, 1966), vol 2, 886.

33. Frederic Thompson, "The Profits from Laughter," in *The Saturday Evening Post Reflections of a Decade: 1901–1910* (Indianapolis: Curtis Publishing Co., 1980), 55.

34. Robert Rydell, *All the World's a Fair: Visions of Empire at American International Expositions, 1876–1976* (Chicago: University of Chicago Press, 1984), 236.

35. The print media's role in cultivating a national interest in sports during the late nineteenth century is examined in Michael Oriard, *Reading Football: How the Popular Press Created an American Spectacle* (Chapel Hill: University of North Carolina Press, 1993). Though the book's focus is on college football, Oriard's insights apply as well to the growing public interest in all sport by the early twentieth century.

36. Griffith Borgeson, *The Golden Age of the American Racing Car* (New York: Bonanza, 1966), 16.

37. A. H. Bruce, "Baseball and National Life," *Outlook* 104 (May 1913): 104–7.

38. Sam Hunter, *Modern American Painting and Sculpture* (New York: Dell, 1959), 37.

39. Steichen would break with Stieglitz's anticommercial ideals to become a leading advocate of the art of photography in advertising. For an analysis of Steichen's role in the debate between the proper goals of art and advertising, see Michele H. Bogart, *Artists, Advertising, and the Borders of Art* (Chicago: University of Chicago Press, 1995), 178–86.

40. Quoted in Hunter, *Modern American Painting and Sculpture*, 49.

41. Indeed, until 1906 and the passage of the Pure Food and Drug Act, patent medicines by the score had been advertised as cures for a nervous condition that neurologist George M. Beard labeled neurasthenia. Those having problems staying abreast of the fast-paced urban lifestyle were considered prime targets for this condition and possible mental illness.

42. For an in-depth study of the Village lifestyle and its sociocultural impact on modernity, see Christine Stansell, *American Moderns: Bohemian New York and the Creation of a New Century* (New York: Metropolitan Books, 2000).

43. Quoted in Tallack, *Twentieth-Century America,* 24.

CHAPTER 3. 1914–1929—FANTASIZING THE PROMISE OF A CONSUMER SOCIETY

1. Quoted in Gilman M. Ostrander, *American Civilization in the First Machine Age: 1890–1940* (New York: Harper and Row, 1970), 210. During these years, then, the automobile's response to enhancing personal mobility was a major sociocultural force in shaping Ostrander's "First Machine Age."

2. Concerning the awesome challenges to a motorist at this time, see Gerald Carson, "Goggles and Side Curtains," *American Heritage* (April 1967): 32–39, 108–11.

3. In 1921 Floyd W. Parsons wrote of this new challenge to the advertising business: "The seller of goods must be a psychologist, a statistician, a personality analyst, and a performer, in addition to possessing the skills of a merchant." See "The New Day in Salesmanship," *Saturday Evening Post,* 4 June 1921, 28.

4. In responding to the private dreams of magazine readers, many advertisers used ploys that attempted "to link their products with adventure, mystery, and romance." See Neil Harris, chap. 2 of *Cultural Excursions: Marketing Appetite and Cultural Tastes in Modern America* (Chicago: University of Chicago Press, 1990), 196–97. Along similar lines, see also Roland Marchand, *Advertising the American Dream: Making Way for Modernity* (Berkeley: University of California Press, 1985).

5. For the pro and con arguments concerning the billboard as "Urban Art," see Michele H. Bogart, *Artists, Advertising, and the Borders of Art* (Chicago: University of Chicago Press, 1995), 89–119.

6. Robert W. Rydell, *All the World's a Fair: Visions of Empire at American Expositions, 1876–1976* (Chicago: University of Chicago Press, 1984), 231.

7. The public reception of these and other war-related films is discussed in Leslie Midkiff DeBauche, *Reel Patriotism: The Movies and World War I* (Madison: University of Wisconsin Press, 1997).

8. Bruce Firestone, "A Man Named Sioux," in *The First Film Makers,* ed. Richard Dyer MacCann (Metuchen, N.J.: Scarecrow Press, 1989), 107.

9. Francis Wyndham has assessed the Chaplin image in light of its innocent appeal as "part of our psychic heritage," that it "seems to belong to some universal, almost abstract concept of childhood, beyond time and space." See the introduction to *My Life in Pictures by Charles Chaplin* (New York: Grosset & Dunlap, 1975), 26.

10. The man behind the revival, theater music director Hugo Riesenfeld, commented in *The New York Times* (23 February 1919) that it was time to "demonstrate the permanent value of good pictures" just as it has been accorded "good music, good books, good painting" (section 4, p. 6).

11. Quoted in The New York Times *at the Movies,* ed. Arleen Keylin and Christine Bent (New York: Arno Press, 1979), 27.

12. John Baxter, *Sixty Years of American Film* (Cranbury, N.J.: A. S. Barnes, 1973), 27.

13. Quoted in *Spellbound in Darkness: A History of the Silent Film*, ed. George C. Pratt (Greenwich, Conn.: New York Graphic Society, 1973), 139. This book's bountiful collection of contemporary reviews, criticism, and film stills proved an invaluable source for this section's development.

14. Vachel Lindsay, *The Art of the Moving Picture* (New York: Macmillan, 1915), 165–66. In *The Photoplay: A Psychology Study* (New York: D. Appleton, 1916), Hugo Munsterberg contended that the "movies crossed the line that separated reality from imagination" (50), anticipating Neal Gabler's argument that, in a sense, reality in the late twentieth century is becoming indistinguishable from the movies. See *Life the Movie: How Entertainment Conquered Reality* (New York: Knopf, 1998).

15. Quoted in Pratt, *Spellbound in Darkness*, 488.

16. Prominent in this kind of filmmaking was the team of Merian C. Cooper and Ernest B. Schoedsack, whose *Grass* (1925) and *Chang* (1927) took viewers to remote areas of the world. Foreshadowing their classic production of *King Kong* (1933) was the Siamese jungle setting in *Chang*, which also had an influence on other fictional films with exotic jungle settings.

17. Quoted in Pratt, *Spellbound in Darkness*, 426. To Grierson, *The Big Parade* (1925) exemplified filmmaking at its best. For its public reception and other postwar films, see DeBauche, *Reel Patriotism*, chapter 6.

18. Quoted in Pratt, *Spellbound in Darkness*, 430.

19. John Margolies and Emily Gwathmey, *Ticket to Paradise: American Movie Theaters and How We Had Fun* (Boston: Little, Brown, 1991), 15. For a firsthand look at some of the nation's most glamorous movie palaces and their lavish decor, see Ben M. Hall's *The Best Remaining Seats: The Golden Age of the Movie Palace* (New York: Bramhall House, 1971).

20. Another influential factor in moviegoers' reception of the Hollywood star system was the studios' public relations departments which mailed out autographed photo portraits on request, coordinated movie tie-ins with their book versions and the covers of popular sheet music songs, radio interviews, and personal appearance tours, and licensed the stars' images to endorse commercial products and promote popular culture items. By the end of the 1920s, the pervasive image of the movie star had invaded the entire province of American media culture.

21. An insightful analysis of the animated cartoon's development during its silent years is Leonard Maltin, *Of Mice and Magic: A History of American Animated Cartoons* (New York: McGraw-Hill, 1980), chapter 1. Disney's early contributions are covered in chapter 2.

22. Douglas Gilbert, *American Vaudeville: Its Life and Times* (New York: Dover, 1963), 393.

23. Morton Minsky and Milt Machlin, *Minsky's Burlesque* (New York: Arbor House, 1986), 26.

24. Richard Ziegfeld and Paulette Ziegfeld, *The Ziegfeld Touch: The Life and Times of Florenz Ziegfeld, Jr.* (New York: Abrams, 1993), 176.

25. Robert Kimball and Alfred Simon, *The Gershwins* (New York: Atheneum, 1973), 35.

26. Lyricist Dorothy Fields and such talented women composers as Ann Ronell, Dana Suesse, and Kay Swift, who turned out some of the most popular songs of the 1920s, proved that Tin Pan Alley was not just a man's world.

27. Although Eugene O'Neill had won three Pulitzer Prizes by 1928, his greatest achievement as a playwright was in bringing international recognition to American drama. For an analysis of O'Neill's impact on Expressionism in the 1920s, see Ronald H. Wainscott, *The Emergence of the Modern American Theater, 1914–1929* (New Haven, Conn.: Yale University Press, 1997).

28. The social significance of this neglected genre as a comedic expression that helped liberate the theater's subject matter and language in the 1920s is examined in ibid.

29. A perceptively original approach to radio as a visual force in challenging the listener's imagination is Susan J. Douglas, *Listening In: Radio and the American Imagination* (New York: Times Books, 1999). See chapter 1, "The Zen of Listening."

30. Commenting on radio's role in this process in the 1920s, Douglas says it "was the agent through which this African American music, for the first time on a mass scale, helped define the rebellion of young whites" (96–97).

31. André Millard, *America on Record: A History of Recorded Sound* (New York: Cambridge University Press, 1995), 96.

32. The role of New York City's social scene in the development of tabloid journalism is examined in John D. Stevens, *Sensationalism and the New York Press* (New York: Columbia University Press, 1991).

33. In addition to other works on the comics cited in this book, this section is indebted to Ron Goulart, *The Funnies: 100 Years of American Comics Strips* (Holbrook, Mass.: Adams Publishing, 1995) and Maurice Horn, ed., *100 Years of Newspaper Comics* (New York: Gramercy Books, 1996).

34. Quoted in Jerry Robinson, introduction to Skippy *and Percy Crosby* (New York: Holt, Rinehart and Winston, 1978), x.

35. A comprehensive source for this section's discussion of the mass magazine's sociocultural impact is Amy Janello and Brennon Jones, *The American Magazine* (New York: Abrams, 1991). For an overview of the popular magazine's heyday, see *The American Magazine: 1890–1940*, ed. Dorey Schmidt (fall 1979), a collection of essays published by the Delaware Art Museum for its 1979 exhibit on the sociocultural role of the magazine in American society.

36. The media culture's visionary concept of a utopian future is entertainingly discussed and illustrated in Joseph J. Corn and Brian Horrigan, *Yesterday's Tomorrows: Past Visions of the American Future* (Baltimore: Johns Hopkins University Press, 1996).

37. Jan Cohn, *Covers of the* Saturday Evening Post (New York: Penguin Books, 1995), 92.

38. Both Parrish and his talented contemporary, Rockwell Kent, saw the advertising field as a way to democratize fine art. For their efforts in this process, see Bogart, 234–55.

39. Biographical pieces of the major artists who contributed to the American tradition of magazine art, along with liberal samplings of their work, are presented in Susan E. Meyer, *America's Great Illustrators* (New York: Galahad Books, 1987).

40. For examples of the pulps' cover art, see Robert Lesser, *Pulp Art: Original Cover Paintings for the Great American Pulp Magazines* (New York: Gramercy Books, 1997).

41. And as Thomas M. Disch observes, science fiction, through the print and visual media, would come to permeate American culture "in ways both trivial and profound." See *The Dreams Our Stuff Is Made Of: How Science Fiction Conquered the World* (New York: Free Press, 1998). For the genre's historical development, see Brooks Landon, *Science Fiction after 1900: From the Steam Man to the Stars* (New York: Twayne, 1997).

42. James D. Hart, *The Popular Book: A History of America's Literary Taste* (Berkeley: University of California Press, 1963), 218.

43. The long popularity of these series as they reflected changing times is recounted in Carole Kismaric and Marvin Heiferman, *The Mysterious Case of Nancy Drew and the Hardy Boys* (New York: Fireside Books, 1998).

44. For examples showing "how art and design were reconciled with commerce," see Steven Heller and Seymour Chwast, *Jackets Required: An Illustrated History of American Book Jacket Design, 1920–1950* (San Francisco: Chronicle Books, 1995).

45. See Janice Radway, *A Feeling for Books: The Book of the Month Club, Literary Taste and Middle-Class Desire* (Chapel Hill: University of North Carolina Press, 1997), in particular chapters 8 and 9.

46. The growth in college enrollment, which by 1926 saw one out of every eight youths in college, reflected a prosperous middle class's growing faith in higher education. But these same youths, by emphasizing the social side of college life, developed their own fantasized notions as to what should also comprise the educational process. The democratization of

American higher education and its implications are discussed in Daniel J. Boorstin, *The Americans: The Democratic Experience* (New York: Vintage Books, 1974), 478–90.

47. The literary genre is examined in John Lyons, *The College Novel in America* (Carbondale: Southern Illinois University Press, 1962); the film genre, in Wiley Lee Umphlett, *The Movies Go to College: Hollywood and the World of the College-Life Film* (Madison, N.J.: Fairleigh Dickinson University Press, 1984).

48. On the major American writers of this era, Alfred Kazin, *On Native Grounds: An Interpretation of Modern American Prose Literature* (Garden City, N.Y.: Anchor Books, 1956) is still a highly reliable source. For poetry and drama, see Frederick J. Hoffman, *The Twenties: American Writing in the Postwar Decade* (New York: Collier Books, 1962).

49. This form as a cultural force is analyzed in David Glassberg, *American Historical Pageantry: The Uses of Tradition in the Early 20th Century* (Chapel Hill: University of North Carolina Press, 1990).

50. This sport's little-known background is examined in Kristine Fredriksson, *American Rodeo: From Buffalo Bill to Big Business* (College Station: Texas A&M University Press, 1985).

51. Sport's nationalistic import and the military's positive posture toward athletics during this era are discussed in S. W. Pope, *Patriotic Games: Sporting Tradition in the American Imagination, 1876–1926* (New York: Oxford University Press, 1997).

52. Cited in ibid., 157. See also Murray Sperber, introduction to *Onward to Victory: The Crises That Shaped College Sports* (New York: Henry Holt, 1998), xix–xxv.

53. Until the advent of Prohibition in 1920, the urban saloon augmented its all-male escapist aura by functioning as a center for gambling activity and the related reporting of sporting results as well as the staging of boxing matches. See Madelon Powers, *Faces along the Bar: Lore and Order in the Workingman's Saloon, 1870–1920* (Chicago: University of Chicago Press, 1998), 159–61.

54. While baseball and boxing were the sports that created an air of both bonding and dispute among their all-male community of fans, segregation policies were maintained against blacks as spectators and participants, except occasionally as boxers. See David Nasaw, *Going Out: The Rise and Fall of Public Amusements* (New York: Basic Books, 1993), 96–103.

55. This "new image" is aptly described in Richard Maltby, ed., *Passing Parade: A History of Popular Culture in the Twentieth Century* (New York: Oxford University Press, 1989), 77.

56. For an insider's views on life in the Village during this time, see Malcolm Cowley, *Exile's Return: A Literary Odyssey of the 1920s* (New York: Viking Press edition, 1956), 48–65.

57. Literary symbolism in the offbeat realism of Hopper and Burchfield is discussed in Sam Hunter, *Modern American Painting and Sculpture* (New York: Dell, 1959), 108–15.

58. The facts that precipitated the trial and its outcome's ironic impact on modernist thought are pointed out in Hoffman, 313–15.

59. But radical change was on the way in modernist architecture's International Style. While the concept of a building as "a machine for living," posited by the Swiss artist/architect Le Corbusier, had significant influence on the design of inner and outer architectural space, Mies van der Rohe's concept of "less is more" would have a greater impact on the future of the American skyline's appearance.

Chapter 4. 1930–1945—Testing the Dream in the Great Depression and World War II

1. Joseph Alsop, *FDR: A Centenary Remembrance* (New York: Viking Press, 1982), 254.

2. For a sociocultural analysis of the American people's growing attraction to flight, see Joseph J. Corn, *The Winged Gospel: America's Romance with Aviation, 1900–1950* (New York: Oxford University Press, 1983).

3. John E. Findling, *Chicago's Great World Fairs* (New York: Manchester University Press, 1994), 154. As Findling notes, Chicago's modernist-styled 1933–34 fair also provided the model for upcoming fairs in San Diego (1935) and in New York and San Francisco (1939–40). But Michael Horsham designates the New York Fair as "The Endnote of 1920s and 1930s Style." See *20s & 30s Style* (North Dighton, Mass.: JG Press, 1996), 112–21.

4. See Rita Barnard, *The Great Depression and the Culture of Abundance: Kenneth Fearing, Nathanael West and Mass Culture in the 1930s* (New York: Cambridge University Press, 1995), 166–67. The epitome of California style was Sid Grauman's Chinese Theater, which opened in 1927 as a Hollywood movie palace.

5. Gary Dean Best, *The Nickel and Dime Decade: American Popular Culture during the 1930s* (Westport, Conn.: Praeger, 1993), 15–16.

6. Although by the 1920s Prohibition had brought an end to the workingman's saloon, its escapist atmosphere lived on in the neighborhood tavern after the legalization of alcohol in 1933. For a well-documented account of some earlier drinking traditions that also lived on, see Madelon Powers, *Faces along the Bar: Lore and Order in the Workingman's Saloon, 1879–1920* (Chicago: University of Chicago Press, 1998).

7. An entertaining as well as informative look at Factor's impact on movie culture is Fred E. Basten, *Max Factor's Hollywood* (Santa Monica, Calif.: General Publishing Group, 1995). The book's visual appeal is enhanced by an abundance of rare photographs.

8. See introduction to *The Nickel and Dime Decade*, Best, xiv. But the uncertainties of a time poised between a debilitating Depression and the threat of another war is poignantly captured in Ross Gregory, *America 1941—A Nation at the Crossroads* (New York: Free Press, 1989).

9. A unique study of the wartime relationship between grocer and consumer is Barbara McLean Ward, ed., *Produce and Conserve, Share and Play Square* (Hanover: University Press of New England, 1994). For the public's reaction to gas rationing regulations and related issues, see Robert Heide and John Gilman, *Home Front America: Popular Culture of the World War II Era* (San Francisco: Chronicle Books, 1993), 56–57.

10. Susan J. Douglas has noted how radio "cultivated both a sense of nationhood and a validation of subcultures, often simultaneously." See *Listening In: Radio and the American Imagination* (New York: Times Books, 1999), 11.

11. Melvin Patrick Ely has shown how listeners were inclined to interpret these characters not so much as black as they were merged versions of everyman. See *The Adventures of Amos 'n' Andy: A Social History of an American Phenomenon* (New York: Free Press, 1991). A similar posture helps explain the appeal of the Jewish family depicted in *The Rise of the Goldbergs* and the rural types in *Lum and Abner*. Quite often, the humorous situations these shows' characters were involved in reminded listeners of themselves and their own concerns, which was undoubtedly a major reason for their popularity. Though radio introduced its audience to diverse cultural lifestyles, they were dramatized within the larger sphere created by the democratization process.

12. For the integral role that sound effects played in both radio drama and comedy, see Leonard Maltin, *The Great American Broadcast: A Celebration of Radio's Golden Age* (New York: Dutton, 1997), 87–112.

13. The degree that the soaps' role identification had on women listeners is discussed in Douglas, *Listening In*, 144–45.

14. Prior to the war a nightly ritual of radio buffs was tracking international news on shortwave radio and during the war picking up the Voice of America's messages to the world. To Douglas, World War II was a radio listener's war that prompted the invention of broadcast journalism, the import of which is analyzed in chapter 7 of *Listening In*.

15. J. Fred MacDonald, *Don't Touch That Dial! Radio Programming in American Life, 1920–1960* (Nelson-Hall: Chicago, 1979), 50. MacDonald's sociocultural approach to his subject matter also applies to other topics in this section.

16. Quoted in Amy Henderson, *On the Air: Pioneers of American Broadcasting* (Washington, D.C.: Smithsonian Institute Press, 1988), 48.

17. Donald Clarke, *The Rise and Fall of Popular Music* (New York: St. Martin's Griffin, 1995), 165.

18. For a comprehensive source on the development of Swing music, its international appeal, and cultural impact during the war years, see Albert McCarthy, *The Dance Band Era: From Ragtime to Swing* (Radnor, Pa.: Chilton Books, 1982), 121–62.

19. Cecelia Tichi has produced an impressive study of country music's indigenous relationship to American culture. See *High Lonesome: The American Culture of Country Music* (Chapel Hill: University of North Carolina Press, 1994).

20. Frank Miller, *Censored Hollywood: Sex, Sin, and Violence on the Screen* (Atlanta: Turner, 1994), 51. Chapters 4, 5, and 6 have particular import for the years 1930–45. Influential in arousing public opinion against the movies as a contributor to deviant behavior among youth during this time were the findings of *Our Movie Made Children* (1933), commissioned by the Motion Picture Research Council.

21. In the early years of sound, producer Darryl F. Zanuck made effective use of the public vernacular, particularly in Warners' crime films. This method revolutionized film's role as a cultural force by recognizing that sound not only "made the movies the primary carrier of mass culture" but "reshaped the very way film production was orchestrated." See George F. Custen, *Twentieth Century's Fox: Darryl F. Zanuck and the Culture of Hollywood* (New York: Basic Books, 1997), 90–91.

22. For the studios' attraction to the subject of crime, particularly Warner Brothers, see Colin Shindler, *Hollywood in Crisis: Cinema and American Society, 1929–1939* (New York: Routledge, 1996), chapter 7.

23. For a complete list of prohibitions, see Miller, *Censored Hollywood*, 51.

24. The escapist fascination with the exploitation film in the 1930s and 40s is scrutinized in Eddie Muller and Daniel Faris, *Grindhouse: The Forbidden World of "Adults Only" Cinema* (New York: St. Martin's Griffin, 1996), 13–53. The "porn" film is documented in Al Di Lauro and Gerald Rabkin, *Dirty Movies: An Illustrated History of the Stag Film, 1915–1970* (New York: Chelsea House, 1976).

25. This section's opinions about comedy and the social message film of the 1930s were influenced by chapters 11 and 12 in Robert Sklar, *Movie-Made America: A Cultural History of American Movies*, rev. ed. (New York: Vintage Books, 1994).

26. Darryl Zanuck, who had departed Warners in 1933, was the architect behind this merger. Ever sensitive to the mediated vision's evolving outlook and what it desired to see on the screen, Zanuck now headed up a studio that would produce many of Hollywood's classic films as well as a bountiful output of B-movie favorites.

27. Shirley Temple's positive image pervaded 1930s' mediated culture, appearing on the covers of sheet music and magazines, as a model for little-girl fashions, and in the form of numerous merchandising items. The Shirley Temple doll, in fact, became a revered icon of the American girl during this time.

28. Screen biography, or the biopic, was a strong suit of Fox's Zanuck, especially in the musical films of entertainment figures that emphasized visual spectacle and nostalgic identity with turn of the century lifestyles. But in such historical biopics as *Clive of India* (1935) and *Wilson* (1942), he took a more serious bent by encoding a personal sense of values he assumed was also that of the mediated vision.

29. Richard Fehr and Frederick G. Vogel, *Lullabies of Hollywood: Movie Music and the Movie Musical* (Jefferson, N.C.: McFarland, 1993), 208. This book is a highly informative source on the integral role music has played in the movies.

30. Regarding the import of music's emotional role in film narrative, André Millard has observed: "The Golden Age of Hollywood represented more than the creation of a perfect illu-

sion; it marked a high point of recorded-sound technology in the service of this illusion." See *America on Record: A History of Recorded Sound* (New York: Cambridge University Press, 1995), 284.

31. For some screenwriters the studio production system inspired a satirical posture reflected in the novels they would write about Hollywood, as in Nathanael West's *The Day of the Locust* (1939), F. Scott Fitzgerald's posthumously published *The Last Tycoon* (1941), and Budd Schulberg's *What Makes Sammy Run?* (1941) and *The Disenchanted* (1950).

32. For a generous sampling of fan magazine stories and their photographs, see Barbara Gelman, ed., Photoplay *Treasury* (New York: Crown, 1972).

33. Robert S. Sennett examines the fan magazine and the Hollywood gossip reporter's role in *Hollywood Hoopla: Creating Stars and Selling Movies in the Golden Age of Hollywood* (New York: Billboard Books, 1998), 46–63.

34. This section dealing with the Western, the serial, and the series film respectively is indebted to the following sources for its direction: George N. Fenin and William K. Everson, *The Western: From Silents to Cinerama* (New York: Orion Press, 1962); Ken Weiss and Ed Goodgold, *To Be Continued . . .* (New York: Bonanza Books, 1972); and James Robert Parish, ed., *The Great Movie Series* (New York: A. S. Barnes, 1971).

35. The most informative book on these and other two-reel shorts of the 1930s and 40s is Leonard Maltin, *The Great Movie Shorts* (New York: Crown, 1972).

36. For an expanded look at the time's war-related films, in both their escapist and realistic postures, see Joe Morella, Edward Z. Epstein, and John Griggs, *The Films of World War II* (Secaucus, N.J.: Citadel Press, 1973).

37. Quoted in Arleen Keylin and Christine Bent, The New York Times *at the Movies* (New York: Arno Press, 1979), 51.

38. The productions of Micheaux and Williams comprised only a few of the hundreds of so-called "race" movies that were made by black film companies between 1910 and the early 50s for distribution to black-owned theaters and their audiences. The racial problems that the black film industry faced in the early years of the century are pointed out in Gary Null, *Black Hollywood: The Black Performer in Motion Pictures* (Secaucus, N.J.: Citadel Press, 1975). The performers' growing proactive role since the 1930s is recounted in Alan Pomerance, *Repeal of the Blues: How Black Entertainers Influenced Civil Rights* (Secaucus, N.J.: Citadel Press, 1988). See, in particular, chapter 5.

39. A major reason the Disney studio outdid MGM's competition in the annual Academy Award derby for best cartoon short during 1931–46 (nine Disney Oscars to MGM's five) was its creation of such memorable productions as *Ferdinand the Bull* (1938), *The Ugly Duckling* (1939), and *Der Führer's Face* (1942), Donald Duck's antic takeoff on the Hitler regime. Though this cartoon was a big boost to wartime morale, MGM's zany cat/mouse team, Tom and Jerry, also garnered a large following during this time.

40. According to Steven Watts, Disney's intent of appealing to both high- and low-culture sectors derived from his Midwest populist origins. See chapter 4 in Steven Watts, *The Magic Kingdom: Walt Disney and the American Way of Life* (Boston: Houghton Mifflin, 1997). *Fantasia*, Disney's idealistic attempt to bring high culture to the people and democratize it in the eyes of the mediated vision, resulted in a lively critical debate. Its contested viewpoints underscored the realization that by 1940 American culture was indeed undergoing a transformation into a more egalitarian milieu. See Watts, 113–19.

41. Nevertheless, the fact that the concerns of the real world were not too far removed from those of the fantasized cartoon was reflected in the opinions of those offended by the sexist innuendos of MGM's *Red Hot Riding Hood* and the racial stereotyping of Warners' *Coal Black and de Sebben Dwarfs* (both 1943). For background analyses of these two cartoons and others in the great tradition of the animated cartoon, see Jerry Beck, ed., *The 50 Greatest Cartoons* (Atlanta: Turner, 1994).

42. A well-documented survey of this prolific period is Stanley Green, *Ring Bells! Sing Songs! Broadway Musicals of the 1930s* (New Rochelle, N.Y.: Arlington House, 1971).

43. Quoted in Null, *Black Hollywood,* 67. Flanagan's remarks were made in the context of a new consciousness in the 1930s of black acting in the American theater. Singer/actor Paul Robeson, for example, had played the title role in Eugene O'Neill's *The Emperor Jones* and its film version in 1933. He also appeared in numerous other film roles until he became disillusioned with the American way of life due mainly to its pervasive racism.

44. Morton Minsky and Milt Machlin, *Minsky's Burlesque* (New York: Arbor House, 1986), 97.

45. Robert C. Allen, *Horrible Prettiness: Burlesque and American Culture* (Chapel Hill: University of North Carolina Press, 1991), 258–59. In this light, Allen also observed that the burlesque performer assumed a special power on stage that she was denied off, thus dramatizing the transcendence of fantasy over reality.

46. In referring to the American people as "guinea pigs" duped by the advertising industry, authors F. J. Schlink and Arthur Kellet, officials of a consumer research organization that published their book, spawned a number of such books in the muckraking vein. The investigative journal *Consumer Reports,* with its product evaluations, grew out of such efforts.

47. John Margolies and Emily Gwathmey, *Signs of Our Time* (New York: Abbeville Press, 1993), 9.

48. For the origins of "roadfood" catering, see John Mariani, *America Eats Out* (New York: Morrow, 1991), 105–31.

49. The colorful travel brochure that experienced its golden age during the years prior to World War II was so much ballyhoo compared to the factualness of the state travel guides produced during the Depression. Indeed, Alfred Kazin contends that they offer "evidence . . . born of the crisis to recover America *as an idea*" in order "to build a better society in the shell of the old." See *On Native Grounds* (Garden City, N.Y.: Doubleday Anchor Books, 1956), 381. For roadside tourist culture, see John Margolies, *Fun along the Road: American Tourist Attractions* (Boston: Bulfinch Books, 1998).

50. Ronald Primeau, *Romance of the Road: The Literature of the American Highway* (Bowling Green, Ohio: Popular Press, 1996), 1. Thus, as the metaphor of the "road journey" has influenced the literary vision of American writers, so then, by extension, it has mirrored the nostalgic reveries and questing dreams of the mediated vision.

51. This point is underscored by the many exemplary posters presented in William L. Bird Jr. and Harry R. Rubenstein, *Design for Victory: World War II Posters on the American Home Front* (New York: Princeton Architectural Press, 1998). On page 1 the authors state: "Addressing every citizen as a combatant in a war of production, wartime posters united the power of art with the power of advertising to sell the idea that the factory and the home were also arenas of war."

52. The era of the drive-in restaurant, extending from the 1920s to the 1960s, was another offshoot of American car culture. Expressing itself in a variety of flamboyant architectural styles, the drive-in came into its own in the 1930s and early 40s as a pleasant gathering place of temporary escape, particularly for youth. Thus, as a familiar cultural institution that the mediated vision readily identified with, its setting frequently appeared in both the movies and fiction. See Jim Heimann, *Car Hops and Curb Service: A History of American Drive-In Restaurants, 1920–1960* (San Francisco: Chronicle Books, 1996).

53. For an analysis of the night life milieu, See Sennett, *Hollywood Hoopla,* chapter 6. Café society's desire to be seen and see others of its kind during this era is detailed in Ralph Blumenthal, *Stork Club: America's Most Famous Nightspot and the Lost World of Café Society* (Boston: Little, Brown, 2000).

54. Steven Heller and Louise Fili, *Cover Story: The Art of American Magazine Covers, 1900–1950* (San Francisco: Chronicle, 1996), 10.

55. William Owen, *Modern Magazine Design* (New York: Rizzoli, 1991), 44. Accordingly, art director T. M. Cleland's format "epitomized the best in the American typographic vernacular" to achieve a unique modernist look.

56. Quoted in Loudon Wainwright, *The Great American Magazine: An Inside History of* Life (New York: Knopf, 1986), 33.

57. "The U.S. at War," *Time*, Special 60th Anniversary Issue, 1983, 34.

58. In the 10 June 1939 issue, Macfadden based his prediction on his view that "the German people do not want war and they do not believe that a war is imminent." Clearly, he underestimated the power Adolph Hitler wielded over the German people. In three months World War II would be underway.

59. Peter Canning, *American Dreamers: The Wallaces and* Reader's Digest (New York: Simon & Schuster, 1996), 87

60. The root years of the exploitation magazine are examined, with a profuse display of their covers, in Alan Betrock, *Unseen America: The Greatest Cult Exploitation Magazines* (New York: Shake Books, 1990), 8–22.

61. For a sampling of these kinds of stories that were published in the 1930s and 40s, see Florence Moriarty, ed., *True Confessions: Sixty Years of Sin, Suffering and Sorrow, 1919–1979* (New York: Fireside Books, 1979).

62. Quoted in James Playsted Wood, *Magazines in the United States*, 3d ed. (New York: Ronald Press, 1971), 452.

63. Books on the pulp magazine have proliferated in recent years. One of the first is a reliable source for a sampling of pulp stories and their cover art: Tony Goodstone, ed., *The Pulps: Fifty Years of American Pop Culture* (New York: Chelsea House, 1970). See also Peter Haining, ed., *The Fantastic Pulps* (New York: Vintage Books, 1976).

64. Chris Steinbrunner, preface to Walter Gibson, *The Shadow Scrapbook* (New York: Harcourt Brace Jovanovich, 1979, v.

65. The legendary careers of the most popular pulp heroes are delineated in Don Hutchinson, *The Great Pulp Heroes* (Buffalo, N.Y.: Orion Press, 1996).

66. For an overview of Gardner's writing career, see Jeff Siegel, *The American Detective: An Illustrated History* (Dallas: Taylor Publishing, 1993), 106–12.

67. Quoted in Miles Orvell, *The Real Thing: Imitation and Authenticity in American Culture, 1880–1940* (Chapel Hill: University of North Carolina Press, 1989), 260.

68. Thomas L. Bonn attends to cover art's role in serving the commercial ends of the paperback in *Undercover: An Illustrated History of American Mass Market Paperbacks* (New York: Penguin Books, 1982).

69. At a time when many of the Sunday comics' popular features appeared in full-page dress, some carried a two-tiered strip by the same artist. Called a topper, it showed up above the main feature, as Raymond's *Jungle Jim* did to *Flash Gordon*. For a more detailed assessment of this era's major comics artists, as well as samples of their work, see Richard Marschall, *America's Great Comic-Strip Artists* (New York: Abbeville Press, 1989).

70. For example, the title character of *Joe Palooka*, who was heavyweight champion of the comics world, joined the Army; *Barney Google*, which was now dominated by the hillbilly character Snuffy Smith, had both Barney and Snuffy serving in the military, with the expected comical results; Tillie the Toiler departed her office job for the WACS; and even Little Orphan Annie headed up a group of juvenile "commandos" who fought their own war against Nazi spies.

71. Milton Caniff, *Male Call, 1942–46* (Princeton, Wis.: Kitchen Sink Press, 1987), 12. Caniff was particularly adept at this sort of thing, as from *Terry and the Pirates* to *Steve Canyon*, which began in 1947, sex played an integral role in his plotting.

72. The universality of *Blondie*'s humor is thematically organized with bountiful examples from the comic strip in Dean Young and Rick Marschall, *Blondie and Dagwood's America* (New

York: Harper & Row, 1981). *Blondie*'s popularity was evidenced in its radio and film series versions, comic book reprints, and numerous merchandising spin-offs.

73. Of relevance to a basic premise of this book is Arthur Asa Berger's scholarly analysis of Al Capp's contribution to American mediated culture—*Li'l Abner: A Study in American Satire* (New York: Twayne, 1969). It was reprinted in 1994 in the Studies in Popular Culture series of the University Press of Mississippi. Berger defends his serious study of such a non-academic subject because, as he notes in the introduction, *Li'l Abner* is not "simple" or "mindless," as its critics charge. It, in fact, "mirrors many of the tensions that exist in our thinking and reflects many of our ideological commitments and values" (see p. 15). His book is among the first to recognize mediated culture in general and the comic strip in particular as fruitful areas of scholarly pursuit.

74. Other Pulitzer winners during this era were Jacob Burck, whose work for the *Chicago Times* revealed a shift away from his earlier Leftist leanings; the *Baltimore Sun*'s Edmund Duffy, whose cartoons looked ahead to a new wave of uncluttered graphics; and Daniel Fitzpatrick of the *St. Louis Post-Dispatch*, whose expert control of the grease crayon helped invigorate his art.

75. In fact, the demand for comic strip ads had grown so great in the 1930s that the Johnstone and Cushing studio in New York was established to supply them. In addition to Caniff and Sickles, such comics artists as Austin Briggs, Lou Fine, and Stan Drake worked for the studio at one time or another.

76. In 1996, Eros Comix revived these once contraband publications as *The Tijuana Bibles: America's Forgotten Comic Strips*. In its introduction, comics historian R. C. Harvey describes them as "joyous celebrations of sex" that focus on a fantasized, purely escapist "world in which sex preoccupies everyone's every waking moment" (6). Serving mainly as nostalgic titillation for those who remember them from younger days, these crude little booklets remain as curiosities to eyes that are now conditioned to more explicitly realistic images of a sexual nature.

77. For the origins and early years of the comic book, see Ron Goulart, *Over 50 Years of American Comic Books* (Lincolnwood, Ill.: Mallard Press, 1991). Updated in 2001 as *Great American Comic Books*.

78. Gary Engle, "What Makes Superman So Darned American?" in *Superman at Fifty: The Persistence of a Legend* (Cleveland: Octavia Press, 1987), 80.

79. Quoted in Mike Benton, *Masters of Imagination: The Comic Book Artists Hall of Fame* (Dallas: Taylor Publishing, 1994), 33, 35.

80. Both Jack Cole's and Will Eisner's contributions to the art of the comic book have been well documented, in particular in Ron Goulart, *Focus on Jack Cole* (Agoura, Calif.: Fantagraphic Books, 1986), and in Art Spiegelman and Chip Kidd, *Jack Cole and Plastic Man: Forms Stretched to Their Limits* (San Francisco: Chronicle Books, 2001); Catherine Yronwode, *The Art of Will Eisner* (Princeton, Wis.: Kitchen Sink Press, 1982): and Robert C. Harvey, *The Art of the Comic Book: An Aesthetic History* (Jackson: University Press of Mississippi, 1996), 66–99.

81. Marston, who wrote his stories under the pen name of Charles Moulton, was the inventor of the polygraph lie detector. His use of feminist theory to counter the status quo of male domination offers psychological insights into the early controversy surrounding the Wonder Woman character. That costumed women characters have had a surprisingly long history in the comic book is attested to in Trina Robbins, *The Great Women Superheroes* (Northampton, Mass.: Kitchen Sink Press, 1996).

82. Not only did women perform as superheroes during this era but funny animals, like Mighty Mouse, also appeared as spoofs of the genre in both the comic book and film. In fact, the time's animated cartoon characters became comic book stars. Animal characters were always popular in the comics, and in 1930 Mickey Mouse, anticipating the popularity of the continuity strip, began appearing in the adventure genre. In 1940, the model for the funny an-

imal publications appeared in *Walt Disney's Comics and Stories*, followed in 1941 by Warners' lineup of characters in *Looney Tunes and Merrie Melodies*. Their success spawned dozens of funny animal titles. Unsung artists, who would achieve recognition down the road, honed their skills drawing for these comic books—most notably, Walt Kelly, who introduced his Pogo character in *Animal Comics* in 1942, and Carl Barks, whose popular version of Donald Duck began appearing in the Disney comic book the same year.

83. Les Daniels, *Marvel: Five Fabulous Decades of the World's Greatest Comics* (New York: Abrams, 1991), 15.

84. The development of college football as commercialized public spectacle and the coaching fraternity's role in promoting it are examined in Wiley Lee Umphlett, *Creating the Big Game: John W. Heisman and the Invention of American Football* (Westport, Conn.: Greenwood, 1992). For the mythology of the game as the media have perpetuated it, see Sperber, cited 292 n. 52, parts 1–3.

85. Ironicallly, a major cultural achievement of the Berlin Olympics initiated a new way to view sport through film's power to capture the visually aesthetic side of athletic competition. Leni Riefenstahl shot much of her documentary film *Olympia* from sublevel views in slow motion to capture the intensity of physical effort in track, field, and diving events. Granted project funds from the Nazi government, the former German film star produced a classic work that transcended the commercialized spectacle of sport to focus on its heretofore concealed side. On the implications of her work and the 1936 Olympics, see Richard D. Mandell, *Sport: A Cultural History* (New York: Columbia University Press, 1984), 241–45.

86. The significant role that sports have played in the movies is attested to in Jeffrey H. Wallenfeldt, ed., *Sports Movies: A Review of Nearly 500 Films* (Evanston, Ill.: CineBooks, 1989).

EPILOGUE: DETECTING THE SIGNS OF A COMING POSTMODERN ERA

1. Senior citizen Anna Mary Robertson Moses, a self-taught practitioner of folk art, better known as Grandma Moses, found a large audience just when the abstract style was coming into prominence in the 1940s. H. H. Arnason, in the *History of Modern Art* (New York: Abrams, 1998), comments that her popularity "proves that there was a large sector of the American public [i.e., the mediated vision] that preferred this art to the more radical statements of the avant-garde." See the 4th edition, 423.

Bibliography

Adams, Judith A. *The American Amusement Park Industry: A History of Technology and Thrills.* Boston: Twayne, 1991.

Allen, Robert C. *Horrible Prettiness: Burlesque and American Culture.* Chapel Hill: University of North Carolina Press, 1991.

Alsop, Joseph. *FDR: A Centenary Remembrance.* New York: Viking Press, 1982.

Andrist, Ralph K. "Paladin of Purity." *American Heritage* (October 1973): 4–7, 84–89.

Anger, Kenneth. *Hollywood Babylon.* San Francisco: Straight Arrow Books, 1975.

Armitage, Shelley. *Kewpies and Beyond: The World of Rose O'Neill.* Jackson: University Press of Mississippi, 1994.

Arnason, H. H. *History of Modern Art.* 4th ed. New York: Abrams, 1998.

Aron, Cindy S. *Working at Play: A History of Vacations in the United States.* New York: Oxford University Press, 1999.

Badger, Reid. *The Great American Fair: The World's Columbian Exposition and American Culture.* Chicago: Nelson-Hall, 1979.

Balio, Tino, ed. *The American Film Industry.* Madison: University of Wisconsin Press, 1976.

Barnard, Rita. *The Great Depression and the Culture of Abundance: Kenneth Fearing, Nathanael West, and Mass Culture in the 1930s.* New York: Cambridge University Press, 1995.

Barnouw, Erik. *Documentary: A History of the Non-fiction Film.* Rev. ed. New York: Oxford University Press, 1993.

Basten, Fred E. *Max Factor's Hollywood.* Santa Monica, Calif.: General Publishing Group, 1995.

Baum, L. Frank. *The Wonderful Wizard of Oz.* 1900. Reprint, New York: Airmont Classic, 1965.

Baxter, John. *Sixty Years of Hollywood.* Cranbury, N.J.: A. S. Barnes, 1973.

Beck, Jerry. *The 50 Greatest Cartoons.* Atlanta: Turner, 1994.

Belton, John, ed. *Movies and Mass Culture.* New Brunswick: Rutgers University Press, 1996.

Benton, Mike. *Masters of Imagination: The Comic Book Artists Hall of Fame.* Dallas: Taylor Publishing, 1994.

Berger, Arthur Asa. *Li'l Abner: A Study in American Satire.* Jackson: University Press of Mississippi, 1994.

Bergergren, Ralph. "The Humor of the Colored Supplement." *Atlantic Monthly* (August 1906): 270–273.

Best, Gary Dean. *The Nickel and Dime Decade: American Popular Culture during the 1930s.* Westport, Conn.: Praeger, 1993.

Betrock, Alan. *Unseen America: The Greatest Cult Exploitation Magazines.* New York: Shake Books, 1990.

300

Bird, William L. Jr., and Harry R. Rubenstein. *Design for Victory: World War II Posters of the American Home Front.* New York: Princeton Architectural Press, 1998.

Blackbeard, Bill. *R. F. Outcault's* The Yellow Kid. Northampton, MA: Kitchen Sink Press, 1995.

Blair, Walter et al., eds. *The Literature of the United States.* 2 vols. 3d ed. New York: Scott, Foresman, 1966.

Blumenthal, Ralph. *Stork Club: America's Most Famous Nightspot and the Lost World of Café Society.* Boston: Little, Brown, 2000.

Bogart, Michele H. *Artists, Advertising, and the Borders of Art.* Chicago: University of Chicago Press, 1995.

Bonn, Thomas L. *An Illustrated History of American Mass Market Paperbacks.* New York: Penguin, 1982.

Boorstin, Daniel J. *The Americans: The Democratic Experience.* New York: Vintage Books, 1974.

———. *The Image: A Guide to Pseudo-Events in America.* 2d. ed. New York: Atheneum, 1980.

Borgeson, Griffith. *The Golden Age of the American Racing Car.* New York: Bonanza, 1966.

Bruce, A. H. "Baseball and National Life." *Outlook* 104 (May 1913): 104–7.

Canemaker, John. *Winsor McCay: His Life and Art.* New York: Abbeville Press, 1987.

Caniff, Milton. *Male Call, 1942–46.* Princeton, Wis.: Kitchen Sink Press, 1987.

Canning, Peter. *The Wallaces and* Reader's Digest. New York: Simon and Schuster, 1996.

Cantor, Norman F. *The American Century: Varieties of Culture in Modern Times.* New York: Harper Collins, 1997.

Carr, Roy. *A Century of Jazz.* New York: Da Capo Press, 1997.

Carson, Gerald. "Goggles and Side Curtains." *American Heritage* (April 1967): 32–39, 108–11.

———. "The Piano in the Parlor." *American Heritage* (December 1965): 54–59, 91.

Cashman, Sean Dennis. *America in the Twenties and Thirties: The Olympian Age of FDR.* New York: New York University Press, 1989.

Cather, Willa. Preface to *The Country of the Pointed Firs,* by Sarah Orne Jewett. Garden City, N.Y.: Doubleday Anchor, 1956.

Churchill, Allen. *The Improper Bohemians.* New York: Ace Books, 1959.

Clarke, Donald. *The Rise and Fall of Popular Music.* New York: St. Martin's Griffin, 1995.

Cohn, Jan. *Covers of the* Saturday Evening Post. New York: Penguin Books, 1995.

Conrad, Peter. *Modern Times, Modern Places.* New York: Knopf, 1999.

Constantino, Maria. *Men's Fashion in the Twentieth Century.* New York: Costume & Fashion Press, 1997.

Cooney, Terry A. *Balancing Acts: American Thought and Culture in the 1930s.* New York: Twayne, 1995.

Corn, Joseph J. *The Winged Gospel: America's Romance with Aviation, 1900–1950.* New York: Oxford University Press, 1983.

Corn, Joseph J., and Brian Horrigan. *Yesterday's Tomorrows: Past Visions of the American Future.* Baltimore: Johns Hopkins University Press, 1996.

Cotkin, George. *Reluctant Modernism: American Thought and Culture, 1880–1900.* New York: Twayne, 1992.

Couperie, Pierre, and Maurice C. Horn. *A History of the Comic Strip*. New York: Crown, 1968.

Cowley, Malcolm. *Exile's Return: A Literary Odyssey of the 1920s*. New York: Viking Press, 1956.

Crafton, Donald. *Before Mickey: The Animated Film, 1898–1928*. Cambridge: MIT Press, 1982.

Csida, Joseph, and June Bundy. *American Entertainment: A Unique History of Popular Show Business*. New York: Watson-Guptil, 1978.

Custen, George F. *Twentieth Century's Fox: Darryl F. Zanuck and the Culture of Hollywood*. New York: Basic Books, 1997.

Cztrom, Daniel J. *Media and the American Mind: From Morse to McLuhan*. Chapel Hill: University of North Carolina Press, 1982.

Daniels, Les. *Marvel: Five Fabulous Decades of the World's Greatest Comics*. New York: Abrams, 1991.

Davidson, Sander. "Wish You Were Here." *American Heritage* (October 1962): 97–112.

DeBauche, Leslie Midkiff. *Reel Patriotism: The Movies and World War I*. Madison: University of Wisconsin Press, 1997.

Denning Michael. *Mechanic Accents: Dime Novels and Working-Class Culture in America*. London: Verso, 1987.

DiLauro, Al, and Gerald Rabkin. *Dirty Movies: An Illustrated History of the Stag Film, 1915–1970*. New York: Chelsea House, 1976.

Disch, Thomas M. *The Dreams Our Stuff Is Made Of: How Science Fiction Conquered the World*. New York: Free Press, 1998.

Douglas, Susan J. *Listening In: Radio and the American Imagination*. New York: Times Books, 1999.

Dreiser, Theodore. *Sister Carrie*. 1900. Reprint, New York: New American Library, 1961.

Ely, Melvin Patrick. *The Adventures of Amos 'n' Andy: A Social History of an American Phenomenon*. New York: Free Press, 1991.

Engle, Gary. "What Makes Superman So Darned American?" In *Superman at Fifty: The Persistence of a Legend*, edited by Dennis Dooley and Gary Engle, 79–87. Cleveland: Octavia Press, 1987.

Erenberg, Lewis A. *Steppin' Out: New York Nightlife and the Transformation of American Culture, 1890–1930*. Chicago: University of Chicago Press, 1984.

Everson, William K. *American Silent Film*. New York: Oxford University Press, 1978.

Eyles, Allen. *The World of Oz*. Tucson: HP Books, 1985.

Fehr, Richard, and Frederick G. Vogel. *Lullabies of Hollywood: Movie Music and the Movie Musical, 1915–1992*. Jefferson, N.C.: McFarland, 1993.

Fenin, George N., and William K. Everson. *The Western: From Silents to Cinerama*. New York: Orin Press, 1962.

Findling, John E. *Chicago's Great Fairs*. New York: Manchester University Press, 1994.

Firestone, Bruce. "A Man Named Sioux." In *The First Film Makers*, edited by Richard Dyer MacCann, 102–7. Metuchen, N.J.: Scarecrow Press, 1989.

Forma, Warren. *They Were Ragtime*. New York: Grosset & Dunlap, 1976.

Fraser, James. *The American Billboard 100 Years*. New York: Abrams, 1991.

Fredriksson, Kristine. *American Rodeo: From Buffalo Bill to Big Business*. College Station: Texas A&M University Press 1985.

Gabler, Neal. *Life the Movie: How Entertainment Conquered Reality*. New York: Knopf, 1998.

Gelman, Barbara, ed. Photoplay *Treasury.* New York: Crown, 1972.

Gilbert, Douglas. *American Vaudeville: Its Life and Times.* New York: Dover, 1963.

Glassberg, David. *American Historical Pageantry: The Uses of Tradition in the Early 20th Century.* Chapel Hill: University of North Carolina Press, 1990.

Goodrum, Charles, and Helen Dalrymple. *Advertising in America: The First Two Hundred Years.* New York: Abrams, 1990.

Goodstone, Tony, ed. *The Pulps: Fifty Years of American Pop Culture.* New York: Chelsea House, 1970.

Goulart, Ron. *The Dime Detectives.* New York: Mysterious Press, 1988.

———. *Focus on Jack Cole.* Agoura, Calif.: Fantagraphics Books, 1986.

———. *The Funnies: 100 Years of American Comic Strips.* Holbrook, Mass.: Adams Publishing, 1995.

———. *Over 50 Years of American Comic Books.* Lincolnwood, Ill.: Publications International, 1991.

Green, Stanley. *Ring Bells! Sing Songs! Broadway Musicals of the Thirties.* New Rochelle: Arlington House, 1971.

Greene, Theodore P. *America's Heroes: The Changing Models of Success in American Magazines.* New York: Oxford University Press, 1970.

Gregory, Ross. *America 1941—A Nation at the Crossroads.* New York: Free Press, 1989.

Guimond, James. *American Photography and the American Dream.* Chapel Hill: University of North Carolina Press, 1991.

Hackett, Alice Payne. *70 Years of Best Sellers, 1895–1965.* New York: Bowker, 1967.

Haining, Peter, ed. *The Fantastic Pulps.* New York: Vintage, 1976.

Hall, Ben M. *The Best Remaining Seats: The Golden Age of the Movie Palace.* New York: Bramhall House, 1971.

Harris, Neil. *Cultural Excursions: Marketing Appetites and Cultural Tastes in Modern America.* Chicago: University of Chicago Press, 1990.

———, ed. *The Land of Contrasts: 1880–1901.* New York: Braziller, 1970.

Hart, James D. *The Popular Book: A History of America's Literary Taste.* Berkeley: University of California Press, 1963.

Harvey, Robert C. *The Art of the Comic Book: An Aesthetic History.* Jackson: University Press Mississipi, 1996.

———. *The Art of the Funnies: An Aesthetic History.* Jackson: University Press of Mississippi, 1994.

———. Introduction to *The Tijuana Bibles: America's Forgotten Comic Strips,* 4–6. Seattle, Wash.: Eros Comix, 1996.

Heide, Robert, and John Gilman. *Home Front America: Popular Culture of the World War II Era.* San Francisco: Chronicle Books, 1993.

Heimann, Jim. *Car Hops and Curb Service: A History of American Drive-In Restaurants, 1920–1960.* San Francisco: Chronicle Books, 1996.

Heller, Steven, and Seymour Chwast. *Jackets Required: An Illustrated History of American Book Jacket Design, 1920–1950.* San Francisco: Chronicle Books, 1995.

Heller, Steven, and Louise Fili. *Cover Story: The Art of American Magazine Covers, 1900–1950.* San Francisco: Chronicle Books, 1996.

Henderson, Amy. *On the Air: Pioneers of American Broadcasting.* Washington, D.C.: Smithsonian Institute Press, 1988.

Heyman, Therese Thau. *Posters American Style.* New York: Abrams, 1998.

Hoffman, Frederick J. *The Twenties: American Writing in the Postwar Decade.* Rev. ed. New York: Collier Books, 1962.

Horn, Maurice, ed. *100 Years of Newspaper Comics.* New York: Gramercy Books, 1996.

Horsham, Michael. *20s and 30s Style.* N. Dighton, Mass.: J. G. Press, 1996.

Howells, William Dean. *A Hazard of New Fortunes.* 1890. Reprint, New York: New American Library, 1965.

Hoyt, Harlowe R. *Town Hall Tonight.* Englewood Cliffs, N.J.: Prentice-Hall, 1955.

Hunter, Sam. *Modern American Painting and Sculpture.* New York: Dell, 1959.

Hutchinson, Don. *The Great Pulp Heroes.* Buffalo, N.Y.: Orion Press, 1996.

Janello, Amy, and Brennon Jones. *The American Magazine.* New York: Abrams, 1991.

Jensen, Oliver, ed. *The Nineties.* New York: American Heritage Publishing Co., 1967.

Jewett, Sarah Orne. *The Country of the Pointed Firs and Other Stories.* 1986. Reprint, Garden City, N.Y.: Doubleday Anchor, 1956.

Joselit, Jenna Weissman. *A Perfect Fit: Clothes, Character, and the Promise of America.* New York: Metropolitan Books, 2001.

Kammen, Michael. *Mystic Chords of Memory: The Transformation of Tradition in American Culture.* New York: Vintage, 1993.

Kasson, John F. *Amusing the Million: Coney Island at the Turn of the Century.* New York: Hill and Wang, 1978.

Kazin, Alfred. *On Native Grounds: An Interpretation of Modern American Prose Literature.* 1942. Reprint, Garden City, N.Y.: Doubleday Anchor, 1956.

Keylin, Arleen, and Christine Bent. The New York Times *at the Movies.* New York: Arno Press, 1979.

Kimball, Robert, and Alfred Simon. *The Gershwins.* New York: Atheneum, 1973.

Kismaric, Carole, and Marvin Heiferman. *The Mysterious Case of Nancy Drew & the Hardy Boys.* New York: Fireside Books, 1998.

Klein, Marcus. *Easterns, Westerns, and Private Eyes: American Matters, 1870–1900.* Madison: University of Wisconsin Press, 1994.

Kluger, Richard. *The Paper: The Life and Death of the* New York Herald Tribune. New York: Knopf, 1986.

Knight, Arthur. *The Liveliest Art: A Panoramic History of the Movies.* 3d ed. New York: New American Library, 1957.

Landon, Brooks. *Science Fiction after 1900: From the Steam Man to the Stars.* New York: Twayne, 1997.

Lencek, Lena, and Gideon Bosker. *Making Waves: Swimsuits and the Undressing of America.* San Francisco: Chronicle Books, 1989.

Lesser, Robert. *Pulp Art: Original Cover Paintings for the Great American Pulp Magazines.* New York: Gramercy Books, 1997.

Levine, Lawrence W. *Highbrow/Lowbrow: The Emergence of Cultural Hierarchy in America.* Cambridge: Harvard University Press, 1988.

Lindsay, Vachel. *The Art of the Moving Picture.* New York: Macmillan, 1915.

Loth, David. *The Erotic in Literature.* New York: Julian Messner, 1961.

Lupoff, Richard A. *Edgar Rice Burroughs: Master of Adventure.* New York: Ace Books, 1968.

Lyons, John. *The College Novel in America.* Carbondale: Southern Illinois University Press, 1962.

MacCann, Richard Dyer, ed. *The First Film Makers*. Metuchen, N.J.: Scarecrow Press, 1989.

MacDonald, J. Fred. *Don't Touch That Dial! Radio Programming in American Life, 1920–1960*. Chicago: Nelson-Hall, 1979.

Maltby, Richard, ed. *Passing Parade: A History of Popular Culture in the 20th Century*. New York: Oxford University Press, 1989.

Maltin, Leonard. *The Great American Broadcast: A Celebration of Radio's Golden Age*. New York: Dutton, 1997.

———. *The Great Movie Shorts*. New York: Crown, 1972.

———. *Of Mice and Magic: A History of American Animated Cartoons*. New York: McGraw-Hill, 1980.

Mandell, Richard D. *Sport: A Cultural History*. New York: Columbia University Press, 1984.

Marchand, Roland. *Advertising the American Dream: Making Way for Modernity*. Berkeley: University of California Press, 1985.

Margolies, John. *Fun along the Road: American Tourist Attractions*. Boston: Bulfinch Press, 1998.

Margolies, John, and Emily Gwathmey. *Signs of Our Times*. New York: Abbeville Press, 1993.

———. *Ticket to Paradise: American Movie Theaters and How We Had Fun*. Boston: Bulfinch Press, 1991.

Mariani, John. *America Eats Out*. New York: Morrow, 1991.

Marquis, Alice G. *Hopes and Ashes: The Birth of Modern Times, 1929–1939*. New York: Free Press, 1986.

Marschall, Richard. *America's Great Comic-Strip Artists*. New York: Abbeville Press, 1989.

Marschall, Rick. *Blondie & Dagwood's America*. New York: Harper & Row, 1981.

Matlaw, Myron, ed. *American Popular Entertainment*. Westport, Conn.: Greenwood, 1979.

McCarthy, Albert. *The Dance Band Era: From Ragtime to Swing*. Radnor, Pa.: Chilton Books, 1982.

McDonnell, Patrick, et al., eds. *Krazy Kat: The Comic Art of George Herriman*. New York: Abrams, 1986.

Merlis, Bob, and Davin Seay. *Heart & Soul: A Celebration of Black Music Style in America, 1930–1975*. New York: Stewart, Tabori & Chang, 1997.

Meyer, Susan E. *America's Great Illustrators*. New York: Galahad, 1987.

Millard, André. *America on Record: A History of Recorded Sound*. New York: Cambridge University Press, 1995.

Miller, Don. *B Movies*. New York: Curtis Books, 1973.

Miller, Donald L. "The White City." *American Heritage* 44 (July/August 1993): 70–87.

Miller, Frank. *Censored Hollywood: Sex, Sin, & Violence on Screen*. Atlanta: Turner Publishing, 1994.

Minsky, Morton, and Milt Machlin. *Minsky's Burlesque*. New York: Arbor House, 1986.

Mizejewski, Linda. *Ziegfeld Girl: Image and Icon in Culture and Cinema*. Durham, N.C.: Duke University Press, 1999.

Morella, Joe, et al. *The Films of World War II*. Secaucus, N.J.: Citadel Press, 1973.

Morgan, Hal. *Symbols of America*. New York: Penguin Books, 1986.

Morgan, Thomas L., and William Barlow. *From Cakewalks to Concert Halls: African American Popular Music from 1895 to 1930*. Washington, D.C.: Elliott and Clark, 1992.

Moriarty, Florence, ed. *True Confessions: Sixty Years of Sin, Suffering & Sorrow, 1919–1979.* New York: Fireside Books, 1979.

Mott, Frank Luther. *Golden Multitudes: The Story of Best Sellers in the United States.* New York: Macmillan, 1947.

Muller, Eddie, and Daniel Faris. *Grindhouse: The Forbidden World of "Adults Only" Cinema.* New York: St. Martin's Griffin, 1996.

Munsterberg, Hugo. *The Photoplay: A Psychology Study.* New York: D. Appleton, 1916.

Nasaw, David. *Going Out: The Rise and Fall of Public Amusements.* New York: Basic Books, 1993.

Nash, Roderick, ed. *The Call of the Wild, 1900–1916.* New York: Braziller, 1970.

Null, Gary. *Black Hollywood: The Black Performer in Motion Pictures.* Secaucus, N.J.: Citadel Press, 1975.

Nye, David E. *Narrative and Spaces: Technology and the Construction of American Culture.* New York: Columbia University Press, 1997.

Olderman, Murray. "The Sporting Life." *Hogan's Alley: The Magazine of the Cartoon Arts* 6 (1999): 122–36.

Oriard, Michael. *Reading Football: How the Popular Press Created an American Spectacle.* Chapel Hill: University of North Carolina Press, 1993.

Orvell, Miles. *The Real Thing: Imitation and Authenticity in American Culture.* Chapel Hill: University of North Carolina Press, 1989.

Ostrander, Gilman M. *American Civilization in the First Machine Age: 1890– 1940.* New York: Harper & Row, 1970.

O'Sullivan, Judith. *The Great American Comic Strip: One Hundred Years of Cartoon Art.* Boston: Bulfinch Press, 1990.

Owen, William. *Modern Magazine Design.* New York: Rizzoli, 1991.

Palmer, Tony. *All You Need Is Love: The Story of Popular Music.* New York: Penguin Books, 1977.

Parish, James Robert. *The Great Movie Series.* New York: A. S. Barnes, 1971.

Parsons, Floyd W. "The New Day in Salesmanship." *Saturday Evening Post,* 4 June 1921, 28.

Pascal, David. "The Art of the Comic Strip." *Graphis* 28, no. 159 (1972–73): 6.

Petersen, James R. *The Century of Sex:* Playboy's *History of the Sexual Revolution, 1900–1999.* New York: Grove Press, 1999.

Pomerance, Alan. *Repeal of the Blues: How Black Entertainers Influenced Civil Rights.* Secaucus, N.J.: Citadel Press.

Pomeroy, Earl. *In Search of the Golden West: The Tourist in Western America.* Lincoln: University of Nebraska Press, 1990.

Pope, S. W. *Patriotic Games: Sporting Tradition in the American Imagination, 1876–1926.* New York: Oxford University Press, 1997.

Powell, Richard J. *Black Art and Culture in the 20th Century.* New York: Thames and Hudson, 1997.

Powers, Madelon. *Faces along the Bar: Lore and Order in the Workingman's Saloon, 1870–1920.* Chicago: University of Chicago Press, 1998.

Pratt, George C., ed. *Spellbound in Darkness: A History of the Silent Film.* Greenwich, Conn.: New York Graphic Society, 1973.

Primeau, Ronald. *Romance of the Road: The Literature of the American Highway.* Bowling Green, Ohio: Popular Press, 1996.

Radway, Janice A. *A Feeling for Books: The Book of the Month Club, Literary Taste, and Middle-Class Desire.* Chapel Hill: University of North Carolina Press, 1997.

Rebello, Stephen, and Richard Allen. *Great Posters from the Golden Age of the Silver Screen.* New York: Artebras, 1988.

Robbins, Trina. *The Great Women Superheroes.* Northampton, Mass. Kitchen Sink Press, 1996.

Robinson, Jerry. *The Comics: An Ilustrated History of Comic Strip Art.* New York: Putnam's, 1974.

———. Skippy *and Percy Crosby.* New York: Holt, Rinehart and Winston, 1978.

Robinson, Julian. *Body Packaging: A Guide to Human Sexual Display.* Los Angeles: Elysium Press, 1988.

Rosenberg, Bernard, and David Manning White, eds. *Mass Culture: The Popular Arts in America.* Glencoe, Ill.: Free Press, 1957.

Rydell, Robert W. *All the World's a Fair: Visions of Empire at American International Expositions, 1876–1916.* Chicago: University of Chicago Press, 1984.

Sanjak, Russell. *American Popular Music and Its Business.* 3 vols. New York: Oxford University Press, 1988.

Schmidt, Dorey, ed. *The American Magazine: 1890–1940.* Wilmington: Delaware Art Museum, 1979.

Schwartzman, Arnold. *Phono-Graphics: The Visual Paraphernalia of the Talking Machine.* San Francisco: Chronicle Books, 1993.

Sennett, Robert S. *Hollywood Hoopla: Creating Stars and Selling Movies in the Golden Age of Hollywood.* New York: Billboard Books, 1998.

Server, Lee. *Danger Is My Business: An Illustrated History of the Fabulous Pulp Magazines: 1896–1953.* San Francisco: Chronicle Books, 1993.

Shindler, Colin. *Hollywood in Crisis: Cinema and American Society, 1929–1939.* New York: Routledge, 1996.

Siegel, Jeff. *The American Detective: An Ilustrated History.* Dallas: Taylor Publishing, 1993.

Sims, Newman, ed. *Literary Journalism in the Twentieth Century.* New York: Oxford University Press, 1990.

Sklar, Robert. *Movie-Made America: A Cultural History of American Movies.* Rev. ed. New York: Vintage Books, 1994.

Slide, Anthony. *Early American Cinema.* Rev. ed. Metuchen, N.J.: Scarecrow Press, 1994.

———. *The Silent Feminists: America's First Women Directors.* Lanham, Md.: Scarecrow Press, 1996.

Slotkin, Richard. *Gunfighter Nation. The Myth of the Frontier in Twentieth-Century America.* New York: Atheneum, 1992.

Smith, Gene. "A Little Visit to the Lower Depths via the *Police Gazette.*" *American Heritage* (October 1972): 65–73.

Sperber, Murray. *Onward to Victory: The Crises That Shaped College Sports.* New York: Henry Holt, 1998.

Spiegelman, Art, and Chip Kidd. *Jack Cole and Plastic Man: Forms Stretched to Their Limits.* San Francisco: Chronicle Books: 2001.

Stansell, Christine. *American Moderns: Bohemian New York and the Creation of a New Century.* New York: Metropolitan Books, 2000.

Steinbrunner, Chris. Preface to *The Shadow Scrapbook,* by Walter Gibson. New York: Harcourt Brace Jovanovich, 1979.

Stevens, John D. *Sensationalism and the New York Press.* New York: Columbia University Press, 1991.

Tallack, Douglas. *Twentieth-Century America: The Intellectual and Cultural Context.* New York: Longman, 1991.

Thompson, Frederic. "The Profits from Laughter." In *The Saturday Evening Post Reflections of a Decade, 1901–1910,* 54–55. Indianapolis: Curtis Publishing Co., 1980.

Tichi, Cecelia. *High Lonesome: The American Culture of Country Music.* Chapel Hill: University of North Carolina, 1994.

Toll, Robert C. *On with the Show: The First Hundred Years of American Show Business.* New York: Oxford University Press, 1976.

———. "Show Biz in Blackface: The Evolution of the Minstrel Show as a Theatrical Form." In *American Popular Entertainment,* edited by Myron Matlaw, 19–32. Westport, Conn.: Greenwood, 1979.

Twain, Mark. *Autobiography.* 2 vols. New York: Harper & Brothers, 1924.

Twitchell, James B. *ADCULT USA: The Triumph of Advertising in American Culture.* New York: Columbia University Press, 1996.

Umphlett, Wiley Lee. *Creating the Big Game: John W. Heisman and the Invention of American Football.* Westport, Conn.: Greenwood, 1992.

———. *The Movies Go to College: Hollywood and the World of the College-Life Film.* Madison, N.J.: Fairleigh Dickinson University Press, 1984.

"The U.S. at War." *Time.* Special 60th Anniversary Issue (1983): 34.

Vidal, Gore. "Tarzan Revisited." *Esquire* 80 (October 1973): 281–83, 484–86. (This is the 40th anniversary issue.)

Wainscott, Ronald H. *The Emergence of the Modern American Theater, 1914–1929.* New Haven: Yale University Press, 1997.

Wainwright, Loudon. *The Great American Magazine: An Inside History of* Life. New York: Knopf, 1986.

Wallenfeldt, Jeffrey H. ed., *Sports Movies: A Review of Nearly 500 Films.* Evanston, Ill.: Cine-Books, 1989.

Ward, Barbara McLean, ed. *Produce & Conserve, Share & Play Square.* Hanover: University Press of New England, 1994.

Warner Jr., Sam Bass. *The Urban Wilderness: A History of the American City.* Berkeley: University of California Press, 1995.

Watts, Steven. *The Magic Kingdom: Walt Disney and the American Way of Life.* Boston: Houghton Mifflin, 1997.

Waugh, Coulton. *The Comics.* Macmillan, 1947.

Weiss, Ken, and Ed Goodgold. *To Be Continued . . .* New York: Bonanza Books, 1972.

Wenzel, Lynn, and Carol J. Binkowski. *I Hear America Singing: A Nostalgic Tour of Popular Sheet Music.* New York: Crown, 1989.

Wilson, Garff B. *Three Hundred Years of American Drama and Theatre.* 2d ed. Englewood Cliffs, N.J.: Prentice-Hall, 1982.

Wood, James Playsted. *Magazines in the United States,* 3d ed. New York: Ronald Press, 1971.

Wood, Norton, ed., *The Spectacle of Sport.* Englewood Cliffs, N.J.: Prentice-Hall, 1957.

Wyndham, Francis. Introduction, *My Life in Pictures by Charles Chaplin.* New York: Grosset & Dunlap, 1975.

Yronwode, Catherine. *The Art of Will Eisner.* Princeton, Wisc.: Kitchen Sink Press, 1982.

Ziegfeld, Florenz. "What Makes a Woman Beautiful." Liberty: *Then and Now* (summer 1974): 45–47.

Ziegfeld, Richard, and Paulette Ziegfeld. *The Ziegfeld Touch: The Life and Times of Florenz Ziegfeld, Jr.* New York: Abrams, 1993.

Zurier, Rebecca et al., eds. *Metropolitan Lives: The Ashcan Artists and Their New York.* New York: W. W. Norton, 1995.

Index

Illustrated pages are indicated with boldface